COMMON PHRASES AND QUICK REFERENCE

ANSWER Y
Conteste sí
(Kohn-TEH

CALM DOW
¡Cálmese!
(KAHL-meh-seh)

COME HERE.?
Venga aquí.
(VEHN-gah ah-KEE)

UNDERSTAND?
¿Comprende?
(kom-PREN-day)

CONTRABAND
contrabando
(kohn-trah-BAHN-doh)

EMPTY YOUR POCKETS.
Vacíe sus bolsillos.
(Vah-SEE-eh soos bohl-SEE-yohs)

FALSE   **DID YOU KNOW?**
¿falso?   Supo?
(FAHL-soh)   (SOO-poh)

I SAW YOU_____.
Le ví _____.
(Lay VEE _____.)

IS THIS YOURS?
¿Es suyo?
(ehs SOO-yoh)

IT'S NOT TRUE
No es verdad
(noh ehs behr-DAHD)

LEAVE   vayase
(VAH-yah-say)

OPEN!   **CLOSE!**
¡Abra!   ¡Cierra!
(AH-brah)   (see-AIR-ah)

POINT! ¡Apunte! (ah-POON-tay)

PULL OFF THE ROAD.
Estaciónese fuera del camino.
(Ay-stah-SYOHN-ay-say
foo-AYR-ah dayl kah-MEE-noh)

QUIET!
¡Silencio!
(see-LEHN-see-oh)

SIT!   **WAIT!**
¡Siéntese!   ¡Espere!
(see-EHN-tay-say) (ehs-PEHR-ay)

SMUGGLER -coyote (koh-YOH-tay)
-contrabandista
(kohn-trah-bahn-DEES-tah)

SPEAK LOUDER
Hable en voz más alta
(AH-blay ehn vohz mahs ahl-tah)

SPEAK SLOWER.
Hable más despacio
(AH-blay mahs days-PAH-see-oh)

STAND HERE.
Párese aquí.
(PAH-reh-say ah-KEE)

TELL ME THE TRUTH.
Dígame la verdad.
(DEE-gah-may lah vehr-DAHD)

THANK YOU
Gracias
(GRAH-see-ahs)

TITLE   título   (TEE-too-loh)

WALLET PURSE COAT
cartera   bolsa   abrigo
(kar-TEH-ra) (BOHL-sa) (ah-BREE-go)

YES   **NO**   **PLEASE**
sí   no   por favor
(see)   (noh)   (pohr fah-VOHR)

YOU DO NOT FOOL ME!
¡Usted no me engaña!
(oo-STEHD noh may ehn-GAHN-yah)

YOU PRETEND TO NOT UNDERSTAND!
¡Finge no entender, se hace no más!
(FEEN-hay noh ehn-tehn-DEHR
say ah-say noh MAHS)

SPEAK ENGLISH!
¡Habla Inglés!
(AH-blay een-GLAYS)

TABLE OF CONTENTS PAGE 7

FIELD INTERVIEW / WITNESSES

LICENSE?
¿licencia?
(lee-SEHN-syah)

PAPERS?
¿Papeles?
(pah-PEH-lays)

DO YOU HAVE A DRIVERS LICENSE?
¿Tiene usted licencia de manejar?
(tee-EH-neh oo-STEHD lee-SEHN-see-ah deh mah-neh-HAHR)

WRITE YOUR NAME
Escribe su nombre con letras de molde.
(Ehs-KREE-bay soo NOHM-bray kohn LEH-trahs day MOHL-day)

FIRST NAME	SURNAME		MATERNAL
nombre de pila	apellido	/	paterno	materna
NOHM-bray day PEE-lah	(ah-peh-YEE-doh)		(pah-TEHR-noh)	(mah-TEHR-nah)

(Note: PATERNAL / MATERNAL under SURNAME)

DATE OF BIRTH — **WRITE**
Fecha de nacimiento — (escriba)
(FEH-chah day nah-see-mee-EHN-toh) (ehs-KREE-bah)

(Fetch the day!) *(Scribe)*

day	month	year
día	mes	año
(DEE-ah)	(mehs)	(AHN-yoh)

CAN YOU READ?
¿Puede leer?
(PWAY-day lay-AYR)

WRITE?
escribir
(ehs-kree-BEER)

WHAT IS THE NAME OF YOUR PATRON SAINT? — **PRINT**
¿Qué es el nombre de su santo? — imprenta
(Kay ays ehl NOHM-bray day soo SAHN-toh) (eem-PREHN-tah)

WHAT IS YOUR ADDRESS? — Or — **ADDRESS**
¿Cuál es su domicilio? — dirección
(Kwahl es soo doh-mee-SEE-lyoh) (dee-rehk-SYOHN)

HOUSE NO.-	número de casa	(NOO-may-roh day KAH-sah)
APARTMENT #	número de apartamento	(ah-pahr-tah-MEHN-toh)
STREET	calle	(KAH-yay)
CITY	ciudad	(see-oo-DAHD)
STATE	estado	(ehs-TAH-doh)
COUNTRY	país;	(pah-EES); (or) - patria (PAH-tree-ah)
SQUARE	plaza	(PLAH-sah)
TOWN	pueblo	(PWEH-bloh)
ZONE	zona	(ZOH-nah)

SOCIAL SECURITY NUMBER?
¿Número de seguro social?
(NOO-may-roh day say-GOO-roh soh-see-AHL)

WHAT IS YOUR TELEPHONE NUMBER?
¿Cuál su número de teléfono?
(Kwahl ess soo NOO-may-roh day tay-LAY-foh-noh)

BASIC GRAMMAR / FAMILIAR VERSUS FORMAL

VOWELS
(Sounds)
- A (AH)
- E (EH)
- I (EE)
- O (OH)
- U (OO) Usted (oo-STEHD)
- Y (EE)

(Tu vs. Usted)
Subject's responses will be enhanced by proper usage of "**Tu**" or "**Usted**" and to put oneself on an equal level with the person you are interviewing.

Use **Tu (you)** for familiar form for friends, young men/women, children.

Use **Usted** (formal for you) to show respect:ie: Community Leader, Priest, older people, boss, head of the household, Gang or Organization Leader. Vd.(s) and Ud.(s) are abbrev. for Usted(es).

HE	El	(Ehl)
I	Yo	(YOH)
SHE	Ella	(AY-yah)
THAT	Aquel	(ah-KAYL)
THESE	Estos	(AYS-tohs)
THEY(masc.)	Ellos	(EH-yohs)
THIS	Este	(AHS-tay)
THOSE	Aquellos	(ah-KAY-yohs)
YOU	Usted	(oo-STEHD)
YOU (sing.)	Tú	(TOO) (familiar)
YOU (plural)	Ustedes	(oo-STEH-days)
WE	Nosotros	(Noh-SOH-trohs)

WORDS ENDING IN:
"O" are basically **masculine**
"A" are basically **feminine**
"El" means the singular masculine
"La" means the singular feminine
IE: **El** muchach**o**, **La** muchach**a**
(NOTE: Most articles agree in gender and number with the noun).

SINGULAR
*The man   El hombre   (ehl OHM-bray)
*The girl   La muchacha
             (Lah moo-CHAH-chah)

**A man   Un hombre (oon OHM-bray)
**A girl   Una muchacha
             (OO-nah moo-CHAH-chah)

PLURAL
*The men   Los hombres (Lohs OHM-brays)
*The girls Las muchachas
            (Lahs moo-CHAH-chahs)

**Some men Unos hombres
            (OO-nohs OHM-brays)
**Some girls Unas muchachas
            (OO-nahs moo-CHAH-chahs)

NOTE: * **DEFINITE ARTICLE**
       ** **INDEFINITE ARTICLE** (a/an)

(NOTE: Most often, nouns ending in a vowel add **s** to form the plural; nouns ending in a consonant add **es**).

IS THERE OR ARE THERE?
¿Hay?
(eye)   Pronounced like:

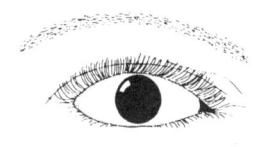

THERE IS OR THERE ARE! ¡Hay! (EYE)

THERE ISN'T OR AREN'T   No hay
                             (noh eye)

ISN'T THERE? OR AREN'T THERE?
¿No hay?   (Form a question by the
(no EYE)   intonation of the voice).

HOW?	¿Cómo?	(KOH-moh)
WHAT?	¿Qué?	(KAY)
WHEN?	¿Cuándo?	(KWAHN-doh)
WHERE?	¿Dónde?	(DOHN-day)

WHERE IS THE _____?
Dónde está el/la _____?
(DOHN-day ess-TAH el/lah_____?

WHICH?	¿Cuál?	(KWAHL)
WHICH ONE?	¿Cuál?	(KWAHL)
WHO?	¿Quien?	(kee-EHN)
WHOSE?	¿De Quién es?	
	(Day kee-EHN ess)	

WHY?	¿Por que?	(pohr KAY)
WRITE!	¡Escriba!	(ehs-KREE-bah)

NOTE: Remember to make a question sound like a question and a statement like a statement.

IT IS....	Es	(ehs)
IS IT?	¿Es?	(EHS)
IT ISN'T...	No es	(noh ehs)
ISN'T IT?	¿No es?	(noh EHS)

EMPHASIS ON SYLLABLES
The acute accent (´) is used to indicate a syllable that is stressed, IE: día (DEE-ah).

Words ending with a consonant, the last syllable is emphasized IE: señor
                                       (seh-**NYOHR**)

Words ending with a vowel, the next to the last syllable is stressed, IE: mañana
                                       (mahn-**YAHN**-nah)

ADJECTIVES agree with the noun in gender and number. If the masculine form ends in "O" the feminine ends in "A". Most often, the adjective comes after the noun. IE:

THE SMALL BOY
El niño pequeño
(ehl NEEN-yoh pay-KAY-nyoh)

THE SMALL GIRL
La niña pequeña
(lah NEEN-yah pay-KAY-nyah)

Possessive Adj. (Singular) (Plural)

my -	mi	(mee)	mis (mees)
your(fam.)	tu	(too)	tus (toos)
your (form.)	su	(soo)	sus (soos)
his, her, its	su	(soo)	sus (soos)
their	su	(soo)	sus (soos)

(ex: Su casa - Your house)

our (sing.)	nuestro	(NWEHS-troh)
our (pl.)	nuestros	(NWEHS-trohs)

Demonstrative Pronouns (Neutral)

this -	esto	(ESS-toh)
that -	eso	(EH-soh)
that -	aquello	(ah-KAY-yoh)

Plural

these	estos	(EHS-tohs)
those -	esos	(EH-sohs)
those -	aquellos	(ah-KAY-yohs)

MISCELLANEOUS

and -	y	(ee)
although-	aunque	(ah-OON-kay)
because -	porque	(POHR-kay)
but -	pero	(PAY-roh)
if -	si	(see)
or -	o	(oo)
since-	pues	(pways)
well then-	pues bien	(pways BEE-ehn)

SOME BASIC PREPOSITIONS

a	to, at
ante	before, in the presence of, in the face of
bajo	under
con	with
contra	against, opposite, facing
de	of, from
desde	from, since
durante	during
en	in, into, on, upon, at
entre	among, between, in the midst of
hacia	towards, in the direction of, about
hasta	as far as, up to, down to, till, until
para	for, intended for, in order to
por	for, because of
según	according to, in accordance with, in line with
sin	without, not including
so	thus
sobre	on, upon, on top of, over, above
detrás de	behind, after

TIPS ABOUT MASCULINE NOUNS

Names of male beings are masculine.

Nouns ending in "O" are masculine with the exception of "the hand" (la mano) and "the radio" (la radio).

Days of the week, months, rivers, oceans and mountains are masculine.

Most nouns ending in "L" and "R" and nouns of Greek origin ending in "MA" are masculine (there are exceptions).

TIPS ABOUT FEMININE NOUNS

Names of female beings are feminine.

Nouns ending in "A" are feminine (there are exceptions IE: "the day" (el día).

Letters of the Spanish alphabet are feminine IE: "M" (la eme) (The letter "M" is slang for "The Mexican Mafia").

Nouns ending in (ión, tad, tud, & umbre) are feminine IE: la ciudad ("the city"). There are exceptions.

TIPS ON FORMING THE FEMININE

Nouns and adjectives ending in "O" change to "A".

PLURAL OF NOUNS

Nouns ending in an unaccented vowel add "S" to form the plural IE: The house. (la casa) to the houses (las casas).

Nouns ending in a consonant, in "Y", or in an accented vowel add "es".
IE: The paper, (el papel)
the papers (los papeles).

Nouns ending in the unaccented "es" and "is" don't change in the plural, IE: Monday (el lunes) to Mondays (los lunes).

Note: Some nouns (and their plurals) have different genders according to their meanings and some nouns have invariable endings which are both used for both the masculine and feminine).

Nouns ending in: (ón, or, and án) add "A".
IE: patrón to patrona (there are exceptions).

OFFICER SAFETY and "RED FLAG" WORDS

DON'T SHOOT!
¡No dispare!
(No dees-**PAH**-ray)

POINT
Apunte
(ah-**POON**-tay)

DON"T DO IT!
¡No lo haga!
(noh loh **AH**-gah)

RUN!
¡Corre!
(**KOHR**-ray)

FAST
Rápido
(**RAH**-pee-doh)

KILL HIM!
Matele
(**MAH**-tay-lay)

I HAVE A FAMILY!
¡Tengo una familia!
(**TEHN-**goh oo-nah fah-**MEE**-lee-ah)

PLEASE!   **NO!**
¡Por favor,   No!
(pohr fah-**VOHR**,   noh)

THINK OF MY FAMILY!
¡Piense de mi familia!
(Pee-**EHN**-say day mee fam-**MEE**-lee-ah)

WHEN HE LOOKS AWAY!
¡Cuando mira para otro lado!
(**KWAHN**-doh mee-**RAH PAH**-rah oh-troh lah-**DOH**)

KILL
Máte
(**MAH**-tay)

PUSH HIM!
¡Empújalo!
(em-**POO**-hah-loh)

SHOOT
tira   or   dispáre
(**TEE**-rah)   (dees-**PAH**-ray)

SHOOT HIM!
¡Tírale!   or   ¡Dispárele!
(**TEE**-rah-lay)   (dees-**PAH**-ray-lay)

STAB HIM!
¡Déle!   or   ¡Pícale!
(**DAY**-lay)   (**PEE**-kah-lay)

GRAB HIM!
¡Agárrele!
(ah-**GAH**-ray-lay)

GET HIS GUN. (THE GUN)
Agarra su arma. (el arma)
(ah-**GAH**-rah soo **AHR**-mah [el ____])

GET THE KNIFE.
Agarra la navaja.
(ah-**GAH**-rah lah nah-**VAH**-hah)

HANDS UP!
¡Manos arriba!
(**MAH**-nohs ah-**REE**-bah)

HIT HIM!
¡Pégale!
(**PAY**-gah-lay)

JUMP ON HIM.   **LET'S GO!**
Sáltele.   ¡Vamos!
(**SAHL**-tay-lay) (**VAH**-mohs)

GUN
arma
(**AHR**-mah)

KNIFE
cuchillo   or   navaja
(koo-**CHEE**-yoh)   (nah-**VAH**-ha)

(Or)

PICA
(**PEE**-kah)

PISTOL
pistola   or   escuadra
(pees-**TOH**-lah)   (es-**KWAH**-drah)

REVOLVER
fusil
(foo-**SEEL**)

RIFLE   rifle   (**REE**-fleh)

WEAPON   arma   (**AHR**-mah)
HELP!   ¡Socorro!   (soh-**KOH**-rroh)

HE DOESN'T SPEAK SPANISH
¡El no habla español!
(ehl noh AH-blah ehs-pah-NYOHL)

HE DOESN'T UNDERSTAND
¡El no entiende!
(ehl noh ehn-tee-EHN-doh)

HE FOUND IT!
¡El lo encontró!
(ehl loh ehn-kohn-TROH)

DAMN IT!
¡Maldito!
(mahl-DEE-toh)

DON'T TALK!
¡No hables!
(noh AH-blehs)

PRETEND NOT TO UNDERSTAND!
¡Finge no entender
(FEEN-hay noh ehn-tehn-DEHR)

I'M BEGGING!
¡Le estoy rogando!
(leh ehs-TOH-ee roh-GAHN-doh)

MY FAMILY!
¡Mi familia!
(mee fah-MEE-lyah)

YOU LIE! ¡Miente! (MYEHN-teh)

OFFER A BRIBE!
¡Ofrece una mordida!
(oh-FREH-seh OO-nah mohr-DEE-dah)

DON'T CONFESS!
¡No confiesa!
(noh kohn-fee-EHS-ah)

WATCH HIM!
¡Wáchale!
(Whoo-AH-chah-lay)

HE IS STUPID!
¡El es estupido!
(ehl ehs ehs-TOO-pee-doh)

DISTRACT HIM!
¡Distráelo!
(dees-TRAH-eh-loh)

GET READY!
¡Prepárese!
(Pray-PAHR-ray-say)

READY?
¿Listo?
(LEES-toh)

MY CHILDREN!
¡Mis niños!
(mees NEE-nyohs)

WHEN I SAY NOW!
¡Cuando digo ahora!
(KWAHN-doh DEE-goh ah-OH-rah)

HIDE IT!
¡Escóndela!
(ehs-KOHN-deh-lah)

PUSH HIM!
¡Empujalo!
(em-POO-hah-loh)

GET RID OF IT!
¡Tíralo!
(TEE-rah-loh)

DON'T! PLEASE! (NO)
¡No! ¡Por favor, ¡No!
(pohr fah-VOHR, noh)

STAB HIM!
¡Dele! or ¡Pícale!
(DAY-lay) (PEE-kah-lay)

(Take an ice pick and lay him down).

TABLE OF CONTENTS

About the Author	158
Constable Public Safety Memorial Foundation	173
Dedication	172
Endorsements	157
Other language training materials	176-177
Purpose	159

ABUSE	12-29
ACCIDENTS AND ACCIDENT INTERVIEWS	10
ADDRESS (Asking for)	11
ADVICE OF RIGHTS (Consent to Search on page 195)	194-195
ALCOHOL AND OPEN ALCOHOLIC CONTAINERS	11
ARREST (YOUR ARE UNDER ARREST FOR)	11
ASSAULT AND DOMESTIC VIOLENCE	12-29
ASSOCIATES and FRIENDS	58
ATTITUDES	38-39
BACKGROUND / BIOG. INVEST.	11
BODY PARTS and VOCABULARY	52
BLOOD AND URINE SAMPLES (Requesting and Test Results)	128
CALENDAR DIVISIONS	15
CARS & VEHICLES (Types of and Determining ownership)	15
CASH	56-57
CITIZEN'S ARREST	16
CLOTHING (Types of)	17
COLORS	17
COMMANDS	17
COMMON PHRASES (Quick Reference)	1
CONCEALMENT AREA (Show me the)	20
CONSCIENCE (Having to do with thoughts.....)	23-24
CONSENT TO SEARCH AND CONTRABAND INTERVIEWS	24,195
CONTRABAND	24
CORRECTIONS (Terminology)	47-50
CULTURAL DIVERSITY (A Matter of Honor)	160
CRIMES (List of), Victim interview and suspect descriptions	29
DATE OF BIRTH	2
DATES TO REMEMBER	101
DEATH MESSAGE (Delivery of)	33
DECEPTION	23-24
DESCRIPTIONS	29-33
DIABETICS	34
DOGS (Animal control phrases)	141,37
DOMESTIC DISTURBANCES (Shelters for abused women)	12,29
DIRECTIONS	33-34
DRAWINGS & DIAGRAMS OF HOUSES	17
DRIVING WHILE INTOXICATED and SOBRIETY TESTS	34-37
DRUG GLOSSARY	130-139
Drug Dogs	37
Drug Interviews	24, 89, 90
Drug Pricing and Packaging	137-139
Drug Slang	130-139
Meth Labs (Precursors, Reagents and Solvents)	139-141
DYING DECLARATIONS	38
EDUCATION (Determining education and reading / writing ability)	38
EMERGENCY 911 DISPATCH PHRASES	196 AND INSIDE BACK COVER
EMOTIONS (Determining emotional state)	38-39
ENGLISH (Do you speak? Understand?)	39-40
EQUIPMENT (Vehicle)	69-70
EXPRESSIONS	23-24
FALSE IDENTIFICATION	47

FALSE NAMES	58
FELONY ARREST	(INSIDE FRONT COVER)
F.I.R. (Quick reference for basic identification of person(s))	2
FIRE & ARSON	40
FORGERY / FRAUD	29
FOREIGN CURRENCY	46
FRIENDS & ASSOCIATES	58
FRUITS & VEGETABLES	40-41
GANGS (Street) (A Profile)	84-87
GANG AFFILIATIONS	12-14
GANG NICKNAMES	88
GANG ORGANIZATIONAL STRUCTURE CHART	109
GANGS (Prison) (A Profile)	89
GANG TATTOOS (Prison and Street)	112-127
GANG SLANG (Street, Jail, Prison and Drug)	89-108
Cuban Criminals - The Marielitos	103-104
Latin Kings (LK)	105
Mara Salvatrucha (MS)	106-108
Mexican Mafia (MM)	90-92
Mexikanemi (Mexican Mafia - Texas)	93-96
My Race United (MR) Mi Raza Unida	105
Nuestra Familia (NF)	101-102
Texas Syndicate (TS)	96-100
GRAMMAR (Basic) and helpful hints for the field	3, 4
Alphabet	142
Errors when speaking	143
Nicknames	88
Shortcuts (Survival Spanish® - No conjugation)	148
Similar words	145
Survival Spanish® learning cognates	144
Verbs and simple conjugation	146-151
GREETINGS	43-44
HANDS & ARMS (Phrases for controlling)	44
HEART (attack)	55
HOME (We are taking you home)	44
HOUSE (Parts of and common household items)	44-46
HOW (Questions)	46
IDENTIFICATION (Do you have?)	46
IMMIGRATION QUESTIONS	12-14
Deportation / Parole / Probation / Bail Hearings	129
INTERPRETER (Do you want one? - Page 47) Selection of	167
INTERVIEWS (Suspects, Victims, and Witnesses)	29
INTERVIEWING EXPRESSIONS	23-24
JUVENILE	50
LAWYER	50
LICENSE (Driver's)	50
LOCATIONS (Determining specific)	44-46
MEDICAL	51-56
MEDICAL (Emergency Quick Reference)	INSIDE OF BACK COVER
MEXICAN CITIES and STATES	62
MEXICAN and HISPANIC FAMILY VALUES	160
MISSING OR LOST CHILD	55
MONEY (Banking & Commerce; Foreign Currency)	56-57
MOODS	38-39
MOTORIST ASSIST	15
NAMES (Name and date of birth structure)	57-58
Hints on Hispanic name structure	156
NATIONALITIES	152
NUMBERS (Ordinal & Cardinal)	59-60
OCCUPATIONS (List of)	60
OFFICER SAFETY PHRASES AND "RED FLAG" WORDS	5, 6, 122

Entry	Page
OPEN CONTAINER (alcohol)	11
PAROLE AND PROBATION (To Do With)	127-
PATRON SAINTS (List on pages 153-155)	2
PHOTOGRAPHS / Mug Shots	61
POLICE (International terms for)	109
POLICE / POLICE STATIONS	64
POSSESSION (Culpability)	195
PUPIL DILATION CHART	(BACK COVER)
RACE (Determining race of suspects)	62
RADIO CODES (& Morse Code)	58-59
RAID BRIEFINGS (Delegation of assignments checklist)	111
RAPE	29
RECALL UNDER HIGH STRESS (Learning Tips)	168
RELATIONSHIPS (Determining)	58
RELATIVES (Is this your........?)	61
RESTRAINING AND STALKING ORDERS	128
ROBBERY	29
SCARS, MARKS, & TATTOOS	12-14
SEARCH & SEIZURE	195
SEARCH WARRANTS ("Knock and Announce phrases")	FRONT COVER
SHOPLIFTING	29
SOCIAL SECURITY NUMBERS	110
SUICIDE PREVENTION (also see "COMMANDS")	63
TAPE RECORDING (Pre-Advisal)	63
TELEPHONE (Use of)	63
THEFT	29
TIME CONCEPTIONS AND TIME QUESTIONS	20-23
TOW TRUCK	64
TRAFFIC STOPS (Car Parts on page 68)	65-72
TRANSLATIONS	152
TRAVEL (MODES OF)	80-81
TRUCK INSPECTIONS	73-80
Initial Contact (Inspection Terms)	73-76
Brakes	78
Common Terms	77
Contraband and Smuggling	76
Coupling and Towing Devices	78
Driver (Condition of)	80
Frames and Chasis	78
Fuel Systems	78
Hours of Service	80
Inspections (Proof of)	80
License Requirements and Standards	80
Log Book Violations	80
Other Vehicle Defects	79
Suspension	78
Tires	79
Wheels and Studs	79
TRESPASS	29
TRUTH AND DECEPTION	51
VICTIM INTERVIEWS	29
VICTIMS ASSISTANCE PHONE NUMBERS	175
VOCABULARY	179-192
WARRANTS (Arrest and Search)	81
WHAT QUESTIONS	81-82
WHEN QUESTIONS	82
WHERE QUESTIONS	82-83
WHICH QUESTIONS	83
WHO QUESTIONS	83
WHY	84
WILDLIFE INVESTIGATIONS (Fish and Game)	41-43
WITNESSES	2, 83

ACCIDENTS

AMBULANCE
ambulancia
(ahm-boo-LAHN-see-ah)

CALL AN AMBULANCE
Llamar una ambulancia
(yah-MAHR OO-nah ahm-boo-LAHN-syah)

EMERGENCY ROOM-
Sala de emergencia
(SAH-lah day eh-mehr-GEHN-see-ah)

CALL A DOCTOR
llamar a un médico
(yah-MAHR ah oon MEH-dee-koh)

HELP! ¡Socorro!
(soh-KOH-roh)

HOSPITAL
hospital
(ohs-pee-TAHL)

SERIOUS ACCIDENT
accidente grave
(ahk-see-DEHN-tay GRAH-vay)

TRAFFIC ACCIDENT
Accidente de tránsito
(ahk-see-DEHN-tay day TRAHN-see-toh)

SHOCK choque (CHOH-kay)
WOUND herida (eh-REE-dah)

ARE YOU OK?
¿Está bien?
(Ess-TAH bee-YEHN)

I WILL HELP YOU.
Yo le ayudaré.
(Yoh lay ah-yoo-dah-RAY)

CALM DOWN!
¡Cálmese!
(KAHL-meh-seh)

ARE YOU HURT/INJURED?
¿Está lastimado/herido?
(Ess-TAH lahs-tee-MAH-doh / ehr-EE-doh)

SHOW ME THE PLACE.
Enséñeme el lugar.
(En-SEHN-yeh-may ehl LOO-gahr)

WANT TO GO TO THE HOSPITAL?
¿Quiere ir al hospital?
(Kee-EH-ray eer ahl ohs-pee-TAHL)

LAY DOWN HERE.
Acuéstese aquí.
(ah-Koo-AYS-tay-say ah-KEE)

THE AMBULANCE IS COMING
La ambulancia viene
(La ahm-boo-LAHN-syah vee-EHN-nay)

YOU WILL BE OK.
Estará bien.
(Ess-tahr-AH bee-YEHN)

CALM DOWN!
¡Cálmese!
(KAHL-meh-seh)

YOUR WIFE / CHILD /HUSBAND IS OK.
Su esposa / niño / esposo / está bien.
(Soo ess-POH-sah\ NEEN-yoh\ ess-POH-soh\ ess-TAH bee-YEHN)

DID YOU SEE THE ACCIDENT?
¿Vió usted el accidente?
(vee-OH oo-STED ayl ahk-see-DEN-tay)

WHO WAS THE DRIVER?
¿Quién era el chofer?
(Kee-EHN ay-rah el chof-FAYR)

HOW FAST WERE YOU GOING?
A qué velocidad iba usted
manejando su carro?
(ah kay veh-loh-see-DAHD EE-bah oo-STEHD mah-neh-HAHN-doh soo KAHR-roh)

WERE YOU DRIVING THE CAR?
¿Usted estaba manejando este carro?
(oo-STEHD ehs-TAH-bah mah-neh-HAHN-doh EHS-tay KAHR-roh)

HAVE YOU BEEN DRINKING?
(SEE DWI IF DRINKING)
¿Ha estado usted tomando?
(Ah ess-TAH-doh oo-STEHD toh-MAHN-doh)

GIVE ME YOUR LICENSE & REG.
Déme su licencia y circulación
(DEH-may soo lee-SEHN-see-ah ee seer-koo-lah-SYOHN)

DO YOU HAVE A LICENSE?
¿Tiene usted licencia?
(Tee-EHN-ay oo-STED lee-SEHN-syah)

(see "NAMES" for name & address)

IS THIS YOUR CAR?
Es este su carro?
(Ess ESS-tay soo KAHR-roh)

WHO IS THE OWNER OF THE CAR?
¿Quién es el dueño del carro?
(Kee-EHN es ayl DWEH-nyoh dayl KAHR-roh)

MAY I SEE YOUR INSURANCE PAPERS?
Déjeme ver los papeles de aseguranza de su carro.
(DAY-hay-may behr lohs pah-PAY-lays day ah-say-goo-RAHN-zah day soo KAHR-roh)

DO YOU WANT A TOW TRUCK?
¿Quiere usted una grua?
(Kee-AYR-ay oo-STEHD OO-nah GROO-ah)

HERE IT STATES WHERE YOUR CAR IS.
Aquí dice donde está su carro.
(Ah-KEE DEE-say DOHN-day ess-TAH soo KAHR-roh

ADDRESS

WHAT IS YOUR ADDRESS?
¿Cuál es su domicilio?
(Kwahl es soo doh-mee-SEE-lyoh)
  or   dirección (dee-rehk-SYOHN)

AVENUE avenida (ah-beh-NEE-dah)
BLOCK manzana (mahn-ZAH-nah)
CITY ciudad (see-oo-DAHD)
COUNTRY país (pah-EES);
  (or) S.America patria (PAH-tree-ah)

DEPARTMENT departamento
  (deh-pahr-tah-MEHN-toh)
HOUSE NO. número de casa
  (NOO-may-roh day KAH-sah)
  or   dirección (dee-rehk-SYOHN)
SQUARE plaza (PLAH-sah)
STATE estado (ehs-TAH-doh)
STREET calle (KAH-yay)
TOWN pueblo (PWEH-bloh)
ZONE zona (ZOH-nah)

ALCOHOL

HAVE YOU BEEN DRINKING LIQUOR? ALCOHOL?
¿Ha estado tomando licor?
(Ah ays-TAH-doh toh-MAHN-doh lee-KOHR)   (alcohol) (ahl-koh-OHL)

IT IS UNLAWFUL TO HAVE AN OPEN ALCOHOL CONTAINER IN THE CAR
Es prohibido tener un bote abierto (licor) (alcohol) en el carro)
(Ess proh-EE-bee-doh tay-NAYR oon BOH-tay ah-bee-AYR-toh [lee-KOHR] (ahl-koh-OHL) ehn ayl KAHR-roh)

ARREST

YOU ARE UNDER ARREST FOR....
Usted está arrestado por....
(Oo-STEHD ess-TAH ah-reh-STAH-doh pohr....)

POSSESSION OF NARCOTICS
Posesión de narcóticos
(poh-sez-SYOHN day nahr-KOH-tee-kohs)

DRIVING WITH A SUSPENDED DRIVER'S LICENSE
Manejando con licencia suspendida
(mah-neh-HAHN-doh kohn lee-SEHN-see-ah soos-PEHN-dee-dah)

THERE IS A WARRANT FOR YOUR ARREST.
Hay una orden para su arresto.
(I OO-nah OHR-dehn PAH-rah soo ah-REHS-toh)

ASSAULT Asalto (ah-SAHL-toh)

CARRYING A CONCEALED WEAPON
Llevar arma ocultada (escondida)
(yeh-VAHR AHR-mah oh-kool-TAH-dah [ays-kohn-DEE-dah])

(refer "CRIMES" for other crimes)

ASSAULT AND DOMESTIC VIOLENCE

CALM DOWN!	¡Cálmese!	DOES ANYONE HAVE A WEAPON (GUN)?	¿Tiene alguien un arma?
	(KAHL-meh-seh)		(Tee-EHN-ay ahl-GOO-ee-ehn oon AHR-mah)

DID HE / SHE STRIKE YOU? WERE YOU BEATEN? *(See "Crimes.")*
¿El/ella le pegó? ¿Le golpearon?
(ehl/EH-yah leh peh-GOH?) (Lay gohl-peh-AH-rohn)

DID HE HIT YOU WITH HIS FIST?
¿Le pegó a usted con su puño?
(Lay peh-GOH ah oo-STEHD kohn soo poo-NYOH)

DID HE STAB YOU? WHO DID THIS TO YOU?
¿El te apuñaló? ¿Quién te hizo esto?
(El tay ah-poo-nyah-LOH) (Kee-EHN tay HEE-zoh ESS-toh)

WHAT DOES HE OR SHE LOOK LIKE?
¿Como se parece el o ella?
(KOH-moh say pah-RAY-say ayl oh AY-yah)

DO YOU WISH TO BE PROTECTED IN A SHELTER FOR WOMEN?
¿Desea protección en un asilo para mujeres?
(deh-SEH-ah pro-tehk-see-SYOHN ehn oon ah-SEE-loh PAH-rah moo-HEH-rehs?)

(For DESCRIPTIONS see Crimes, Descriptions, Associates & Names)

BACKGROUND - BIOGRAPHICAL INVESTIGATIONS & GANGS

NAME	nombre	(NOHM-bray)
NICKNAME	sobrenombre/apodo	(soh-bray-NOHM-bray / ah-POH-doh)
ALIAS	alias	(ah-LEE-ahs)
OTHER NAME	otro nombre	(OH-troh NOHM-bray)
DOB	fecha de nacimiento	(fay-CHAH day nah-SEE-mee-EHN-toh)
ADDRESS	domicilio de correos	(doh-mee-SEE-lee-oh day koh-RAY-ohs)
STREET	calle	(KAH-yah)
POST OFFICE BOX	casilla de correo apartado postal	(kah-SEE-yah day koh-RAY-ohs) (ah-pahr-TAH-doh pohs-TAHL)
AVENUE	avenida	(ah-vayn-EE-dah)
CITY	ciudad	(SEE-oo-dahd)
COUNTY	condado	(kohn-DAH-doh)
STATE	estado	(ays-TAH-doh)
COUNTRY	país	(pah-EES)
DRIVERS LICENSE NO.	número de licencia	(NOO-may-roh day lee-SEHN-see-ah)
STATE	estado	(ays-TAH-doh)
LAST KNOWN LOCATION	domicilio más reciente	(doh-mee-SEE-lee-oh mahs ray-see-EHN-tay)

NATIONALITY	nacionalidad	
	(nah-syohn-**AHL**-ee-dahd)	
GANG AFFILIATION	afiliación de pandilla	
	(ah-**FEE**-lee-**AH**-syohn day pahn-**DEE**-yah)	
PLACE OF BIRTH	lugar de nacimiento	
	(loo-**GAHR** day nah-**SEE**-mee-**EHN**-toh)	
HEIGHT	altura	(ahl-**TOO**-roh)
WEIGHT	peso	(**PAY**-soh)
EYE COLOR	color de ojos	(koh-**LOHR** day **OH**-hohs)
HAIR COLOR	color de pelo	(koh-**LOHR** day **PAY**-loh)
SOCIAL SECURITY No.	número de seguro social	
	(**NOO**-may-roh day say-**GOO**-roh soh-see-**AHL**)	
ALIEN REG. CARD No.	número de su mica	
	(**NOO**-may-roh day soo **MEE**-kah)	

ARE YOU AN AMERICAN CITIZEN? ¿Es usted un ciudadano americano?
(Ays oo-**STEHD** oon see-oo-dahd-**DAH**-noh ah-may-ree-**KAH**-noh)

DO YOU HAVE IMMIGRATION PAPERS?
¿Tiene usted papeles de imigración / mica?
(tee-**EHN**-ay oo-**STEHD** pah-**PEHL**-ays day eem-ee-grah-**SYOHN** / **MEE**-kah)

IMMIGRATION CARD, SHOW ME YOUR	Enséñeme su mica.	
	(ehn-seh-**NYEH**-may soo **MEE**-kah)	
GREEN CARD, SHOW ME YOUR	Enséñeme su mica.	
	(ehn-seh-**NYEH**-may soo **MEE**-kah)	
DO YOU HAVE A PASSPORT?	¿Tiene un pasaporte?	
	(Tee-**EHN**-nay oon pah-sah-**POHR**-tay)	
HOME ADDRESS	dirección de casa	
	(dee-rehk-**SYOHN** day **KAH**-sah)	
EMPLOYER	patrón	(pah-**TROHN**)
OCCUPATION-	ocupación	(oh-koo-pah-**SYOHN**)
YEARS EMPLOYED-	años empleado	(**AHN**-yohs ehm-play-**AH**-doh)
NAME OF SUPV.-	nombre del supervisor	
	(**NOHM**-bray dayl soo-**PAYR**-vee-sohr)	
REFERENCES	referencias	(ray-fayr-**EHN**-see-ahs)
TELEPHONE NUMBER	número de teléfono	
	(**NOO**-may-roh day tay-**LAY**-foh-noh)	
BUSINESS PHONE No.	número de teléfono del trabajo	
	(**NOO** may-roh day tay-**LAY**-foh-noh dayl trah-**BAH**-hoh)	
MARITAL STATUS	estado legal matrimonial	
	(ay-**STAH**-doh lay-**GAHL** mah-tree-mohn-ee-**AHL**)	
MARRIED, SINGLE, DIVORCED	casado, soltero, divorciado	
	(kah-**SAH**-doh, sohl-**TAY**-roh, dee-**VOHR**-see-ah-doh)	
SPOUSE NAME	nombre de esposo / esposa	
	(**NOHM**-bray day ays-**POH**-soh / ays-**POH**-sah)	

ADDRESS/ EMPLOYER/ PHONE NUMBER
dirección, patrón, número de teléfono
(dee-rehk-SYOHN, pah-TROHN, NOO-may-roh day tay-LAY-foh-noh)

DRIVERS LICENSE NUMBER & STATE
número de su licencia y de cuál estado
(NOO-may-roh day soo lee-SEHN-see-ah ee day koo-AHL ays-TAH-doh)

VEHICLE PLATE NO. número de placa
(NOO-may-roh day PLAH-kah)

MOTHER'S NAME nombre de madre
(NOHM-bray day MAH-dray)

FATHER'S NAME nombre de padre
(NOHM-bray day PAH-dray)

ADDRESS/PHONE NO. dirección y número de teléfono
(dee-rehk-SYOHN ee NOO-may-roh day tay-LAY-foh-noh)

CLOSE FRIENDS & ASSOCIATES NAMES
nombres de amigos cercanos y socios
(nohm-BRAYS day ah-MEE-gohs sayr-KAH-nohs ee soh-SEE-ohs)

ADDRESS/PHONE #s dirección y número de teléfono
(dee-rehk-SYOHN ee NOO-may-roh day tay-LAY-foh-noh)

VEHICLE PLATE NO. número de la placa
(NOO-may-roh day lah PLAH-kah)

PRIOR ARRESTS	¿Arrestos previos?	
	(Ah-REHS-tohs pray-VEE-ohs)	
WHEN; WHERE:	¿cuándo? ¿dónde?	(KWAHN-doh; DOHN-day)
WHAT CHARGE?	¿acusado de?	(ah-koo-SAH-doh day)
SCARS	¿cicatrices?	(see-KAH-tree-says)

DO YOU HAVE ANY SCARS OR TATTOOS?
¿Tiene usted cicatrices o tatuajes?
(Tee-EHN-ay oo-STEHD see-kah-TREE-says oh tah-TWAH-ays)

MARKS [TATTOOS]	marcas [tatuajes]	
	(MAHR-kahs [tah-too-AH-hays])	
[BIRTHMARKS]	[estigmas]	(ays-TEEG-mahs)
REMARKS	observaciones	(ohb-sayr-VAH-syohn-ays)

FALSE TEETH/PIERCED EARS(S)/JEWELRY/ETC.-
Dientes falsos / perforaciones en los oidos/joyas/etc.
(dee-EHN-tays FAHL-sohs / payr-foh-RAH-syohn-ays ehn lohs
oh-EE-dohs/HOH-yahs)

"Never get into fist fights with ugly people as they have nothing to lose".

CALENDAR DIVISIONS

MONTHS OF THE YEAR

January	enero	(eh-**NEH**-roh)
February	febrero	(feh-**BREH**-roh)
March	marzo	(**MAHR**-soh)
April	abril	(ah-**BREEL**)
May	mayo	(**MAH**-yoh)
June	junio	(**HOO**-nyoh)
July	julio	(**HOO**-lyoh)
August	agosto	(ah-**GOHS**-stoh)
Sept.	septiembre	(sep-**TYEM**-breh)
October	octubre	(ohk-**TOO**-breh)
Nov.	noviembre	(noh-**VYEM**-breh)
Dec.	diciembre	(dee-**SYEM**-breh)

DAYS OF THE WEEK

Sunday	domingo	(Doh-**MEEN**-goh)
Monday	lunes	(**LOO**-nehs)
Tuesday	mártes	(**MAHR**-tehs)
Wed.	miércoles	(mee-**EHR**-koh-lehs)
Thurs.	jueves	(**HWEH**-behs)
Friday	viernes	(bee-**EHR**-nehs)
Sat.	sábado	(**SAH**-bah-doh)

SEASONS OF THE YEAR

Spring	primavera	(pree-mah-**BEH**-rah)
Summer	verano	(beh-**RAH**-noh)
Autumn	otoño	(oh-**TOH**-nyoh)
Winter	invierno	(een-vee-**EHR**-noh)

Day of the week
día de la semana
(**DEE**-ah day lah seh-**MAH**-nah)

Day día (**DEE**-ah)
Week- semana (seh-**MAHN**-nah)
Month mes (mehs)
Year- año (**AHN**-nyoh)
Weekend fin de semana
(feen day seh-**MAH**-nah)
Workday día entre semana
(**DEE**-ah **EHN**-tray say-**MAH**-nah)

HOLIDAY fiesta (fee-**EHS**-tah)
VACATION vacaciones
(vah-**KAH**-syohn-ays)
TIME tiempo (**TYEHM**-poh)

WHEN? ¿Cuándo? (**KWAHN**-doh)

WHAT DAY? ¿Qué día? (kay **DEE**-ah)

WHAT WEEKDAY?
¿Qué dia de semana?
(kay **DEE**-ah day seh-**MAH**-nah)

WHAT MONTH?
¿Qué mes?
(Kay mehs)

WHAT YEAR?
¿Qué año?
(kay **AHN**-yoh)

WHAT TIME DID YOU LEAVE?
¿A qué hora salió?
(ah kay **OH**-rah sah-lee-**OH**)

WHAT TIME DID YOU ARRIVE?
¿A qué hora llegó?
(ah kay **OH**-rah yay-**GOH**)

WHEN DID HE LEAVE?
¿Cuándo salió?
(**KWAHN**-doh sah-lee-**OH**)

WHEN DID HE ARRIVE?
¿Cuándo llegó?
(**KWAHN**-doh yay-**GOH**)

WHEN WILL HE RETURN?
¿Cuándo volverá?
(**KWAHN**-doh vohl-vehr-**AH**)

WHEN DID THEY ARRIVE?
¿Cuándo llegaron?
(**KWAHN**-doh yay-**GAH**-rohn)

WHEN WERE YOU TO MEET?
¿Cuándo se iban a juntar?
KWAHN-doh say **EE**-bahn
ah hoon-**TAHR**

CAR and VEHICLES

CAR carro (**KAHR**-roh)
BUS- bús (**BOOS**);
camión (kah-mee-**OHN**)

COMPACT CAR- coche pequeño
(**KOH**-chay peh-**KAY**-nyoh)
MOTORCYCLE motocicleta
(moh-toh-see-**KLEH**-tah)
MOTORHOME- casa rodante
(**KAH**-sah roh-**DAHN**-tay)
PICKUP- camioneta
(kah-myoh-**NEH**-tah)
RENTED CAR- coche alquilado
(**KOH**-chay ahl-kee-**LAH**-doh)
SPORTS CAR- coche deportivo
(**KOH**-chay deh-pohr-**TEE**-voh)
TAXI- taxi (**TAHK**-see)
TRAILER- traila (trah-**EE**-lah)
- remolque (reh-**MOHL**-kay)
TRUCK- camión (kah-**MYOHN**)
VEHICLE vehículo (beh-**EE**-koo-loh)
VAN- furgón (foor-**GOHN**);
van (vahn)

FOUR DOOR	de cuatro puertas	¿Kwahl ehs deh keh ehs-TAH-doh ehs?
FOUR WHEELS	cuatro ruedas (day KWAH-troh PWEHR-tahs)	
TWO DOOR	de dos puertas (day KWAH-troh roo-AY-dahs)	**WHO IS THE OWNER OF THE CAR?**
TWO WHEELS	dos ruedas (day dohs PWEHR-tahs)	¿Quién es el dueño del vehículo?
	(dohs roo-AY-dahs)	(kee-EHN ehs ehl DOO-EH-nyoh dehl veh-EE-koo-loh?)

DID YOUR CAR QUIT?
¿Falló su carro? (fah-YOH soo KAHR-roh) or
¿Ya no trabaja su carro?
(yah noh trah-BAH-hoh soo KAHR-roh)

WHAT IS THAT PERSON'S NAME?
¿Cómo se llama esa persona?
(KOH-moh seh YAH-mah EH-sah pehr-SOH-nah?)

ANYTHING WRONG WITH THE CAR?
¿Hay algo malo con su carro?
(I AHL-go MAH-lo kon soo KAHR-roh)

SIGN (V) firme (FEER-meh) (for stolen)

STOP YOUR MOTOR
Apague su motor
(Ah-PAH-gay soo moh-TOHR)

CITIZEN'S ARREST

GET OUT OF THE CAR.
Bájate del carro.
(BAH-hah-tay dayl KAHR-roh)

IF YOU SIGN THIS, I WILL ARREST HIM
Si usted firma esto, lo detendré.
(see oo-STEHD FEER-mah ays-toh,
loh day-tehn-DRAY)

IS THIS YOUR CAR?
¿Es este su carro?
(Ess ESS-teh soo KAHR-roh)

CLOTHING

WHOSE CAR IS THIS?
¿De quién es este carro?
(Day Kee-EHN ays ESS-teh KAHR-roh)

TAKE OFF ALL YOUR CLOTHES.
Quítese toda la ropa.
(KEE-teh-say TOH-dah lah ROH-pah)

GET INTO THE CAR.
Súbase al carro.
(SOO-bah-say ahi KAHR-roh)

GIVE ME YOUR CLOTHES
Deme su ropa
(DEH-may soo ROH-pah)

HERE IT STATES WHERE YOUR CAR IS. (TOWED).
Aquí dice dónde está su carro.
(Ah-KEE DEE-say DOHN-day ess-TAH soo KAHR-roh) [reh-mohl-KAH-doh] (remolcado)

GIVE ME YOUR .... Déme su(s) ....
(DEH-may soo[s]......)

BAG	bolsa	(BOHL-sah)
BELT	faja	(FAH-zhah)
BLOUSE	blusa	(BLOO-sah)
BOOTS	botas	(BOH-tahs)
BRA	sostén	(sohs-TEHN)
	brasier	(brah-SEE-ayr)
BRIEFCASE	maletín	(mah-leh-TEEN)
COAT	saco	(SAH-koh)
DRESS	vestido	(bens-TEE-doh)
GARMENT BAG	bolsa	(BOHL-sah)
HAT	sombrero	(sohm-BREH-roh)
JACKET	chaqueta	(chah-KAY-tah)
	chamarra	(chah-MAH-rah)
JEWELRY	joyas	(HOY-ahs)
PANTIES	pantaletas	(pahn-tah-LAY-tahs)
	calzones	(kahl-ZOH-nays)
PURSE	bolsa	(BOHL-sah)
SHIRT	camisa	(kah-MEE-sah)
SHOES	zapatos	(sah-PAH-tohs)
SKIRT	falda	(FAHL-dah)
STOCKINGS	medias	(MEH-dee-ahs)
SUITCASE	maleta	(mah-LEH-tah)
TRAVEL	viajar	(vee-ah-HAHR)

DEFECTIVE . (POINT AT PART). (SEE TRAFFIC STOPS)
Defectivo _____.
(dee-FEHK-tee-voh)

DID YOU GET A VEHICLE LICENSE PLATE NUMBER?
¿Obtuviste su número de placa del vehículo?
(Ohb-too-VEES-tay soo NOO-may-roh day PLAH-kahs dayl beh-EE-koo-loh)

WHAT IS THE LICENSE PLATE NUMBER AND STATE?
¿Cuál es el número de la placa y de qué estado es?

UNDERWEAR ropa interior
 (ROH-pah een-teh-ree-OHR)
WALLET   cartera (kahr-TEH-rah)

COLORS

WHAT COLOR? ¿De qué color?
 (Day kay koh-LOHR)

black-	negro	(**NEH**-groh)
blue-	azúl	(ah-**SOOL**)
dark blue-	azúl oscuro	
	(ah-**SOOL** ohs-**KOO**-roh)	
light blue-	azúl claro	
	(ah-**SOOL** **KLAH**-roh)	
navy blue-	azúl marino	
	(ah-**SOOL** mah-**REE**-noh)	
bright-	vivo	(**BEE**-boh)
brown-	café	(kah-**FAY**)
dark-	oscuro	(ohs-**KOO**-roh)
dull-	apagado	(ah-pah-**GAH**-doh)
gold-	dorado	(doh-**RAH**-doh)
gray-	gris	(grees)
green-	verde	(**BEHR**-day)
light-	claro	(**KLAH**-roh)
orange-	anaranjado	
	(ah-nah-rahn-**HAH**-doh)	
pink-	rosado	(roh-**SAH**-doh)
purple-	púrpuro	(**POOR**-poo-roh)
	morado	(moh-**RAH**-doh)
red-	colorado	(koh-loh-**RAH**-doh)
	rojo	(**ROH**-hoh)
silver-	plateado	(plah-teh-**AH**-doh)
transparent-	transparente	
	(trahns-pah-**REHN**-tay)	
white-	blanco	(**BLAHN**-koh)
yellow-	amarillo	(ah-mah-**REE**-yoh)

COMMANDS

ANSWER YES OR NO.
Conteste si o no.
(Kohn-**TEHS**-tay see oh noh)

BEND OVER!
¡Agáchate!
(ah-**GAH**-chah-tay)

BRING IT!
¡Traigalo!
(**TRAH**-ee-gah-loh

CALM DOWN!
¡Cálmese!
(**KAHL**-meh-seh)

CARRY IT! ¡Llevalo!
 (**YAY**-vah-loh)

CLOSE! ¡Cierra! (see-**AIR**-ah)

COME- Venga   (**VEHN**-gah)

COME HERE. Venga aquí
 (**VEHN**-gah ah-**KEE**)

COME WITH ME- Venga conmigo.
 (**VEHN**-gah kohn-**MEE**-goh)

DESCRIBE-   describe
 (days-**KREE**-bay)

DO WHAT HE SAYS-
 Haga lo que el diga.
 (**AH**-gah loh kay ayl **DEE**-gah)

DON'T BE AFRAID. No tenga miedo.
 (noh **TEHN**-gah mee-**AY**-doh)

DON'T HANG UP! ¡No cuelgues!
 (Noh koo-**EHL**-gays)

Don't jump No salte. (no **SAHL**-tay)

DON'T MOVE. No se mueva.
 (Noh say moo-**EH**-vah)

DON'T SHOOT.   No dispare.
 (Noh dees-**PAH**-ray)

DRAW IT-   dibujemelo
 (dee-**BOO**-hay-may-loh)

DRAW ME THE INSIDE & OUTSIDE OF THE HOUSE.
Dibújeme el interior y exterior de la casa.
(Dee-**BOO**-hay-may ehl
ehn-tee-ree-**OHR** ee ehl
ex-tee-ree-**OHR** day lah **KAH**-sah)

LABEL THE ROOMS AND DOORS.
(North at top)
Nombre los cuartos y las puertas.
[Norte a la parte de arriba]
(**NOHM**-bray lohs **KWAHR**-tohs ee
lahs **PWEHR**-tahs [**NOHR**-tay ah lah
PAHR-tay day ahr-**REE**-bah])

DRIVE- Maneja (mah-**NAY**-hah)

DROP IT! ¡Déjela caer!
 (**DEH**-hay-lah kah-**EHR**)

DROP YOUR PANTS-
 Baje sus pantalones.
 (**BAH**-hay soos pahn-tah-**LOHN**-nays)

EMPTY YOUR POCKETS
Vacie sus bolsillos.
(Vah-**SEE**-eh soos bohl-**SEE**-yohs)

FOLLOW ME Sígame (**SEE**-gah-may)

18

FREEZE!	¡Quieto!	(kee-ET-oh)
GET DRESSED!	¡Vístese!	(VEES-tay-say)
GET INTO THE CAR	Súbase al carro.	(SOO-bay-say ahl KAHR-roh)
GET OUT OF THE CAR	Salga del carro	(SAHL-gah dayl KAHR-roh)
GET UP	Levántese	(lay-VAHN-tay-say)
GIVE ME THAT	Déme eso	(DEH-may ESS-oh)
GIVE ME YOUR ___.	Déme su ___.	(DEH-may soo ___.)
PRINT YOUR NAME	Escriba su nombre con letras de molde.	(ehs-KREE-bah soo NOHM-bray kohn LEH-trahs day MOHL-day)
GIVE THEM TO ME	Démelos a mí	(DEH-may-lohs ah mee)
PULL OFF THE ROAD.	Conduzca fuera del camino.	(Kohn-DOOZ-kah foo-AYR-ah dayl kah-MEE-noh)
PUSH!	¡Empuje!	(ehm-POO-hay)
PUT-	ponga	(POHN-gah)
PUT YOUR HANDS ON YOUR HEAD.	Ponga las manos sobre la cabeza.	(POHN-gah lahs MAH-nohs SOH-bray lah kah-BAY-sah)
PUT YOUR HANDS BEHIND YOU.	Ponga las manos detrás de usted.	(POHN-gah lahs MAH-nohs day-TRAHS oo-STEHD)
PUT YOUR THINGS ON THE TABLE.	Ponga sus cosas en la mesa	(POHN-gah soos KOH-sahs ehn lah MAY-sah)
QUICK!	¡Rápido!	(RAH-pee-doh)
QUIET!	¡Silencio!	(see-LEHN-see-oh)
READ THIS	Lea esto	(LAY-ah AY-stoh)
RELAX	relájese	(ray-LAH-hes-say)
REPEAT	repita	(ray-PEE-tah)
RETURN (ITEM)	devolver	(deh-bohl-BEHR)
I WILL RETURN	Yo volveré.	(yoh vohl-veh-RAY)
RETURN TOMORROW	vuelva mañana	(VAYL-vah man-NYAN-yah)
MOVE	muevese	(moo-AY-vay-say)
DON'T MOVE!	¡No se mueva!	(noh say moo-EH-vah)
LOOK FOR IT	Búsquelo	(BOOS-kay-loh)
LISTEN!	¡Escuche!	(ehs-KOO-chay)
LIFT	levántelo	(lay-VAHN-tay-loh)
LIE DOWN!	¡Acuéstese!	(ah-KWEHS-tay-say)
LET'S GO!	¡Vámonos!	(VAH-mah-nohs)
LET ME DO IT	Déjame hacerlo	(DEH-hay-may ah-SEHR-loh)
RELAX YOUR HAND	Descanse la mano.	(Dehs-KAHN-say lah MAH-noh)
LEAVE IT	Déjalo	(DAY-hah-loh)
LEAVE!	¡Váyase!	(VIE-yah-say)
KNEEL!	¡Híncate!	(EEN-kah-tay)
I ORDER YOU TO HELP ME!	¡Te ordeno que me ayudes!	(Tay ohr-DAY-noh kay may ah-YOO-days)
LET ME SEE YOUR HANDS.	Déjeme ver las manos.	(DAY-hay-may behr lahs MAH-nohs)
HANDS UP-	Manos arriba	(MAH-nohs ah-REE-bah)
HAND OVER	Entregue(en-TRAY-gay)	
GO OVER THERE	Vaya allí	(VAH-yah ah-YEE)
LET'S GO	Vámonos.	(VAH-mah-nohs)
GO!	¡Váyase!	(VIE-yah-say)
GIVE UP!	¡Ríndete!	(REEN-day-tay)
POINT-	apunte	(ah-POON-tay)
POINT HIM OUT	Apúntele	(Ah-POON-tay-lay)
POINT IT OUT	Apúntelo	(ah-POON-tay-loh)
OPEN!	¡Abra!	(AH-brah)
NOW!	¡Ahora!	(ah-OH-rah)
NO TALKING!	¡No hablen!	(nohAH-blehn)
OPEN IT!	¡Ábralo!	(AH-brah-loh)
OPEN THE DOOR!	¡Abra la puerta!	(AH-brah lah PWEYR-tah)
OPEN YOUR PURSE!	¡Abra su bolsa!	(AH-brah soo BOHL-sah)
OUT!	¡Fuera!	(FWEH-rah)
EVERYBODY OUT!	¡Todos afuera!	(TOH-dohs ah-FWEH-rah)

RUN! ¡Corre! (koh-**RAY**)

SEPARATE YOUR FEET.
Separe los pies.
(Seh-**PAHR**-ay lohs pee-**ESS**)

SHOW ME Muéstreme.
(**MWEHS**-treh-may)

SHOW ME THE PLACE.
Enséñeme el lugar.
(En-**SEHN**-yeh-may al **LOO**-gahr)

SHOW ME YOUR ARMS!
¡Enséñeme sus brazos!
(En-**SEHN**-yeh-may soos **BRAH**-sohs)

LIFT YOUR ARMS UP.
Levánte los brazos.
(Leh-**VAHN**-tay soos **BRAH**-sohs)

LET ME SEE THE BOTTOMS OF YOUR FEET.
Dejeme ver los fondos de sus pies.
(**DEH**-hay-may vehr lohs **FOHN**-dohs day soos **PEE**-ehs)

SIGN HERE
Firme aquí.
(**FEER**-may ah-**KEE**)

SIGN HERE FOR YOUR PROPERTY.
Firme aquí por su propiedad.
(**FEER**-may ah-**KEE** pohr soo pro-pee-eh-**DAHD**)

SIT DOWN!
¡Siéntese!
(See-**EHN**-teh-say)

SLOW despacito (dehs-pah-**SEE**-toh)

SPEAK SLOWER
Hable más despacio.
(**AH**-blay mahs days-**PAH**-see-oh)

SPEAK LOUDER
Hable en voz más alta
(**AH**-blay ehn vohs mahs **AHL**-toh)

YOU SPEAK Usted habla.
(oo-**STEHD** AH-blah)

YOU DO NOT SPEAK! ¡No habla!
(Noh **AH**-blah)

SPELL YOUR NAME FOR ME.
Deletréeme su nombre.
(Day-lay-**TRAY**-ay-may soo **NOHM**-bray)

SPREAD YOUR BUTTOCKS WITH YOUR HANDS.
Separa sus nalgas con sus manos.
(Seh-**PAHR**-ah soos **NAHL**-gahs kohn soos **MAH**-nohs)

SPREAD YOUR LEGS AND ARMS WELL APART.
Separe bien las piernas y los brazos.
(Seh-**PAH**-ray bee-**EHN** lahs pee-**EHR**-nahs ee lohs **BRAH**-zohs)

STAND! ¡Párese! (**PAH**-ray-say)

STAND HERE- Párese aquí.
(**PAH**-ray-say ah-**KEE**)

START comience (koh-mee-**EHN**-say)
STAY! ¡Qúedese! (**KAY**-day-say)

STEP FORWARD
Tome un paso para adelante.
(**TOH**-may oon **PAH**-soh **PAH**-rah **AH**-day-**LAHN**-tay)

STEP BACK Pase para atras
(**PAH**-say **PAH**-rah ah-**TRAHS**)

STOP alto (**AHL**-toh)

STOP OR I WILL SHOOT.
Alto o disparo.
(**AHL**-toh oh dees-**PAH**-roh)

STOP YOUR MOTOR Pare su motor.
(**PAH**-ray soo moh-**TOHR**)

TAKE ME WHERE HE LIVES OR IS.
Lléveme a dónde el vive o donde está.
(**YAY**-vay-may ah **DOHN**-day ayl **VEE**-vay oh **DOHN**-day ays-**TAH**)

TAKE OFF ALL YOUR CLOTHES.
Quítese toda la ropa.
(**KEE**-teh-say **TOH**-dah lah **ROH**-pah)

TALKING (NO) no hable (noh **AH**-blay)
TELL ME! ¡Dígame! (**DEE**-gah-may)
TELL THE TRUTH Diga la verdad.
(**DEE**-gah lah vehr-**DAHD**)

THROW IT OUT! ¡Tirelo afuera!
(tee-**RAY**-loh ah-**FWEHR**-ah)
KEYS llaves (**YAH**-vays)

TURN AROUND- Voltéese.
(Vohl-**TEE**-ess-ay)

TURN AROUND & FACE THE WALL.
Voltéese cara a la pared.
(Vohl-**TEE**-ess-ay **KAH**-rah ah lah pah-**REHD**)

TURN OFF THE ENGINE	apaga el motor	(ah-PAH-gah el moh-TOR)
	Ah-POON-tay loh kay	
	oh-koo-ree-OH DEHZ-day	
	ayl preen-SEE-pee-oh,	
	el principio.	
		"OR"
WAIT!	¡Espere!	(ehs-PEHR-ay)
WALK!	¡Camine!	(kah-MEE-nay)
WRITE-	Escribe	(ehs-KREE-bay)
WRITE DOWN WHAT HAPPENED FROM THE BEGINNING	Apúntese lo que ocurrió desde al principio.	(ehs-KREE-bah loh kay pah-SOH DEHS-day al preen-SEE-pee-oh)

CONCEALMENT AREA

SHOW ME WHERE YOU HID THE _____! **SU CLAVO** (Nail of clove)
Enséñeme dónde escondiste el/la _____ ¡
(Ehn-SEHN-yay-may DOHN-day ays-kohn-DEES-tay ayl _____.)

CONCEPTS OF TIME

-after.	después de	(dehs-PWAYS day)
-(or)-	luego	(LWEH-goh)
-afterwards-	después	(dehs-PWAYS)
-ago.	hace	(AH-say)
-afternoon-	tarde	(TAHR-day)
-in the afternoon-	por la tarde	(pohr lah TAHR-day)
-this afternoon-	esta tarde	(EHS-tah TAHR-day)
-tomorrow afternoon-	mañana la tarde	(mah-NYAH-nah lah TAHR-day)
-already-	ya	(yah)
-always-	siempre	(see-EHM-pray)

AS SOON AS POSSIBLE -
Tan pronto como sea posible
(tahn PROHN-toh KOH-moh say-ah pah-SEE-blay)   (or)
lo más pronto posible
(loh mahs PROHN-toh pah-SEE-blay)

-at the same time-	al mismo tiempo	(ahl MEES-moh tee-EHM-poh)
AT WHAT TIME?	¿A qué hora?	(ah kay OH-rah)
-be on time-	llegar a tiempo	(yay-GAHR ah tee-EHM-poh)
-on time-	a tiempo	(ah tee-EHM-poh)
-before-	antes de	(AHN-tays day)
-begin-	empezar	(ehm-peh-SAHR)
-beginning-	al principio	(ahl preen-SEE-pee-oh)
	principiando	(preen-see-pee-AHN-doh)
	comenzando	(koh-mehn-ZAHN-doh)
-brief-	breve	(BREH-vay)
-briefly-	brevemente	(breh-vay-MEHN-tay)
-by now-	ya	(yah)
-continually-	continuamente	(kohn-tee-nwah-MEHN-tay)
-continue-	continuar	(kohn-tee-NWAHR)
-dawn-	amanecer	(ah-mah-neh-SEHR)
-day-	día	(DEE-ah)
-all day-	todo el día	(TOH-doh ehl DEE-ah)
-daily-	diario	(dee-AH-ree-oh)
-a few days-	unos días	(OO-nohs DEE-ahs)
-decade-	década	(DAY-kah-dah)
-during-	durante	(doo-RAHN-tay)
-dusk-	el anochecer	(ayl ah-NOH-chay-sayr)
-early-	temprano	(tehm-PRAH-noh)
-earlier -	más temprano	(mahs tehm-PRAH-noh)
-to be early-	llegar temprano	(yay-GAHR tehm-PRAH-noh)
-evening-	tarde	(TAHR-day)
-in the evening-	por la tarde	(POHR lah TAHR-day)

English	Spanish	Pronunciation
this evening-	Esta tarde	(EHS-tah TAHR-day)
tomorrow evening-	mañana por la tarde	(mah-NYAH-nah pohr lah TAHR-day)
finish-	terminar	(tehr-mee-NAHR)
frequent-	frecuente	(freh-KWEHN-tay)
frequently-	frecuentemente	(freh-KWEHN-teh-MEHN-tay)
hour-	hora	(OH-rah)
in an hour's time-	dentro de una hora	(DEHN-troh day OO-nah OH-rah)
per hour-	por hora	(pohr OH-rah)
instant-	instante	(eens-TAHN-tay)
last (to)-	durar	(doo-RAHR)
last (the)-	el último	(ehl OOL-tee-moh)
last month-	el mes pasado	(ehl mehs pah-SAH-doh)
last time-	última vez	(OOL-tee-mah vehz)
last year-	el año pasado	(ehl AH-nyoh pah-SAH-doh)
late-	tarde	(TAHR-day)
to be late-	llegar tarde	(yay-GAHR TAHR-day)
long term-	a largo plazo	(ah LAHR-goh PLAH-soh)
look forward to-	esperar con placer	(ehs-peh-RAHR kohn plah-SEHR)
	anticipar	(ahn-tee-see-PAHR)
meantime (in the)-	mientras tanto	(mee-EHN-trahs TAHN-toh)
midnight-	medianoche	(meh-dee-ah-NOH-chay)
at midnight-	a la medianoche	(ah lah meh-dee-ah-NOH-chay)
minute-	minuto	(mee-NOO-toh)
moment-	momento	(moh-MEHN-toh)
month-	mes	(mehs)
monthly-	mensual	(mehn-SWAHL)
morning-	mañana	(mahn-YAH-nah)
in the morning-	por la mañana	(pohr lah mahn-YAH-nah)
this morning-	esta mañana	(EHS-tah mahn-YAH-nah)
tomorrow morning-	mañana por la mañana	(mah-NYAN-nah pohr lah mahn-YAH-nah)
yesterday morning-	ayer por la mañana	(ah-YAYR pohr lah mahn-YAH-nah)
never-	nunca	(NOON-kah)
almost never-	casi nunca	(KAH-see NOON-kah)
night-	noche	(NOH-chay)
at night-	de noche	(day NOH-chay)
last night-	anoche	(ah-NOH-chay)
tomorrow night-	mañana por la noche	(mah-NYAH-nah pohr lah NOH-chay)
tonight-	esta noche	(EHS-tah NOH-chay)
noon-	mediodía	(meh-dee-oh-DEE-ah)
at noon-	al mediodía	(ahl meh-dee-oh-DEE-ah)
now-	ahora	(ah-OH-rah)
from now on-	de ahora en adelante	(day ah-OH-rah ehn ah-deh-LAHN-tay)
for now-	por ahora	(pohr ah-OH-rah)
occasionally-	de vez en cuando	(day vehs ehn KWAHN-doh)
occur-	ocurrir	(oh-koo-REER)
often-	con frecuencia	(kohn freh-KWEHN-see-ah)
once-	una vez	(OO-nah vehs)
twice-	dos veces	(dohs VEH-sehs)
once in a while-	de vez en cuando	(day vehs ehn KWAHN-doh)
only-	sólo	(SOH-loh)
past-	pasado	(pah-SAH-doh)
present-	actual	(ahk-TWAHL)
presently-	actualmente	(ahk-twahl-MEHN-tay)
previous-	anterior	(ahn-teh-ree-OHR)
previously-	anteriormente	(ahn-teh-ree-ohr-MEHN-tay)
quickly-	pronto	(PROHN-toh)
rare-	raro	(RAH-roh)
rarely-	raramente	(rah-rah-MEHN-tay)
recent-	reciente	(reh-see-EHN-tay)
recently-	recientemente	(reh-see-ehn-teh-MEHN-tay)

English	Spanish	Pronunciation
-regular	regular	(reh-goo-LAHR)
-regularly	regularmente	(reh-goo-lahr-MEHN-tay)
-right away	ahora mismo	(ah-Oh-rah MEES-moh)
-second	segundo	(seh-GOON-doh)
-short term	a corto plazo	(ah KOHR-toh PLAH-soh)
-simultaneous	simultáneo	(see-mool-TAH-nay-oh)
-simultaneously	simultáneamente	(see-mool-TAH-nay-ah-MEHN-tay)
-since	desde	(DEHS-day)
-since yesterday	desde ayer	(DEHS-day ah-YEHR)
-slow	lento	(LEHN-toh)
-slowly	lentamente	(lehn-tah-MEHN-tay)
(or)	despacio	(dehs-pah-SEE-toh)
-soon	pronto	(PROHN-toh)
-as soon as	asi que	(ah-SEE kay)
-sooner or later	tarde o temprano	(TAHR-day oh tehm-PRAH-noh)
-spend time	pasar	(pah-SAHR)
-sporadic	esporádico	(ehs-poh-RAH-dee-koh)
-sporadically	esporádicamente	(ehs-poh-RAH-dee-kah-MEHN-tay)
-still	aún	(ah-OON)
-sunrise	el amanecer	(ayl ah-MAHN-ay-sayr)
-sun up	salida del sol	(sah-LEE-dah dayl sohl)
-sundown	puesta del sol	(POO-ehs-tah dayl sohl)
-take place	tener lugar	(teh-NEHR loo-GAHR)
-temporary	temporáneo	(tehm-poh-RAH-nay-oh)
-temporarily	temporáneamente	(tehm-poh-RAH-nay-ah-mehn-tay)
-then	entonces	(ehn-TOHN-says)
-time	tiempo	(tee-EHM-poh)
-at the same time	al mismo tiempo	(ahl MEES-moh tee-EHM-poh)
-be on time	llegar a tiempo	(yay-GAHR ah tee-EHM-poh)
(or)	ser puntual	(sehr poon-TWAHL)
-first time	primera vez	(pree-MAY-rah vehs)
-in an hour's time	dentro de una hora	(DEHN-troh day OO-nah Oh-rah)
-in the meantime	mientras tanto	(mee-EHN-trahs TAHN-toh)
-in time	a tiempo	(ah tee-EHM-poh)
-last time	última vez	(OOL-tee-mah vehz)
-on time	a tiempo	(ah tee-EHM-poh)
-spend time	pasar	(pah-SAHR)
-time is up	Es la hora	(ays lah Oh-rah)
-timetable	horario	(oh-RAH-ree-oh)
-today	hoy	(oy)
-tomorrow	mañana	(mahn-YAH-nah)
-day after tomorrow	pasado mañana	(pah-SAH-doh mahn-YAH-nah)
-tonight	esta noche	(EHS-tah NOH-chay)
-twice	dos veces	(dohs BEH-says)
-until	hasta	(AHS-tah)
-usually	normalmente	(nohr-mahl-MEHN-tay)
-wait for	esperar	(ehs-peh-RAHR)
-week	semana	(seh-MAH-nah)
-weekly	semanalmente	(seh-mah-nahl-MEHN-tay)
-next week	la semana que entra	(lah seh-MAH-nah kay EHN-trah)
(or)	la próxima semana	(lah PROHK-see-mah seh-MAH-nah)
-a few weeks	unas semanas	(OON-ahs seh-MAH-nahs)

WHAT TIME IS IT GOING TO HAPPEN?	¿A que hora va a pasar?	(Ah KAY Oh-rah vah ah pah-SAHR)
AMERICAN TIME	(Hora Americana)	(Slang: Be on time)
-WHEN-	Cuándo	(KWAHN-doh)
WHEN DID YOU LEAVE?	¿Cuándo salió?	(KWAHN-doh sah-lee-OH)
WHEN DID HE LEAVE?	¿Cuándo salió?	(KWAHN-doh sah-lee-OH)
WHEN DID THEY LEAVE?	¿Cuándo salieron?	(KWAHN-doh sah-LEE-ayr-ohn)
WHEN DID YOU ARRIVE?	¿Cuándo llegó?	(KWAHN-doh yah-GOH)
WHEN DID HE ARRIVE?	¿Cuándo llegó?	(KWAHN-doh yah-GOH)

WHEN DID THEY ARRIVE?	¿Cuándo llegáron?	(KWAHN-doh yaw-GAW-RAHN)
WHEN WERE YOU TO MEET?	¿Cuándo se iban a encontrar?	
	(KWAHN-doh say EE-bahn ah ehn-kohn-TRAHR)	
WHEN WILL HE LEAVE?	¿Cuándo saldrá?	(KWAHN-doh sahl-DRAH)
WHEN WILL HE RETURN?	¿Cuándo volverá?	(KWAHN-doh vahl-vehr-AH)

while-	mientras	(mee-EHN-trahs)
within-	dentro de	(DEHN-troh day)
year-	año	(AH-nyoh)
yearly-	anual	(ah-NWAHL)
yesterday-	ayer	(ah-YEHR)
day before yesterday-	anteayer	(ahn-teh-ah-YEHR)
since yesterday	desde ayer	(DEHS-day ah-YEHR)
yesterday morning-	ayer por la mañana	(ah-YEHR pohr lah mah-NYAH-nah)
yet-	todavía	(toh-dah-BEE-ah)

CONSCIENCE & EXPRESSIONS

ACCORDING TO según
(seh-**GOON**)

ADMIT IT! ¡Admitelo!
(ahd-**MEE**-tay-loh)

BE A MAN! ¡Pórtese como hombre!
(POHR-tay-say KOH-moh OHM-bray)

BY THE WAY A propósito
(ah proh-**POH**-see-toh)

DO WHAT IS RIGHT!
¡Haz lo que es correcto!
(Hahz loh kay ays koh-**REHK**-toh)

ENOUGH! ¡Basta! (**BAHS**-tah)
EXCUSE ME. Perdóneme.
(Payr-**DOH**-nay-may)

FALSE falso (**FAHL**-soh)

THAT IS NOT TRUE.
Eso no es verdad.
(ess-oh noh ess vehr-**DAHD**)

HOW CAN YOU SAY YOU DIDN'T DO IT?
¿Como puede decir que no lo hizo?
(KOH-moh PWAY-day day-SEER kay noh loh EE-zoh)

WE FOUND IT IN YOUR ....!
¡Lo hallamos en su _____!
(Loh ah-**YAH**-mohs ehn soo _____)

WE FOUND YOUR _____ THERE.
Hallamos su _____ alli.
(ah-**YAH**-mohs soo _____ ah-**YEE**)

IMPOSSIBLE.
Imposible.
(eem-poh-**SEE**-blay)

I DIDN'T UNDERSTAND. No entendí.
(noh ehn-tehn-**DEE**)

I DOUBT THAT...
Dudo que...
(**DOO**-doh kay)

WE KNOW THAT YOU DID IT.
Sabemos que ud. lo hizo.
(Sah-**BAY**-mohs kay oo-STED lo EE-zo)

I KNOW YOU ARE A GOOD PERSON.
Yo se que ud. es una buena persona.
(Yoh **SAY** kay oo-STEHD ess OO-nah BWAY-nah pehr-SOH-nah)

I SAW YOU DO IT.
Yo le ví hacerlo.
(Yoh lay **VEE** ah-**SAYR**-loh)

THEY SAW YOU DO IT.
Ellos le vieron hacerlo.
(AY-yohs lay VEE-ayr-ohn ah-SAYR-loh)

I SAW YOU TAKE IT.
Yo le vi tomarlo.
(Yoh lay **VEE** toh-**MAHR**-loh)

I'M SURE.
Estoy seguro.
(Ay-**STOY** see-**GOO**-roh)

I THINK THAT...
Pienso que...
(pee-**EHN**-soh kay)

WE WILL TELL THE STATE PROSECUTOR YOU COOPERATED.
Vamos a decir al fiscal del Estado que ud. cooperó.
(VAH-mohs ah day-SEER ahl fees-KAHL dayl ess-TAH-doh kay oo-STEHD koh-oh-pay-ROH)

WE CAN'T MAKE ANY PROMISES.
No podemos hacer promesas.
(Noh poh-DAY-mohs ah-SAYR
proh-MAY-sahs)

WILL YOU HELP US CATCH _____?
¿Nos ayudará ud. a pescar ah pehs-KAHR
_____?
(Nohs ah-yoo-dah-RAH oo-STEHD
ah pehs-KAHR)

I WILL KEEP MY WORD.
Confíe en mi palabra.
(kohn-FEE-ay ehn mee pah-LAH-brah)

I WON'T HURT YOU! ¡No le dañaré!
(Noh lay dahn-yah-YAH-ray)

ISN'T IT SO? ¿Verdad? (vehr-DAHD)

IT DOESN'T MATTER. No importa.
(noh eem-POHR-tah)

IT'S CLEAR. Es claro.(Ays KLAH-roh)

IT'S NOT TRUE. No es verdad.
(noh ehs vehr-DAHD)

IT'S TRUE Es verdad(es vehr-DAHD)

NOW ahora (ah-OH-rah)

REALLY ¿De veras? (day BEH-rahs)

THAT'S IT! ¡Eso es! (AYS-oh ays)

UNBELIEVABLE! ¡Increíble!
(een-kreh-EE-blay)

WE HAVE FINGERPRINTS/ FOOTPRINTS.
Tenemos huella / huellas.
(Tay-NAY-mohs oo-AY-yah /oo-AY-yahs)

WE CAN PROVE YOU DID IT!
Podemos probar que ud. lo hizo.
(Poh-DAY-mohs prob-BAHR kay
oo-STEHD loh EE-soh)

YOU WILL HEAT THE CEMENT! (slang) ¡Calentarás el cemento!
(kah-lehn-tahr-AHS el say-MEHN-toh)

POSSIBLY- Posiblemente
(poh-SEE-bleh-MEHN-tay)

WHAT DO YOU THINK?
¿Qué opina usted?
(Kay oh-PEE-nah oo-STEHD)

WHO KNOWS? ¿Quién sabe?
(Kee-EHN SAH-bay)

WOULD YOU TAKE A LIE DETECTOR TEST?
¿Tomará ud. un exámen de mentiras?
(Toh-mah-RAH oo-STEHD oon ex-
SAH-mehn day mehn-TEER-ahs)

IF YOU'RE TROUBLED COME SEE ME.
Si esta apenado venga a verme.
(see ESS-tah ah-pehn-AH-doh
vehn-GAH ah VEHR-may)

slang- Si se le volteen las tripas dame un quemazon o ven a verme.
[Literally: If your guts are turning over give me a horn or come see me]
(see say lay vohl-teh-EHN lahs
TREE-pahs DAH-may oon kwehr-
NAH-zoh oh vehn ah VEHR-may)

CONSENT

YOU ARE FREE TO GO. DO YOU UNDERSTAND?
Es libre para irse. ¿Comprende?
(Ays LEE-bray PAH-rah EER-say.
Kohm-PREHN-day)

DO YOU SPEAK ENGLISH?
¿Habla usted inglés?
(AH-blah oo-STEHD een-GLAYS)

I DON'T UNDERSTAND
No comprendo
(noh kohm-PREHN-doh)

IS THERE ANYONE HERE WHO SPEAKS ENGLISH?
¿Hay alguien aquí que habla inglés?
(AH-ee AHL-ghee-EHN ah-KEE kay
AH-blay een-GLAYS)

MAY I ASK YOU A FEW QUESTIONS?
¿Le puedo hacer algunas preguntas?
(Lay PWAY-doh ah-SAYR
ahl-GOO-nahs pray-GOON-tahs)

ARE THERE GUNS, NARCOTICS, OR LARGE AMOUNTS OF CASH IN THE CAR? HOUSE? (ETC.)
¿Hay armas, drogas, o cantidades grandes de dinero en el carro? casa?
(Ay AHR-mahs, DROH-gahs, oh
kahn-TEE-dah-days GRAHN-days day
dee-NAY-roh en el KAH-roh, KAH-sah)

slang: ¿Hay cohetes, jale o lana en el carro? ¿Casa?
[Literally: Are there rockets, pull, or wool in the car?]
(Ay koh-EH-tays, HAH-lay oh
LAH-nah ehn el KAH, roh, KAH-sah)

DRUGS Drogas (DROH-gahs)

24

TAKE DRUGS- tomar drogas
(toh-**MAHR** **DROH**-gahs)

DRUG ADDICT
drogadicto(a)
(droh-gah-**DEEK**-toh [-tah])

DRUG PUSHER-
traficante de drogas
(trah-fee-**KAHN**-tay day **DROH**-gahs)

DRIVER- chofer (**CHOH**-fehr)
PASSENGER pasajero
(pah-sah-**HAY**-roh)

TITLE OF OWNERSHIP título
(**TEE**-too-loh)

MAY I SEARCH YOUR CAR?
¿Puedo registrar su carro?
(**PWAY**-doh ray-hees-**TRAHR** soo **KAHR**-roh)

MAY I SEARCH YOUR _____?
¿(Me permite)
Puedo registrar su_____?
([May payr-**MEE**-tay] **PWAY**-doh ray-hees-**TRAHR** soo _____?)

LUGGAGE? ¿Equipaje?
(Ay-**KEE**-pah-hay)
RESIDENCE? ¿Residencia?
(ray-see-**DEHN**-see-ah)

PERSON? Persona? (payr-**SOHN**-ah)

IS THERE ANY ____ IN THE____?
Hay ____ en el ____?
(Ay ____ ehn ayl ____)

**I AM GOING TO SEARCH YOUR
____ WITH A DRUG DOG?**
Voy ir a registrar su ____ con un
perro de drogas?
(Boy eer ah ray-hees-**TRAHR** soo ____ kohn oon **PAY**-roh day **DROH**-gahs)

**I WILL FIRST REMOVE FOOD OR
VALUABLES SO THEY WILL NOT
BE DAMAGED.**
Primero voy a quitar comida o cosas
de valor para que no se dañan.
(Pree-**MAY**-roh boy ah kee-**TAHR** koh-**MEE**-dah oh **KOH**-zahs day vah-**LOHR** **PAH**-rah kay noh say **DAHN**-yahn)

DO NOT TOUCH THE DOG.
No toque el perro.
(Noh **TOH**-kay ayl **PAY**-roh)

GIVE ME YOUR ____.   KEYS
Deme su (sus)____.   llaves
(**DEH**-may soo(s)____.) (**YAH**-vays)

IS THIS YOURS? WHO OWNS IT?
¿Es suyo?   ¿De quién es?
(es **SOO**-yoh)   Day kee-**EHN** ehs)

(If evidence found, advise of rights)

**THE DRUG DOG ALERTED TO THE
SCENT OF DRUGS ON YOUR ____.**
El perro de droga puso sobre aviso el
olor de narcóticos en su ____.
(El **PAY**-roh day **DROH**-gahs **POO**-soh **SOH**-bray ah-**VEE**-soh ayl oh-**LOHR** day nahr-**KOH**-tee-kohs ehn soo ____)

THE ____ WILL BE SEIZED.
El ____ será confiscado.
(Ayl ____ say-**RAH** kohn-fees-**KAH**-doh)

DOG FOUND DRUGS IN YOUR CAR.
El perro halló drogas en su carro.
(Ayl **PAY**-roh ah-**YOH** **DROH**-gahs ehn soo **KAHR**-roh)

YOU ARE UNDER ARREST FOR:
Usted está arrestado por:
(Oo-**STEHD** ess-**TAH** ah-reh-**STAH**-doh pohr:)

POSSESSION OF NARCOTICS
Posesión de narcóticos (drogas)
(Poh-sez-**SYOHN** day nahr-**KOH**-tee-kohs)

**DRIVING WITH A SUSPENDED
DRIVER'S LICENSE.**
Manejando con licencia suspendida.
(Mahn-nay-**HAHN**-doh kohn lee-**SEHN**-see-ah soos-pehn-**DEE**-dah)

THERE IS A WARRANT FOR YOUR ARREST.	**WHEN?**	**FOR WHAT?**
Hay una orden de arresto para usted.	¿Cuándo?	¿Por qué?
(Eye OO-nah OHR-dehn day ah-SREHS-toh PAH-rah oo-STEHD)	(KWAHN-doh)	(Pohr kay)

HOW MUCH DO YOU WEIGH?
¿Cuánto pesa usted?
(KWAHN-toh PEH-sah oo-STEHD)

CARRYING A CONCEALED WEAPON.
Lleva una arma oculta.
(YAY-vah oona AHR-mah oh-KOOL-tah)

HOW TALL ARE YOU?
¿Cuánto mide usted?
(KWAHN-toh MEE-day oo-STEHD)

ASSAULT
asalto
(ah-SAHL-toh)

VISIBLE MARKS OR SCARS?
Tiene Usted marcas o cicatrices visibles?
(Tee-EHN-ay oo-STEHD MAHR-kahs oh see-kah-TREE-says vee-SEE-blays)

(refer "CRIMES" for other crimes)

PUT YOUR HANDS BEHIND YOU.
Ponga las manos detrás de usted.
(POHN-gah lahs MAH-nohs deh-TRAHS day oo-STEHD)

SHOW ME YOUR ARMS.
Enséñeme sus brazos
(Ehn-SEH-nyeh-may soos BRAH-sohs)

WHERE WERE YOU BORN?
¿(En) dónde nació usted?
(Ehn DOHN-day nah-SEE-oh oo-STEHD)

FOLLOW ME Sígame (SEE-gah-may)

WHERE DO YOU WORK?
¿Dónde trabaja?
(DOHN-day trah-BAH-hah)

STAND HERE. Párese aquí.
(PAH-reh-say ah-KEE)

WHAT CITY? ¿Qué ciudad?
(KAY SEE-oo-dahd)

WAIT HERE
Espere aquí.
(ehs-PEHR-ay ah-KEE)

NAME OF YOUR EMPLOYER?
¿Cuál es el nombre de su patrón?
(Kwahl es el NOHM-bray day soo pah-TROHN)

GET INTO THE CAR!
¡Súbase al carro!
(SOO-bah-say ahl KAHR-roh)

PHONE # ? ¿Número de teléfono?
(NOO-may-roh day tay-LAY-foh-noh)

I AM GOING TO ASK YOU SOME QUESTIONS
Voy a hacerle algunas preguntas.
(Boy ah ah-SAYR-lay ahl-GOO-nahs pray-GOON-tahs)

ADDRESS? ¿Dirección?
(Dee-rehk-SYOHN)

HAVE YOU EVER BEEN IN JAIL?
¿Ha estado en la cárcel alguna vez?
(Ah ess-TAH-doh ehn lah KAHR-sehl ahl-GOO-nah vehs)

HOW MUCH ARE YOU COMPENSATED WEEKLY?
¿Cuánto ganas por semana?
(KWAHN-toh GAH-nahs pohr say-MAH-nah)

WHAT IS YOUR SOCIAL SECURITY #.
¿Cuál es el número de su seguro social?
(Kwahl ess el NOO-may-roh day soo seh-GOO-roh soh-see-AHL)

HOW MUCH MONEY DO YOU HAVE WITH YOU NOW?
¿Cuánto dinero tiene con usted ahora?
(KWAHN-toh dee-NAY-roh tee-EHN-ay kohn oo-STEHD ah-OH-rah)

ARE YOU NOW OR HAVE YOU EVER BEEN A MEMBER OF ANY CRIMINAL ORGANIZATION?
¿Eres o has sido miembro de una organización criminal?
(AYR-ays oh ahs SEE-doh mee-EHM-broh day oona ohr-gah-nee-zah-SYOHN kree-mee-NAHL)

WHERE DID YOU GET THE DRUGS?
¿Dónde obtuvo las drogas?
(DOHN-day ohb-TOO-oh lahs DROH-gahs)

26

slang: ¿Donde conseguiste jale?
(**DOHN**-day kohn-see-**GEES**-tay **HAH**-lay)

FROM WHOM? ¿De quien?
(Day kee-**EHN**)

WHO PUT IT THERE?
¿Quien lo puso allí?
(Kee-**EHN** loh **POO**-soh ah-**YEE**)

HIS NAME, ADDRESS, & PHONE #
Su nombre, dirección, y número de teléfono
(Soo **NOHM**-bray, dee-rehk-**SYOHN**, ee **NOO**-may-roh day tay-**LAY**-foh-noh)

HOW MUCH DID THEY GIVE YOU FOR TRANSPORTING THE DRUGS?
¿Cuánto le dieron por transportar las drogas?
(**KWAHN**-toh lay dee-**AYR**-ohn pohr trahn-spohr-**TAHR** lahs **DROH**-gahs)

HOW MUCH? ¿Cuánto? (**KWAHN**-toh)

WHO PUT THE CONTRABAND OR CASH IN THE CAR?
¿Quien pusó el contrabando o dinero dentro del carro?
(Kee-**EHN POO**-soh el kohn-trah-**BAHN**-doh oh ayl dee- **NAY**-roh **DEHN**-troh dayl **KAHR**-roh)

DID YOU KNOW? ¿Supo? (**SOO**-poh)

IS THIS YOUR MONEY?
¿Es esto su dinero?
(Ays **ESS**-toh soo dee-**NAY**-roh)

DID YOU ADVISE THE INTERNAL REVENUE OF THIS INCOME?
¿Reportó ese dinero a Impuestos Internos?
(Ray-pohr-**TOH AY**-say dee-**NAY**-roh ah eem-**PWEHS**-tohs een-**TAYR**-nohs)

WHERE DID YOU GET IT?
¿Dónde lo obtuvo?
(**DOHN**-day loh ohb-**TOO**-voh)

WHERE WERE YOU GOING?
¿A dónde iba?
(Ah **DOHN**-day **EE**-bah)

TO WHAT ADDRESS?
¿A cuál dirección?
(Ah kwahl dee-rehk-**SYOHN**)

WHERE DID YOU START FROM?
¿De dónde viene?
(Day **DOHN**-day vee-**EH**-nay)

NAME YOUR BOSS.
Nombre su patrón.
(**NOHM**-bray soo pah-**TROHN**)

NAME HIS BOSS. Nombre su patrón.
(**NOHM**-bray soo pah-**TROHN**)

SEE ORGANIZATIONAL STRUCTURE

WHO IS THE HEAD OF THE ORGANIZATION?
¿Quien es la cabeza de la [familia] organización?
(Kee-**EHN** ays lah kah-**BAY**-sah day lah [fah-**MEE**-lee-ah] ohr-gah-nee-zah-**SYOHN**)

WHERE DOES HE LIVE?
¿Dónde vive?
(**DOHN**-day **VEE**-vah)

WHERE DOES HE KEEP THE ____?
¿Dónde guarda el/la _____?
(**DOHN**-day **GWAHR**-dah ayl/lah __?)

WHERE IS THE _____?
¿Dónde esta el_____?
(**DOHN**-day **ESS**-tah ayl _____?)

WHAT AMOUNT DOES HE HAVE?
¿Qué cantidad tiene?
(Kay kahn-**TEE**-dahd tee-**EHN**-ay)

HAVE YOU SEEN THIS?
¿Ha visto esto?
(Ah **VEES**-toh **AYS**-toh)

WHERE? ¿Dónde? (**DOHN**-day)

DRUGS	Drogas	(**DROH**-gahs)
TAKE DRUGS	tomar drogas	(toh-**MAHR DROH**-gahs)

DRUG ADDICT- drogadicto(a)
(droh-gah-**DEEK**-toh (-tah)

DRUG PUSHER-
traficante de drogas
(trah-fee-**KAHN**-tay day **DROH**-gahs)

SMUGGLE (to)
pasar de contrabando
(pah-**SAHR** day kohn-trah-**BAHN**-doh)

SMUGGLED GOODS Contrabando
(kohn-trah-**BAHN**-doh)

SMUGGLER (things) contrabandista (cohn-trah-bahn-DEES-tah) - (people) coyote (coh-YOH-tay)

HOW LONG HAS HE BEEN A SMUGGLER?
¿Cuánto tiempo ha sido un contrabandista?
(KWAHN-toh tee-EHM-poh ah SEE-doh oon kohn-trah-bahn-DEES-tah)

HOW LONG HAVE YOU WORKED FOR HIM?
¿Cuánto tiempo lleva trabajando con él?
(KWAHN-toh tee-EHM-poh yay-yah trah-bah-HAHN-doh kohn ayl)

HOW MANY TRIPS HAVE YOU MADE FOR HIM?
¿Cuántos viajes has hecho para él?
(KWAHN-tohs vee-AH-hays ahs AY-chah PAH-rah ayl)

WHAT IS THE LARGEST AMT. OF DRUGS/MONEY YOU TRANSPORTED FOR HIM AT ONE TIME?
¿Cuál es la cantidad más grande de drogas o dinero que has transportado para él de una vez?
(Kwahl ays lah kahn-TEE-dahd mahs GRAHN-day day DROH-gahs oh dee-NAY-roh kay ahs trahn-spohr-TAH-doh PAH-rah ayl day OONA vehz)

(REFER WHO, WHAT, WHERE, WHEN, HOW, & WHY INTERVIEW SECTIONS)

IS THIS BOOK FOR WRITING THE NAMES OF THE SMUGGLERS?
¿Este libro es para escribir los nombres de los contrabandistas?
(AY-stay LEE-broh ays PAH-rah ays-KREE-beer lohs NOHM-brays day lohs kohn-trah-bahn-DEES-tahs)

START FROM THE BEGINNING AND (WRITE DOWN) TELL ME EXACTLY WHAT THE ARRANGEMENTS WERE.
Comenze desde el principio (apunte) y dígame exactamente que fueron los arreglos?
(Koh-mee-EHN-say DAYS-day ayl preen-SEE-pee-oh [ah-POON-tay] ee DEE-gah-may ex-ZAHK-tah-MEHN-tay kay FWEHR-ohn lohs ah-REHG-lohs)

INCLUDE NAMES, ADDRESSES, TIMES, LOCATIONS, HIGHWAYS AND STREETS USED, INCLUDING THE NAMES OF THE CITIES AND THE FINANCIAL ARRANGEMENTS AGREED UPON.
Incluye nombres, direcciones, horas, sitios, carreteras y calles usadas, incluso los nombres de las ciudades y los arreglos de dinero acordado.
(Een-KLOO-yay NOHM-brays, dee-rehk-SYOHN-ays, OH-rahs, SEE-tee-ohs, kah-ray-TAY-rahs ee KAH-yays oo-SAH-dahs, een-KLOO-soh NOHM-brays, day lahs see-oo-DAHD-days ee lohs ah-REG-lohs day dee-NAY-roh ah-kohr-DAH-doh)

THE OFFENSE WAS MORE SERIOUS THAN WHAT WE THOUGHT.
La ofensa fué más seria que lo que pensamos.
(Lah oh-FEHN-sah foo-AY mahs SAY-ree-ah kay loh kay pehn-SAH-mohs)

IF CONVICTED YOU MAY GO TO PRISON.
Si lo hallan culpable, usted puede ir a la prisión. ("pinta")
(See loh AH-yahn kool-PAH-blay, oo-STEHD PWAY-day eer ah lah pree-SYOHN [PEEN-tah])

THINK ABOUT IT Piénsalo.
(Pee-EHN-sah-loh)

WILL YOU HELP US CATCH _____ ?
¿Nos ayudas agarrer a _____ ?
(Nohs ah-YOO-dahs ah-ga-RAHR ah ___ ?)

WE WILL TELL THE PROSECUTOR YOU HELPED US.
Nosotros le diremos al fiscal que nos ayudaste.
(Noh-SOH-trohs lay dee-RAY-mohs ahl fees-KAHL kay nohs ah-yoo-DAHS-tay)

DO WHAT IS RIGHT.
Haga lo que es correcto.
(AH-gah loh kay ays kohr-REHK-toh)

YOUR CAR WILL BE SEIZED.
Su carro será confiscado.
(Soo KAHR-roh say-RAH kohn-fees-KAH-doh)

SIGN HERE FOR YOUR PROPERTY.
Firme aquí para su propiedad.
(FEER-may ah-KEE para soo proh-pee-eh-DAHD)

I AM TAKING THE CAR TO THE POLICE STATION.
Voy a llevar el carro a la estación de policía.
(Boy ah yay-VAHR ayl KAHR-roh ah lah ay-stay-SYOHN day poh-lee-SEE-ah)

HERE IT STATES WHERE YOUR CAR IS.
Aquí dice donde está su carro.
(Ah-**KEE** DEE-say **DOHN**-day ess-**TAH** soo **KAHR**-roh)

IF YOU'RE TROUBLED COME SEE ME.
Si está apenado venga a verme.
(see ays-**TAH** ah-peh-**NAH**-doh **VEHN**-gah ah **VAYR**-may)

Slang: Si se volteen las tripas dame un cuernazo o ven a verme.
[Literally: If your guts are turning over give me a horn or come see me.]
(see say vohl-teh-ehn lahs **TREE**-pahs **DAH**-may oon kwehr-**NAH**-zoh oh vehn ah **VEHR**-may)

WAIT ¡Espere! (ehs-**PEHR**-ay)

LET'S GO.   COME WITH ME.
Vamos.   Venga conmigo.
(**VAH**-mohs)(**VEN**-gah kohn-**MEE**-goh)

(A man is never so weak as when a woman is telling him how strong he is.)

CRIMES - DESCRIPTIONS & INTERVIEWS

I AM GOING TO ASK YOU SOME QUESTIONS.
Voy a hacerle unas preguntas
(Boy ah ah-**SAYR**-lay **OO**-nohs preh-**GOON**-tahs)

HE	El	(El)
I	Yo	(Yoh)
SHE	Ella	(**EH**-yah)
THAT	Aquel	(ah-**KAYL**)
THESE	Estos	(**AYS**-tohs)
THEY	Ellos	(**EH**-yohs)
THIS	Este	(**AYS**-tay)
THOSE	Aquellos	(ah-**KAY**-yohs)
YOU	Usted	(Oo-**STEHD**)
YOU(sgl)	Tu(fam)	(Too)
YOU(pl)	Ustedes	(Oo-**STEHD**-days)
WE	Nosotros	(Noh-**SOH**-trohs)

DID YOU CALL THE POLICE?
¿Llamó a la policia?
(Yah-**MOH** ah lah poh-lee-**SEE**-ah)

ARE YOU THE VICTIM?
¿Es usted la víctima?
(ehs oo-**STEHD** lah **VEEK**-tee-mah)

DID YOU WITNESS THE CRIME?
¿Vió el crimen?
(vee-**OH** el **KREE**-mehn)

DID THE PERSON _____ YOU?
¿La persona le _____ a usted?
(La payr-**SOH**-nah lay __ ah oo-**STED**)

(DID YOU) _____ THE PERSON?
¿ _____ la persona?
(_____ lah payr-**SOHN**-ah)

IS THE SUSPECT _____ ?
¿Es el sospechoso _____ ?
(ess ehl sohs-peh-**CHOH**-soh ___?)

HISPANIC	Hispano	(ees-**PAH**-noh)
ANGLO	Anglo	(**AHN**-gloh)
Oriental	oriental	(oh-ree-ehn-**TAHL**)
NEGRO	negro	(**NAY**-groh)
INDIAN	Indio	(**EEN**-dee-oh)

(USE VOCABULARY FOR ADD'L)

abuse-	abuso	(ah-**BOO**-soh)
allow-	permitir	(pehr-mee-**TEER**)
argue-	reñir	(rehn-**YEER**)
ask-	preguntar	(preh-goon-**TAHR**)
assault-	asalto	(ah-**SAHL**-toh)
attempt	tratar de	(trah-**TAHR** day)
burglary-	robo	(**ROH**-boh)
burn-	quemadura	(kay-mah-**DOO**-rah)
buy-	comprar	(kohm-**PRAHR**)
check-	revisar	(reh-bee-**SAHR**)
conceal-	esconder	(ess-kohn-**DEHR**)
consent-	permiso	(pehr-**MEE**-soh)
conspire-	conspirar	(kohns-pee-**RAHR**)
credit card-	tarjeta de crédito	(tahr-**HAY**-tah day **KREH**-dee-toh)
CRIME-	crimen	(**KREE**-mehn)
description-	descripción	(dehs-kreep-**SYOHN**)
drugs-	drogas	(**DROH**-gahs)
fight-	luchar	(loo-**CHAHR**)
firearm-	arma de fuego	(**AHR**-mah day **FWAY**-goh)
forgery-	falso	(**FAHL**-soh)
GUN-	arma	(**AHR**-mah)
harass-	molestar	(moh-lehs-**TAHR**)

English	Spanish	Pronunciation
hit-	golpear	(gohl-PAY-ahr)
hear-	oir	(oh-EER)
injure-	herir	(eh-REER)
intentional-	intencional	(een-tehn-syohn-NAHL)
intercourse-	acto sexual	(AHK-toh sex-soo-AHL)
	-relaciones sexuales	(ray-lah-see-OHN-ays sex-oo-AHL-ays)
	-relaciones íntimas	(ray-lah-see-OHN-ays EEN-tee-mahs)
kidnap-	raptar	(rahp-TAHR)
kill-	matar	(mah-TAHR)
killer-	asesino	(ah-ses-SEE-noh)
know-	conocer	(koh-noh-SEHR)
lie-	mentira	(mehn-TEE-rah)
molest-	molestar	(moh-lehs-TAHR)
murder-	homicidio	(oh-mee-SEE-dee-oh)
	-asesinato	(ah-SAHS-ee-nah-toh)
peace-	paz	(pahs)
penetrate-	penetrar	(pay-neh-TRAHR)
penetration-	penetración	(pay-neh-trah-SYOHN)
permit-	permiso	(pehr-MEE-soh)
permit (to)-	permitir	(pehr-mee-TEER)
point-	apuntar	(ah-poon-TAHR)
possess-	tener	(teh-NEHR)
rape-	violar	(vee-oh-LAHR)
revolver-	fusil	(foo-SEEL)
rob-	robar	(roh-BAHR)
see-	ver	(BEHR)
sell-	vender	(vehn-DEHR)
sex-	sexo	(SEK-soh)
shoot-	disparar	(dees-pah-RAHR)
shoplift-	ratear	(rah-tay-AHR)
shoplifter-	ratero de tienda	(rah-TAY-roh day tee-EHN-dah)
solicit-	solicitar	(soh-lee-see-TAHR)
stab-	apuñalar	(ah-poo-nah-LAHR)
start-	empezar	(ehm-peh-SAHR)
steal-	robar	(roh-BAHR)
supply-	proveer	(pro-vee-EER)
take-	tomar	(toh-MAHR)
touch-	tocar	(toh-KAHR)
trespass-	traspasar	(trahs-pah-SAHR)
victim-	víctima	(VEEK-tee-mah)
wound (v)	herir	(eh-REER)
wound (n)	herida	(eh-REE-dah)
write-	escribir	(ehs-kree-BEER)

I'M LOOKING FOR _____.
Busco a _____. (BOOS-koh ah)

DO YOU KNOW THE VICTIM?
¿Conoce a la víctima?
(Koh-NOH-say ah lah VEEK-tee-mah)

DO YOU KNOW WHO DID IT?
¿Sabe quién lo hizo?
(SAH-bay kee-EHN loh EE-soh)

DO YOU KNOW HIS (HER) NAME?
¿Conoce su nombre?
(Koh-NOH-say soo NOHM-bray)

DO YOU KNOW HIM (HER)?
¿Lo conoce? / ¿La conoce?
(Loh koh-NOH-say / Lah koh-NOH-say)

YOU ARE DISTURBING THE PEACE
Usted está interrumpiendo la paz.
(Oo-STEHD ess-TAH een-tehr-RUMP-pee-EHN-doh lah pahs)

WHERE DID THIS HAPPEN?
¿Dónde ocurrió esto?
(DOHN-day oh-koo-ree-oh AYS-toh)

CITY? ¿Ciudad? (see-oo-DAHD)
ADDRESS Domicilio (doh-mee-SEE-lyoh)

WHEN DID IT HAPPEN?
¿Cuándo pasó?
(KWAHN-doh pah-SOH)

THE NUMBER OF SUSPECTS?
¿El número de sospechosos?
(Ay NOO-may-roh day sohs-peh-CHOH-sohs)

WHERE DID HE GO?
¿A dónde fué?
(Ah DOHN-day foo-AY)

TIME HE LEFT? ¿A qué hora salió?
(Ah kay OH-rah sah-lee-OH)

HOW MANY MILES FROM HERE?
¿A cuántas millas de aquí?
(Ah KWAHN-tahs MEE-yahs day ah-KEE)

ADDRESS OF THE PERSON?
¿Dirección de la persona?
(Dee-rekk-SYOHN day lah payr-SOH-nah)

POINT TO WHERE YOU WERE TOUCHED.
Apunte a dónde fué tocado(a).
(Ah-POON-tay ah DOHN-day foo-AY toh-KAH-dah [doh])

(use anatomically correct doll)

30

DID HE LEAVE ON FOOT?
¿Salió a pie?
(Sah-lee-**OH** ah **PEE**-ay)

SHOW ME WHERE.
Enseñeme dónde.
(Ehn-**SEHN**-yah-may **DOHN**-day)

DID HE LEAVE IN A CAR?
¿Salió en carro?
(Sah-lee-**OH** ehn **KAHR**-roh)

WHAT DIRECTION? ¿Qué rumbo?
(Kay **ROOM**-boh)

POINT Apúnte (ah-**POON**-tay)

WHAT YEAR? ¿Qué año?
(Kay **AHN**-yoh)

MAKE: MODEL: STYLE:
Marca: Modelo: Estilo:
(**MAHR**-kah; Moh-**DAY**-loh; Ays-**TEE**-loh)

COLOR: LICENSE #:   STATE:
Color: Licencia: Estado:
(koh-**LOR**, Lee-**SEN**-see-ah, Es-**TAH**-doh)

CONDITION: Condición
(kohn-dee-**SYOHN**)

GOOD;   AVG.;   POOR
Bueno;   Término Medio, Pobre
(**BWAY**-no; **TEER**-mee-noh may-**DEE**-oh;
POH-bray)

LOUD MUFFLER Mofle ruidoso
(**MOH**-flay roo-ee-**DOH**-soh)

WHO OWNS THE CAR?
¿De quién es el carro?
(Day kee-**EHN** ays ehl **KAHR**-roh)

IS THE PERSON RELATED TO YOU?
¿Es pariente suyo?
(Ehs pah-ree-**EHN**-tay **SOO**-yoh)

WHAT RELATION? ¿Qué relación?
(Kay ray-lah-**SYOHN**)

IS HIS LICENSE SUSPENDED?
¿Esta suspendida su licencia?
(**AYS**-tah soos-**PEHN**-dee-dah soo
lee-**SEHN**-see-ah)

FOR WHAT? ¿Para que?
(**PAH**-rah kay)

HOW OLD? ¿Qué tan viejo?
(Kay tahn vee-**EH**-hoh)

HOW TALL? ¿Qué tan alto?
(Kay tahn **AHL**-toh)

THE NUMBER OF SUSPECTS?
¿El número de sospechosos?
(Ayl **NOO**-may-roh day
sohs-peh-**CHOH**-sohs)

WHERE DID HE GO? ¿A dónde fué?
(Ah **DOHN**-day foo-**AY**)

TIME HE LEFT?
¿A que hora salió?
(Ah kay **OH**-rah sah-lee-**OH**)

HOW MANY MILES FROM HERE?
¿A cuántas millas de aquí?
(Ah **KWAHN**-tahs **MEE**-yahs day
ah-**KEE**)

WEIGHT? ¿Peso? (**PAY**-soh)

THIN, AVERAGE, OR HEAVY?
¿Delgado, término medio, o pesado?
(Dehl-**GAH**-doh, **TEER**-mee-noh
may-**DEE**-oh, oh pay-**SAH**-doh)

HAIR COLOR? ¿Color de pelo?
(koh-**LOHR** day **PAY**-loh)
HOW LONG? ¿Qué tan largo?
(kay tahn **LAHR**-goh)
EYE COLOR? ¿Color de ojos?
(koh-**LOHR** day **OH**-hohs)

COMPLEXION TYPE? ¿Tipo de tez?
(**TEE**-poh day tayz)

WHAT WAS HE WEARING?
¿Qué ropa llevaba/Como estaba
vestido?
(Kay **ROH**-pah yay-**VAH**-bah /
KOH-moh ays-**TAH**-bah vehs-**TEE**-doh)

DESCRIBE WHAT WORN & COLOR.
Describe qué ropa usó y el color.
(Day-**SCREE**-bay kay **ROH**-pah
oo-**SOH** ee ayl koh-**LOHR**)

ANY PHYSICAL ODDITIES?
¿Algunos defectos físicos?
(Ahl-**GOO**-nohs day-**FEHK**-tohs
FEE-see-kohs)

BEARD? ¿Barba? (**BAHR**-bah)
BELT? ¿Faja? (**FAH**-hah);
¿Cinto? (**SEEN**-toh)

COAT? ¿Chamarra? (chah-**MAH**-rah)

EARRINGS? ¿Aretes? (ah-**RAY**-tahs)
¿Pendientes? (pehn-dee-**EHN**-tays)

GLASSES? ¿Lentes/ anteojos? (LEHN-tays/ ahn-tay-OH-hohs)	
GLOVES? ¿Guantes? (oo-AHN-tays)	
HAT? ¿Sombrero? (sohm-BRAY-roh)	
MOLES? ¿Lunares? (loo-NAH-rays)	
MOUSTACHE? ¿Bigotes?(bee-GOH-tays)	
PANTS? ¿Pantalones? (pahn-tah-LOHN-nays)	
RINGS? ¿Anillos? (ah-NEE-yohs)	
OTHER JEWELRY? ¿Otras joyas? (oh-TRAHS HOH-yahs)	
SHIRT? ¿Camisa? (kah-MEE-sah)	
SHOES? ¿Zapatos? (zah-PAH-tohs)	
SOCKS? ¿Calcetines? (kahl-say-TEE-nays)	
WATCH? ¿Reloj? (RAY-loh)	
ABSENT FINGERS, LARGE NOSE, EARS, etc. Le falta dedos, nariz grande, oidos, (Lay FAHL-tah DAY-dohs, nah-REEZ GRAHN-day, oh-EE-dohs,)	
SCARS/ MARKS/ TATTOOS? ¿Cicatrices/ marcas/ tatuajes? (see-kah-TREE-says, MAHR-kahs, tah-too-AH-ays)	
DESCRIBE OR DRAW? (Describir o dibujar) (Day-scree-BEER oh dee-boo-HAHR)	
LABEL THE ROOMS AND DOORS. (North at top) Designe los cuartos y puertas. (Note a la parte de arriba) (Day-SEHN-yay lohs KWAHR-tohs ee PWEHR-tahs [Noh-AHR-tay ah lah PAHR-tay day ah-REE-bah])	
DRAW ME THE INSIDE AND OUTSIDE OF THE HOUSE. Dibujeme el interior y el exterior de la casa. (Dee-BOO-hah-may el een-TEE-ree-or ee el ex-TEE-ree-or day lah KAH-sah)	
IS HE VIOLENT? ¿Es violento? (Ays vee-oh-LEHN-toh)	
HAS HE BEEN ARRESTED PREVIOUSLY? ¿Ha sido detenido anteriormente? (Ah SEE-doh day-TEHN-ee-doh ahn-TEE-ree-ohr-MEHN-tay)	
WHERE? ¿Dónde? (DOHN-day)	
DOES ANYBODY POSSESS A GUN OR KNIFE? ¿Posee alguien un arma (pistola, fusil) o navaja (cuchillo)? (Poh-SAY-ay ahl-GEE-ehn oon AHR-mah [pees-TOH-lah, foo-SEEL] oh nah-VAH-hah [koo-CHEE-yoh)	
WHERE? ¿Dónde? (DOHN-day)	
HOW MUCH? ¿Cuánto? (KWAHN-toh)	
DOES ANYONE HAVE A WEAPON? ¿Tiene alguien un arma? (Tee-EHN-ay ahl-GOO-ee-ehn oon AHR-mah)	
ANY DOGS AT THE HOUSE? ¿Hay perros a la casa? (Ay PAY-rohs ah lah KAH-sah)	
HOW MANY? ¿Cuántos? (KWAHN-tohs)	
DESCRIBE? ¿Describe? (Day-SCREE-bay)	
VICIOUS? ¿Viciosos? (vee-see-OH-sohs)	
HOW MANY PEOPLE ARE THERE? ¿Cuántos personas hay alli? (KWAHN-tohs payr-SOHN-ahs ay ah-YEE)	
WHO? ¿Quién? (kee-EHN)	
CHILDREN? ¿Niños? (NEEN-yohs)	
DOES THE PERSON HAVE ANY PHYSICAL INJURY? ¿Tiene la persona alguna herida físíca? (Tee-EHN-ay lah payr-SOH-nah ahl-GOO-nah ayr-EE-dah FEE-see-kah)	
IS HE DRUNK OR TAKING DRUGS? ¿Está borracho o toma drogas? (Ay-STAH boh-RAH-choh oh TOH-mah DROH-gahs)	
WHAT DRUGS? ¿Cuáles drogas? (KWAHL-ays DROH-gahs)	
DOES HE POSSESS DRUGS OR LARGE AMOUNTS OF MONEY? ¿Posee drogas o cantidades grandes de dinero? (Poh-SAY-ay DROH-gahs oh kahn-tee-DAHD-days GRAHN-days day dee-NAY-roh)	

DO YOU HAVE WITNESSES?
¿Tiene usted testigos?
(Tee-**EHN**-nay oo-**STED**
tehs-**TEE**-gohs)

NAMES, ADDRESSES, & PHONE #'s.
(Nombres, direcciones, y numeros de
teléfono)
(**NOHM**-brays, dee-rehk-**SYOH**-nays, ee
NOO-may-rohs day tay-**LAY**-foh-noh)

WHERE CAN I FIND THEM?
¿En dónde puedo hallarlos?
(Ehn **DOHN**-day **PWAY**-doh
ah-**YAHR**-lohs)

EMPLOYER? ¿Patrón?
(pah-**TROHN**)

WHERE DO THEY OFTEN GO?
¿Van allí a menudo?
(Vahn ah-**YEE** ah may-**NOO**-doh)

**WRITE DOWN WHAT HAPPENED
FROM THE BEGINNING.** (Incl, names,
times, locations, highways, streets, etc.)
Apunte lo que ocurió desde el
principio. [Incluye nombres, horas,
sitios, carreteras, calles, etc.]
(Ah-**POON**-tay loh kay oh-**KOO**-ree-**OH**
DAYS-day ayl preen-**SEE**-pee-oh.
[een-**KLOO**-yay **NOHM**-brays, **OH**-rahs, **SEE**-tee-ohs, kah-rah-**TAY**-rahs, **KAH**-yays, etc])

WHAT ARE THE ARRANGEMENTS?
**(Include names, times, locations,
routes, prices)**
¿Cuales son los arreglos? (Incluye
nombres, horas, sitios, rutas, precios)
(**KWAHL**-ays sohn lohs
ah-**RAY**-glohs [een-**KLOO**-yay
NOHM-brays, **OH**-rahs, see-**TEE**-ohs,
ROO-tahs, **PRAY**-see-ohs])

**YOU WILL BE REQUIRED TO
TESTIFY.**
Usted será requerido atestiguar.
(oo-**STEHD** say-**RAH** ray-**KAY**-ree-doh ah-**TEHS**-tee-gwahr)

TAKE ME TO WHERE HE LIVES/IS.
Lleveme a dónde vive o a dónde está.
(Yay-**VAY**-may ah **DOHN**-day **VEE**-vay oh ah **DOHN**-day ays-**TAH**)

**YOU COMMITTED THE CRIME,
CORRECT?**
¿Cometió usted la ofensa, Verdad?
(koh-**MAY**-tee-**OH** oo-**STEHD**
loh oh-**FEHN**-sah, vehr-**DAHD**)

DEATH MESSAGE

(Note: If at all possible, attempt to
locate a qualified interpreter or
translator and only use these phrases
as a last resort. It is then better to let
the person read the phrases when
possible.)

I'M LOOKING FOR _____.
Busco a _____.
(**BOOZ**-koh ah _____.)

ARE YOU _____?
¿Eres/Estas _____?
(**AY**-rays/ **AY**-stahs _____?)

I AM SORRY, YOUR _____ **WAS
KILLED IN AN ACCIDENT.**
Lo siento, su _____ se
mató en un accidente.
(Loh see-**EHN**-toh, soo _____ say
mah-**TOH** ehn oon ahk-see-**DEHN**-tay)

I AM SORRY, YOUR _____ **DIED.**
Lo siento, su _____ murió.
(Loh see-**EHN**-toh, soo _____
moo-ree-**OH**)

_____ **DIED FROM** _____.
_____ murió por _____.
(_____ moo-ree-**OH** pohr _____)

I DON'T KNOW. No sé. (Noh say)

**IS THERE ANYTHING I CAN DO FOR
YOU?**
Hay algo que puedo hacer por Ud.
(Ay **AHL**-goh kay **PWAY**-doh
ah-**SAYR** pohr oo-**STEHD**)

DIRECTIONS

POINT! ¡Apúnte! (ah-**POON**-tay)

WHAT DIRECTION?
¿Cuál dirección?
(Kwahl dee-rehk-**SYOHN**)

WHERE IS THE _____?
¿Dónde está el/la _____?
(**DOHN**-day ays-**TAH** ehl /lah _____?)

IS IT _____. (insert below)
Es _____?
(ess _____)

EAST este (**ESS**-tay)
 oriente (ohr-ee-**EHN**-tay)
NORTH norte (**NOHR**-tay)
NORTHEAST noreste (Nohr-**ESS**-tay)
N.WEST noroeste (Nohr-**OHWES**-tay)

HAVE YOU BEEN DRINKING?
¿Has tomado licor?
(Ahs toh-MAH-doh lee-KOHR)

DO YOU TAKE SHOTS?
¿Toma inyecciones?
(TOH-mah een-yeck-SYOHN-nays)

ARE YOU A DIABETIC?
¿Es usted diabético(a)?
(Ess oo-STEHD dee-ah-BEH-tee-koh)

FOR WHAT? ¿Para qué cosa?
(PAH-rah kay KOH-sah)

IS A DOCTOR TAKING CARE OF YOU?
¿Está usted bajo cuidado de doctor?
(Ess-TAH oo-STEHD BAH-hoh kwee-DAH-doh day dohk-TOHR)

WHAT KIND OF MEDICINE?
¿Qué clase de medicina?
(Kay KLAH-say day meh-dee-SEE-nah)

ARE YOU TAKING MEDICINE?
¿Está tomando medicina?
(Ess-TAH toh-MAHN-doh meh-dee-SEE-nah)

ARE YOU HURT?
¿Está lastimado(a)?
(Ess-TAH lah-stee-MAH-doh)

IS THERE ANYTHING WRONG WITH THE CAR?
¿Hay algo mal con su carro?
(I AHL-goh mahl kohn soo KAH-roh)

HOW MUCH DID YOU DRINK?
Cuánto tomó?
(KWAHN-toh toh-MOH)

DO YOU FEEL THE EFFECTS OF ALCOHOL?
¿Siente usted los efectos del licor?
(See-EHN-tay oo-STEHD lohs ah-FEHK-tohs dayl lee-KOHR)

YOU ARE BEING TAPE RECORDED.
Se está grabando.
(Say ays-TAH grah-BAHN-doh)

WHAT? ¿Qué? (Kay)	
BEER- cerveza	(sayr-VAY-zah)
BOTTLE- botella	(boh-TAY-yah)
BRANDY-Presidente	(brand name) (pray-see-DEHN-tay)
CAN- bote	(BOH-tay)
QUART- guayama	(goo-AY-ah-mah)
TEQUILA- tequila	(tay-KEI-lah)
WHISKEY- whiskey	(WEES-kee)
WINE- vino	(VEE-noh)

DRIVING WHILE INTOXICATED (DWI)

SOUTH	sud	(Sood)
	sur	(soor)
SOUTHEAST	sudeste	(Soo-DEHS-tay)
SOUTHWEST	sudoeste	(Soo-doh-WEHS-tay)
WEST	oeste	(Oo-WEHS-tay)
	occidente	(ohk-see-DEHN-tay)
ABOVE-	arriba	(ah-REE-bah)
ACROSS-	a través de	(ah trah-VEHS day)
AHEAD-	delante	(deh-LAHN-tay)
BACK-	atras	(ah-TRAHS)
BETWEEN-	entre	(EHN-tray)
BEHIND-	detrás	(day-TRAHS)
BESIDE-	junto a	(HOON-toh ah)
BEYOND-	más allá	(mahs ah-YAH)
BOTTOM-	a fondo de	(ah FOHN-doh day)
DOWN-	abajo	(ah-BAH-hoh)
FRONT-	en frente de	(ehn FREHN-tay day)
INSIDE-	dentro de	(DEHN-troh day)
LEFT-	izquierdo	(ees-kee-EHR-doh)
MIDDLE-	en medio de	(en meh-DEE-oh day)
NEAR-	cerca de	(SEHR-kah day)
RIGHT-	derecho	(deh-REH-choh)
MUCH? ¿Mucho?	(MOO-choh)	
A LITTLE? ¿Poco?	(POH-koh)	
TOP (on)-	encima de	(ehn-SEE-mah day)
TOWARD-	hacia	(AH-see-ah)
UNDER-debajo de	(deh-BAH-hoh day)	
UP-	arriba	(ah-REE-bah)

34

WHEN DID YOU TAKE YOUR LAST SHOT?
¿Cuándo tomó la última inyección?
(KWAHN-doh toh-MOH lah
OOL-tee-mah een-yeck-SYOHN)

WHEN SHOULD YOU TAKE THE NEXT ONE?
¿Cuándo debe tomar la siguiente?
(KWAHN-doh DEH-beh toh-MAHR
lah see-gee-EHN-tah)

ARE YOU EPILEPTIC?
¿Es usted epiléptico(a)?
(Ess oo-STEHD eh-pee-LEHP-tee-koh)

ARE YOU OK? ¿Está bien?
(Ess-TAH bee-YEHN)

DO YOU HAVE HEART TROUBLE?
¿Está malo del corazón?
(ess-TAH MAH-loh dayl kohr-ah-ZOHN)

DO YOU HAVE PILLS FOR YOUR HEART?
¿Tiene pildoras para el corazón?
(Tee-EHN-ay PEEL-door-ahs PAH-rah ehl kohr-ah-ZOHN)

REMOVE THE KEYS FROM THE IGNITION.
Quite las llaves del carro.
(KEE-tay las YAH-vays del KAHR-roh)

THROW YOUR KEYS OUT.
Arroje sus llaves para afuera.
(Ah-ROH-hay soos YAH-vays
PAH-rah ah-FWEH-rah)

IS THIS YOUR CAR?
¿Es este su carro?
(Ess ESS-teh soo KAHR-roh)

WERE YOU DRIVING THE CAR?
¿Usted estaba manejando este carro?
(oo-STEHD ehs-TAH-bah mah-neh-HAHN-doh ESS-tay KAHR-roh)

WHERE WERE YOU GOING?
¿A dónde iba?
(Ah DOHN-day EE-bah)

WHERE DID YOU START?
¿En dónde comenzó?
(Ehn DOHN-day koh-mehn-ZOH)

WHAT TIME IS IT WITHOUT LOOKING AT YOUR WATCH?
¿Que hora es sin mirar a su reloj?
(Kay OH-rah ays seen mee-RAHR
ah soo RAY-loh)

ARE YOU WEARING CONTACTS?
¿Usa usted lentes de contacto?
(OO-sah oo-STEHD LEHN-tays day
kohn-TAHK-toh)

HAVE YOU USED MOUTHWASH TODAY?
¿Ha usado usted un enjuage de su boca hoy?
(Ah oo-SAH-doh oo-STEHD oon ehn-hoo-AH-gay day soo BOH-kah oy)

WHEN DID YOU LAST SLEEP?
¿Cuándo durmió ultimamente?
(KWAHN-doh door-mee-OH
ool-tee-mah-MEHN-tay)

HOW MANY HOURS?
¿Cuántos horas?
(KWAHN-tohs OH-rahs)

I'M NOW GOING TO REQUEST YOU TO PERFORM FIELD TESTS. IF YOU REFUSE OR FAIL TO SUBMIT TO THE FIELD TESTS, EVIDENCE OF THE REFUSAL OR FAILURE TO SUBMIT IS ADMISSIBLE IN ANY CRIMINAL OR CIVIL ACTION OR PROCEEDING ARISING OUT OF ALLEGATIONS THAT YOU WERE DRIVING UNDER THE INFLUENCE OF ALCOHOL OR DRUGS.
Ahora voy a pedirle que haga ciertos examenes. En caso de que usted se niega hacerlos, o no se conforma a hacerlos, esa evidencia se puede usar en contra de usted en corte, sea en un caso criminal o en un caso civil que pueda surgir de lahs alegaciones que usted estaba manejando bajo la influencia de alcohol o de drogas.
(Ah-OH-rah boy ah pay-DEER-lay
kay AH-gah see-AYR-tohs
egs-AH-may-nays. Ehn KAH-soh
day kay oo-STEHD say nee-AY-gah
ah-SAYR-lohs, oh noh say
kohn-FOHR-mah ah ah-SAYR-lohs,
AY-sah eh-vee-DEHN-see-ah say
PWAY-day oo-SAHR ehn
KOHN-trah day oo-STEHD ehn
kohr-TAY, SAY-ah ehn oon KAH-soh
kree-mee-NAHL oh ehn oon
KAH-soh see-VEEL kay PWAY-dah
soor-HEER day lahs
ah-lay-GAH-syohn-ays kay
oo-STEHD ay-STAH-boh
mah-nay-HAHN-doh BAH-hoh lah
een-floo-EHN-see-ah day
ahl-koh-AHL oh day DROH-gahs)

STEP FROM YOUR CAR.
Salga de su carro.
(SAHL-gah day soo KAHR-roh)

FOLLOW ME Sígame (SEE-gah-may)

LET'S GO Vámonos (VAH-moh-nohs)

STAND HERE. Párese aquí.
(PAH-reh-say ah-KEE)

YOUR BREATH SMELLS OF ALCOHOL.
Su aliento huele de alcohol.
(Soo ahl-ee-EHN-toh oo-ELL-ay day ahl-koh-OHL)

BREATH (ahl-lee-EHN-toh) aliento
BREATHE respirar (rehs-pee-RAHR)
MEDICINE medicina (meh-dee-SEE-nah)
TO SPIT escupir (ehs-koo-PEER)
TO VOMIT vomitar (Vohm-ee-TAHR)
-vasquear (vahz-KAY-ar)

STAND WITH THE FEET TOGETHER, LIKE ME.
Párese con los pies juntos como yo.
(PAH-reh-say kohn lohs pee-EHS HOON-tohs KOH-moh yoh)

CLOSE YOUR EYES. Cierre los ojos.
(See-EH-ray lohs OH-hohs)

WALK LIKE ME. Camine como yo.
(Kah-MEE-nay KOH-moh yoh)

DO LIKE ME. Haga como yo.
(AH-gah KOH-moh yoh)

1. PERFORM HORIZONTAL GAZE NYSTAGMUS TEST HERE

Hold your head still and follow my (finger / light) with your eyes.
Tenga su cabeza quieto y sigue mi (dedo / luz) con sus ojos.
(TEHN-gah soo kah-BAY-zah kee-EH-toh ee see-GAY mee [DAY-doh/loos] kohn sus OH-hohs)

2. WALK AND TURN TEST

Walk 10 steps heel to toe in a straight line. Turn and walk back 10 steps heel to toe. Like this.
Camine diez pasos adelante taco a dedo. Voltéese y camine diez pasos para atrás. Haga como yo.
(Kah-MEE-nay dee-AYS PAH-sohs ah-day-LAHN-tay TAH-koh ah DAY-doh TAY-ay-say ee kah-MEE-nay dee-AYS PAH-sohs PAH-rah ah-TRAHS. AH-gah KOH-moh yoh)

LIKE THIS. Como esto.
(KOH-moh AYS-toh)

3. ONE LEG TEST

Lift a foot like me.
Levante un pie como yo.
(Leh-VAHN-tay oon pee-EH KOH-moh yoh)

4. STAND STILL TEST

STAND STILL! ¡Apláguese!
(Ah-PLAH-kay-say)

PUT YOUR FEET TOGETHER.
Ponga sus pies juntos.
(POHN-gah soos PEE-ays HOON-tohs)

PUT YOUR HANDS AT YOUR SIDE.
Ponga sus manos a su lado.
(POHN-gah soos MAH-nohs ah soo LAH-doh)

CLOSE YOUR EYES.
Cierre sus ojos.
(See-AY-ray soos OH-hohs)

5. FINGER TO NOSE TEST
(Demonstrate test)

CLOSE YOUR EYES.
Cierre sus ojos.
(See-AY-ray soos OH-hohs)

TOUCH YOUR (LEFT)(RIGHT) INDEX FINGER TO THE TIP OF YOUR NOSE. (Like this)
Favor de tocar la punta (izquierda/derecho) de la nariz así. (Como esto)
(Fah-VOHR day toh-KAHR lah POON-tah [ees-kee-AYR-dah / day-RAY-choh] day lah nah-REEZ ah-SEE. [KOH-moh AYS-toh])

STAND STILL. Esté quieto.
(ays-TAY kee-EH-toh)

(Or) ¡Apláguese!
(Ah-PLAH-kay-say)

FEET TOGETHER.
Pies juntos.
(pee-ESS HOON-tohs)

HANDS AT YOUR SIDES.
Manos a sus lados.
(**MAH**-nohs ah soos **LAH**-dohs)

CLOSE YOUR EYES
Cierre sus ojos.
(See-**AY**-ray soos **OH**-hohs)

KEEP YOUR EYES CLOSED.
Mantenga sus ojos cerrados.
(Mahn-**TEHN**-gah soos **OH**-hohs say-**RAY**-dohs)

6. TIME TEST
WHAT TIME IS IT WITHOUT LOOKING AT YOUR WATCH?
¿Que hora es sin mirar a su reloj?
(Kay **OH**-rah ays seen mee-**RAHR** ah soo **RAY**-loh)

OPEN LIQUOR IN THE CAR IS AGAINST THE LAW.
Licor abierto en el carro es en contra de la ley.
(Lee-**KOHR** ah-bee-**AYR**-toh ehn ayl **KAHR**-roh ays ehn **KOHN**-trah day lah lay)

YOU ARE UNDER ARREST.
Usted está arrestado.
(Oo-**STEHD** ess-**TAH** ah-reh-**STAH**-doh)

YOU ARE UNDER ARREST FOR DRIVING WHILE UNDER THE INFLUENCE OF AN INTOXICANT.
Usted está arrestado por manejar tomado.
(Oo-**STEHD** ess-**TAH** ah-reh-**STAH**-doh pohr mahn-neh-**HAHR** toh-**MAH**-doh)

SEPARATE YOUR FEET.
Separe los pies.
(Seh-**PAH**-ray lohs pee-**ESS**)

PUT YOUR HANDS UP!
¡Alce las manos!
(**AHL**-say lahs **MAH**-nohs)

PUT YOUR HANDS BEHIND YOU.
Ponga las manos detrás de usted.
(**POHN**-gah lahs **MAH**-nohs deh-**TRAHS** day oo-**STEHD**)

COME WITH ME.
Venga conmigo.
(**VEHN**-gah kohn-**MEE**-goh)

GET INTO THE CAR.
Súbase al carro.
(**SOO**-bay-say ahl **KAHR**-roh)

LET'S GO! ¡Vámos! (**VAH**-mohs)

WAIT- ¡Espére! (ehs-**PEHR**-ay)

THE LAW REQUIRES THAT YOU SUBMIT YOURSELF TO A TEST IN ORDER TO KNOW THE ALCOHOL CONTENT OF YOUR BLOOD
La ley require que usted se someta a una prueba para saber cuanto alcohol contiene su sangre.
(La lay reh-kee-**EHR**-ray kay oo-**STEHD** say soh-**MEE**-tah ah **OO**-nah proo-**EH**-bah **PAH**-rah sah-**BEHR KWAHN**-toh ahl-koh-**OHL** kohn-tee-**EHN**-nay soo **SAHN**-gray)

SIGN HERE FOR YOUR PROPERTY.
Firme aquí para su propiedad.
(**FEER**-may ah-**KEE** pah-rah soo pro-pee-eh-**DAHD**)

BLOW INTO THE MACHINE CONTINUOSLY UNTIL I SAY STOP
Sople en la maquina continuamente hasta que yo le diga que no sople más
(**SOH**-play ehn lah **MAH**-kee-nah kohn-tee-**NOO**-ah-**MEHN**-tay **AHS**-tah kay yoh lay **DEE**-gah kay no **SOH**-play mahs)

IT STATES HERE WHERE YOUR CAR IS. Dice aquí dónde está su carro.
(**DEE**-say ah-**KEE DOHN**-day ays-**TAH** soo **KAHR**-roh)

DRUG DOG

ARE THERE ANY DRUGS IN THE _?
Hay drogas en el _____?
(Ay **DROH**-gahs ehn ayl _____?)

ARE THERE ANY _____?
Hay ¿_____?
(eye)

NEEDLES? ¿Agujas?(ah-GOO-hahs)
POISONS?¿Venenos? (vay-NAY-nohs)

SHARP OBJECTS?
¿Objetos afilosos?
(ohb-HAY-tohs ah-FEE-lohs-sohs)

DOGS IN HEAT? ¿Perros en calor?
(PAY-rohs ehn kah-LOHR)

DO THEY BITE?
¿Muerdan?
(moo-AYR-dahn)

PETS?
¿Animales domesticos?
(ah-nee-MAH-lays doh-MEHS-tee-kohs)

MY DOG SCRATCHES AND BITES WHERE DRUGS ARE.
Mi perro rasguña y muerde dónde hay drogas.
(Mee PAY-roh rahs-GOON-yah ee moo-AYR-day DOHN-day ay DROH-gahs)

THE DOG WILL DAMAGE YOUR PROPERTY.
El perro dañará a su propiedad
(Ay! PAY-roh dahn-YAH-RAH ah soo proh-PEE-ay-dahd)

WHERE ARE THE DRUGS?
¿Dónde están las drogas?
(DOHN-day ays-TAHN lahs DROH-gahs)

MY DOG WILL NOT BITE.
Mi perro no morderá.
(Mee PAY-roh noh mohr-day-RAH)

WOULD YOU LIKE TO PET MY DOG? (child)
¿Quieres acariciarle?
(Kee-AYR-ays ah-KAH-ree-see-AHR-lay)

MY DOG'S NAME IS _____.
El nombre de mi perro es _____.
(Ay! NOHM-bray day mee PAY-roh ays _____.)

MY DOG IS VERY PROTECTIVE OF MY CAR.
Mi perro es muy protectivo de mi carro.
(Mee PAY-roh ays MOO-ee proh-TEHK-tee-voh day mee KAHR-roh)

DON'T PET HIM WHEN HE'S THERE.
No lo acaricies cuando esta allí.
(Noh loh ah-KAH-ree-see-ahs KWAHN-doh AYS-tah ah-YEE)

DO YOU HAVE SOME WATER FOR MY DOG?
¿Tiene ud. agua para mi perro?
(Tee-EHN-ay oo-STEHD ah-GOO-ah PAH-roh mee PAY-roh)

MY DOG IS INJURED.
Mi perro esta herido.
(Mee PAY-roh ays-TOH ay-REE-doh)

IS THERE A VET NEARBY?
¿Hay un veterinario cerca?
(Ay oon vay-tay-ree-NAH-ree-oh SAYR-kah)

DYING DECLARATIONS

DO YOU UNDERSTAND YOU ARE GOING TO DIE?
¿Entiende que ud. va a morir?
(Ehn-tee-EHN-day kay oo-STEHD vah ah moh-REER)

WHO DID THIS TO YOU?
¿Quien hizo este a usted?
(Kee-EHN EE-soh AYS-toh ah oo-STEHD)

HIS / HER NAME?
¿Su nombre?
(Soo NOHM-bray)

EDUCATION

WHAT GRADE DID YOU COMPLETE IN SCHOOL?
¿Hasta qué grado llegaste en la escuela?
(AH-stah kay GRAH-doh Yay-GAHS-tay ehn lah ehs-koo-AY-lah)

CAN YOU READ / WRITE?
¿Puede leer / escribir?
(PWAY-day lay-AYR / ehs-kree-BEER)

EMOTIONS

ACCEPT- aceptar (ah-sehp-TAHR)
ACCEPTABLE- aceptable
(ah-sehp-TAH-bleh)

UNACCEPTABLE- no aceptable
(noh ah-sehp-TAH-bleh)

38

AFFECTION-	cariño (kah-**REEN**-yoh)
AGREE-	acuerdo(ah-**KOO**-air-doh)
ANGER-	enojo (eh-**NOH**-zhoh)
ANXIETY-	ansia (**AHN**-see-ah)
ATTITUDE:	actitúd (ahk-tee-**TOOD**)
CRY-	llorar (yoh-**RAHR**)
CRYING-	llanto (**YAHN**-toh)
DEPRESSED-	deprimido (day-pree-**MEE**-doh)
DEPRESSION-	depresión (day-pray-**SYOHN**)
DESPERATE-	desesperado (deh-sehs-peh-**RAH**-doh)
DETEST-	detestar (deh-tehs-**TAHR**)
DISAGREE-	no estar de acuerdo (noh ehs-**TAHR** day ah-**KOO**-ayr-doh)
DISAPPOINTED-	decepcionado (deh-sehp-**SEE**-oh-**NAH**-doh)
DISGUST-	disgusto (dees-**GOOS**-toh)
DISSATISFIED-	descontento (dehs-kohn-**TEHN**-toh)
FAITH-	fé (**FEH**)
HAPPY-	felíz (feh-**LEES**)
HATE-	odiar(oh-dee-**AHR**)
LIKE-	gustar (goos-**TAHR**)
INDIFFERENT-	indiferente (een-dee-feh-**REHN**-tay)
MOOD-	humor (oo-**MOHR**)
BAD MOOD-	mal humor (mahl oo-**MOHR**)
GOOD MOOD-	buen humor (bwehn oo-**MOHR**)
RELIEF-	alivio (ah-**LEE**-bee-oh)
SAD-	triste (**TREES**-tay)
SADNESS-	tristeza (trees-**TEH**-sah)
SATISFIED-	satisfecho (sah-tees-**FEH**-choh)
SHAME-	verguenza (behr **GWEHN**-sah)
BE ASHAMED	avergonzado (ah-behr-**GOHN**-zah-doh)
SMILE-	sonrisa (sohn-**REE**-sah)
SORROW-	dolor (doh-**LOHR**)
SURPRISE-	sorpresa (sohr-**PREH**-sah)
SYMPATHY-	pésame (**PAY**-sah-may)
SYMPATHY (death)	Condolencia (kohn-doh-**LEHN**-see-ah)
TRUST-	tener confianza (teh-**NEHR** kohn-fee-**AHN**-zah)

ENGLISH - DO YOU SPEAK

DO YOU SPEAK ENGLISH?
¿Habla usted inglés?
(**AH**-blah oo-**STEHD** een-**GLAYS**)

COMPREHEND? ¿Comprende?
(kohm-**PREHN**-day)

I SPEAK A LITTLE SPANISH.
Yo hablo poco español.
(yoh **AH**-bloh **POH**-koh ehs-pah-**NYOHL**)

I DON'T UNDERSTAND
No comprendo.
(noh kohm-**PREHN**-doh)

IS THERE ANYONE HERE WHO SPEAKS ENGLISH?
¿Hay alguien aquí que habla inglés?
(**AH**-ee ahl-ghee-**EHN** ah-**KEE** kay **AH**-blah een-**GLAYS**)

WHAT DO YOU CALL THIS IN SPANISH?
¿Cómo se llama esto en español?
(**KOH**-moh say **YAH**-mah **ESS**-toh ehn ehs-pah-**NYOHL**)

YOU SPEAK ENGLISH!
¡Habla Inglés!
(**AH**-blah een-**GLAYS**)

YOU UNDERSTAND! ¡Entiende!
(Ehn-tee-**EHN**-day)

YOU DO NOT FOOL ME!
¡No me engaña!
(Noh may ehn-**GAHN**-yay)

YOU PRETEND NOT TO UNDERSTAND!
¡Ud. finge no entender!
(oo-**STEHD** **FEEN**-hay noh ehn-tehn-**DAYR**)

FIRE

DANGER - Peligro (Peh-LEE-groh)
FIRE Fuego (FOO-ay-goh)

EVERYBODY OUT!
¡Todos afuera!
(TOH-dohs ah-FWAYR-ah)

JUMP! ¡Salte! (SAHL-tay)

LEAVE! ¡Salga! (SAHL-gah)

IS THERE A FIRE HERE?
¿Hay incendio aquí?
(eye een-SEHN-dee-oh ah-KEE)

IS EVERYBODY OUT OF THE HOUSE?
¿Salieron todos de la casa?
(Sah-lee-EH-rohn TOH-dohs day lah KAH-sah)

I ORDER YOU TO HELP PUT OUT THE FIRE!
¡Ordeno que usted ayude a apagar el fuego!
(Ohr-DAY-noh kay oo-STEHD ah-YOO-day ah ah-pah-GAHR ayl FWAY-goh)

TELL ME THE TRUTH.
Dígame la verdad.
(DEE-gah-may lah vehr-DAHD)

TRUTH verdad (vehr-DAHD)

IT'S NOT TRUE. No es verdad.
(noh ehs vehr-DAHD)

TO BE DOUBTFUL Ser dudoso
(sayr doo-DOH-soh)

FALSE falso (FAHL-soh)

IT'S A LIE! ¡Es mentira!
(ehs mehn-TEE-rah)

LIE (n) - mentira (mehn-TEE-rah)

PUT OUT THAT FIRE. ¡Apáguelo.
(ah-PAH-gay-loh)

DID YOU REPORT THE FIRE?
¿Reportó el incendio?
(Reh-pohr-TOH el een-SEHN-dee-oh)

DON'T INTERFERE WITH FIREMEN.
No estorbe a los bomberos.
(No es-STOHR-bay ah lohs bohm-BEHR-rohs)

HOW DID THE FIRE START?
¿Como empezó el incendio?
(KOH-moh em-pay-ZOH el een-SEHN-dyoh)

DID YOU SET THE FIRE?
¿Ud. prendió el fuego?
(oo-STEHD prehn-dee-OH el FWAY-goh)

YOU CAN NOT PARK IN FRONT OF A FIRE HYDRANT
No se puede estacionar frente a una llave contra-incendio.
(No say poo-EH-day ehs-stah-see-oh-NAHR FREHN-tah ah OO-nah YAH-vay KOHN-trah-een-SEHN-dyoh)

YOU CANNOT DRIVE OVER THE FIREHOSE.
No se permite caminar sobre la manguera.
(No say pehr-MEE-tay kah-mee-NAHR SOH-bray lah mahn-GAY-rah)

THE FIRE IS NOW OUT.
Ya se apagó el incendio.
(yah say ah-pah-GOH el een-SEHN-dyoh)

FIREFIGHTER- bombero (bohm-BAY-roh)

PARAMEDICS- asistentes médicos
(ah-sees-TEHN-tays MEH-dee-kohs)

FRIENDS & ASSOCIATES
(SEE NAMES / RELATIVES)

FRUITS & VEGETABLES
(PLURAL ADD THE LETTER "s".)

FRUIT - fruta (FROO-tah)
APPLE manzana (mahn-ZAH-nah)
APRICOT- albaricoque
(ahl-bah-ree-KOH-kay);
chabacano (chah-bah-KAH-noh)

BANANA-banana(bah-NAH-nah);
   plátano(**PLAH**-tah-noh)
BLACKBERRY- zarzamora
   (zahr-zah-**MOH**-rah);
   mora   (**MOH**-rah)
CHERRY- cereza(she-**REH**-sah);
   guinda   (**GEEN**-dah)
DRIED FRUIT- fruta seca
   (**FROO**-tah **SAY**-kah)
FRUIT-   fruta   (**FROO**-tah)
GRAPEFRUIT-   toronja
   (toh-**ROHN**-hah);
   pomelo (poh-**MEH**-loh)
GRAPES-   uvas   (**OO**-bahs)
LEMON-   limón   (lee-**MOHN**)
MELON- melón   (meh-**LOHN**)
ORANGE- naranja   (nah-**RAHN**-hah)
PEACH- melocotón
   (meh-loh-koh-**TOHN**);
   durazno (doo-**RAHS**-noh)
PEAR-   pera   (**PAY**-rah)
PLUM-   ciruela (seer-**WAY**-lah)
PRUNE- ciruela pasa
   (seer-**WAY**-lah **PAH**-sah)
RAISINS- pasas   (**PAH**-sahs)
RASPBERRY-   frambuesa
   (frahm-**BWEH**-sah)
STRAWBERRY- fresa (**FRAY**-sah)
WALNUT-   nuez (**NOO**-ehz)
WATERMELON sandía(sahn-**DEE**-ah)

VEGETABLES

BEANS- verdes   (**VEHR**-days);
   frijoles   (free-**HOH**-lays);
   porotos   (poh-**ROH**-tohs)

BEET remolacha(reh-moh-**LAH**-chah);
   betaraga (bay-tah-**RAH**-gah);
   betabel   (beh-tah-**BELL**)
CARROT- zanahoria
   (zah-nah-**OH**-ree-ah)
CORN-   maíz   (mah-**EEZ**)
CUCUMBER- pepino (peh-**PEE**-noh)
GARDEN-   jardín   (hahr-**DEEN**)
GREEN PEPPER-   pimenton
   (pee-mehn-**TOHN**)
LETTUCE- lechuga (leh-**CHOO**-gah)
LIMA BEAN- haba   (**AH**-bah)

MUSHROOM- champiñon
   (chahm-pee-**NYOHN**);
   - hongo (**OHN**-goh)

ONION-   cebolla   (seh-**BOH**-yah)

POTATO- papa   (**PAH**-pah);
   patata   (pah-**TAH**-tah)

TOMATO- tomate   (toh-**MAH**-tay)
ZUCCHINI- pepino   (pay-**PEE**-noh)

GAME / FISH / WILDLIFE

I SAW YOU_____.
Le ví usted_____.
(Lay vee oo-**STEHD** _____.)

*YOU ILLEGALLY KILLED THE____.
Ilegalmente mató el _____.
(ee-leh-gahl-**MEHN**-teh mah-**TOH** ehl __.

*I AM GOING TO SEIZE THE _____.
Voy a confiscar el _____.
(Boy ah kohn-fees-**KAHR** ehl ____.)

ACROSS THE ROAD-
Al otro lado del camino
(Ahl **OH**-troh **LAH**-doh dayl
   kah-**MEE**-noh)

*ALLIGATOR cayman (kahy-**MAHN**)
ANIMAL- animal   (ah-nee-**MAHL**)
*ARTIFACTS   artefactos
   (ahr-teh-**FAHK**-tohs)
*ARROWHEADS   puntas de flecha
   (**POON**-tahs deh **FLEH**-chah)
BEAK-   pico   (**PEE**-koh)
BEAR-   oso   (**OH**-soh)
*BEES   abejas   (ah-**BEH**-hahs)
BIRDS-   pájaros   (**PAH**-hah-rohs)
BLACKBIRD- mirlo   (**MEER**-loh)
BLOOD- sangre   (**SAHN**-gray)
BOW AND ARROW- arco y flecha
   (**AHR**-koh ee **FLAY**-chah)
BLOOD   sangre   (**SAHN**-gray)
*BRAINS sesos   (**SEH**-sohs)
BUCK-   venado ciervo
   (veh-**NAH**-doh **SYEHR**-voh)
BULL-   toro   (**TOH**-roh)
*BURIAL SITE (sitio) or cementerio
   (seh-mehn-**TEH**-ryoh)
*CAPE   capa   (**KAH**-pah)
CAT-   gato   (**GAH**-toh)
CATCH-   coger   (koh-**HEHR**)
CHASE- perseguir (payr-say-**GEER**)
CLAM-   almeja   (al-**MAY**-hah)
CLAW-   garra   (**GAH**-rah)

CODFISH- bacalao (bah-kah-LAH-oh)
CONCEAL esconder (ess-kohn-DEHR)
COW- vaca (VAH-kah)
CRAB- cangrejo (kahn-GRAY-hoh)
CROCODILE- cocodrilo
(koh-koh-DREE-loh)

DEER- venado (beh-NAH-doh)
DOE- venada cierva
(veh-NAH-dah SYEHR-voh)
DOG- perro (PAY-roh)
DOLPHIN- delfín (dehl-FEEN)
DOVE- paloma (pah-LOH-mah)
DUCK- pato (PAH-toh)
EAGLE- águila (AH-gee-lah)
EEL- anguila (ahn-GEE-lah)
ELEPHANT- elefante
(eh-leh-FAHN-teh)
ELK- alce (ahl-SAY) (or)
ante (ahn-TAY)
*ENDANGERED Puesto en peligro
(PWAYS-toh ehn peh-LEE-groh)
*NEARLY EXTINCT Casi en extinción
(KAH-see ehn eks-teen-SYOHN)

EXCEEDING THE LIMIT-
Exceda el límite
(Ex-SAY-day ayl LEE-mee-tay)

FEATHER- pluma (PLOO-mah)
FIN- aleta (ah-LAY-tah)
FISH (to)- pescar (pehs-KAHR)
       pez (pehs)
FISHING- pesca (PEHS-kah)
FISHING POLE- palo de pesca
(PAH-loh day PEHZ-kah)
FISHING LICENSE- licencia de pesca
(lee-SEHN-see-ah day pehs-KAH)
FOX- zorro (SOH-roh)
FROG- rana (RAH-nah)
*FUR- piel (pyehl)
*GALL BLADDERS-
Vejigas (beh-HEE-gahs)
GAME WARDEN- guardián
(gwahr-dee-AHN)
GOAT- cabra (KAH-brah)
GOLDFISH- carpa dorada
(KAHR-pah doh-RAH-dah)
GOOSE- ganso (GAHN-soh)
*GORILLA gorila
(goh-REE-lah)
HAWK- halcón (ahl-KOHN)
HEADLIGHTS- cuartos delanteras
(KWAHR-tohs day-lahn-TAY-rohs)
HEN- gallina (gah-YEE-nah)
*HIDE Esconder
(ehs-koon-DEHR)
HOOK- anzuelo (ahn-soo-EH-loh)
HORNS- cuernos (KWAYR-nohs)
HORSE- caballo (kah-BAH-yoh)

HUNT- (to) cazar (kah-SAHR)
HUNTER- cazador(kah-sah-DOHR)
HUNTING- caza (KAH-zah)
HUNTING LICENSE-
licencia de caza
(lee-SEHN-see-ah day KAH-zah)

I AM GOING TO SEIZE THE ___.
Voy a confiscar el ___.
(Boy ah kohn-fees-KAHR el ___.)

*INSECT insecto (een-SAYK-toh)
*IVORY marfil (mahr-FEEL)
KEEP-mantenga (mahn-TEHN-gah)
*KIDNEYS riñones (ree-NYOH-nays)
LAMB- cordero (kohr-DEH-roh)
LEOPARD leopardo
(leh-oh-PAHR-doh)
LIMIT- límite (LEE-mee-tay)
*LION león (lay-OHN)
MALE DEER- venado macho
(vay-NAH-doh MAH-choh)
MAMMAL- mamífero
(mah-MEE-feh-roh)
*MONKEY mono (MOH-noh)
MULE- mula (MOO-lah)
*MUSHROOMS hongos (OHN-gohs)
OWL- telecote (teh-koh-LOH-teh)
(Slang for Cop, undercover cop or the one that watches with big eyes).

OWL- búho (BOO-oh)
PARROT loro (LOH-roh)
PAW- pata (PAH-tah)
PELICAN pelícano (peh-LEE-kah-noh)
*PENIS pene (PEH-neh)
PERMIT- permiso (payr-MEE-soh)
PIG- cerdo (SEHR-doh)
PIGEON- pichón (pee-CHOHN)
PROHIBITED- prohibido
(proh-EE-bee-doh)
RABBIT- conejo (koh-NEH-hoh)
RAT- rata (RAH-tah)
RED SNAPPER- huachinango
(wah-chee-NAHN-goh)
*RHINOCEROS rinoceronte
(ree-noh-seh-ROHN-teh)
ROOSTER- gallo (GAH-yoh)
SEAGULL- gaviota (gah-bee-OH-tah)
SHARK- tiburón (tee-boo-ROHN)

42

SHEEP-	carnero	(kahr-**NEH**-roh);	
	oveja	(oh-**VAY**-hah)	
SHOOT-	disparar	(dees-pah-**RAHR**)	

SHOOTING FROM THE ROAD
Tirando del camino.
(Tee-**RAHN**-doh dayl kah-**MEE**-noh)

SHOW ME-	Enseñeme	(Ehn-**SEHN**-yah-may)
SNAKE-	serpiente	(sehr-pee-**EHN**-tay)
SOLEFISH-	lenguado	(lehn-**GWAH**-doh)
SPARROW-	gorrión	(goh-ree-**OHN**)
SPECIAL	especial	(ays-pehz-see-**AHL**)
SPOT LIGHT-	foco	(**FOH**-koh)
SWAN-	cisne	(**SEEZ**-nay)
*SWARM	enjambre	(ehn-**HAHM**-breh)
SWORDFISH-	pez espada	(pehs ehs-**PAH**-dah
TAG-	etiqueta	(ay-tee-**KAY**-tah
TAIL-	cola	(**KOH**-lah)
*TESTICLES	testículos	(tehs-**TEE**-koo-lohs)
TIGER	tigre	(**TEE**-greh)
TOAD-	sapo	(**SAH**-poh)

(Sapo is also slang for police sap)

TOO BIG- demasiado grande
(day-mah-**SEE**-ah-doh **GRAHN**-day)

TOO EARLY- demasiado temprano
(day-mah-**SEE**-ah-doh tehm-**PRAH**-noh)

TOO LATE- demasiado tarde
(day-mah-**SEE**-ah-doh **TAHR**-day)

TOO LONG- demasiado tiempo
(day-mah-**SEE**-ah-doh tee-**EHM**-poh)

TOO MANY- demasiado
(day-mah-**SEE**-ah-doh)

TOO SHORT- demasiado corto
(day-mah-**SEE**-ah-doh **KOHR**-toh)

TOO SMALL- demasiado pequeño
(day-mah-**SEE**-ah-doh pay-**KAY**-nyoh)

TRAPPING LICENSE-
Licencia de trampa
(lee-**SEHN**-see-ah day **TRAHM**-pah)

TROUT-	trucha	(**TROO**-chah)
TUNA-	atún	(ah-**TOON**)
*TUSKS	colmillos	(kohl-**MEE**-yohs)
TURKEY-	pavo	(**PAH**-boh);
	guajolote	(goo-ah-hoh-**LOH**-tay)
TURTLE-	tortuga	(tohr-**TOO**-gah)
VEHICLE-	vehículo	(beh-**EE**-koo-loh)

VIOLATION-	violación	(bee-oh-lah-**SYOHN**)
VULTURE-	buitre	(**BWEE**-tray)
WASTE-to	desperdiciar	(days-payr-**DEE**-see-ahr)
*WHALE	ballena	(bah-**YEH**-nah)
WING-	ala	(**AH**-lah)
WOLF-	lobo	(**LOH**-boh)

YOU KILLED THE __ UNLAWFULLY.
Usted mató el/la _____ ilegalamente.
(Oo-**STEHD** mah-**TOH** el / lah ____.
ee-lay-gahl-ah-**MEHN**-tay)

GREETINGS

MY NAME IS_____.
Me llamo _____
(May **YAH**-moh _____).

WHAT IS YOUR NAME?
¿Como se llama?
(**KOH**-moh say **YAH**-mah)

ALLOW ME TO INTRODUCE ____.
Presento a _____.
(Preh-**SEHN**-toh ah _____.)

EXCUSE ME. Perdóneme.
(Pehr-**DOHN**-eh-may)

GOOD AFTERNOON/EVENING.
Buenas tardes.
(**BWAY**-nahs **TAHR**-days)

GOOD MORNING.
Buenos días.
(**BWEH**-nohs **DEE**-ahs)

GOOD NIGHT.
Buenas noches.
(**BWEH**-nahs **NOH**-chays)

GOODBYE. Adiós. (ah-dee-**OHS**)

HELLO Hola (**OH**-lah)

HOW ARE YOU?
¿Cómo está Usted?
(**KOH**-moh ehs-**TAH** oo-**STEHD**)

WHAT'S HAPPENING?
¿Qué hubo? (kay oo-boh) **(SLANG)**

I AM.....	estoy...	(ehs-TOY.....)
BAD	malo	(MAH-loh)
FINE	bien	(bee-EHN)

PLEASED TO MEET YOU.
Mucho gusto en conocerlo.
(MOO-choh GOOS-toh en koh-noh-SEHR-loh)

SEE YOU LATER.
Hasta luego.
(AHS-tah LWEH-goh)

SEE YOU TOMORROW
Hasta mañana
(AHS-tah mah-NYAH-nah)

THANK YOU. Gracias.
(GRAH-see-ahs)

YOU'RE WELCOME. De nada.
(day NAH-dah)

HANDS

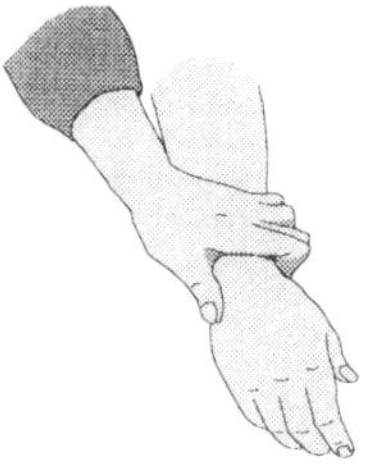

KEEP YOUR HANDS OUT OF YOUR POCKETS.
No se meta las manos en los bolsillos.
(No say MEH-tay lahs MAH-nohs en lohs bohl-SEE-yohs)

KEEP YOUR HANDS VISIBLE.
Mantenga sus manos visibles.
(mahn-TEHN-gah soos MAH-nohs vee-SEE-blays)

PUT YOUR HANDS ON THE WHEEL.
Ponga las manos sobre el volante.
(POHN-gah lahs MAH-nohs SOH-bray el vohl-AHN-tay)

PUT YOUR HANDS ON TOP OF YOUR HEAD.
Ponga sus manos sobre la cabeza.
(POHN-gah soos MAH-nohs SOH-bray lah kah-BAY-sah)

SHOW ME YOUR HANDS.
Enséñeme sus manos.
(Ehn-SEHN-yah-may soos MAH-nohs)

THROW YOUR KEYS OUT.
Arroje sus llaves para afuera.
(Ah-ROH-hay soos YAH-vays PAh-rah ah-FWAY-rah)

COME OUT WITH YOUR HANDS UP.
Salga con las manos arriba.
(SAHL-gah kohn lahs MAH-nohs ah-REE-bah)

HANDS ON TOP OF THE CAR.
Ponga sus manos encima del carro.
(POHN-gah soos MAH-nohs ehn-SEE-mah dayl KAHR-roh)

PUT YOUR HANDS BEHIND YOU.
Ponga las manos detrás de usted.
(POHN-gah lahs MAH-nohs deh-TRAHS day oo-STEHD)

HOME

WE'RE TAKING YOU HOME.
Le vamos a llevar a casa.
(Lay VAH-mohs ah yay-VAHR ah KAH-sah)

WHERE IS YOUR HOME?
¿Dónde está su casa?
(DOHN-day ess-TAH soo KAH-sah)

POINT
¡Apunte!
(ah-POON-tah)

IS IT IN (ON) THE ___? (insert word)
¿Está en (sobre) el ___?
(ess-TAH en [SOH-bray] el ___?)

WHAT ROOM IS (THE) ___ IN?
¿En qué cuarto está (el) ___?
(En kay KWAHR-toh ess-TAH [el] ___?)

IS IT ___?	**¿Está?**	**(ess-TAH)**

above the-	sobre el	(SOH-bray)
back of-	detrás de	(deh-TRAHS day)
behind the-	detrás de	(deh-TRAHS day)
below the-	debajo de	(deh-BAH-zhoh day)
beside the-	al lado de	(ahl LAH-doh day)
between the-	entre el	(AHN-tray el)
bottom of-	al fondo de	(ahl FOHN-doh day)

English	Spanish	Pronunciation
buried underground-	enterrado en la tierra	(ehn-tayr-AH-doh ehn lah tee-AYR-ah)
front of-	frente de	(FREHN-tay day)
inside the-	dentro de	(DEHN-troh day)
middle of-	en medio de	(ehn may-DEE-oh day)
on the-	encima de	(ehn-SEE-mah day)
top of-	parte de arriba de	(PAHR-tay day ah-REE-bah day)
under the-	debajo de	(day-BAH-hoh day)

English	Spanish	Pronunciation
armchair-	sillón	(see-YOHN)
ashtray-	cenicero	(say-nee-SAY-roh)
attic-	ático	(AH-tee-koh)
balcony-	balcón	(bahl-KOHN)
bag-	bolsa	(BOHL-sah)
barrel-	barril	(bah-REEL)
basement	sótano	(SOH-tah-noh)
bathroom	cuarto de baño	(KWAHR-toh day BAHN-yoh)
bathtub-	bañera	(bahn-YEH-rah)
	tina de baño	(TEE-nah day BAHN-yoh)
bed-	cama	(KAH-mah)
bedroom-	alcoba	(ahl-KOH-bah)
	recamara	(ray-KAH-mah-rah)
bedside table-	mesilla de noche	(may-SEE-yah day NOH-chay)
blanket-	manta	(MAHN-tah)
blender-	licuadora	(lee-koo-ah-DOO-rah)
bookcase-	estante	(ay-STAHN-tay)
bottle-	botella	(boh-TAY-yah)
bowl-	tazón	(tah-ZOHN)
box-	caja	(KAH-hah)
can-	lata	(LAH-tah)
	bote	(BOH-tay)
carpet-	alfombra	(ahl-FOHM-brah)
case-	estuche	(ay-STOO-chay)
ceiling-	techo	(TAY-choh)
chair-	silla	(SEE-yah)
chest/drawers-	cómoda	(KOH-moh-dah)
children's room-	cuarto de niños	(KWAHR-toh day NEEN-yohs)
chimney-	chimenea	(CHEE-may-nay-ah)
closet-	closet	(KLOH-zeht)
clothing-	vestidos	(vehs-TEE-dohs)
coffee pot	cafetera	(kah-fay-TAY-rah)
couch-	sofá	(soh-FAH)
cup-	taza	(TAH-zah)
cupboard-	armario	(ahr-MAH-ree-oh)
curtain-	cortina	(kohr-TEE-nah)
cushion-	cojín	(koh-HEEN)
deck-	cubierta	(koo-bee-AYR-tah)
desk-	escritorio	(ays-cree-TOH-ree-oh)
dining room-	comedor	(koh-may-DOHR)
dishwasher	lavaplatos	(lah-vah-PLAH-tohs)
door-	puerta	(PWAYR-tah)
downstairs	piso bajo	(PEE-soh BAH-hoh)
drawer-	cajón	(kah-HOHN)
dresser-	tocador	(toh-kah-DOHR)
dryer-	secadora	(say-kah-DOH-rah)
entrance-	entrada	(ehn-TRAH-dah)
family room-	cuarto de familia	(KWAHR-toh day fah-MEE-lee-ah)
fireplace-	chimenea	(chee-may-NEE-ah)
floor-	suelo	(soo-AY-loh)
freezer	congelador	(kohn-hehl-ah-DOHR)
furniture-	muebles	(MOO-eh-blays)
garage-	garaje	(gah-RAH-hay)
garden-	jardín	(hahr-DEEN)
glass (drink)-	vaso	(VAH-soh)
hall-	vestíbulo	(vehs-TEE-boo-loh)
house-	casa	(KAH-sah)
at home-	en casa	(ehn KAH-sah)
at the house-	en la casa	(en la KAH-sah)
from home-	de casa	(day KAH-sah)
from the house-	de la casa	(day lah KAH-sah)
to home-	a casa	(ah KAH-sah)
to the house-	a la casa	(ah lah KAH-sah)
kitchen-	cocina	(koh-SEE-nah)
lamp-	lámpara	(LAHM-pah-rah)
light-	luz	(loos)
linen closet-	gabinete de lienzo	(gah-bee-NEH-tay day lee-EHN-zoh)
living room-	sala	(SAH-lah)
mailbox-	buzón	(boo-SOHN)
main bedroom-	alcoba principal	(ahl-KOH-bah preen-see-PAHL)
mattress-	colchón	(kohl-CHOHN)
microwave oven-	horno de microndas	(OHR-noh day mee-kroh-OHN-dah)
mirror-	espejo	(ays-PAY-hoh)
night table-	mesilla de noche	(may-SEE-yah day NOH-chay)
painting-	pintura	(peen-TOO-rah)
	cuadro	(koo-AH-droh)
porch-	portal	(pohr-TAHL)
pot-	olla	(OH-yah)
radio-	radio	(RAH-dee-oh)
refrigerator	hielera	(yah-LEE-rah)
roof-	techo	(TAY-choh)
room-	cuarto	(KWAHR-toh)
rug-	alfombra	(ahl-FOHM-brah)
sack-	saco	(SAH-koh)
sofa-	sofá	(soh-FAH)
shed-	cobertizo	(koh-behr-TEE-zoh)
shelf-	repisa	(ray-PEE-sah)
	estante	(ays-TAHN-tay)
shop-	tienda	(tee-EHN-dah)
shower-	ducha	(DOO-chah)
sill-	antepecho de ventana	(ahn-tay-PAY-choh day vehn-TAHN-ah)
sink-	lavabo	(lah-VAH-boh)
spoon-	cuchara	(koo-CHAH-rah)
stairs-	escalera	(ays-kah-LAY-rah)
stove-	estufa	(ays-TOO-fah)
switch-	interruptor	(een-tay-roop-TOHR)
table-	mesa	(MAY-sah)
coffee table-	mesa de centro	(may-SAH day SEHN-troh)
end table-	mesa auxiliar	(may-SAH ah-oo-ex-see-lee-AHR)
television set-	televisor	(the-leh-bee-SOHR)

45

HOW

HOW ARE YOU?	¿Qué tal?	(Kay TAHL)
HOW DO YOU SAY ___ IN SPANISH?	¿Cómo se dice ___ en español?	(KOH-moh say DEE-say ehn ehs-pah-NYOHL)
	wall (inside)- muro	(MOO-roh)
	wall (outside)- pared	(pah-REHD)
	washing machine- lavadora	(lah-bah-DOH-rah)
	washroom- servicios	(sayr-VEE-see-ohs)
	window- ventana	(vehn-TAH-nah)
	window ledge- antepecho de ventana	(ahn-tay-PAY-choh day vehn-TAH-nah)
	writing desk- escritorio	(ays-kree-TOH-ree-oh)
	yard- patio	(PAH-tee-oh)
	yarda	(YAHR-dah)

HOW MANY	¿Cuántos?	(KWAHN-tohs)
HOW MANY METERS/KILOMETERS/MILES?	¿Cuántos metros/kilómetros/millas?	(KWAHN-tohs MAY-trohs / kee-LOH-may-trohs / MEE-yahs)
HOW MANY TIMES HAVE YOU DONE THIS?	¿Cuántas veces ha hecho ha esto?	(KWAHN-tahs VAY-says ah AY-choh ha AYS-toh)
HOW MUCH?	¿Cuánto?	(KWAHN-toh)
HOW OLD ARE YOU?	¿Cuántos años tiene usted?	(KWAHN-tohs AHN-yohs tee-EHN-ay oo-STEHD)

CURRENCY AND EXCHANGE RATES

Country	Currency	Value to U.S. Dol.
Argentina	Austral	.230
Bahamas	Dollar	1.
Bermuda	Dollar	1.
Brazil	Crusado	.015
Caribbean	Dollar	.375
Cayman	Dollar	1.215
Chile	Escudo	.0042
Columbia	Peso	.00038
Costa Rica	Colon	.015
Cuba	Peso	1.317
Dom. Rep	Peso	.203
Ecuador	Sucre	.0027
El Sal.	Colon	.200
Guatemala	Quetal	.395
Jamaica	Dollar	.183
Mexico	Peso	.0047
Paraguay	Guarani	.0012
Peru	Sol	.040
Phillipines	Peso	.047
Portugal	Escudo	.0072
Spain	Peseta	.0087
Uruguay	Peso	.0032
Venezuela	Bolivar	.035

(Rates will vary. Call local bank for current exchange rates.)

threshold- umbral		(oom-BRAH)
toilet- taza de baño		(TAH-zah day BAHN-yoh)
tools- herramientas		(ayr-ah-mee-EHN-tahs)

(NOTE: SLANG FOR WEAPONS)

tool shed- cobertizo de herramientas		(kuh-behr-TEEL-soh day ayr-ah-mee-EHN-tahs)
upstairs- piso de arriba		(PEE-soh day ah-REE-bah)
upholstery- tapizado		(tah-pee-ZAH-doh)

IDENTIFICATION

DO YOU HAVE IDENTIFICATION?
¿Tiene usted identificación?
(Tee-EHN-ay oo-STEHD ee-dehn-tee-fee-kah-SYOHN)

PAPERS?	¿Papeles?	(pah-PEH-lays)
LICENSE?	¿licencia?	(lee-SEHN-syah)

GIVE ME YOUR DRIVER'S LICENSE AND REGISTRATION.
Déme su licencia y la circulación.
(DEH-may soo lee-SEHN-syah ee la seer-koo-lah-SYOHN)

46

DO YOU HAVE A DRIVER'S LICENSE?
¿Tiene usted una licencia?
(Tee-**EHN**-ay oo-**STEHD** **OO**-nah lee-**SEHN**-syah)

ARE YOU AN AMERICAN CITIZEN?
¿Es usted un ciudadano americano?
(Ays oo-**STEHD** oon see-oo-dahd-**DAH**-noh ah-may-ree-**KAH**-noh)

DO YOU HAVE IMMIGRATION PAPERS?
¿Tiene usted papeles de imigración / mica?
(tee-**EHN**-ay oo-**STEHD** pah-**PEHL**-ays day eem-ee-grah-**SYOHN** / **MEE**-kah)

IMMIGRATION CARD, SHOW ME YOUR
Enseñeme su mica.
(ehn-seh-**NYEH**-may soo **MEE**-kah)

GREEN CARD, SHOW ME YOUR
Enseñeme su mica.
(ehn-seh-**NYEH**-may soo **MEE**-kah)

DO YOU HAVE A PASSPORT?
¿Tiene un pasaporte?
(Tee-**EHN**-nay oon pah-sah-**POHR**-tay)

WHAT IS YOUR SOCIAL SECURITY NUMBER?
¿Cuál es su número de seguro social?
(Kwahl ess soo **NOO**-may-roh day seh-**GOO**-roh soh-**SYAHL**)

FALSE IDENTIFICATION.
Identificación falsa.
(ee-dehn-tee-fee-kah-**SYOHN** **FAHL**-sah)

THIS IDENTIFIES IT AS BELONGING TO: (also used re: STOLEN ITEMS)
Esto lo identifica como que es de:
(**AYS**-toh loh ee-dehn-tee-**FEE**-kah **KOH**-moh kay ays day:_____.)

INTERPRETER

DO YOU WANT AN INTERPRETER?
¿Quiere un intérprete?
(Kee-**AYR**-ay oon een-**TAYR**-pray-tay)

JAIL, BOOKINGS and CORRECTIONS

(* Refer to "Backgound - Biographical Investigation")

JAIL	**YOU WILL GO TO JAIL**
Cárcel	Usted irá a la cárcel
(**KAHR**-sehl)	(Oo-**STEHD** eer-**AH** ah lah **KAHR**-sehl)

HAVE YOU EVER BEEN IN JAIL?
¿Ha estado en la cárcel alguna vez?
(Ah ess-TAH-doh en la KAHR-sehl ahl-GOO-nah vehs?)

WHERE?	¿Dónde?	(DOHN-day)
WHEN?	¿Cuándo?	(KWAHN-doh)
FOR WHAT?	¿Por qué estuvo?	(Pohr KAY ess-TOO-voh)

WE WILL KEEP YOUR MONEY AND PROPERTY UNTIL YOU LEAVE THE STATION.
Vamos a guardar su dinero y propiedad hasta que quede usted libre.
(VAH-mohs ah gwahr-DAHR soo dee-NAY-roh ee soo proh-pee-eh-DAHD AHS-tah kay KEH-day oo-STEHD LEE-bray)

WHAT IS YOUR NAME, ADDRESS, DATE OF BIRTH ETC... *(SEE F.I.R. pg)*
¿Cuál es su nombre, dirección, fecha de nacimiento, etc?
(Kwahl ays soo NOHM-bray, dee-reck-SYOHN, FAY-chah day nah-see-mee-EHN-toh)

HOW TALL ARE YOU?	¿Cuánto mide usted?	(KWAHN-doh MEE-day oo-STEHD)
WEIGHT?	pesa	(peh-SAH)

OCCUPATION- profesión (proh-feh-SYOHN)

WHERE WERE YOU BORN?
¿Dónde nació usted?
(DOHN-day nah-see-OH oo-STEHD)

WHERE DO YOU WORK?
¿Dónde trabaja usted?
(DOHN-day trah-BAH-hah oo-STEHD)

IN CASE OF EMERGENCY, WHO DO WE CALL?
¿En caso de emergencia, a quién llamamos?
(En KAH-soh day eh-mayr-HAYN-syah, ah kee-YEHN yah-MAH-mohs)

(See "PHONE" Section for phone usage and numbers)

*TELL THEM YOU ARE IN THE SHERIFF'S STATION
Dígales que usted está en la estación del aguacil
(DEE-gah-lehs keh oo-STHED ess-TAH en la ay-stay-SYOHN del ahl-goo-ahl-SEEL)

*THE POLICE STATION
la estación de policia.
(lah ay-stay-SYOHN day poh-lee-SEE-ah)

I AM GOING TO TAKE YOUR FINGERPRINTS.
Le voy a tomar sus huellas digitales.
(Lay voy ah toh-MAHR soos WEH-yahs dee-hee-TAH-lays)

GIVE ME YOUR RIGHT/LEFT HAND.
Déme la mano derecha/izquierda.
(DEH-may lah MAH-noh deh-REH-chah / ees-kee-EHR-dah)

RELAX YOUR HAND.   **LET ME DO IT.**
Descanse la mano.   Déjeme hacerlo.
(dehs-KAHN-say lah MAH-noh)   (DEH-hay-may ah-SEHR-loh)

SIGN HERE. Firme aquí. (FEER-may ah-KEE)

THIS MEANS YOU HAVE BEEN GIVEN THIS INFORMATION.
Esto quiere decir que se le ha dado esta información.
(**EHS**-toh kee-**AYR**-ay deh-**SEER** kay say lay ah **DAH**-doh **ES**-tah
een-fohr-mah-**SYOHN**)

IT EXPLAINS WHICH DAY AND WHICH COURT YOU WILL GO TO.
Explica qué día y en cuál corte usted debe presentarse.
(Ex-**PLEE**-kah kay **DEE**-ah ee en kwahl **KOHR**-tay oo-**STEHD**
DEH-bay preh-sehn-**TAHR**-say)

WE ARE GOING TO TAKE YOUR PICTURE.
Vamos a tomar su retrato.
(**VAH**-mohs ah toh-**MAHR** soo reh-**TRAH**-toh)

STAND HERE. Párese aqui. (**PAH**-reh-say ah-**KEE**)

THIS FORM SHOWS THAT YOU HAVE RECEIVED YOUR PROPERTY.
Esta forma quiere decir que usted ha recibido su propiedad.
(**ESS**-tah **FOHR**-mah kee-**EH**-ray deh-**SEER** kay oo-**STEHD** ah
reh-see-**BEE**-doh soo pro-pee-eh-**DAHD**)

*ARE YOU WEARING CONTACTS?
¿Usa usted lentes de contacto?
(**OO**-sah oo-**STHED** **LENT**-tehs deh cohn-**TOCK**-tohs)

*OPEN YOUR MOUTH
Abra la boca
(**AH**-brah lah **BOH**-kah)

TAKE OFF ALL YOUR CLOTHES. (see "CLOTHING" page 15)
Quítese toda la ropa.
(**KEE**-tay-say **TOH**-dah lah **ROH**-pah)

NOTE: REFER TO COMMAND SECTION FOR
OTHER COMMANDS AND INSTRUCTIONS

---

*IT IS OUR RESPONSIBILITY TO CHECK EVERYBODY
Es deber nuestro de revisar a todos
(Ess deh-**BEHR** noo-**EHS**-troh deh ray-vees-**AHR** ah **TOH**-dos)

SPREAD YOUR BUTTOCKS WITH YOUR HANDS.
Separe sus nalgas con sus manos.
(Seh-**PAHR**-ay soos **NAHL**-gahs kohn soos **MAH**-nohs)

DO YOU HAVE A MEDICAL PROBLEM? (See "Medical" for more info).
¿Tiene usted algun problema médico?
(Tee-**EHN**-ay oo-**STEHD** ahl-**GOON** pro-**BLEH**-mah **MEH**-dee-koh)

*DO YOU HAVE HEPATITIS B? ¿Tiene hepatitis B?
(**TYEH**-neh eh-pah-**TEE**-tees beh)

*AIDS? ¿Sida? (**SEE** dah)

*TUBERCULOSIS? ¿Tiene tuberculosis?
(**TYEH**-neh too-behr-koo-**LOH**-sees)

*VENEREAL DISEASE? ¿Tiene una enfermedad venérea?
(**TYEH**-neh **OO**-nah ehn-fehr-meh-**DAHD** veh-**NEH**-reh-ah)

HEART TROUBLE? ¿Tiene problemas del corazón?
(**TYEH**-neh proh-**BLEH**-mahs dehl koh-rah-**SOHN**)

*WE ARE TAKING YOU TO A DOCTOR
Le vamos a llevar a un médico
(Lay **VAH**-moose ah yeh-**VAR**- ah oon **MEH**-dee-koh)

YOUR BAIL IS ___. Su fianza es de ___.
(soo **FYAHN**-sah ehs deh ___)

YOU CANNOT BAIL. No puede salir bajo fianza
(noh **PWAY**-deh sah-**LEER BAH**-oh **FYAHN**-sah)

*TELL THEM TO CALL ANY BAIL BONDSMAN
Dígales que llamen a cualquier fiador
(**DEE**-gah-lehs kay yah-mahn ah kwall-kay-**AIR** fee-ah-**DOOR**)

visit (to)- visitar (bee-see-**TAHR**)

VISITING HOURS ARE ___. Las horas de visita son ___.
(Lahs **OH**-rahs day vee-see-**TAH** sohn ___)

NOTE: * Indicates updates and are not on audio tape at this time.

JUVENILE juvenil (hoo-vehn-**NEEL**)

YOUR PARENTS ARE COMING FOR YOU.
Sus padres vienen por usted.
(Soos **PAH**-drays vee-**EHN**-ehn pohr oo-**STEHD**)

LAWYER and ATTORNEY

DO YOU WANT A LAWYER?
¿Quiere un abogado/licenciado?
(Kee-**AYR**-ay oon ah-boh-**GAH**-doh/ lee-sehn-see-**AH**-doh)

LICENSE licencia (lee-**SEHN**-see-ah)

(EXAMPLE): JUAN CAMPOLI-LOPEZ (OR)
JUAN C. LOPEZ

(ASK WHAT FATHER'S LAST NAME IS: SHOULD BE: CAMPOLI
" " MOTHER'S " " : SHOULD BE: LOPEZ

THE REAL LAST NAME IS: CAMPOLI

Official U.S. I.N.S. Gov't Listing would be: CAMPOLI-Lopez
(Paternal is uppercase and underlined; maternal is lowercase, not underlined)

50

LIE mentir (mehn-TEER)

IT'S A LIE	¡Es mentira!	(ehs mehn-TEE-rah)
IT'S NOT TRUE.	No es verdad	(noh ehs behr-DAHD)
TELL THE TRUTH.	Díga la verdad.	(DEE-gah lah vehr-DAHD)

LIVE (Where do you?)

WITH WHOM DO YOU LIVE?
¿Con quiéne vive usted?
(kohn kee-**EHN**-ay **VEE**-vay oo-**STEHD**)

WHERE DO YOU LIVE?
¿Dónde vive?
(**DOHN**-day **VEE**-vay)

MEDICAL - ACCIDENTS - DISASTERS

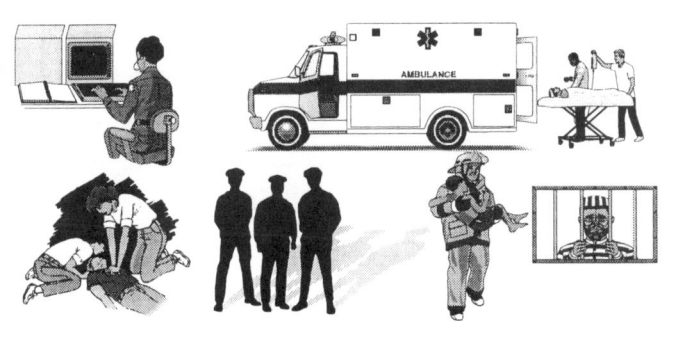

DON'T HANG UP!
¡No cuelgues!
(Noh koo-**EHL**-gays)

I WILL HELP YOU.
Yo le ayudaré.
(Yoh lay ah-yoo-dah-**RAY**)

I AM TRAINED TO HELP YOU.
Estoy entrenado para ayudarle.
(**EHS**-toy ehn-**TRAYN**-ah-doh pah-rah ah-yoo-**DAHR**-lay)

ARE YOU HURT?
¿Está herido?
(Ess-**TAH** ehr-**EE**-doh)

SHOW ME THE PLACE.
Enséñeme el lugar.
(En-**SEH**-nyeh-may ehl **LOO**-gahr)

LAY DOWN HERE.
Acuéstese aqui.
(ah-koo-**AYS**-tay-say ah-**KEE**)

ACCIDENT	accidente	(ahk-see-**DEHN**-tay)
AMBULANCE	ambulancia	(ahm-boo-**LAHN**-see-ah)

CALL AN AMBULANCE
llamar a una ambulancia.
(yah-**MAHR** ah **OO**-nah ahm-boo-**LAHN**-see-ah)

CALL THE POLICE
llamar a la policía.
(yah-**MAHR** ah lah poh-lee-**SEE**-ah)

EMERGENCY ROOM
Sala de Emergencia
(SAH-lah day eh-mehr-GEHN-see-ah)

CALL A DOCTOR
llamar a un médico.
(yah-MAHR ah oon MEH-dee-koh)

YOU WILL BE O.K.
Estará bien.
(Ess-tahr-AH bee-YEHN)

YOUR WIFE \	CHILD \	HUSBAND \	IS O.K.
Su esposa \	niño \	esposo \	está bien
(Soo ess-POH-sah \	NEEN-yoh \	ess-POH-soh \	ess-TAH bee-YEHN)

WHEN IS THE BABY DUE?
¿Para cuándo espera a su niño?;
(Pah-rah KWAHN-doh ehs-PAYR-rah ah soo NEEN-yoh)
- ¿Cuando se va a aliviar?
(KWAHN-doh say vah ah ah-lee-vee-AHR)

FOLLOW ME. Sígame. (SEE-gah-may)

DO YOU HAVE A MEDICAL PROBLEM?
¿Tiene usted algún problema médico?
(Tee-EHN-ay oo-STEHD ahl-GOON ahl-BLEH-mah MEH-dee-koh)

BODY PARTS and VOCABULARY

BANDAGES	vendas	(Vehn-DAHS)
BEARD	barba	(BAHR-bah)
*BEDS.	camas	(KAH-mahs)
*BLANKETS	cobija	(koh-BEE-hah)
BLEEDING	sangrando	(sahn-GRAHN-doh)
BLOOD	sangre	(SAHN-gray)
BLIND	ciego	(See-AY-goh)
BODY	cuerpo	(KWEHR-poh)
BOMB	bomba	(BOM-bah)
BONE	hueso	(WEH-soh)
BRAIN	cerebro	(seh-REH-broh)
BREAST	pecho	(PAY-choh)
BREATHE	respirar	(rehs-pee-RAHR)
BROKEN	quebrado(a)	(kay-BRAH-doh)
BROKEN BONE	hueso quebrado	(WEH-soh kay-BRAH-doh)
BRUISE	contusión	(kohn-too-SYOHN)
BUMP	golpe	(GOHL-pay)
BUTTOCKS nalgas	pantorrilla	(NAHL-gahs)
CALF	pantorrilla(pahn-toh-REE-yah)	
CHEEK	mejilla	(meh-HEE-yah)
CHEST	pecho	(PEH-choh)
CHIN	barba	(BAHR-bah)
*COLD (to freeze)	Congelar	
*CONSCIOUS	conciente	(kohn-LAHR)
*UNCONSCIOUS	Inconciente	(kohn-SYEHN-teh)
CROTCH	bragadura(brah-gah-DOO-rah)	(een-NHKN-SYEHN-teh)
CUT	cortada	(kohr-TAH-dah)
*DANGEROUS	peligroso	(peh-lee-GROH-soh)
*SAFE	No es peligroso	(noh ehs peh-lee-GROH-soh)
*DANGEROUS ANIMAL		
animal peligroso		
(ah-nee-MAHL peh-lee-GROH-soh)		

BACK	espalda	(ehs-SPAHL-dah)
	(ah-bah-LAHN-chah)	
*AVALANCHE	avalancha	(BRAH-soh)
ARM	brazo	(ah-pehn-dee-SEE-tees)
*APPENDICITIS	Apendicitis	
ANKLE	tobillo	(toh-BEE-yoh)
*AIRPLANE CRASH Accidente aéreo		
(ahk-see-DEHN-teh ah-EH-reh-oh)		
*FIRST AID	Primeros auxilios	
(pree-MEH-rohs ow-SEE-lyohs)		
*AID (ah-YOO-dah) Ayuda		
*TRAFFIC ACCIDENT		
Accidente de tránsito		
(ahk-see-DEHN-tay day TRAHN-see-toh)		
*ACCIDENT	accidente	
ABDOMEN (ahb-DOH-mehn) abdomen		
(ahk-see-DEHN-tay)		

INSERT APPROPRIATE WORD:

NOTE: It is impossible to provide all of the necessary phrases for medical emergencies or disasters. By using the two phrases with the appropriate word inserted will assist in providing very basic communication.

COMING! _____
¡Viene! (VYEH-neh)

THERE IS or ARE _____ .
Hay
(eye)

52

*PERSON Persona (pehr-SOH-nah)
*DEAD? ¿muerto? (MWAYR-toh)
*ALIVE? ¿vivo? (BEE-boh)
DEAF sordo (SOHR-doh)
*DISASTER desastre (deh-SAHS-treh)
*DISEASE enfermedad
 (ehn-fehr-meh-DAHD)
DOCTOR doctor (dohk-TOHR)
*NURSE enfermera (o)
 (ehn-fehr-MEH-rah [roh])
DROUGHT sequía (seh-KYAH)
EAR oreja (oh-REH-hah)
*EARTHQUAKE terremoto
 (the-rreh-MOH-toh)
ELBOW codo (KOH-doh)
*EMERGENCY ROOM
 Sala de emergencia
 (SAH-lah deh eh-mehr-HEHN-syah)
*ENEMY enemigo (eh-neh-MEE-goh)
*EVACUATE! ¡evacuar!
 (eh-vah-KWAHR)
EXAM exámen (ays-AH-mahn)
EYE(s) ojo(s) (OH-hoh[s])
EYEBROW ceja (SEH-hah)
EYELASH pestaña (pehs-TAH-nyah)
EYELID párpado (PAHR-pah-doh)
FACE cara (KAH-rah)
*FAMILY familia (fah-MEE-lyah)
*FAMINE hambre (AHM-breh)
FEET pies (pee-EHS)
FINGERS dedos (DEH-dohs)
FINGERNAIL uña (OO-nyah)
*FIRE fuego (FWAY-goh)
*FIRE TRUCK carro de bomberos
 (KAH-rroh deh bohm-BEH-rohs)
*FOREST FIRE incendio forestal
 (een-SEHN-dyoh foh-rehs-TAHL)
 *RANGE FIRE campo de fuego
 (KAHM-poh deh FWAY-goh)
FLOOD inundación
 (ee-noon-dah-SYOHN)
FOOD comida (koh-MEE-dah)
FOOT pie (PEE-eh)
FOREHEAD frente (FREHN-tay)
FRACTURE fractura (frahk-TOO-rah)
*GOOD bueno (BWAY-noh)
 *BAD malo (MAH-loh)
*GRAB IT! agárrelo (ah-GAH-rreh-loh)
HAIR pelo (PEH-loh)
HAND mano (MAH-noh)
 Right hand- mano derecha
 (MAH-noh deh-REH-chah)
 Left hand mano izquierda
 (MAH-noh ess-kee-EHR-dah)
HEAD cabeza (kah-BAY-sah)
HEART corazón (kohr-ah-SOHN)

*HEAT WAVE ola de calor
 (OH-lah deh kah-LOHR)
*HEAT calor (kah-LOHR)
*HEAT STROKE ataque de calor
 (ah-TAH-keh deh kah-LOHR)
*HELICOPTER helicóptero
 (eh-lee-KOHP-teh-roh)
*HELP! ¡socorro! (soh-KOH-rroh)
*HERE? ¿aquí? (ah-KEE)
*HIGH TIDE marea alta
 (mah-REH-ah AHL-tah)
HIP cadera (kah-DEH-rah)
HOSPITAL hospital (ohs-pee-TAHL)
*HOW MANY? ¿Cuántos? (KWAHN-tohs)
*ON YOUR FINGERS! ¡En sus dedos!
 (ehn soos DEH-dohs)
HURTING doliendo(doh-lee-EHN-doh)
*IMPORTANT importante
 (eem-pohr-TAHN-teh)
 *UNIMPORTANT Sin importancia
 (seen eem-pohr-TAHN-syah)
INDEX FINGER dedo índice
 (DEH-doh EEN-dee-say)
INFECTION infección
 (een-feck-SYOHN)
*INSURANCE? ¿seguro?(seh-GOO-roh)

*INTERNATIONAL. RED CROSS
Cruz Roja International
(kroos ROH-hah
 een-tehr-nah-syoh-NAHL)
*INVASION invasión (een-vah-SYOHN)
*I DON'T KNOW! ¡No sé! (noh SEH)
JAW mandíbula (mahn-DEE-boo-lah)
KNEE rodilla (roh-DEE-yah)
KNUCKLE nudillo (noo-DEE-yoh)
LEG pierna (pee-YEHR-nah)
LIPS labios (LAH-byohs)
*LITTLE pequeño (peh-KEH-nyoh)
 *BIG grande (GRAHN-deh)
LITTLE FINGER dedo meñique
 (DEH-doh meh-NYEE-kay)
*LOST perdido (pehr-DEE-doh)
 *FOUND encontrado
 (ehn-kohn-TRAH-doh)
LUNG pulmón (pool-MOHN)
*MEDICAL médico (MEH-dee-koh)
*MEDICAL TEST Exámen médico
 (EHKSAH-mehn MEH-dee-koh)
MEDICINE medicina (meh-deh-SEE-nah)
MIDDLE FINGER dedo medio
 (DEH-doh MEH-dee-oh)
*MORE mas (mahs)
 *LESS menos (MEH-nohs)
*MOVE mover (moh-BEHR)
 *DON'T MOVE No se mueva
 (noh seh MWAY-vah)
MOUSTACHE bigote (bee-GOH-tay)
MOUTH boca (BOH-kah)
MUSCLE músculo (MOOS-koo-loh)
*NECESSARY necesario
 (neh-seh-SAH-ryoh)
 *UNNECESSARY innecesario
 (een-neh-seh-SAH-ryoh)

53

NECK	cuello	(KWAY-yoh)
NEVER	nunca	(NOON-kah)
ALWAYS	siempre	(SYEM-preh)
NEXT próximo	(PROHK-see-moh)
NOBODY	nadie	(nah-DYEH)
NONE	ninguno	(neen-GOO-noh)
NOSE	nariz	(nah-REES)
NOSTRIL	nariz	(nah-REES)
NURSE	enfermera	(ehn-fayr-MAY-rah)
NUCLEAR WAR	Guerra nuclear	(GEH-rrah noo-kleh-AHR)
ONE	uno	(OO-noh)
OPEN YOUR MOUTH Abra su boca	(AH-brah soo BOH-kah)
OVER HERE aquí	(ah-KEE)
OVER THERE allá	(ah-YAH)
PALM	palma	(PAHL-mah)
PAIN	dolor	(doh-LOHR)

THIS WILL HURT A LITTLE
Esto dolerá un poco
(EHS-toh doh-leh-RAH oon POH-koh)

PENIS	pene	(PAY-nee)
***PLAGUE**	plaga	(PLAH-gah)
***POISON**	veneno	(beh-NEH-noh)
***POSSIBLE**	posible	(poh-SEE-bleh)
***IMPOSSIBLE**	imposible	(eem-poh-SEE-bleh)
***PREGNANT** embarazada	(ehm-bah-rah-SAH-dah)
***PRIEST** sacerdote (sah-sehr-DOH-teh)
***PULSE**	pulso	(POOL-soh)
***RAIN**	lluvia	(YOO-vyah)
***RECTUM**	recto	(REHK-toh)
***RELAX**	relajar	(reh-lah-HAHR)

***RELIEF WORKERS**
trabajadores de rescate

***REPEAT**	repetir	(reh-peh-TEER)
***RESCUE** rescatar	(rehs-kah-TAHR)
RIBS	costillas	(kohs-TEE-yahs)
RING FINGER dedo anular	(DEH-doh ah-noo-LAHR)
SCALP	craneo	(krah-NEE-oh)
***SEEK SHELTER!** Busque refugio (BOOS-keh reh-FOO-hyoh)
SEX	sexo	(SEK-soh)
***SHOCK**	susto	(SOOS-toh)
SHOULDER	hombro	(OHM-broh)
SKIN	piel	(pee-EHL)
***SOLDIER**	soldado	(sohl-DAH-doh)
SOON	Pronto	(PROHN-toh)

SHOW ME THE PLACE.
Enséñeme el lugar.
(Ehn-SEHN-yeh-may ayl loo-GAHR)

ARE YOU HURT?
¿Está herido?
(Ess-TAH ayr-EE-doh)

I WILL HELP YOU.
Yo le ayudaré.
(Yoh lay ah-yoo-dah-RAY)

HELP - MAY I HELP YOU?
¿En qué puedo servirlo?
(ehn kay PWAY-doh sehr-BEER-loh)

X-RAY radiografía	(rah-dee-oh-grah-FEE-ah)
WRIST	muñeca	(moo-NYAY-kah)
WOUND (v)- herir	(heh-REER)
WOUND (n) - herida	(heh-REE-dah)
***WATER**	agua	(ah-GWAH)
WASH	lavar	(lah-VAHR)
WAR	guerra	(GEH-rrah)
WAIST	cintura	(seen-TOO-rah)
VOMIT	vomitar	(vohm-mee-TAHR)

VOLCANIC ERUPTION
erupción volcánica
(eh-ruhp-SYOHN vohl-KAH-nee-kah)

VAGINA	vagina	(vah-HEE-nah)
URINATE	orinar	(oh-ree-NAHR)
***TREMOR**	temblor	(tehm-BLOHR)
***TORNADO**	tornado	(tohr-NAH-doh)
TOOTH	diente	(dee-EHN-tay)
TONGUE	lengua	(LEHN-gwah)
TOES dedos del pie	(DEH-dohs day PEE-eh)
***TIDAL WAVE** Mar de fondo	(mahr deh FOHN-doh)
THUMB	pulgar	(pool-GAHR)
THROAT	garganta	(gahr-GAHN-tah)
THIGH , muslo	(MOOS-loh)
TESTICLES testiculos	(tehs-TEE-koo-lohs)
TEETH	dientes	(dee-AYN-tays)
SYRINGE	jeringa	(heh-REEN-gah)
***SWARM**	enjambre	(ehn-HAHM-breh)
SUTURE	sutura	(soo-TOO-rah)
SURVIVORS sobrevivientes (soh-breh-bee-BYEHN-tehs)
SURGERY cirugía	(see-roo-HEE-ah)
SUNBURN quemadura de sol (keh-mah-DOO-rah deh sohl)
***STRETCHER** camilla	(kah-MEE-yah)
***STORM** tormenta	(tohr-MEHN-tah)
STOMACH estómago (ess-TOH-mah-goh)
***UNSTABLE**	inestable	(ee-nehs-TAH-bleh)
STABLE estable	(ehs-TAH-bleh)
SPRAIN torcedura	(tohr-see-DOO-rah)
SPIT (TO) escupir	(ehs-koo-PEER)
***LATER** Mas tarde (mahs TAHR-deh)

54

LAY DOWN HERE.
Acuestese aqui.
(ah-**KWAYS**-teh-say ah-**KEE**)

DID YOU FALL?
¿Se cayó usted?
(say kah-**YOH** oo-**STEHD**)

IS A DOCTOR TAKING CARE OF YOU?
¿Está usted bajo cuidado de doctor?
(Ess-**TAH** oo-**STEHD** **BAH**-hoh kwee-**DAH**-doh day dohk-**TOHR**)

NAME OF YOUR DOCTOR?
PHONE NUMBER?
¿Nombre de su médico?
(**NOHM**-bray day soo **MEH**-dee-koh)

¿Número de teléfono?
(**NOO**-may-roh day tay-**LAY**-foh-noh)

ARE YOU TAKING MEDICINE?
¿Está tomando medicina?
(Ess-**TAH** toh-**MAHN**-doh meh-dee-**SEE**-nah)

WHAT KIND OF MEDICINE?
¿Qué clase de medicina?
(Kay **KLAH**-say day meh-dee-**SEE**-nah)

FOR WHAT?
¿Para qué cosa?
(**PAH**-rah kay **KOH**-sah)

ARE YOU A DIABETIC?
¿Es usted diabético?
(Ess oo-**STEHD** dee-ah-**BEH**-tee-koh)

DO YOU TAKE SHOTS?
¿Toma inyecciones?
(**TOH**-mah een-yeck-**SYOHN**-nays)

WHEN DID YOU TAKE YOUR LAST SHOT? (refer TIME header)
¿Cuándo tomó la última inyección?
(**KWAHN**-doh toh-**MOH** lah **OOL**-tee-mah een-yeck-**SYOHN**)

WHEN SHOULD YOU TAKE THE NEXT ONE?
¿Cuándo debe tomar la siguiente?
(**KWAHN**-doh **DEH**-bay toh **MAHR** lah see-gee-**EHN**-tay)

ARE YOU EPILEPTIC?
¿Es usted epiléptico?
(Ess oo-**STEHD** eh-pee-**LEHP**-tee-koh)

ARE YOU OK?
¿Está bien?
(Ess-**TAH** bee-**YEHN**)

DO YOU HAVE HEART TROUBLE?
¿Tiene usted enfermedad del corazón?
(Tee-**EHN**-ay oo-**STEHD** en-fayr-may-**DAHD** dayl kohr-ah-**SOHN**)

DO YOU HAVE PILLS FOR YOUR HEART?
Tiene píldoras para el corazón?
(Tee-**EHN**-ay **PEEL**-door-ahs **PAH**-rah el kohr-ah-**SOHN**)

DO YOU WANT TO GO TO THE HOSPITAL?
¿Quiere ir al hospital?
(Kee-**AY**-ray eer ahl ohs-pee-**TAHL**)

THE AMBULANCE IS COMING.
La ambulancia viene.
La ahm-boo-**LAHN**-see-ah vee-**EHN**-ay

YOU WILL BE OK.
Estará bien.
(Ess-tahr-**AH** bee-**YEHN**)

YOUR WIFE/ CHILD/ HUSBAND IS O.K.
Su esposa/ niño/ esposo está bien.
(Soo ess-**POH**-sah/ **NEEN**-yoh/ ess-**POH**-soh ess-**TAH** bee-**YEHN**)

MENSTRUATION - ARE YOU HAVING A PERIOD?
¿Está en su menstruación?
/ ¿Bajó su regla?
(Ess-**TAH** en soo mehn-stroo-ah-**SYOHN** / **BAH**-hoh soo **REG**-lah)

ARE YOU WEARING A TAMPON?
¿Trae toalla o tampón sanitario?
(Try toh-**WY**-yah oh tahm-**POHN** sah-nee-**TAHR**-ee-oh)

TAKE IT OUT Sáqueselo
(**SAH**-kay-say-loh)

I WILL GIVE YOU A PAD.
Yo le daré un nuevo tampón o una toalla
(Yoh lay dahr-**AY** oon noo-**AY**-voh tahm-**POHN** oh **OO**-nah toh-**AHL**-yah)

DID YOU TAKE PILLS?
¿Tomó usted píldoras?
(Toh-**MOH** oo-**STEHD** **PEEL**-door-ahs)

WHAT COLOR?
¿De qué color?
(Day kay koh-**LOHR**)

HOW MANY DID YOU TAKE?
¿Cuántas tomó?
(**KWAHN**-tahs toh-**MOH**)

WHAT DID YOU TAKE?
¿Qué tomó usted?
(Kay toh-MOH oo-STEHD)

ACID?
¿Ácido?
(AH-see-doh)

MISSING OR LOST CHILD
(Refer to name section for name, DOB, address, etc.)

DO YOU GO TO SCHOOL?
¿Vas a la escuela?
(Vahs ah lah ess-KWEH-lah)

IS THIS YOUR BROTHER (SISTER)?
¿Es tu hermano (hermana)?
(Ess too ehr-MAH-noh(ehr-MAH-nah))

MONEY

MONEY Dinero (dee-NAY-roh);
(slang) Lana (LAH-nah);
(slang) Feria (FAY-ree-ah)

YOU HAVE NO MONEY?
¿No tiene dinero?
(noh tee-EH-nay dee-NAY-roh)

HOW MUCH MONEY DO YOU EARN?
¿Cuánto dinero gana?
(KWAHN-toh dee-NAY-roh GAH-nah)

WHERE DID YOU GET THE MONEY?
¿Dónde obtuvo el dinero?
(DOHN-day ohb-TOO-voh ay!
dee-NAY-roh)

HOW MUCH MONEY IS HERE / THERE?
¿Cuánto dinero hay aquí / allí?
(KWAHN-toh dee-NAY-roh ay
ah-KEE / ah-YEE)

IS THIS YOURS?
¿Es esto suyo?
(Ays AYS-toh SOO-yoh)

account-	cuenta	(KWEHN-tah)
bank-	banco	(BAHN-koh)
bank book-	libreta de depósitos	(lee-BREH-tah day deh-POH-see-tohs)
bill-	billete	(bee-YAY-tay)
large bill-	billete grande	(bee-YAY-tay GRAHN-day)
small bill-	billete pequeño	(bee-YEH-tay peh-KAY-nyoh)
cash-	dinero en efectivo	(dee-NAY-roh ehn ay-fehk-TEE-voh)
	cobrar	(koh-BRAHR)
	cambiar	(kahm-bee-AHR)
cash payment-	pago al contado	(PAH-goh ahl kohn-TAH-doh)
	pago en efectivo	(PAH-goh ehn ay-fehk-TEE-voh)
check (bank)-	cheque bancario	(CHAY-kay bahn-KAH-ree-oh)
checkbook-	libro de cheques	(LEE-broh day CHAY-kays)
checking acct.-	cuenta corriente	(KWEHN-tah koh-ree-EHN-tay)
	chequera	(chay-KAY-rah)
	cuenta bancaria	(KWEHN-tah bahn-KAH-ree-oh)
coin	monedas	(moh-NEH-dahs)
credit card-	tarjeta de crédito	(tahr-HAY-tah day KRAY-dee-toh)
currency-	dinero en circulación	(dee-NAY-roh en seer-koo-lah-SYOHN)
	billetes	(bee-YAY-tays)
customer-	cliente	(klee-EHN-tay)
debt-	deuda	(day-OO-dah)
deposit-	depósito	(deh-POH-see-toh)
discount-	descuento	(dehs-KWEHN-toh)
draft-	giro	(HEE-roh)
	letra de cambio	(LEH-trah day KAHM-bee-oh)
endorse-	endosar	(ehn-doh-SAHR)
	firmar	(feer-MAHR)
endorsement-	endoso	(ehn-DOH-soh)
income-	ingresos	(een-GREH-sohs)
investment-	inversión	(een-vehr-SYOHN)
loan-	préstamo	(PREHS-tah-moh)
loss-	pérdida	(PEHR-dee-dah)
money order-	giro	(HEE-roh)
pay-	pagar	(pah-GAHR)
payment-	pago	(PAH-goh)
pay off debts-	saldar las deudas	(sahl-DAHR lahs dee-OO-dahs)
profit-	ganancia	(gah-NAHN-see-ah)
real estate	propiedad	(proh-pee-ay-DAHD)
	- bienes raíces	(bee-EH-nays rah-EE-says)
receipt-	recibo	(ray-SEE-boh)
safe-	caja fuerte	(KAH-hah FWEHR-tay)
safe deposit box-	caja de seguridad	(KAH-hah day seh-goo-ree-DAHD)
	- caja de depósitos	(KAH-sah day dee-POH-see-tohs)

56

salary-	salario	(sah-**LAH**-ree-oh)
savings-	ahorros	(ah-**OH**-rohs)
savings acct.-	cuenta de ahorros	
	(**KWEHN**-tah day ah-**OH**-rohs)	
securities-	valores	(bah-**LOH**-rays)
	bonos	(**BOH**-nohs)
wholesale-	venta al por mayor	
	(**BEHN**-tah ahl pohr mah-**YOHR**)	
withdraw-	retirar	(ray-tee-**RAHR**)
withdrawal-	retiro	(ray-**TEE**-roh)

NAMES
(address & date of birth)

NAME- nombre (**NOHM**-bray)

TITLES

Mr. -Señor (seh-**NYOHR**)

Mrs. -Señora (seh-**NYOH**-rah)

Miss -Señorita (seh-nyoh-**REE**-tah)

WHAT IS YOUR NAME? (write)
¿Cómo se llama usted? (escribe)
(**KOH**-moh say **YAH**-mah
oo-**STEHD** [ehs-**KREE**-bay])

WHAT IS HIS NAME?
¿Cuál es su nombre?
(Kwahl ays soo **NOHM**-bray)

MY NAME IS _____.
Me llamo _____.
(May **YAH**-moh _____.)

HOW DO YOU SPELL YOUR NAME?
¿Cómo se deletrea su nombre?
(**KOH**-moh say deh-leh-**TREH**-ah
soo **NOHM**-bray)

PRINT YOUR NAME, PLEASE
Escribe su nombre con letras de
molde.
(Ays-**KREE**-bay soo **NOHM**-bray kohn
LEH-trahs day **MOHL**-day)

_____ _____ _____
FIRST NAME / SURNAME / PATERNAL
nombre de pila/
(**NOHM**-bray day **PEE**-lah)

    SURNAME
    apellido
    (ah-peh-**YEE**-doh)

    PATERNAL
    paterno
    (pah-**TEHR**-noh)

    MATERNAL
    materna
    (mah-**TEHR**-nah)

DO YOU HAVE A NICKNAME?
¿Tiene usted sobrenombre / apodo?
(Tee-**EHN**-ay oo-**STEHD**
soh-bray-**NOHM**-bray / ah-**POH**-doh)

NAMES AND ADDRESSES
NOTE EXAMPLE:

JUAN CAMPOLI-LOPEZ (or)
JUAN-LOPEZ

ASK FATHER'S NAME:
(Should be: CAMPOLI)

ASK MOTHER'S NAME:
(Should be: Lopez)

HIS TRUE NAME IS:

  CAMPOLI - Lopez

(Official U.S. I.N.S. Gov.
Listing of last name).

Paternal should be
uppercase/underlined

Maternal should be
lowercase/ no underline

DATE OF BIRTH (WRITE)
Fecha de nacimiento (escriba)
(**FEH**-chah day nah-see-mee-**EHN**-toh)
([ays-**KREE**-bah])

____	____	____
day	month	year
día	mes	año
(**DEE**-ah)	(mehs)	(**AHN**-yoh)

HOW OLD ARE YOU?
¿Cuántos años tiene?
(**KWAHN**-tohs **AHN**-yohs tee-**EHN**-ay)

WHERE WERE YOU BORN?
¿Dónde nació usted?
(**DOHN**-day nah-see-**OH** oo-**STEHD**)

PLACE OF BIRTH.
Lugar de nacimiento.
(Loo-**GAHR** day nah-see-mee-**EHN**-toh)

____	____	____
CITY	STATE	COUNTRY
ciudad	estado	país
(see-oo-**DAHD**)	(ehs-**TAH**-doh)	(pah-**EES**)

> **ARE YOU AN AMERICAN CITIZEN?**
> ¿Es un ciudadano Americano?
> (Ays oon see-oo-**DAH**-dah-noh
>   Ah-mayr-ee-**KAH**-noh)

PASSPORT NUMBER
Número de pasaporte
(NOO-may-roh day pah-sah-POHR-tay)

REFER TO PATRON SAINTS

WHAT IS THE NAME OF YOUR PATRON SAINT?
¿Qué es el nombre de su santo?
(Kay ays eh! NOHm-bray day soo SAHN-toh)

WHAT IS YOUR ADDRESS?
¿Cuál es su domicilio?
(kwahl es soo doh-mee-SEE-Iyoh)

HOUSE NUMBER
Número de casa
(NOO-may-roh day KAH-sah)

STREET	CITY	STATE	COUNTRY
calle	ciudad	estado	país
(KAY-yay)	(see-oo-DAHD)	(ehs-TAH-doh)	(pah-EES)

AVENUE avenida (ah-beh-NEE-dah)
SQUARE plaza (PLAH-sah)
STREET calle (KAY-yay)
HOUSE NUMBER número de casa
(NOO-may-roh day KAH-sah)
TOWN pueblo (PWEH-bloh)
ZONE zona (SOH-nah)

RADIO ALPHABET

	(Military)	(Police)
A	Alpha (or)	Adam
B	Bravo	Boy
C	Charlie	
D	Delta	David
E	Echo	Edward
F	Foxtrot	Frank
G	Golf	George
H	Hotel	Henry
I	India	Ida
J	Juliet	John
K	Kilo	King
L	Lima	Lincoln
M	Mike	Mary
N	November	Nora
O	Oscar	Ocean
P	Papa	Paul
Q	Quebec	Queen
R	Romeo	Robert
S	Sierra	Sand
T	Tango	Tom
U	Uniform	Union
V	Victor	Victor
W	Whiskey	William
X	X-Ray	X-Ray
Y	Yankee	Yellow
Z	Zulu	Zebra

WHAT IS YOUR ___'s NAME?
¿Cómo se llama tu ___?
(KOH-moh say YAH-mah too ___?)

WHAT IS THAT PERSON'S NAME?
¿Cómo se llama esa persona?
(KOH-mah ES-sah pehr-SOH-nah?)

IS THIS YOUR ___?
¿Es este tu ___?
(Ess ESS-tay too ___?)

acquaintance conocido
(Koh-noh-SEE-doh)
boyfriend- novio (NOH-bee-oh)
colleague- colega (koh-LEH-gah)
enemy- enemigo (eh-neh-MEE-goh)
fiancé- novio (NOH-bee-oh)
friend- amigo (ah-MEE-goh)
girlfriend novia (NOH-bee-ah)
 amiga (ah-MEE-gah)
lover amante (ah-MAHN-tay)
love affair- amorío(a) (ah-moh-REE-oh)

To break off a friendship
Romper una amistad
(Rohm-PEHR OO-nah ah-mees-TAHD)

Close friends
Amigos íntimos
(ah-MEE-gohs EEN-tee-mohs)

Family friend
Amigo de familia
(ah-MEE-goh day fah-MEE-Iyah)

MORSE CODE

A ·—
B —···
C —·—·
D —··
E ·
F ··—·
G ——·
H ····
I ··
J ·———
K —·—
L ·—··
M ——
N —·
O ———
P ·——·
Q ——·—
R ·—·
S ···
T —
U ··—
V ···—
W ·——
X —··—
Y —·——

Error ....
Wait .-...
Eng Msg .-.-.

MORSE CODE # 's

1 .----
2 ..---
3 ...--
4 ....-
5 .....
6 -....
7 --...
8 ---..
9 ----.
0 -----

MISC. CODES

Period .-.-.-
Comma --..--
? ..--..

NUMBERS

0	cero	(SEH-roh)
1	uno	(OO-noh)
2	dos	(dohs)
3	tres	(trehs)
4	cuatro	(KWAH-troh)
5	cinco	(SEEN-koh)
6	seis	(sayehs)
7	siete	(see-EH-teh)
8	ocho	(OH-choh)
9	nueve	(noo-EH-veh)
10	diez	(DEE-ess)

11	once	(OHN-seh)
12	doce	(DOH-seh)
13	trece	(TREH-seh)
14	catorce	(kah-TOHR-seh)
15	quince	(KEEN-seh)
16	dieciséis	(dee-eh-see-SAY-ees)

(Modern Variation:
   Diecisels, Diecisiete, ETC.)

17 diecisiete (dee-eh-see-**SEE**-eh-teh)
18 dieciocho (dee-eh-see-**OH**-choh)
19 diecinueve
   (dee-eh-see-**NWEH**-beh)

20 veinte (**VEH**-een-teh)
21 veintiuno (**VEH**-een-tee-**OO**-noh)
22 veintidós (**VEH**-een-tee-**DOHS)**
23 veintitrés (**VEH**-een-tee-**TREHS)**
24 veinticuatro
   (**VEH**-een-tee-**KWAH**-troh)
25 veinticinco
   (**VEH**-een-tee-**SEEN**-koh)
26 veintiséis (**VEH**-een-tee-**SEH**-ees)
27 veintisiete
   (**VEH**-een-tee-see-**EH**-teh)
28 veintiocho
   (**VEH**-een-tee-**OH**-choh)
29 veintinueve
   (**VEH**-een-tee-**NWEH**-beh)
30 treinta (**TREH**-een-tah)
31 treinta y uno
   (**TREH**-een-tah ee **OO**-noh)
32 treinta y dos
   (**TREH**-een-tah ee **Dohs**)
33 treinta y tres
   (**TREH**-een-tah ee trehs)
40 cuarenta (kwah-**REHN**-tah)
41 cuarenta y uno
   (kwah-**REHN**-tah ee **OO**-noh)
42 cuarenta y dos
   (kwah-**REHN**-tah ee dohs)
44 cuarenta y cuatro
   (kwah-**REHN**-tah ee **KWAH**-troh)
50 cincuenta (seen-**KWEHN**-tah)
55 cincuenta y cinco
   (seen-**KWEHN**-tah ee **SEEN**-koh)
60 sesenta (seh-**SEHN**-tah)
61 sesenta y uno
   (seh-**SEHN**-tah ee **OO**-noh)
66 sesenta y seis
   (seh-**SEHN**-tah ee **SEH**-ees)
70 setenta (seh-**TEHN**-tah)
77 setenta y siete
   (seh-**TEHN**-tah ee see-**EH**-teh)
80 ochenta (oh-**CHEHN**-tah)
90 noventa (noh-**BEHN**-tah)
100 cien (**SEE**-ehn)
200 doscientos (dohs-see-**EHN**-tohs)
300 trescientos (trehs-see-**EHN**-tohs)
400 cuatrocientos
   (kwah-troh-see-**EHN**-tohs)
500 quinientos (kee-nee-**EHN**-tohs)
600 seiscientos
   (eh-ees-see-**EHN**-tohs)
700 setecientos
   (seh-teh-see-**EHN**-tohs)
800 ochocientos
   (oh-choh-see-**EHN**-tohs)

900 novecientos
   (noh-beh-see-**EHN**-tohs)

1,000 mil (meel)
2,000 dos mil (dohs meel)
1 Million- un millón (oon mee-**YOHN)**

ORDINAL NUMBERS

first	primero	(pree-MEH-roh)
second	segundo	(seh-GOON-doh)
third	tercero	(tehr-SEH-roh)
fourth	cuarto	(KWAHR-toh)
fifth	quinto	(KEEN-toh)
sixth	sexto	(SEKS-toh)
seventh	séptimo	(SEHP-tee moh)
eighth	octavo	(ohk-TAH-boh)
ninth	noveno	(noh-BEH-noh)
tenth	décimo	(DEH-see-moh)
twentieth	vigésimo	(bee-HEH-see-moh)

OCCUPATIONS

WHERE DO YOU WORK?
¿Donde trabaja? (DOHN-day tra-BAH-hah)

JOB: profesión (pro-feh-SYOHN);
- trabajo (trah-BAH-hoh)

TELL ME YOUR BOSS'S NAME.
Digame el nombre de su patrón.
(DEE-gah-may ehl NOHM-bray day soo pah-TROHN).

Have subject point		
artist	artista	(ahr-TEES-tah)
aviator;	aviador;(ah-vee-ah-DOHR)	
- piloto	(pee-LOH-toh)	
ballplayer- pelotero	(pay-loh-TAY-roh)	
barber - peluquero	(pay-loo-KAY-roh)	
blacksmith- herrero	(ay-RAYR-oh)	
butcher - carnicero(kahr-nee-SAY-roh)		
carpenter carpintero		
(kahr-peen-TAY-roh)		
cattleman- vaquero	(vah-KAY-roh)	
chauffeur - chófer	(CHOH-fahr)	
clerk - dependiente		
(day-pehn-dee-EHN-tay)		
constable- alguacil	(ahl-oo-ah-SEEL)	
cook - cocinero (koh-see-NAY-roh)		
cowboy - vaquero	(vah-KAY-roh)	
customs agent- agente de aduana		
(ah-HEHN-tay day ah-doo-AHN-ah)		
dairyman - lechero	(lay-CHAY-roh)	
dentist - dentista	(dehn-TEES-tah)	
doctor - doctor	(dohk-TOHR)	
DRIVER- chófer	(CHOH-fayr)	
drug smuggler- contrabandista		
(kohn-trah-bahn-DEES-tah)		
druggist- farmaceutico		
(fahr-mah-say-OO-tee-koh)		
engineer - ingeniero	(een-gehn-ee-AY-roh)	
farmer - ranchero	(rahn-CHAY-roh)	
fisherman- pescador	(PEHS-kah-dohr)	
gardener - jardinero	(hahr-deen-AY-roh)	
guide - guia	(GHEE-ah)	
hatmaker- sombrerero		
(sohm-bray-AY-roh)		
irrigator- regador	(ray-gah-DOHR)	
jeweler - joyero	(hoy-AY-roh)	
laborer - labrador	(lah-brah-DOHR)	
lawyer - abogado(ah-boh-GAH-doh)		
machinist- maquinista		
(mah-keen-EES-tah)		
This can also mean a havy equipment operator.		
mailcarrier- cartero	(kahr-TAY-roh)	
mason - albanil	(ahl-bahn-YEEL)	
merchant - comerciante		
(koh-mayr-see-AHN-tay)		
mechanic- mecánico		
(may-KAH-nee-koh)		
miner - minero	(mee-NAY-roh)	
musician - músico	(MOO-see-koh)	
official - oficial	(oh-fee-see-AHL)	
painter - pintor	(peen-TOHR)	
pilot - piloto	(pee-LOH-toh)	
pimp - palo blanco Lit: White Stick		
(PAH-loh BLAHN-koh) (slang)		
alcahuete		
(ahl-kah-HOO-AY-tay)		
plumber - plomero	(ploh-MAY-roh)	
porter - portero	(pohr-TAY-roh)	
priest - cura;	(KOO-rah)	
padre;	(PAH-dray)	
sacerdote(sah-sayr-DOH-tay)		
promoter - promotor (proh-moh-TOHR)		
rancher - ranchero	(rahn-CHAY-roh)	
sailor - marinero	(mah-ree-NAY-roh)	
seller - vendedor	(vehn-day-DOHR)	
servant - criado	(kree-AH-doh)	
seamstress- costurera		
(kohs-too-RAY-rah)		
sharecropper- mediero		
(may-dee-AYR-oh)		
sheriff - alguacil	(ahl-oo-ah-SEEL)	
shoemaker- zapatero	(zah-pah-TAY-roh)	
shoplifter - ratero de tienda		
(rah-TAY-roh day tee-EHN-dah)		
smuggler - contrabandista		
(kahn-trah-bahn-DEES-tah)		
soldier - soldado	(sohl-DAH-doh)	
stenographer- taquigrafo		
(tah-KEE-grah-foh)		
surgeon - cirujano	(see-roo-HAHN-oh)	
tailor - sastre	(SAHS-tray)	
teacher - profesor;	(proh-FAY-sohr)	
- maestro	(mah-ESS-troh)	
tinsmith - hojalatero	(oh-hah-LAH-tay-roh)	
usher - conserje;	(kohn-SAYR-hay)	
- acomodador		
(ah-koh-mah-dah-DOHR)		
waiter - mozo;	(MOH-zoh)	
- mesero	(may-SAY-roh)	
watchmaker- relojero	(ray-loh-HAY-roh)	
worker - trabajador;		
(trah-bah-hah-DOHR)		
- obrero	(oh-BRAY-roh)	

PHOTOGRAPHS

WE ARE GOING TO TAKE YOUR PICTURE.
Vamos a tomar su retrato.
(**VAH**-mohs ah toh-**MAHR** soo reh-**TRAH**-toh)

POLICE

POLICE
policía
(poh-lee-**SEE**-ah)

I AM A POLICE OFFICER.
Yo soy policía.
(Yo soy poh-lee-**SEE**-ah)

POLICE!
WE HAVE A SEARCH WARRANT.
¡Policia!
Tenemos una orden de registro / cateo.
(Poh-lee-**SEE**-ah!
Tay-**NAY**-mohs **OO**-nah **OHR**-dehn day ray-**HEE**-stroh / kah-**TAY**-oh)

RELATIVES

WHAT IS YOUR _____'s NAME?
¿Como se llama su _____?
(**KOH**-moh say **YAH**-mah soo___?)

IS THIS YOUR _____?
¿Es este su _____?
(Ess **ESS**-tay soo _____?)

aunt-	tía	(**TEE**-ah)
brother-	hermano	(ayr-**MAHN**-oh)
brother-in-law	cuñado	(koo-**NYAH**-doh)
child-	niño	(**NEEN**-yoh)
children-	niños	(**NEEN**-yohs)
cousin-	primo	(**PREE**-moh)
dad-	papá	(pah-**PAH**)
daughter-	hija	(**EE**-hah)
daughter in law-	nuera	(**NWEH**-rah)
family-	familia	(fah-**MEE**-lee-ah)
father-	padre	(**PAH**-dray)
father in law-	suegro	(**SWEH**-groh)
grandchild-	nieto	(nee-**EH**-toh)
grandfather-	abuelo	(ah-**BWEH**-loh)
grandmother-	abuela	(ah-**BWEH**-lah)
grandparents-	abuelos	(ah-boo-**AY**-lohs)
great aunt-	tía abuela	(**TEE**-ah ah-**BWEH**-lah)
great grandchild-	bisnieto	(bees-nee-**EH**-toh)
great grandfather-	bisabuelo	(bees-ah-**BWEH**-loh)
great grandmother-	bisabuela	(bees-ah-**BWEH**-lah)
great uncle-	tío abuelo	(**TEE**-oh ah-**BWEH**-loh)
husband-	esposo	(Ess-**POH**-soh)
mother-	mamá	(mah-**MAH**)
mother in law-	suegra	(**SWEH**-grah)
nephew-	sobrino	(soh-**BREE**-noh)
niece-	sobrina	(soh-**BREE**-nah)
parents-	padres	(**PAH**-drays)
relatives-	parientes	(pah-ree-**EHN**-tays)
sister-	hermana	(ayr-**MAHN**-ah)
son-	hijo	(**EE**-hoh)
son in law-	yerno	(**YEHR**-noh)
sons-	hijos	(**EE**-hohs)
step brother-	hermanastro	(ehr-mah-**NAHS**-troh)
step daughter-	hijastra	(ee-**HAHS**-trah)
stepfather-	padrastro	(pah-**DRAHS**-troh)
stepmother-	madrastra	(mah-**DRAHS**-trah)
stepsister-	hermanastra	(ehr-mah-**NAHS**-trah)
stepson-	hijastro	(ee-**HAHS**-troh)
uncle-	tío	(**TEE**-oh)
wife-	esposa	(ess-**POH**-sah)

STATES OF MEXICO AND THEIR ABBR.

Aguascalientes - Ags	Morelos	- Mor.
Baja California - B.C.	Nayarit	- Nay.
Campeche - Camp.	Nuevo Leon	- Nay.
Chiapas - Chis.	Nuevo Leon	- N.L.
Chihuahua - Chih.	Oaxaca	- Oax.
Coahuila - Coah.	Puebla	- Pueb.
Colima - Col.	Queretaro	- Qto.
Distrito Federal - D.F.	San Luis Potosi	- S.L.P.
Durango - Dgo.	Sinaloa	- Sin.
Guanajuato - Gto.	Sonora	- Sin.
Guerrero - Gro.	Tabasco	- Tab.
Hidalgo - Hgo.	Tamaulipas	- Tamps.
Jalisco - Jal.	Veracruz	- Ver.
Mexico - Mex.	Yucatan	- Yuc.
Michoacan - Mich.	Zacatecas	- Zac.
Morelos		
- Mor.		

MAJ. CITIES	POP.	LAT./LONG.	INTERNAT. PHONE CODE
Mexico City	14,000,000	19.25N, 99.10W	52-5
Guadalajara	3,000,000	20.40N,103.20W	52-36
Monterrey	2,700,000	25.40N,100.20W	52-83
Ciudad Juarez	1,120,000	31.42N,106.29W	52-16
Puebla de Zaragoza	1,100,000	28.31N,100.54W	52-22
Leon	1,000,000	21.10N,101.42W	52-
Tijuana	600,000	32.29N,117.10W	52-66
Acapulco	500,000	16.51N, 99.56W	52-748
Chihuahua	400,000	28.40N,106.06W	52-14
Mexicali	350,000	32.36N,115.30W	52-748
San Luis Potosi	330,000	22.10N,101.00W	52-481

Telex Access Code(s) 383 Ham Radio Prefixes: XE

SUICIDE PREVENTION (also see "COMMANDS")

DON'T!
¡No!
(noh)

PLEASE!
!Por favor!
(pohr fah-**VOHR**)

YOUR FAMILY NAME WILL BE DISGRACED!
¡Su familia quedará en desgracia!
(Soo fah-**MEE**-lee-ah kay-dah-**RAH** ehn days-**GRAH**-see-ah)

GOD DOESN'T WANT THIS.
Dios no permite esto.
(**DEE**-ohs noh payr-**MEE**-tay **AYS**-toh)

BLESS YOU!
!Salud!
(sah-**LOOD**)

TAPE RECORDINGS

THIS CONVERSATION IS BEING TAPE RECORDED.
Estamos grabando esta conversación.
(Ay-**STAH**-mohs grah-**BAHN**-doh **ESS**-tah kohn-behr-sah-**SYOHN**)
* **(Refer local laws governing tape recordings)**

TELEPHONE

DON'T HANG UP!
¡No cuelgues!
(Noh koo-**EHL**-gays)

CALM DOWN!
¡Cálmese!
(**KAHL**-meh-seh)

WHAT IS YOUR TELEPHONE NUMBER?
¿Cuál es su número de teléfono?
(Kwahl ess soo **NOO**-may-roh day tay-**LAY**-foh-noh)

WHAT IS THE PHONE NUMBER?
¿Cuál es el número del teléfono?
(Kwahl ess el **NOO**-may-roh del tay-**LAY**-foh-noh)

IS THERE ANOTHER NUMBER I CAN CALL?
¿Hay otro número a dónde puedo llamar?
(Eye **OH**-troh **NOO**-may-roh ah **DOHN**-day poo-**AYD**-oh yah-**MAHR**)

IN CASE OF EMERGENCY, WHO DO WE CALL?
En caso de emergencia, a quién llamamos?
(En **KAH**-soh day ay-mayr-**HAYN**-see-ah, ah kee-**YEHN** yah-**MAH**-mohs)

WE WILL TRY TO CALL LATER.
Trataremos de llamar más tarde.
(Trah-tah-**RAY**-mohs day yah-**MAHR** mahs **TAHR**-day)

DO YOU HAVE A TELEPHONE?
¿Tiene usted teléfono?
(Tee-EHN-ay oo-STEHD tay-LAY-foh-noh)

WHAT IS THE PHONE NUMBER OF YOUR WORK?
¿Cuál es el teléfono de su trabajo?
(Kwahl ess el tay-LAY-foh-noh day soo trah-BAH-hoh)

TELL THEM YOU ARE IN THE SHERIFF'S STATION.
Dígales que usted está en la estación del sherife. (alguacil mayor)
(DEE-gah-lays kay oo-STEHD ess-TAH en la ess-tah-SYOHN del shay-REE-fay) [ahl-gwah-SEEL mah-YOHR]) (or at the _____)

POLICE STATION
Estación de policia
(ess-tah-SYOHN day poh-lee-SEE-ah)

STATE POLICE
Policía del Estado
(Poh-lee-SEE-ah dayl ays-TAH-doh)

TELL THEM TO CALL THIS NUMBER:
Dígales que llamen a este número: _____.
(DEE-gah-lays kay YAH-mehn ah ESS-tay NOO-may-roh _____.)

TELL THEM TO CALL ANY BAIL BONDSMAN.
Dígales que llamen a cualquier fiador.
(DEE-gah-lays kay YAH-mehn ah kwahl-kee-AYR fee-ah-DOHR)

TOW TRUCK

DO YOU WANT A TOW TRUCK?
¿Quiere usted una grua?
(Kee-AYR-ay oo-STEHD OO-nah GROO-ah)

I AM GOING TO TOW YOUR CAR FOR (Appropriate Offense).
Voy a llevar su carro por grua, por _____.
(Voy ah yeh-VAR soo KAHR-roh pohr GROO-ah pohr _____.)

YOUR CAR IS BEING CONFISCATED.
Su carro es confiscado.
(Soo KAHR-roh ays KOHN-fess-kah-doh)

64

TRAFFIC STOPS

HELLO, HOW ARE YOU?
Hola ¿Como esta Usted?
(OH-lah, KOH-moh ays-TAH oo-STEHD)

WHO WAS THE DRIVER?
¿Quién era el chofer?
(Kee-EHN AYR-ah ayl CHOH-fayr)

PARK OVER THERE. (POINT)
Estacione alli.
(Ay-stah-see-OH-nay ah-YEE)

WERE YOU DRIVING?
¿Estaba manejando Ud.?
(Ay-STAH-bah mah-nay-HAHN-doh Ud.)

TURN OFF THE ENGINE.
Apague el motor.
(ah-PAH-queh el moh-TOHR)

RIGHT- correcto (koh-REHK-toh)
WRONG- incorrecto
(een-koh-REHK-toh)

PULL OFF THE ROAD.
Estaciónese fuera del camino.
(Ay-stah-SYOH-nay-say FOO-AIR-ah del kah-MEE-noh)

BACK UP-	retroceder	(ray-troh-say-DEHR)
BRAKE (v)	frenar	(freh-NAHR)
DANGER	¡peligro!	(pay-LEE-groh)
ENOUGH!	¡basta!	(BAHS-tah)
FOLLOW (v)	¡seguir!	(seh-GEER)
FOLLOW ME	¡sígame!	(SEE-gah-may)
FORWARD	adelantarse	(ah-day-lahn-TAHR-say)

GO OVER THERE.
Vaya allí
(VAH-yah ah-YEE)

KEEP TO THE RIGHT-
conserve su derecha
(kohn-SEHR-vay soo day-RAY-chah)

RETURN- I WILL RETURN
Ya vuelvo
(yah voo-AYL-voh); or Ya volveré (yah voll-vehr-AY)

SLOW
Despacio
(days-PAH-see-oh)

START THE CAR.
Arrancar el carro
(ah-rahn-KAHR el KAHR-roh)

STOP Alto (AHL-toh)

TURN	Dar la vuelta	(dahr lah BWEHL-tah)
TO THE LEFT-	a la izquierda	(ah lah ees-kee-EHR-dah)
TO THE RIGHT-	a la derecha	(ah lah day-REH-chah)
YIELD	ceder (v) el paso	(seh-DEHR ayl PAH-soh)

ANSWER YES OR NO.
Conteste si o no.
(Kohn-tays-tay SEE oh noh)

EXCUSE ME	Perdóneme	(payr-DOH-nay-may)
FALSE	Falso	(FAHL-soh)
GO	Vaya.	(VAH-yah)

I DIDN'T UNDERSTAND.	**IT DOESN'T MATTER.**
No entendí.	No importa.
(noh ehn-tehn-DEE)	(Noh eem-POHR-tah)

| **NOW** | ahora | (ah-OH-rah) |
| **REALLY** | ¿De veras? | (day BEH-rahs) |

SPEAK SLOWER.
Hable más despacio.
(AH-blay mahs pah-SEE-toh)

SPEAK LOUDER.
Hable en voz más alta.
(AH-blay ehn vohz mahs AHL-tah)

| **THAT'S IT** | ¡Eso es! | (AY-soh ays) |
| **UNBELIEVABLE!** | ¡increíble! | (een-kreh-EE-bleh) |

DO YOU SPEAK ENGLISH?
¿Habla usted inglés?
(AH-blah oo-STEHD een-GLAYS)

IS THERE ANYONE HERE WHO SPEAKS ENGLISH?
¿Hay alguien aquí que habla inglés?
(AH-ee ahl-GHEE-ehn ah-KEE kay AH-blah een-GLAYS)

I DON'T UNDERSTAND.
No comprendo.
(noh kohm-PREHN-doh)

| **DRIVER** | chofer | (CHOH-fayr) |
| **PASSENGER** | pasajero | (pah-sah-HAY-roh) |

YOU HAVE BEEN STOPPED FOR _____.
Usted ha sido parado por _____.
(oo-STEHD ah SEE-doh pah-RAH-doh pohr _____)

YOU HAVE VIOLATED A TRAFFIC LAW.
Usted ha violado una ley de tránsito.
(Oo-STEHD ah vee-oh-LAH-doh OO-nah lay day TRAHN-see-toh)

FAILURE TO WEAR YOUR SEAT BELT.
Falta de usar su cinturon de segundad.
(FAHL-tah day oo-ZAHR soo seen-too-ROHN day say-goo-REE-dahd)

SLOW DOWN. Ir más despacio.
(eer mahs days-PAH-see-oh)

SPEED LIMIT IS _____ MILES PER HOUR.
El limite de velocidad es _____ millas por hora.
(Ayl LEE-mee-tay day vah-loh-see-DAHD ays _____ MEE-yahs pohr OH-nah)

99

SPEED
Velocidad
(Vay-loh-see-DAHD)

HIGH SPEED
Alta velocidad
(AHL-tah vay-loh-see-DAHD)

YOU WERE GOING TOO SLOW.
Ud. iba demasiado lento.
(oo-STEHD EE-bah day-mahs-ee-AH-doh LEHN-toh)

YOUR SPEED WAS _____MILES PER HR.   RADAR
Su velocidad fué _____ millas por hora.   radar
(Soo vay-loh-see-DAHD foo-AY ____ MEE-yahs pohr OH-rah) (rah-DAHR)

ABOUT HOW FAST WERE YOU GOING?
¿Que tan rápido iba Ud.?
(Kay tahn RAH-pee-doh EE-bah oo-STEHD)

RED LIGHT
La luz roja
(Lah loos ROH-hah)

YOUR CAR WAS WEAVING.
Su coche estuvo moviendo de lado a lado.
(Soo KOH-chay ay-STOO-voh moh-vee-EHN-doh day LAH-doh ah LAH-doh)

EXPIRED CAR LICENSE.
Placa vencida.
(PLAH-kah vehn-SEE-dah)

FAILURE TO USE SIGNALS.
Por no usar los señaleros.
(Pohr noh oo-SAHR lohs sehn-yah-LAY-rohs)

FAILURE TO STOP AT THE TRAFFIC LIGHT/STOP SIGN.
Por no parar en el semáforo. (o alto)
(Pohr noh pah-RAHR ehn el say-MAH-fohr-oh [oh AHL-toh])

TINTED WINDOWS.
Ventanas obscuras.
(vehn-TAH-nahs ohb-SKOO-rahs)

OTHER USEFUL TERMS

BE CAREFUL!
¡Cuidado!
(kwee-DAH-doh)

DANGEROUS CROSSING-
cruce peligroso
(KROO-say pay-lee-GROH-soh)

DETOUR- desvío (days-BEE-oh)

INTERSECTION-
intersección (bocacalle)
(een-tayr-sehk-SYOHN
 [boh-kah-KAH-yay])

KEEP TO THE RIGHT.
Mantenga su derecha.
(Mahn-TEHN-gah soo day-RAY-chah)

NO ENTRY-
Entrada prohibida.
(Ehn-TRAH-dah pro-hee-BEE-dah)

NO LEFT TURN-
Prohibido girar a la izquierda.
(proh-ee-BEE-doh hee-RAHR
 ah lah ess-kee-EHR-dah)

NO PARKING- prohibido estacionar.
(proh-ee-BEE-dah
 ays-tah-see-oh-NAHR)

NO PASSING-
prohibido adelantar.
(proh-ee-BEE-dah ah-day-lahn-TAHR)

NO RIGHT TURN-
Prohibido girar a la derecha.
(proh-ee-BEE-doh hee-RAHR
 ah lah day-REH-chah)

NO U-TURN.
Prohibida dar la vuelta.
(proh-ee-BEE-dah dahr la BWEHL-tah)

NO STOPPING-
Prohibido parar.
(proh-ee-BEE-doh pah-RAHR)

ONE WAY-
dirección única.
(dee-rehk-SYOHN OO-nee-kah);
- tránsito (with arrow)
(TRAHN-see-toh)

PEDESTRIAN CROSSWALK-
Cruce de peatones
(KROO-say day peh-ah-TOH-nays)

TOLL- peaje (peh-AH-hay)

TOW AWAY ZONE-
zona de remolque
(SOH-nah day reh-MOHL-kay)

POINT AT DEFECTIVE PART OR SEE BELOW

DEFECTIVE
Defectuoso
(day-feck-too-OH-soh)

IS IT IN THE _____ ?
Está en el _____ ?
(Ay-STAH ehn el _____ ?)

door- puerta (PWEHR-tah)
electrical system- sistema eléctrico
(sees-TAY-mah eh-LEHK-tree-koh)
fan- ventilador (behn-tee-lah-DOHR)
dashboard- tablero (tah-BLEH-roh)
instruments- instrumentos
(eens-troo-MEHN-tohs)
compartment- compartimiento
(kohm-pahr-tee-mee-EHN-toh)
clutch- embrague
(ehm-BRAH-gweh);
- cluchay (KLOOT-chay)
carburetor- carburador
(kahr-boo-rah-DOHR)
car window- ventanilla
(behn-tah-NEE-yah)
car body- carrocería
(kah-roh-say-REE-ah)
bumper- parachoques
(pah-rah-CHOH-kays)
brake- freno (FREH-noh)
battery- batería (bah-tay-REE-ah)
steering wheel- volante (voh-LAHN-tay)
tire- llanta (YAHN-tah)
flat tire- pinchazo,
llanta desinflada
(peen-CHA-soh
YAHN-ta dehs-een-FLAH-da)
transmission- transmisión
(trahs-mee-SYOHN)
turn signal-
cajuela (kah-HOO-AY-lah)
trunk-
indicador de dirección / señalizador
(een-dee-kah-DOHR day dee-rehk-
SYOHN / say-nyah-lee-sah-DOHR)
vent- abertura (ah-behr-TOO-rah)
vent window- ventanilla
(vehn-tah-NEE-yah)
wheel- la rueda
(lah roo-WAY-dah)
windshield- parabrisas
(pah-rah-BREE-sahs)
wipers-
limpiaparabrisas
(LEEM-pee-ah-pah-rah-bree-sahs)

fan belt- correa de ventilador
(Koh-RAY-ah day behn-tee-lah-DOHR)
gas tank- tanque (TAHN-kay)
gasoline- gasolina (gah-soh-LEE-nah)
gearshift- cambio de velocidad
(KAHM-bee-oh day beh-loh-see-DAHD)
glove compartment- guantera
(gwahn-TAY-rah)
handle- manija (mah-NEE-hah)
headlight- faro delantero
/cuarto delantero
(FAH-roh day-lahn-TAY-roh /
KWAHR-toh day-lahn-TAY-roh)
heater- calefacción
(kah-leh-fahk-SYOHN)
hood- capó (kah-POH)
- cofre (KOH-fray)
horn- bocina (boh-SEE-nah)
- pito (PEE-toh)
ignition- encendido
(ehn-sehn-DEE-doh)
jack- gato (GAH-toh)
license plate- placa (PLAH-kah)
lights- luces (LOO-says)
motor- motor (moh-TOHR)
muffler- mofle (MOH-flay)
- arranque (ah-RAHN-kay)

89

GIVE ME YOUR DRIVER'S LICENSE AND REGISTRATION.
Déme su licencia y la circulación.
(**DAY**-may soo lee-**SEHN**-syah ee la seer-koo-lah-**SYOHN**)

TITLE OF OWNERSHIP. Título. (**TEE**-too-loh)

DO YOU HAVE A DRIVER'S LICENSE?
¿Tiene usted una licencia?
(Tee-**EHN**-ay oo-**STEHD** **OO**-nah lee-**SEHN**-see-ah)

TAKE IT OUT. Sáquelo (**SAH**-kay-loh)

IS THIS YOUR CURRENT ADDRESS?
¿Es este su domicilio actual?
(ehs **EH**-steh so doh-mee-**SEE**-lee-oh ahk-too-**AHL**)

YOUR LICENSE IS SUSPENDED (EXPIRED)
Su licencia está suspendida (vencida)
(Soo lee-**SEHN**-see-ah **AY**-stah soo-spehn-**DEE**-dah [vehn-**SEE**-dah])

YOU CAN'T DRIVE THE CAR
Ud. no puede manejar el carro.
(Oo-**STEHD** noh **PWAY**-day mah-**NAY**-hahr el **KAHR**-roh)

IS THIS YOUR CAR? ¿Es este su carro?
(Ess **ESS**-teh soo **KAHR**-roh)

WHO IS THE OWNER OF THE CAR?
¿Quién es el dueño del carro?
(Kee-**EHN** ess ehl **DWEH**-nyoh dehl **KAHR**-roh)

WHAT YEAR IS THE CAR?
De qué año es el carro?
(Day kay **AHN**-yoh ays ayl **KAHR**-roh)

WHERE DO YOU LIVE?	**DO YOU HAVE INSURANCE?**
¿Dónde vive?	¿tíene seguro?
(**DOHN**-day **VEE**-vay)	(tee-**YEH**-nay say-**GOO**-roh)
INSURANCE	**INSURANCE CARD**
seguro	Tarjeta de seguro
(say-**GOO**-roh)	(tahr-**HAY**-tah day seh-**GOO**-roh)

DO YOU HAVE IDENTIFICATION?
¿Tiene usted identificación?
(Tee-**EHN**-ay oo-**STEHD** ee-dehn-tee-fee-kah-**SYOHN**)

WHAT IS YOUR NAME?	**WRITE**
¿Cómo se llama usted?	escriba
(**KOH**-moh say **YAH**-mah oo-**STEHD**)	(ehs-**KREE**-bah)

MY NAME IS _____. Me llamo _____. (may **YAH**-moh)

HOW DO YOU SPELL YOUR NAME?
¿Cómo se escribe (deletrea) su nombre?
(**KOH**-moh say ehs-**KREE**-bay [deh-leh-tray-ah] soo **NOHM**-bray)

DO YOU HAVE A NICKNAME?
¿Tiene usted sobrenombre?/apodo?
(Tee-**EHN**-ay oo-**STEHD** soh-bray-**NOHM**-bray / ah-**POH**-doh)

WRITE YOUR NAME.
Escriba su nombre con letras de molde.
(ehs-**KREE**-bah soo **NOHM**-bray kohn **LEH**-trahs day **MOHL**-day)

PRINT- imprenta (eem-**PREHN**-tah); (v) imprimir (eem-pree-**MEER**)

FIRST NAME	**SURNAME**	**NICKNAME**
nombre de pila	apellido	apodo/sobrenombre
(**NOHM**-bray day **PEE**-lah)	(ah-peh-**YEE**-doh)	(ah-**POH**-doh/soh-bray-**NOHM**-bray)

NOTE: IF IDENTIFICATION IS AS FOLLOWS:

(EXAMPLE): JUAN CAMPOLI-LOPEZ (OR)
JUAN C. LOPEZ

ASK WHAT FATHER'S LAST NAME IS. (SHOULD BE): CAMPOLI

ASK WHAT MOTHER'S LAST NAME IS. (SHOULD BE): LOPEZ

THE TRUE LAST NAME IS: CAMPOLI
Official U.S. Gov't listing of last name would be: CAMPOLI-LOPEZ

DATE OF BIRTH.
Fecha de nacimiento.
(**FEH**-chah day nah-see-mee-**EHN**-toh)

WHEN WERE YOU BORN?
¿Cuándo nació usted?
(**KWAHN**-doh nah-see-**OH** oo-**STEHD**)

day	month	year
día	mes	año
(**DEE**-ah)	(mehs)	(**AHN**-yoh)

WHAT IS YOUR ADDRESS?
¿Cuál es su domicilio?
(Kwahl es soo doh-mee-**SEE**-lyoh)

HOUSE NUMBER-
Número de casa
(**NOO**-may-roh day **KAH**-sah)

STREET	**CITY**	**STATE**	**AVENUE**
calle	ciudad	estado	avenida
(**KAY**-yay)	(see-oo-**DAHD**)	(ehs-**TAH**-doh)	(ah-veh-**NEE**-dah)

PLACE OF BIRTH
Lugar de nacimiento
(Loo-**GAHR** day nah-see-mee-**EHN**-toh)

CITY	**COUNTY**	**STATE**	**COUNTRY**
ciudad	condado	estado	país
(see-oo-**DAHD**)	(kohn-**DAH**-doh)	(ehs-**TAH**-doh)	(pah-**EES**)

PASSPORT NUMBER ?
Número de pasaporte ?
(**NOO**-may-roh day pah-sah-**POHR**-tay ?)

GREEN CARD, SHOW ME YOUR-
Enséñeme su mica.
(Ayn-**SEHN**-yah-may soo **MEE**-kah)

WHAT IS YOUR _____'s NAME?
¿Como se llama su _____?
(**KOH**-moh say **YAH**-mah soo _____?)

WHAT IS YOUR MOTHER'S SURNAME?
¿Cual es el apellido de su madre / mamá?
(Kwahl ays el ah-pay-**YEE**-doh day soo **MAH**-dray / mah-**MAH**)

HAVE YOU EVER USED ANY OTHER NAMES?
Ha usado Usted algunos otros nombres alguna vez?
(Ah oo-**SAH**-doh oo-**STEHD** ahl-**GOO**-nohs **OH**-trohs **NOHM**-brays ahl-**GOO**-nah vehz)

WRITE YOUR ADDRESS IN THE U.S.
Enscribe su dirección en los Estados Unidos.
(Ay-**SCREE**-bay soo dee-rehk-**SYOHN** ehn lohs aysTAH-dohs oo-**NEE**-dohs)

WHERE DO YOU WORK? (Refer to: Occupations)
¿Dónde trabaja usted?
(**DOHN**-day tra-**BAH**-hah oo-**STEHD**)

WHAT KIND OF WORK DO YOU DO?
¿Que clase de trabajo hace Usted?
(Kay **KLAH**-say day trah-**BAH**-hoh **AH**-say oo-**STEHD**)

WHAT IS YOUR SOCIAL SECURITY NUMBER?
¿Cúal es el número de su seguro social?
(Kwahl ays el **NOO**-may-roh day soo say-**GOO**-roh soh-see-**AHL**)

I AM GOING TO GIVE YOU A CITATION FOR SPEEDING
Voy a darle un tiquete por exceso de velocidad.
(Voy ah **DAHR**-lay oon **TEE**-kay-tay _____ pohr ex-**SES**-soh day vehl-oh-see-**DAHD**)

SIGN HERE.
Favor de firmar aquí.
(fah-**VOHR** day feer-**MAHR** ah-**KEE**)

WHEN YOU SIGN THE TICKET YOU ARE NOT ADMITTING GUILT.
Cuando usted firma el aviso de su infracción, usted no afirma su culpabilidad.
(**KWAHN**-doh oo-**STEHD** **FEER**-mah ehl ah-**VEE**-soh day soo een-frahk-**SYOHN**, oo-**STEHD** noh ah-**FEER**-mah soo kool-pah-bee-lee-**DAHD**)

YOUR SIGNATURE IS A PROMISE TO APPEAR IN COURT OR PAY THE FINE.
Su firma es promesa de presentarse en la corte o pagar la multa.
(Soo **FEER**-mah ehs proh-**MEH**-sah day preh-sehn-**TAHR**-say ehn lah **KOHR**-tay oh pah-**GAHR** lah **MOOL**-tah)

THIS IS A MECHANICAL WARNING.
Esta es una advertencia de que su carro necesita reparación.
(**ESS**-tah ess **OO**-nah ahd-vehr-**TEHN**-syah day kay soo **KAHR**-roh neh-sess-**SEE**-tah reh-pahr-rah-**SYOHN**)

YOU DIDN'T STOP AT THE STOP SIGNAL.
Usted no hizo alto en el semáforo.
(Oo-**STEHD** noh **EE**-soh **AHL**-toh en ehl seh-**MAH**-foh-roh)

THIS IS A CITATION	**THIS IS NOT A CITATION**
Esta es un tiquete.	Esta no es un tiquete.
(ESS-tah ess oon TEE-kay-tay)	(ESS-tah ess oon no TEE-kay-tay)

I AM GOING TO GIVE YOU A BREAK
Voy a darle una quebrada
(Voy ah DARH-lay OO-nah kay BRAH-dah)

THIS IS A WARNING.
Esta es una advertencia
(EHS-tah ehs OO-nah ahd-behr-TEHN-syah)

WAIT HERE!	**WAIT**
¡Espere aquí!	¡Espere!
(ehs-PEHR-ay ah-KEE)	(ehs-PEHR-ay)

FOLLOW ME-	**GIVE ME YOUR ___.**
Sígame	Deme su ___.
(SEE-gah-may)	(DAY-may soo ___)

GO TO THIS COURT
Vaya a esta corte.
(VAH-yah ah ESS-tah KOHR-tay)

OR (oh)

SEND THE AMOUNT BY MAIL
Mande la cantidad por correo
(MAHN-day lah CAHN-tee-dad pohr kor-RAY-oh)

AT THIS ADDRESS-	En esta dirección.	(Ehn ESS-tah dee-rehk-SYOHN)
IN THIS TOWN-	En este pueblo.	(Ah ESS-tay poo-EH-bloh)
ON THIS DATE-	En esta fecha.	(Ehn ESS-tah FEH-chah)
AT THIS HOUR-	A esta hora.	(Ah ESS-tah OHR-ah)

YOU ARE FREE TO GO.	**DO YOU UNDERSTAND?**
Usted es libre para irse.	¿Entiende?
(Oo-STEHD ays LEE-bray PAH-rah EER-say)	(Ehn-TEE-ehn-day)

72

TRUCK INSPECTIONS

(Due to the length of this section the phonetics have been omitted to save space. Many of the phonetic words are listed elsewhere in the manual).

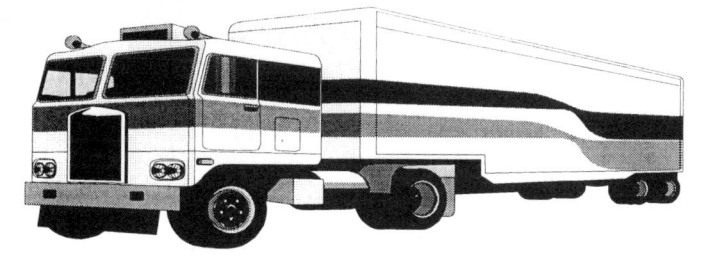

GENERAL INSPECTION TERMS

YOU HAVE BEEN STOPPED FOR ....
Usted ha sido parado por .... (For additional violations see " Traffic Stops")

SPEEDING   Exceso de velocidad

I AM GOING TO GIVE YOU A CITATION FOR SPEEDING
Voy a darle un tiquete por exceso de velocidad.

DEFECTIVE _____.   Defectuoso _____. (Insert appropriate word).

YOU WERE GOING TOO SLOW.
Ud. iba demasiado lento.

FAILURE TO STOP AT THE TRAFFIC LIGHT OR STOP SIGN.
Por no parar en el semáforo.   (o alto)

FAILURE TO: Falta de   (or select violation from list)

DIM HEAD LIGHTS	Reducir la intensidad de los focos
DRIVER OBEY H/M LAWS	Chofer obedecer las leyes de materiales peligrosos
SECURE VEHICLE EQUIPMENT	Falta de asegurar el equipo del vehículo
FOLLOWING TOO CLOSELY	Siguiendo muy cerca
HAZARDOUS WARNING FLASHERS	Uso de las luces de emergencia

INSPECT/USE EMERGENCY EQUIPMENT
Falta de inspección/uso de equipo de emergencia

IMPROPER BLOCKING/BRACING	Bloquear/atar/ligamiento inapropiado
IMPROPER LANE CHANGE	Mal cambio de carril
IMPROPER STORAGE OF BAGGAGE	Almacenamiento de equipaje /carga inapropiado
LAMPS/REFLECTORS OBSCURED	Lámparas/reflectores obscurecidos
NO/IMPROPER LOAD SECUREMENT	Carga no asegurada o inapropiadamente asegurada
OPERATING OOS VEHICLE	Operando un vehículo que fue puesto fuera-de-servicio
PARKING BRAKE NOT SET	Freno de mano no esta puesto
RECKLESS DRIVING	Manejando descuidadamente

STOPPED VEHICLE/	Vehículo parado
INTERFERE TRAFFIC	interfiriendo con el tráfico
USE OF SEATBELTS	Uso de el cinturón de seguridad
USE OF TURN SIGNALS	Uso de la direccional
USING/EQUIPPED WITH RADAR DETECTOR	Uso de detector de radar
VIEW / MOVEMENT OBSTRUCTED	Obstrucción de la vista o movimiento del chofer
WARNING DEVICES	Posición y uso de los avisos de emergencia
PARK OVER THERE.	Estacione allí.
BACKUP !	¡Retrocede!

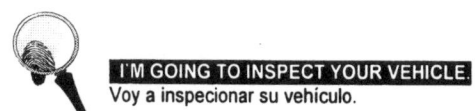

I'M GOING TO INSPECT YOUR VEHICLE.
Voy a inspeccionar su vehículo.

GIVE ME YOUR _____ .	Déme su _____ .
SHOW ME YOUR _____ .	Enséñeme su _____ .
DO YOU HAVE _____ ?	¿Tiene usted _____ ?
GREEN CARD	Mica
IDENTIFICATION	
DO YOU HAVE IDENTIFICATION?	¿Tiene usted identificación?
INSURANCE CARD	Tarjeta de seguro
DO YOU HAVE INSURANCE?	¿Tiene seguro?
LICENSE	Licencia
DO YOU HAVE A DRIVER'S LICENSE?	¿Tiene usted una licencia?
LOG BOOK	Libro de horario.
MEDICAL CERTIFICATE	Certificado Médico
PAPERS	Papeles.
PASSPORT	Pasaporte
SOCIAL SECURITY NUMBER	Número de seguro social
VEHICLE REGISTRATION FOR THE TRACTOR & TRAILER.	Tarjeta de circulación (registro del camion) para el tractor/ camion y el trailer.
YOUR LICENSE IS SUSPENDED	Su licencia está suspendida
(EXPIRED)	(vencida)
CAN YOU READ?	¿Puede leer?
WRITE?	¿escribir?
WHAT IS YOUR NAME?	¿Como se llama?
WRITE	Escriba
FIRST NAME / SURNAME / PATERNAL / MATERNAL	nombre de pila / apellido / paterno / materna
WHAT IS YOUR BIRTHDATE? DAY MONTH YEAR	¿En que fecha nació? día mes año
WHAT IS YOUR ADDRESS?	¿Cuál es su domicilio?

HOUSE NUMBER	número de casa
APARTMENT NUMBER	número de apartamento
STREET	calle
CITY	ciudad
COUNTY	condado
STATE	estado
COUNTRY	país

WHAT IS YOUR AGE? ¿Cuantos años tienes?
WHAT IS YOUR HEIGHT? ¿Que es su altura?
WHAT IS YOUR WEIGHT? ¿Que es su peso?

TURN OFF YOUR ENGINE. Apague su motor.

PLACE THE TRANSMISSION IN NEUTRAL.
Ponga la transmissión en neutral.

RELEASE ALL BRAKES. Suelte todos los frenos.

TURN THE KEY ON. Prenda la llave.
TURN ON ALL LIGHTS. Prenda todas la luces.

WATCH OFFICER FOR HAND AND VERBAL INSTRUCTIONS.
Vea al official para instrucciones manuales y verbales.

APPLY THE FOOT BRAKE. Aplique el freno de pie.

HOLD THE BRAKE PEDAL DOWN. Mantenga puesto el freno de pie.

PUMP THE BRAKES DOWN. Bombea los frenos.

TURN ON THE LEFT TURN SIGNAL. Ponga la direccional izquierda.
TURN ON THE RIGHT TURN SIGNAL. Ponga la direccional derecha.

START VEHICLE. **BUILD UP AIR PRESSURE TO 100PSI.**
Prenda el motor. Suba la presión de aire a 100 libras.

WHERE ARE YOU GOING TO? ¿A donde va?
WHERE ARE YOU COMING FROM? ¿De donde viene?
WHERE DID YOU ENTER? ¿En donde entró?
ENTRY DATE? ¿Fecha de entrada?
YOU MUST GO THROUGH CUSTOMS Tiene que pasar por la aduana.
    ANYTHING TO DECLARE? ¿Tiene algo que declarar?

WHEN DID YOU LEAVE? ¿Cuándo salió?
WHEN DID YOU ARRIVE? ¿Cuándo llegaron?
WHERE HAVE YOU BEEN? ¿Dónde ha estado?
WHERE IS YOUR _____? ¿Dónde está su __?
WHERE WAS IT OBTAINED? ¿Dónde lo obtuvo?

ARE YOU SICK OR FATIGUED? ¿Esta enfermo o cansado?

WHERE IS YOUR EMERGENCY EQUIPMENT
¿Donde esta tu equipo de emergencia?

   (FIRE ESTINGUISHER, TRIANGLES)? (extinguidor, reflectores)?

THIS IS AN EQUIPMENT REPAIR NOTICE, NOT A CITATION.
Este es un aviso para que repare su vehículo y no es una tiquete.

GIVE THIS TO THE MECHANIC OR BOSS.	Dále esto al mecánico o a su jefe.
THIS VEHICLE IS OUT-OF-SERVICE.	Este vehículo esta fuera-de-servicio.
THIS VEHICLE CANNOT BE MOVED UNTIL IT IS REPAIRED.	Este vehículo no puede ser movido hasta que se haya reparado.
DO YOU WANT A TOW TRUCK?	¿Desea una grúa?
THIS IS NOT A CITATION.	Esta no es un tiquete.
THIS IS A WARNING.	Esta es una advertencia
THIS IS A CITATION.	Esta es un tiquete.
I AM GOING TO GIVE YOU A CITATION FOR _____.	Voy a darle un tiquete por _____.
SIGN HERE.	Favor de firmar aquí.
WHEN YOU SIGN THE TICKET YOU ARE NOT ADMITTING GUILT.	Cuando usted firma el aviso de su infracción, usted no afirma su culpabilidad.
SIGNING THIS IS A PROMISE TO APPEAR IN COURT OR PAY THE AMOUNT	Su firma es promesa de presentarse en la corte o pagar la cantidad.
GO TO THIS COURT-	Vaya a esta corte.
AT THIS ADDRESS-	En esta dirección.
IN THIS TOWN-	En este pueblo.
ON THIS DATE-	En esta fecha.
AT THIS HOUR-	A esta hora.
YOU ARE FREE TO GO.	Usted es libre para irse.
DO YOU UNDERSTAND?	¿Entiende?
MAY I ASK A FEW QUESTIONS?	¿Quisiera hacerle unas pocas preguntas?
ARE THERE ANY GUNS, DRUGS, OR LARGE AMOUNTS OF CASH IN THE VEHICLE? HOUSE? OR HERE?	¿Tiene armas, drogas, o grandes cantidades de dinero en el vehículo? ¿Casa? o ¿aquí?
ARE YOU SURE?	¿Está seguro?
WHERE ARE THEY?	¿Dónde están?

MISC. COMMON SPANISH TERMS FOR MOTOR CARRIER INSPECTIONS

DEFECTIVE _____.	Defectuoso _____.
Air Hose	Manguera de aire
Axle/Rear/Front	Eje Trasero / DeFrente
Battery	Batería
Bill of Lading	Conocimiento de embarque
Brake Adjusters	Adjustadores del freno
Brake Chamber	Cámara del freno
Brake Shoe	Zapata del freno
Brake Drum	Tambor del freno
Brake Lining	Balata del freno
Brakes	Frenos
Braking Lights	Luces de freno
Bumper	Parachoques
Cargo	Carga (also slang for Durgs)
Clutch	Embrague (or) cluchay
Daily Inspection Report	Informe de inspección diario
Dashboard	Tablero
Door	Puerta
Driver Out-of-Service	Choferes (fuera-de-servicio)
Driver	Chofér
Electrical system	Sistéma eléctrico
False	Falso
Fan belt	Correa de ventilador
Fan	Ventilador
Flat tire	Pinchazo (or) llanta desinflada
Frame	Estructura
Gas tank	Tanque
Gearshift	Cambio de velocidad
Glove compartment	Guantera
Handle	Manija
Haz/Mat Placard	Aviso de material peligroso
Headlight	Foco delantero (or) /cuarto delantero
Headlights (high/low beam)	Focos (altas/bajas)
Heater	Calefacción
Hood	Capó (or) cofre
Horn	Bocina (or) pito
Ignition	Encendido
Instruments	Instrumentos
Jack	Gato
Leak	Gotera
License plate	Placa (Slang for law enforcement officer)
Lights	Luces
Motor	Motor
Muffler	Mofle
Passenger	Pasajero
Record of Duty Status	Registro de horas de servicio
Starter	Arranque
Steering wheel	Volante
Tire	Llanta
Tires	Llantas
Tractor	Camión
Trailer	Remolque
Transmission	Transmisión
Trunk	Cajuela
Turn signal	Indicador de dirección / señalizador
Vehicle Out-of-Service	Vehiculos (fuera-de-servicio)
Wheel	Rueda
Windshield Wiper	Limpiaparabrisas

COMMON SPANISH TERMS - MOTOR CARRIER INSPECTIONS

BRAKES (FRENOS)

Adequate Tubing Aid (Hanging)	Mangueras de frenos de aire adecuados; mangueras de aire arrastrando
Air Compressor	Compressor del freno de aire
Air/Vacuum System	Aire/sistema de freno de aire
Airbrake Restrictions	Restricción para freno de aire
Brake Drum	Tambor del freno
Brakes Required	Frenos obligatorios
Breakaway Device (Emergency)	Dispositivo de desenganche de emergencia
Front Wheel Brakes	Frenos en las ruedas delanteras
Hose/Tube Damage/Leak	Manguera de freno dañado o escape de aire
Hose/Tube Touching Exhaust Inoperative	Manguera de frenos tocando el escape Frenos inoperativos
Limiting Device (manual brake)	Freno de mano
Linings	Balatas
No Breakaway Protection	Protección de desenganche, obligatorio
Out of Adjustment	Freno fuera de ajuste
Parking Brake Required	Freno para estacionarse, obligatorio
Required All Wheels	Frenos en todas los ejes, obligatorio
Reservoir Pressure Loss	Pérdida de presión en los depósitos de aire
Warning Device (low air)	Aviso de emergencia de bajo presión de aire

COUPLING DEVICES/TOWING METHODS (DEPOSITIVO DE ENGANCHE)

Coupling (Towing of Full Trailer)	Enganche (remolcando un trailer completo)
Coupling Drive/Towaway	Método de cerrojo/operacion de remolques
Fifth Wheel Assemblies (Mounting)	Ensamblaje de la quinta rueda (montadura)
Fifth Wheel (Locking Mechanism)	Mecanismo de cerrojo de la quinta rueda
Safety Chains/Cables (towbar failure)	Cadenas de seguridad/cables. Cadenas o cables de seguridad en caso de que se desconecte o que no opere la barra para remolcar.
Towbar Requirements (chains, etc)	Requirimiento para la barra para remolcar

FRAMES - CHASIS

Accessories Must Be Bolted	Accesorios tienen que ser fijados con tornillo y tuercas
Cab Securement	Aseguramiento de la cabina
Cracked/Broken/Bent/Loose	Chasis quebrado/suelto/rajada/torcida
Frame Rail Flanges	Reborde del chassis
No holes drilled	Sin hoyos aujerados

FUEL SYSTEM (SISTEMA DE COMBUSTIBLE)

Line Protection	Protección de la línea del combustible
Safety Vent	Sistema de ventilación de seguridad para el tanque
Tank Cap Missing	Le falta el tapón del tanque de combustible
Tank Securement	Aseguramiento del tanque de combustible

SUSPENSION (SUSPENSION)

Adjustable Axle-Locking Device	Ajuste de eje, dispositivo para la cerradura
Air Suspension Pressure Loss	Pérdida de aire en la suspensión de aire
Axle Positioning Parts	Posición de las partes de los ejes
Coil Spring Cracked/Broken	Resorte de muelle quebrado o fracturado
Leaf Spring Assembly	Assemblaje del muelle
Torsion Bar	Violación de la barra de torción

TIRES (LLANTAS)

Exceed Tire Weight Rating	Excedir el peso especificado en la llanta
Exposed Fabric	Lona de la llanta expuesta
Flat/Audible Air Leak	Llanta ponchada/escape de aire de la llanta
Front Tread Depth	Llanta delantera; la profudida que le queda la llanta
Regrooved on Front	Delanteras que hayan sido regrurviadas
Tread/Sidewall Separation	Separación de la cara de la llanta de corredera o riel
Under-inflated	Llanta no inflada al peso normal

WHEEL/STUDS/ETC (RUEDAS/TORNILLOS/ETC)

Elongated Stud Holes	hollo del tablique distorcionado (tuercas de las llantas)
Fasteners Loose/Missing	Tuercas de las ruedas flojas o faltantes
Wheel/Rim Cracked	Rueda, rin rajada

OTHER VEHICLE DEFECTS (OTROS DEFECTOS DEL VEHICULO)

Accessories Must Be Bolted	Accesorios tienen que ser fijados con tornillos y tuercas
Battery Installation	Instalación del pilas/baterias
Chafing Hoses	Mangueras de los frenos desgastados
Defroster Inoperative	Descongelador del parabrisas inoperativo
DOT Markings	Número del Departmento de Transportes
Driver View Obstructed	Obstrucción de la vista o movimiento del chofér
Exhaust Discharge Rear or Cab	Descarga de gases del escape atras de la cabina
Exhaust System Location	Posición del sistema de escape
Exhaust Securely Fastened	Sistema de escape aseguarado y fijo
Exhaust Leak Under Cab/Sleeper	Descarga de gases del escape atrás de la cabina
Fire Extinguisher	No esta equipado con extinguidor de incendios
Floor Condition	Condiciones del piso
Front End Structure/Headboard	Estructura delantera/cabecera
Grease/Oil Leaks	Grasa y pérdida de aciete (goteando)
Heaters	Calentador
Horn Inoperative	Claxón inoperativo
Improper Blocking and Bracing	Bloquear / atar / ligamento inappropiado
No Flag on Projecting Load	Uso de bandera para carga sobredimensión
Not Equipped with Seatbelts	Camion no esta equipado con cinturones de seguridad
Overweight	Pasado de peso
Rearend Protection	Protección trasera (parachoces)
Rearvision Mirrors	Espejos retrovisores
Securement Systems	Sistema de aseguramiento: todo tipo de equipo para asegurar la carga sobre el vehículo:ejemplo: cadenas, cables, cuerda, .
Sleeper Berth Requirements	Reglamento del camarote
Speedometer Inoperative	Velocimetro inoperativo
Splashguards - Local Law	Guardafangos ley local
Truck Side Window	Ventana lateral del camion
Vehicle Access Requirements	Requerimiento de acceso al vehículo; tener suficientes escalones y agarraderas y / o plataforma
Warning Devices/Stopped Vehicles	No esta equipado con avisos de emergencia/vehiculo parado
Window Obstructed	Obstrucción en la ventana
Windshield Condition	Condiciones del parabrisas
Windshield Wipers Inoperative	Limpiaparabrisas imperativo
Worn/Welded Universal Joint	Juntura universal gastado o soldado

INSPECTIONS (INSPECCIONES)

No Post-trip Inspection — No se hizo inspección después del viaje
No Pre-trip Inspection — No se hizo inspección antes del viaje
Periodic Inspection — Inspecciones periódicamente
Proof of Annual Inspection — Prueba de la inspección anual del vehículo

LICENSE REQUIREMENTS/STANDARDS - (REQUERIMIENTOS DE LA LICENCIA/NORMAS)

Driver Under 21 — Chofer menor de 21 años
Driving While Disqualified — Manejando cuanda esta descalificado
No/Invalid Commercial License — Sin licencia comercial (Licencia Federal)
Non-English Speaking — Chofer no sabe hablar ingles
Unauthorized Passenger — Pasajero no autorizado
Unauthorized Driver — Chofer no autorizado

HOURS OF SERVICE (HORAS DE SERVICIO)

10-Hour Rule — Regla de 10 horas
15-Hour Rule — Regla de 15 horas
60/70 Hour Rule — Regla 60/70 horas
Failed to Retain 7 Previous Days — Falta de tener el libro de horario de los últimos 7 días
False Log — Libro de horario falso
Log Not Current — Libro de horario no esta al corriente
Log Not in Possession — No estar en posseccion el libro de horario actual
No Log — No tener libro de horario

CONDITION OF DRIVER (CONDICIONES DEL CHOFER)

Driver Use/Possess Drugs/Alcohol
Uso/Possesión de drogas/alcohol por parte del chofer

Ill/Fatigued — Enfermo/cansado

(Thanks to the Arizona DPS who assisted in providing terms for the truck inspection section)

TRAVEL AND MODES OF TRAVEL

ABROAD - el extranjero
(eh! ex-trahn-HAY-roh)

BAGGAGE - equipaje (ay-kee-PAH-hay)
HAND LUGGAGE - equipaje de mano
(ay-kee-PAH-hay day MAH-noh)
LUGGAGE - equipaje (ay-kee-PAH-hay)
KNAPSACK - mochila (moh-CHEE-lah); - saco (SAH-koh)
SUITCASE - maleta (mah-LAY-tah)
CHARTER FLIGHT - vuelo fletado
(BWEH-loh fleh-TAH-doh)

CITY - ciudad (see-oo-DAHD)
KILOMETERS FROM CLOSEST CITY - Kilómetros a la ciudad mas cercana
(kee-LOH-may-trohs ah lah see-oo-DAHD mahs sayr-KAH-nah)

COMPASS DIRECTION - Dirección a la brujula
(dee-rehk-SYOHN ah lah BROO-hoo-lah)

LANDING SITE - sitio de aterrizaje
(SEE-tee-oh day ah-TAYR-ee-ZAH-hay)

NAMES OF PASSENGERS - Nombres de pasajeros
(NOHM-brays day pah-sah-HAY-rohs)
STOP OVERS - parada (bus/train) pah-RAH-dah
Air travel[(ays-KAH-lah)] (escala)
CARGO - carga (KAHR-gah)
COUNTRY - pais (pah-EES)
DOWNTOWN - centro (SEHN-troh)
OUTSKIRTS - afueras (ah-FWAY-rahs); or - alrededores
(ahl-ray-day-DOOR-ays)
FLIGHT - vuelo (voo-AY-loh)
FLIGHT INFORMATION
AIRLINE - linea aérea
(LEE-nay-ah ah-AYR-ee-ah)
AIRPLANE - avión (ah-vee-OHN)
DESCRIPTION - descripción
(days-kreep-SYOHN)

AIRPORT- aeropuerto; or
   (ah-ayr-oh-**PWEHR**-toh)
   - puerto aéreo (S. Amer.)
   (poo-**AIR**-toh ah-**AYR**-ee-oh)

ARRIVAL- llegada (yay-**GAH**-dah)

BOARDING PASS-
tarjeta de embarque
(tahr-**HAY**-tah day ehm-**BAHR**-kay)

CANCELED-
cancelado
(kahn-say-**LAH**-doh)

CO-PILOT- co-piloto (koh-pee-**LOH**-toh)
CREW- tripulación
   (tree-poo-lah-**SYOHN**)
DEPARTURE- salida (sah-**LEE**-dah)
DESTINATION- destino
   (day-**STEE**-noh)
DIRECT FLIGHT- vuelo directo
   (voo-**AY**-loh dee-**REHK**-toh)

EARLY- temprano (tehm-**PRAH**-noh)

ECONOMY CLASS- clase de economia
   turista (S. Amer.)
(**KLAH**-say day ee-koh-noh-**MEE**-ah /
   too-**REE**-stah)
FIRST CLASS- primera clase
   (pree-**MAY**-rah **KLAH**-say)

FLIGHT- vuelo (voo-**AY**-loh)

GATE #- número de puerta
   (**NOO**-may-roh day **PWEHR**-tah)

GROUND CREW- tripulación de tierra
(tree-poo-lah-**SYOHN** day tee-**AYR**-ah)

LATE- atrasado (ah-trah-**SAH**-doh)
ON TIME- a tiempo (ah tee-**EHM**-poh)

PASSENGER LIST- lista de pasajeros
   (**LEE**-stah day pah-sah-**HAY**-rohs)

RESERVATIONS- reservas
   (ray-**SAYR**-vahs)

RETURN TICKET- de regreso
   (day ray-**GRAY**-soh)

R/T TICKET- de ida y vuelta
   (day **EE**-dah ee **BWEHL**-tah)

SEAT- asiento (ah-see-**EHN**-toh)
SEAT NUMBER- número de asiento
(**NOO**-may-roh day ah-see-**EHN**-toh)

TERMINAL- terminal (tayr-mee-**NAHL**)
TICKET- boleto (boh-**LAY**-toh)

TIME OF ARRIVAL- hora de llegada
   (**OH**-rah day yay-**GAH**-dah)

TOURIST CLASS- clase de turista
(S. A.)   (**KLAH**-say day too-**REES**-tah)

FLY- volar (voh-**LAHR**)

TRAVEL- (v) viajar (bee-ah-**HAHR**)

   BY BICYCLE- en bicicleta
      (ehn bee-see-**KLAY**-tah)

   BY BOAT- en barco (ehn **BAHR**-koh)
   BY CAR- en carro (ehn **KAHR**-roh)
   BY FOOT- a pie (ah **PEE**-ay)
   BY PLANE- en avión (ehn ah-vee-**OHN**)

   COMMERCIAL? ¿Comercial?
      (koh-mayr-see-**AHL**)
   PRIVATE? ¿Privado? (pree-**VAH**-doh)
   BY TRAIN- en tren (ehn trehn)
TRAVEL AGENCY- Agencia de viajes
   (ah-**HEHN**-see-ah day bee-**AH**-hays)

TRIP- Viaje (bee-**AH**-hay)

WARRANTS

THERE IS A WARRANT FOR YOUR ARREST.
Hay una orden de arresto para usted.
(Eye **OO**-nah **OHR**-dehn day ah-**REHS**-toh **PAH**-rah oo-**STEHD**)

WE HAVE A SEARCH WARRANT.
Tenemos una orden de registro / cateo.
(Tehn-**EH**-mohs **OO**-nah **OHR**-dehn day reh-**HEE**-stroh / kah-**TAY**-oh)

WHAT

WHAT?	¿Qué?	(Kay)
WHAT? (say again?)	¿Cómo?	(**KOH**-moh)
WHAT CAR IS HE DRIVING?-	¿Qué carro lleva?	(Kay **KAHR**-roh **YAY**-vah)
WHAT COLOR?-	¿De qué color?	(Day kay koh-**LOHR**)
WHAT DID HE/YOU SAY?-	¿Qué dijo?	(Kay **DEE**-hoh)
WHAT DO YOU HAVE?	¿Qué tiene usted?	(keh **TEE-EH**-neh oo-**STEHD**)
WHAT FOR?-	¿Para qué?	(**PAH**-rah kay)
WHAT HAPPENED?	¿Qué ocurrió?	(kay oh-koo-rree-**OH?**)

WHAT IS THAT PERSON'S NAME? ¿Cómo se llama esa persona?
(KOH-mah ES-sah pehr-SOH-nah?)
WHAT IS THAT? ¿Qué es? (Kay ays)
WHAT IS THIS? ¿Qué es esto? (Kay ays AY-stoh)

WHAT IS YOUR ADDRESS AT WORK?
¿Cuál es la dirección de su trabajo?
(Kwahl ehs lah dee-rehk-SEE-OHN deh soo trah-BAH-hoh?)

WHAT KIND OF DRUGS HAVE YOU TAKEN TODAY?
¿Qué clase de drogas ha tomado hoy?
(Keh KLAH-seh deh DROH-gahs ah toh-MAH-doh oy?)

WHAT MONTH? ¿Qué mes? (Kay mays)
WHAT PRICE? ¿Qué precio? (Kay PRAY-see-oh)

WHAT TIME DID YOU ARRIVE? ¿A qué hora llegó?
(Ah Kay OH-rah yay-GOH)

WHAT TIME DID YOU LEAVE?
¿A qué hora salio?
(Ah kay OH-rah sah-lee-OH)

WHAT TIME IS IT GOING TO HAPPEN?   **AMERICAN TIME**
¿A qué hora va a pasar?   (Hora Americana)
(Ah KAY OH-rah vah ah pah-SAHR)

WHAT WAS STOLEN? ¿Qué fue robado? (Kay foo-AH roh-BAH-doh)

WHAT WEEKDAY?
¿Qué día de la semana?
(Kay DEE-ah deh lah say-MAH-nah)

WHAT YEAR? ¿Qué año? (Kay AHN-yoh)
WHAT'S UP? ¿Qué hay? (Kay eye)

WHEN

WHEN? ¿Cuándo? (KWAHN-doh)
WHEN DID YOU LEAVE? ¿Cuándo salió? (KWAHN-doh sah-lee-OH)
WHEN DID HE LEAVE? ¿Cuándo salió? (KWAHN-doh sah-lee-OH)
WHEN DID THEY LEAVE? ¿Cuándo salieron? (KWAHN-doh sah-lee-AY-rohn)
WHEN DID YOU ARRIVE? ¿Cuándo llegaron? (KWAHN-doh yay-GAH-rohn)
WHEN DID HE ARRIVE? ¿Cuándo llegó? (KWAHN-doh yay-GOH)
WHEN DID THEY ARRIVE? ¿Cuándo llegaron? (KWAHN-doh yay-GAH-rohn)
WHEN WERE YOU TO MEET? ¿Cuándo se iban a juntar?
(KWAHN-doh say EE-bahn ah hoon-TAHR)
WHEN WILL HE LEAVE? ¿Cuándo saldrá? (KWAHN-doh sahl-DRAH)
WHEN IS HE COMING BACK? ¿Cuándo vuelve? (KWAHN-doh voo-EHL-vay)
WHEN WILL HE RETURN? ¿Cuándo volverá? (KWAHN-doh vohl-vehr-AH)

WHERE

WHERE? ¿Dónde? (DOHN-day)
WHERE ARE YOU GOING? ¿A dónde va usted? (Ah DOHN-day vah oo-STEHD)
WHERE ARE YOU STAYING? ¿En dónde se queda? (Ehn DOHN-day say KAY-dah)
WHERE ARE THEY STAYING? ¿Dónde están quedando?
(DOHN-day ays-TAHN Kay-DAHN-doh)
WHERE CAN YOU BE CONTACTED DURING THE DAY?
¿Dónde podemos ponernos en contacto con usted durante el día?
(DOHN-deh poh-DEH-mohs poh-NEHR-nohs ehn kohn-TAK-toh kohn
oo-STHED doh-RAHN-teh ehl DEE-ah?)

WHERE DID HE GO?	¿A dónde fué?	(Ah **DOHN**-day foo-**AY**)
WHERE DID YOU COME FROM?	¿De dónde vino?	(Day **DOHN**-day **VEE**-noh)
WHERE DID YOU GET THIS CAR?	¿Dónde compró este carro?	
	(DONDE-deh kom-**PROH** EHS-teh **KAR**-rroh)	

WHERE DID YOU PUT IT?	¿Dónde lo puso?	(**DOHN**-day loh **POO**-soh)
WHERE DID YOU HIDE IT?	¿Dónde lo escondió?	
	(**DOHN**-day loh ays-kahn-dee-**OH**)	
WHERE DO YOU WORK?	¿Dónde trabaja?	(**DOHN**-deh trah-**BAH**-hah?)
WHERE DO YOU LIVE?	¿Dónde vive?	(**DOHN**-day **VEE**-vay)
WHERE HAVE YOU BEEN?	¿Dónde ha estado?	(**DOHN**-day ah ays-**TAH**-doh)
WHERE IS?	¿Dónde está ___ ?	(**DOHN**-day ess-**TAH** _____)
WHERE IS HE GOING?	¿A dónde va?	(Ah **DOHN**-day vah)
WHERE IS IT?	¿Dónde está?	(**DOHN**-day ays-**TAH**)
WHERE IS YOUR _____?	¿Dónde está su __?	(**DOHN**-day ays-**TAH** soo___?
WHERE WAS IT OBTAINED?	¿Dónde lo obtuvo?	(**DOHN**-day loh ohb-**TOO**-voh)
WHERE WAS IT PURCHASED?	¿Dónde fué comprado?	
	(**DOHN**-day foo-**AY** kohm-**PRAH**-doh)	
WHERE WERE YOU LOCATED?	¿Dónde estaba Ud.?	
	(**DOHN**-day ays-**TAH**-bah oo-**STEHD**)	

WHICH

WHICH ¿Cuál? (KWAHL)
WHICH ONE? ¿Cuál? (KWAHL)
WHICH DATE? ¿Qué fecha? (keh **FEH**-chah)

WHO

WHO?	¿Quién?	(Kee-**EHN**)
WHO CALLED THE POLICE?	¿Quién llamó a la policia?	
	(kay-**YEHN** yah-**MOH** ah lah poh-lee-**SEE**-ah)	
WHO DID IT?	¿Quién lo hizo?	(Kee-**EHN** loh **EE**-zoh)
WHO GAVE IT TO YOU?	¿Quién se lo dió?	(Kee-**EHN** say loh dee-**OH**)
WHO IS THE BOSS?	¿Quién es el jefe?	(Kee-**EHN** ays ayl **HAY**-fay)
WHO IS THE VICTIM?	¿Quién es la víctima?	(Kee-**EHN** ehs la **VEEK**-tee-mah)
WHO OWNS IT?	¿Quién es el dueño?	(Kee-**EHN** ays ayl **DWAY**-noh)

WHO SAW WHAT HAPPENED?
¿Quién vió lo que pasó?
(Kee-**EN** vee-**OH** lo keh pah-**SOH**)

WHO SOLD IT TO YOU?
¿Quién se lo vendió a Ud.?
(Kee-**EHN** say loh vehn-dee-**OH** ah oo-**STEHD**)

WHO WAS IT?	¿Quién fué?	(Kee-**EHN** foo-**AY**)
WHO WAS THERE?	¿Quién estuvó allí?	(Kee-**EHN** ays-too-**VOH** ah-**YEE**)
WHOSE?	¿De quién es?	(Day kee-**EHN** ess)

WHY ¿Por Qué? (Pohr kay)

WITNESSES

DO YOU HAVE WITNESSES?
¿Tiene usted testigos?
(Tee-**EHN**-nay oo-**STEHD** tehs-**TEE**-gohs)

WHO WITNESSED THIS?
¿Quién presenció esto?
(Kee-**EHN** pray-**SEHN**-see-**OH** **AYS**-toh)

WHO SAW WHAT HAPPENED?
¿Quién vió lo que pasó?
(Kee-**EHN** vee-**OH** loh keh pah-**SOH**)

WHO DID IT?
¿Quién lo hizo?
(Kee-**EHN** loh **EE**-zoh)

HISPANIC STREET GANGS

Although black street gangs receive the most media attention, Hispanic gang members far out-number the Bloods and Crips and, in some areas of the country, are increasing faster than all of the other gangs. Contributing to the growth of Hispanic gangs is an expanding population, an extremely high school dropout rate, and denial of the problem by some authorities and institutions.

HISTORY

Hispanic or Mexican groups first formed in California in the early 1900's in an effort to protect their neighborhood; they called themselves, "**soldiers of the neighborhood.**" By the end of the 1930's and into the early 1940's these groups evolved into street gangs, similar to what exits now. It was not long before gang rivalries grew, and violence over turf boundaries became a way of life. In fact, much of the violence among the Hispanic gangs today is attributed to turf loyalty, a philosophy held so deeply that they will, as they proudly proclaim, "**Die for the dirt.**"

PROFILE

Age: Although the average age of Hispanic gang members is 11-22 years, there are members who are younger and members who are older. Older members may not be actively "**gang banging**" in the street, but they nonetheless maintain the philosophy of the gang and continue to live by its traditions

SEX: Hispanic gang members are primarily male. Equal rights for females in Hispanic gangs **does not** exist.

RACE: Some whites and blacks belong to Hispanic gangs, but they are never fully accepted by the predominant Hispanic membership. Whites and blacks in Hispanic gangs are often culturally Hispanic, a result of having been raised in the neighborhood.

HAIR: Short hair has become popular. Some shave their heads bald but leave a small "tail" in the back. Many gang members wear mustaches and goatees.

CLOTHING: Clothes are generally three to four sizes too large. White tee-shirts are popular, sometimes worn tucked in, or so oversized that they extend below the buttocks. "**Dickies**" brand tan or black oversized pants are popular, as are baggy shorts that extend below the knees. Stocking caps are often worn to create the illusion of hair when the gang member is shaved.

TATTOOS: Most Hispanic gang members wear religious and gang tattoos from their neck to their feet. The name of the member's gang is almost always found somewhere on the body, as well as his street moniker. First names are also common, as is the first name of the member's mother. The numbers "**13**" and "**14**" indicate which side of Bakersfield, California the member is from. The number "13" sometimes written with the word "**Sur,**" indicates the member is from Southern California, below Bakersfield. The number "14", sometimes seen with the word "**Norte**", means the gang member is from northern California. (These directional designations can apply to other cities. Tattoos of prison gangs will be discussed later).

MONIKERS: Street names are usually associated with the member's physical features or some macho characteristic. Sometimes members who are from different cliques, but still within the same gang, will use the same moniker. **(See Spanish Nicknames.** The nicknames will aid in reading graffiti).

84

FEMALE HISPANIC GANG MEMBERS

Hispanic gangs are predominately male. Female gang members are tolerated by the males as long as they follow the rules of the male structured gang, know their place, and do not try to go beyond it. In a way, females are a separate clique from male members. Completely separate female gangs are rare.

LEADERSHIP AND STRUCTURE

As in the case with most all other street gangs, there is no formal leadership such as president and vice-president that are common in hard-core prison gangs. Leadership, such as it is, is generally assumed by a person who has demonstrated leadership qualities or skills in a given area. For example, if a gang is going to attack another gang, the member with the best fighting skills will assume leadership for the attack. But the role will be short lived, usually just long enough to carry out the mission.

In smaller gangs and in communities with relatively fewer Hispanic gang members, leadership may be more pronounced. Still, leadership will be transitory, since leaders are generally criminally active and get arrested.

Many Hispanic gangs are so large that they have become unwieldy. Out of necessity, cliques have formed, dividing the gangs into more manageable groupings, usually by age, a specific area within the turf, and specialty. For example, one clique may consist of members 16-18 years of age who specialize in drive-by shootings.

Although gang members will claim a particular gang and a specific clique, they often will identify themselves just be the name of their clique.

Once a member, they will remain in the clique throughout their gang career.

"Pee Wees," are likely to use PCP, LSD, speed, and crack Cocaine; many veteranos graduate to Heroin.

MIND SET

A Hispanic gang member is 100% loyal to his gang, and will maintain his loyalty to the death. His membership is who he is, what he is about, and what he exists for; he is proud of it and he brags about it. Even if he moves, he will maintain loyalty to his old gang, while he fights the gang in the new neighborhood.

Hispanic gang members are more mentally entrenched in the gang than black gang members are. Although the gang format provides the young Hispanic his identify and a feeling of belonging to family - the same elements young blacks seek in the gang - it is for the Hispanic a complete approach to life. It is not something he does just to hand out. Many of them believe fervently that their gang is more important than themselves.

Some male gang members want to be seen by others as a **"vato loco,"** a crazy guy. They will act out so as to be perceived as the craziest and the most feared member in the gang. Some will tattoo three dots on the back of their hand indicating **"mi vida loca,"** my crazy life.

From time to time there will be a weak member who will inform police, but a hard-core traditional Hispanic gang member will not **"rata,"** or rat, on other gang members. He will go to prison or die, but he will not inform on his home boys. To be an informant to the police is to bring disgrace to himself and to his family members. In fact, most gangs will not complain about, nor testify against, rival gangs, preferring to handle the dispute themselves.

TURF

In cities like Los Angeles where there are large Hispanic neighborhoods, gang members view themselves as protectors of the turf. They live by the motto, **"to die for the dirt,"** meaning they will stand up to, and defend against, rival gangs, government authorities, anyone who ventures across their boundary lines. Their turf is where they exist; it is part of their identity; it is their world. Many Hispanic gangs are names after their turf, for example 18th Street, Pine Street Cholos, 14th Street Cholos, and Eastside.

Some young Hispanic refuse to go to school because to get to it they would have to leave their turf and cross a rival gang's turf. To make the journey would be too dangerous, so many young people do not attend school.

In smaller cities where Hispanic gangs are increasing rapidly but there is not yet a Hispanic turf, gang members tend to cruise all over the city, into the suburbs, then out further to connecting towns, all in the same night.

GRAFFITI

Hispanic gang members have a reputation for creating stylistic, sometimes beautiful graffiti they call "**placasso**," or "**placa**," meaning sign or plaque. In fact, so great is their reputation, black gangs will occasionally ask Hispanic graffiti artists to illustrate their gang names on walls.

Hispanic gangs use their graffiti to show turf ownership and as a way of glorifying the gang. It illustrates clearly who controls the turf, and it sends a warning and a challenge to rival gangs.

Hispanic gang graffiti is typically written in large block or outline-style lettering. It generally includes the name of the gang, the name of the artist, and great claims as to the gang's strength. For example, the word "**rifa**," which means to rule, or "**por vida**," meaning, for life. The number "**13**" is commonly used t proclaim that the gang is crazy, but it can also mean that they are from Southern California or the southern section of a geographic location.

In cities where there is a heavy concentration of Hispanic turf, gang graffiti that has not been crossed out or written over indicates that the gang rules the area. When a second gang has crossed out or written over another gang's graffiti, an act that is referred to as a "**puto mark**," the territory is being contested. This often leads to a confrontation between the two gangs.

HOUSING AND APARTMENTS

It is not uncommon for a Hispanic gang member to live with his parents. Since the gang lifestyle is often third and fourth generation, parents accept their children's gang involvement. In fact, some parents are still active in various criminal activities such as drug sales.

Drive-by shootings against houses and apartments are common where a gang member lives with his parents. Sometimes when members are anticipating a drive-by, they will set up defensively in the house, on the roof or in the yard. When the drive-by takes place, they return fire.

INTERACTION WITH OTHER GANGS

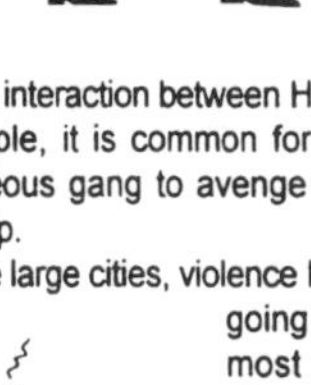

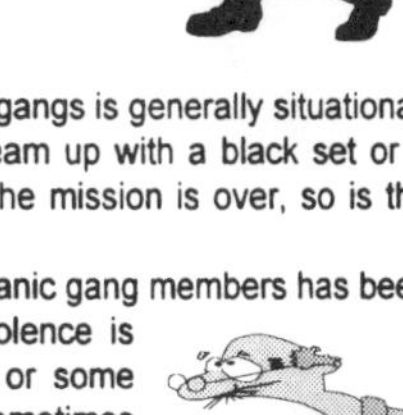

Nonviolent interaction between Hispanic gangs and other gangs is generally situational. For example, it is common for a Hispanic clique to team up with a black set or a miscellaneous gang to avenge another gang. When the mission is over, so is the relationship.

In some large cities, violence between black and Hispanic gang members has been going on for years. The violence is most often over drugs, turf, or some disrespectful act or words. Sometimes the violence is short lived, such as when a Hispanic gang helps another gang to fight a rival. Violence can break out instantly in a shopping mall after no more provocation than a glare from a rival gang member toward a Hispanic gang member. ("*Mad Dogging*.")

SCHOOL

Generally, Hispanic gang members do poorly in school and either get kicked out or drop out. Some end up in alternative schools that work with students who cannot function in mainstream schooling. Others never return to school at all.

In schools where Hispanic gang members attend alongside other gangs, there will almost always be gang activity. In mild form it will consist of graffiti and other acts of vandalism. Violence will consist of fights, knifings and shootings. Unfortunately, and it happens often, innocent students and teachers get caught in the middle.

THE FUTURE OF HISPANIC GANGS

In Los Angeles and other large cities, Hispanic gangs are entrenched. Many of them consist of second, third, and fourth generation gang members who know no other way of life. If it were even possible to eradicate Hispanic gangs in these areas, it would be a monumental task that would take years.

There is probably a greater chance for some success in those smaller communities just now experiencing a Hispanic gang problem. However, it requires a strong response from the schools, police, the juvenile justice system and the community. If the effort is not there, if people deny that there is a problem or minimize its seriousness, outside Hispanic gangs will quickly infest an area and recruit at-risk youth. In a short time there will be Hispanic gangs unyielding to the best efforts to eradicate them. *(Excerpts reprinted from Street Gangs ©1993 by permission of the publisher: Pocket Press Inc., 9220 SW Barbur Blvd., Portland, Oregon 503-291-9308).*

GANG HANDSIGNS

To the gang member, communication with handsigns is just as important as written or verbal forms of communication. Handsigns have become a non- verbal form of speech for the gang member and the **"throwing of handsigns"** has resulted in gang violence. Throwing or flashing handsigns is another way to announce your presence or offer a challenge. Some gang members view the flashing or handsigns as an insult. For every challenge or insult demands a response.

Handsigns are letters of the alphabet formed with the hand and fingers. Usually the letters represent the gang name or affiliation. In groups several letters can be formed to send a message. Like graffiti and stylized clothing, handsigns are a form of gang advertisement. Remember all these characteristics have three functions: to peer gang members they are a form of greeting; to rival gang members they are a form of challenge or threat, and to non-gang members they can be a form of intimidation.
(Excerpt from "Gangs - A Guide to Understanding Street Gangs" by Al Valdez. 3233 Grand Ave., Suite N-326, Chino Hills, CA 91709-1489).

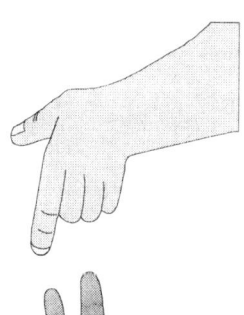

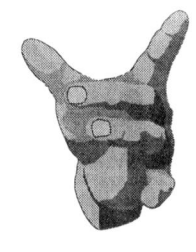

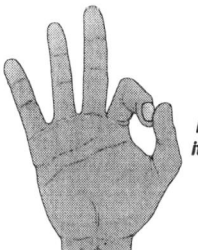

Be careful using this "O.K." symbol as in many countries it has a very derogatory meaning such as "ass hole".

Characteristic "Nicknames" sometimes used by Hispanics

Aguila -	sharp or alert		Japones -	slanted eyes
Alemán -	blonde and big		Joker -	One who jokes
Angel -	Angel		Judio -	stingy
Apache -	dark		Junior -	Little guy
Babos-	dummy		La Chista -	small
Bebe -	baby faced		La Marrana -	fat, big eater (pig)
Bino -	wine		La Reina -	clean (the queen)
Bizco -	crossed-eyed		La Liebre -	fast, or long ears (rabbit)
Blackie -	dark skinned		La Lija -	tall and slender (file)
Bobo -	dummy		La Rata -	thief, informant (the rat)
Borrado -	hazel eyes		La Prieta -	dark skinned
Borrego -	very curly hair		La Pachona -	hairy
Brujo -	witch doctor		Ladrón -	thief
Cabezón -	big head		Lencho -	short for "Florencio"
Camalaco -	big and blonde		Lil' Man -	Short or has little influence
Camaron -	red, scaly skin		Loco -	crazy
Capitán -	captain or leader		Maestro -	teacher
Chacho -	boy		Malo -	the bad one
Chango -	ape-looking (Chango is also the African diety for Violence and Death). Chango in the Afro-Carribean cults are representative of the Catholic saint, St. Barbara. Cuban criminals will often have the dipiction of St. Barbara be holding a chalice in her hand and is represented by the color red (blood).		Manco -	crippled or lame
			Mocho -	amputee
			Mondo -	Short for "Armando"
			Moreno -	dark
			Mosca -	"Fly" One who hangs around
			Muñeco -	babyface, handsome (doll)
			Negro -	black or dark
			Neto -	the truthful one
			Orejón -	big ears
Chaparro -	short		Oso -	hairy (bear)
Chato -	guy		Pájaro -	small (bird)
Chico -	small		Panzón -	large stomach
Chico -	little guy		Papa -	Dad
China -	girl		Patro -	Patron or "boss"
Chino -	curly hair		Payaso -	the clown
Chivo -	young guy or head like a goat		Pee Wee -	A Pee Wee
Chopo -	short		Pelón -	bald
Choto -	bug-nosed		Pocho -	Tex-Mex
Chueco -	physically impaired		Porky -	fat
Chuey -	short for Jesus		Profe -	teacher
Colorado -	red hair		Ratón -	small built (big rat)
Conejo -	long ears		Raunchy -	gross dude
Cowboy -	wild white guy		Rostro -	big and strong
Coyote -	sly		Sapo -	One with big eyes (toad)
Cuajo Largo -	big eater			(Also slang for a "police sap".)
Curandero -	witch doctor/herb healer		Seco -	The quiet one (dry one)
Diablo -	"Devil"		Snake -	sneaky like a snake
Doche -	Dutch		Sordo -	deaf
Spider -	One who is nimble or			
Elefante -	big ears or fat			can spin a web of influence
Falcón -	hooked nose		Tigre -	fighter (tiger)
Flaco -	skinny		Topo -	dumb looking
Flojo -	lazy		Tlacuache -	sneaky
Frog -	like a frog		La Trpa -	tall and thin
General -	general \ leader		Tuerto -	one-eyed
Genio -	genius		Turkey -	a dummy or thin neck
Giro -	fighting cock		La Tusa -	wise (owl)
Gordo -	fat		La Venada -	fast and sleek (deer)
Guero -	blonde or white guy		Viejo -	old or an experienced man.
Guerrero -	Warrior or Soldier		Wino -	one who drinks wine alot
Huero -	blonde		La Zorra -	smart (fox)
Indio -	Indian looking			

Nicknames will assist in reading graffiti

HISPANIC PRISON GANG TATTOOS

As far back as we have had penal institutions *("Pinta" Spanish for penitentiary)*, there have always been a tendency for inmates to band together and form gangs in an attempt to gain control and/or intimidate weaker or less aggressive inmates as well as attempting to cause disruption of prison authority *(other slang for Jail include: Bote, Carcel, Torcida and Tanque).*

These inmate groups are very distinctive from other inmate groups in that they demand absolute obedience and have fierce loyalty to the parent group. When a problem or situation develops *(known as a "Muleta"),* this loyalty has always and predictably materialized in the form of swift and absolute retaliation without regard for their own safety or consequences. They obtain this obedience compelling every potential member *("Carnal" meaning brother or "Camarada" meaning friend or associate)* to make a *"death oath"* of allegiance to the group. The belief behind most of the Hispanic prison gangs is based on the premise *"Blood In, Blood Out."* Once inmates become members of these prison gangs, they are in them forever, *("Sempre")* for life *(Por Vida).* No one gets out - alive. This ensures that only those individuals who are cold-hearted, violent and loyal enough are taken in as a member. They must demonstrate their loyalty to the group by fulfilling a *"hit" or "contract"* on an inmate marked by the group (Other synonyms include: "Give him the big picture", "Give him a bus ticket home", "Green Light", "He got out of the car" (defector from the gang). Once he has taken his oath a *(a "Juramento")* and demonstrated his loyalty to the gang's rules known as *"Movidas"*, a meeting (**"Junta"**) is called. A vote is taken to see if he is accepted. (In some gangs the members will kill anyone wearing their gang tattoo without authorization).

The goals of most prison gangs are control all drug trafficking into penal institutions. They are also involved in murder, robbery, assault *(inside and outside of the prison),* protections rackets, attempting to force weaker inmates into prostitution and extortion. As mentioned their illegal activities are not just limited within the prison walls. They function outside in the community upon release and are commonly involved in murder, contracts of assassinations, burglary, money laundering, the transportation of illegal aliens, guns *("armas")*, narcotics *(drogas)*, prostitution, protection rackets involving small Mexican businesses. Often a paroled member *("Pinto")* when released from prison is ordered to call a *"contact"* in the area the member is paroled to. The "contact" in turn gets the parolee help in getting criminally involved in the community. Any profits obtained from their illegal activities are sent to other incarcerated members. Part of the illicit profits are used to pay attorneys for legal advice and to post bail for other arrested members. (Many prison gangs are involved in an ever continuing effort to undermine prison officials by filing frivolous law suits charging false allegations of prison mismanagement, harassment, brutality by correctional employees often referred to as ***"Maranos" (pigs), "Perros" (dogs), "La Jura", "Pinches" (bastards and other derogatory synonyms).***

Following is a brief synopsis of the varied Hispanic prison gangs considered to be the most violent and dangerous to public safety officers. The list is not intended to be all inclusive but to give the reader a basic understanding of the group and the tattoos they wear. These tattoos *("placas" slang for tattoo, police, graffiti, badge or car license plate)* serve as a *"Red Flag" or "Trip Wire"* that the wearer should be considered extremely dangerous and poses a potential threat.

These tattoos *(or "Cupia" meaning copy)* are those that are known to be the most often used by mentioned Hispanic prison gangs members. They are subject to change by gang members as they become identifiable by public safety officials.

Some members are tattooing over their prison gang tattoo to cover *"track marks" (drug injection marks)* or some are placing the tattoo *(also known as "Marcas" or "Tatuajes")* on lesser exposed parts of the body such as the inside of the upper arm, ankle or neck. A good method to determine if a prison gang tattoo has been tattooed over, is to take a damp cloth and wet the tattooed area, the original tattoo can often be identified.

Officers should keep in mid that the tattoo is a *"silent language"* used to communicate information from one gang member to another often to indicate gang affiliation, intimidation how "bad or violent" the wearer is (is part of their *"machismo"* or maleness). It can also send a statement of resentment or feeling toward another such as the tattooed word *"AZTLAN"* or "Lost Land", meaning according to many Hispanics the occupied Mexican land unlawfully seized, by the U.S. including California,

New Mexico, Texas and Arizona IE: The Treaty of Guadalupe.

(Note: Keep in mind that these inmates are aware that law enforcement officers are identifying members by their tattoos. In certain instances the gang hierarchy is allowing some members to not wear the tattoo at all. These members can be given special assignments without others knowing their affiliation with the organization.)

The Mexican Mafia (Fig. 1)

Considered the most violent, dangerous, and well organized group in the U.S. Prison population. Formed at a California Vocational Institution in the 1950's, the Mexican Mafia, or EME (the letter M in Spanish), is comprised primarily of Mexican-Americans. It is common for members in California and Texas to refer to each other as **"MERECIDOS"** meaning the **"deserved ones."** Outside the prison system, the Mexican Mafia is reportedly involved in criminal activity such as contract killings and narcotics' trafficking. Thee following is a representative collection of Mexican Mafia tattoos. (Fig. 1. The above tattoo the "EME" symbol, means, "I am" proud to be a Mexican).

EME Mexicana (Fig. 2)

The 'EME" Mexicana" symbols is used by the Mexican Mafia on many of their tattoos.

EME Mexicana
Fig. 3

A variation of the "EME Mexicana" symbol. Note the hand which signifies the hitting of the chest indicating, "I am proud to be a Mexican."

Mexican Flag
Fig. 4

The "Mexican Flag" tattoo above is very similar to the actual flag of Mexico. The flag signifies an eagle sitting on a cactus with a serpent in its mouth. (Gang members define this tattoo as the triumph of Good over Evil. Good being the Mexican Mafia and the Evil being their enemies or law enforcement officers).

Mexican Flag
Fig. 5.

The 'Mexican Flag' tattoo is another rendition of the actual Mexican Flag.

Eternal War
Fig. 6.

The tattoo is the Mexican Mafia symbol for "Eternal War."

Mexikanemi (Mexican Mafia - Texas)

(Fig 7). is the largest and fastest growing prison gangs in Texas. Mexikanemi translated means "Free Mexicans" but are better known as the Mexican Mafia. The group is involved in murder and narcotic trafficking both inside and outside of prison. Mexikanemi are rivals of the Texas Syndicate.

Mexikanemi (Mexican Mafia - Texas) Fig 7A

Another rendition of a Mexikanemi tattoo. The daggers indicate violence and death.

Aztland (Knife) Fig. 8.

"*AZTLAN*" or 'Lost Land', meaning according to many Mexicans the occupied Mexican land unlawfully seized, by the U.S. including California, New Mexico, Texas and Arizona IE: The Treaty of Guadalupe).

Mafia Mexicana (Fig 9.)

Note the Virgin Mary in the tattoo which has much religious significance. Also note the bars and chain and ball with the number 15. (15th letter in the Spanish alphabet is "M".

Again the significance of the knives. A symbol of violence and death.

Aztland with sombrero
(Fig. 10)

Note the "M" on the handles of each of the knives.

Mafia Mexicana
(Fig 11).

The significance of the woman in the background is of particular importance to law enforcement officers.

The women in Mexican culture are expected to be supportive of the men. In the criminal element she is more and more playing the role of supplier of contraband and arms. Keep in mind the danger that the female Hispanic poses to law enforcement officers.

"M" Knife
(Fig. 12)

Note the "M" on this tattoo which of course stands for the "Mexican Mafia".

TEXAS SYNDICATE (TS)
(Fig. 13.)

Contrary to their name, The Texas Syndicate or "TS" (ESE TE) Spanish for the letters "T" and "S" is used by members to identify their gang) was actually formed at Folsom Prison in California ("Califas" is slang for the state of California) by inmates from Texas. Comprised of inmates of Mexican-American descent, the Texas Syndicate was formed in the 1970's to keep other gangs from preying on Texas native inmates. On the outside the "TS" involved in drug trafficking, contract murders, and the smuggling of illegal aliens. The "T.S. is among their most often used symbols for tattoos. Within most Texas Syndicate tattoos, you can usually observe a subliminal "T.S." The "TS" may be very ornate or a crude 'jailhouse tattoo'.

Dragon Heads
(Fig. 14.)

In the TS tattoo, the "T" is in the form of "Dragon Heads." Dragons are also very popular symbols on Texas Syndicate tattoos.

Dragon Heads
(Fig 15.)

Another example of the TS tattoo. Here the S is in the form of "Dragon Heads." (Note the bottom dragon is grasping a dagger which is representative of violence and death).

Dragon and T
(Fig. 16.)

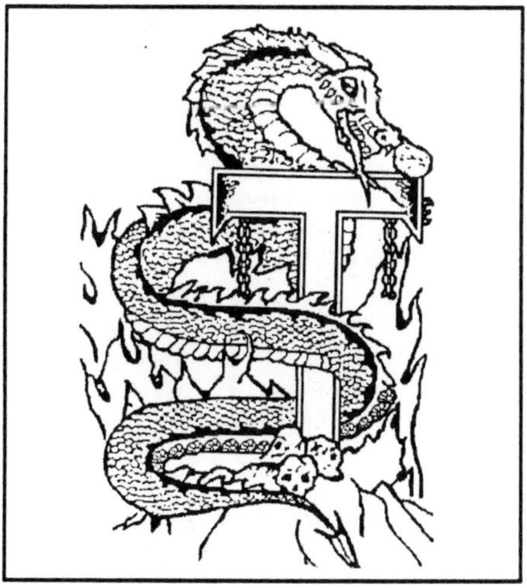

In the "Dragon and T" tattoo above, the S is in the form of a Dragon. The T is obvious but the S is subliminal. Note the skulls heads at the base of the T which again represents violence and death.

Flower and Ribbon
(Fig. 17)

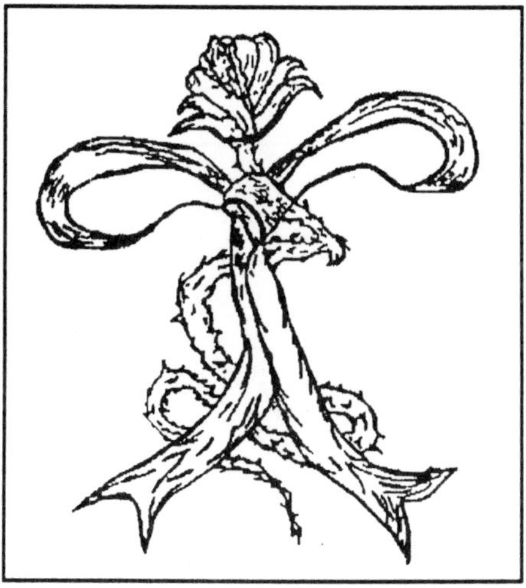

The TS is in the form of a "Flower and Ribbon: in the tattoo above.

MACHO
(Fig. 18.)

The naked women in the tattoo above indicates that the owner is "Macho". Note again the subliminal TS.

Skulls and T
(Fig. 19.)

In the "Skulls and T" tattoo above, note the skull at one end of the S and the dragon at the other end. It takes close scrutiny to make out the TS in this tattoo. Note the female in the background. The message here is that the criminal Hispanic female always stands behind of and supports the men. Women are often used to transport weapons and illegal drugs and contraband.

"TS" and Prison
(Fig. 20.)

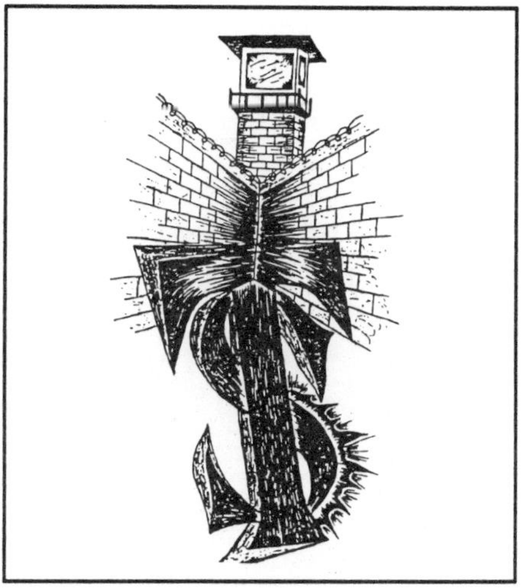

Note the guard tower and prison walls in the background indicating incarceration.

"TS" Sombrero and Prison
(Fig. 21.)

Note the subliminal "TS" on the sombrero. Again the knife indicates violence and death.

NUESTRA FAMILIA (NF)
(Fig. 22.)

Nuestra Familia in the mid- 1960's, a group of Mexican-American inmates, incarcerated at Solidad Prison in California, established the Nuestra Familia. Formed to protect the younger rural inmates *(so called "Farmers" or "Farmeros")* from the older, more experienced criminals including the Mexican Mafia. The NF soon became a well organized prison gang and an adversary of the Mexican Mafia.

The NF is well organized and incorporates robbery, narcotics' trafficking, and murder into their illegal enterprises.

The "Sombrero and Dagger" tattoo is a common symbol among members of the "NF". The tattoo represents death and violence as indicated by the blood dripping from the dagger.

Sombrero and Dagger (NF)
(Fig. 23.)

The above tattoo is another example of the "Sombrero and Dagger" symbol used by the "NF".

NF
(Fig. 24.)

The "NF" stands for Nuestra Familia (Our Family) and is common on their tattoos. Again the dagger indicates death and violence.

BULLETS AND BANDOLIER (NF)
(Fig. 24.)

The number of bullets on the bandolier indicates how many killings the wearer has made. This tattoo is only worn by Generals, Captains, and Lieutenants.

CUBAN CRIMINALS

With the Mariel Boatlift several years ago, public safety officers in the U.S. faced a new breed of criminal. Castro expelled from Cuba their unwanted criminal force to the shores of the U.S.

Into the U.S. came thousands of ex-prisoners with their own brand of problems. Criminals who had robbed, raped, and murdered in Cuba, were now on the streets of America. The difference with these criminals was not only did they possess the criminal mentality of violence but possessed prior military training, and physical and psychological abuse while incarcerated in deplorable Cuban prisons. Because of Cuba's system of extreme brutality, Mariel (*Escoria or Scum* as Castro described the criminal element) make the perfect criminal; no remorse or emotion.

The Cuban prison system was a brutal system of punishment and abuse, and only the strongest survived unspeakable treatment. The torturous abuse included physical punishment as well as psychological attacks. Add to this mandatory 3 years of military service and continued training in Cuba's militia, and our public safety officers now had criminals with an extremely sharp knowledge of weaponry and tactics on their hands.

As with any other known criminals, officers should take extra precautions when confronting a criminal Marielito. The following physical attributes and known Cuban tattoos may help you identify the dangerous criminal Marielito: 19-50 years of age; white to black skin tones; poor hygiene; body scars (either from self inflicted during Santeria rituals) or due to poor medical care in Cuba; although not athletically motivated, usually in good physical shape and muscular.

In addition to this new criminal mind, we found ourselves with a new system of identification, the Cuban prisoner's tattoos, which are considered a disgrace among the law abiding Mariel population. Primarily found on the hand, between the thumb and first finger, these tattoos are an indication of the types of crime in which subjects may have been involved. Some of the Cuban criminals may alter or cover up their tattoos to evade identification. They may also say that they are from a different Hispanic background that Cuban. It is not uncommon for the criminal Cuban Marielito to be tattooed on the inside of the lower lip with a series of numbers. Castro found that it was difficult to cover up or remove the lip tattoo due to the risk of infection. The following pages reflect examples of some of these Cuban Government Incarceration Tattoos and their meanings:

Heart and Madre
(Fig. 25.)

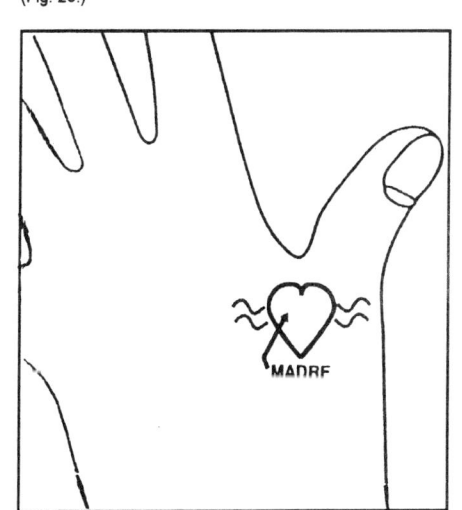

The "Heart and Madre" tattoo represents an executioner.

As mentioned previously, primarily found on the hand, between the thumb and first finger, these tattoos are an indication of the types of crime in which subjects may have been involved. The following tattoo's will be a greenish blue and will be located on the web of the hand as indicated on the previous page:

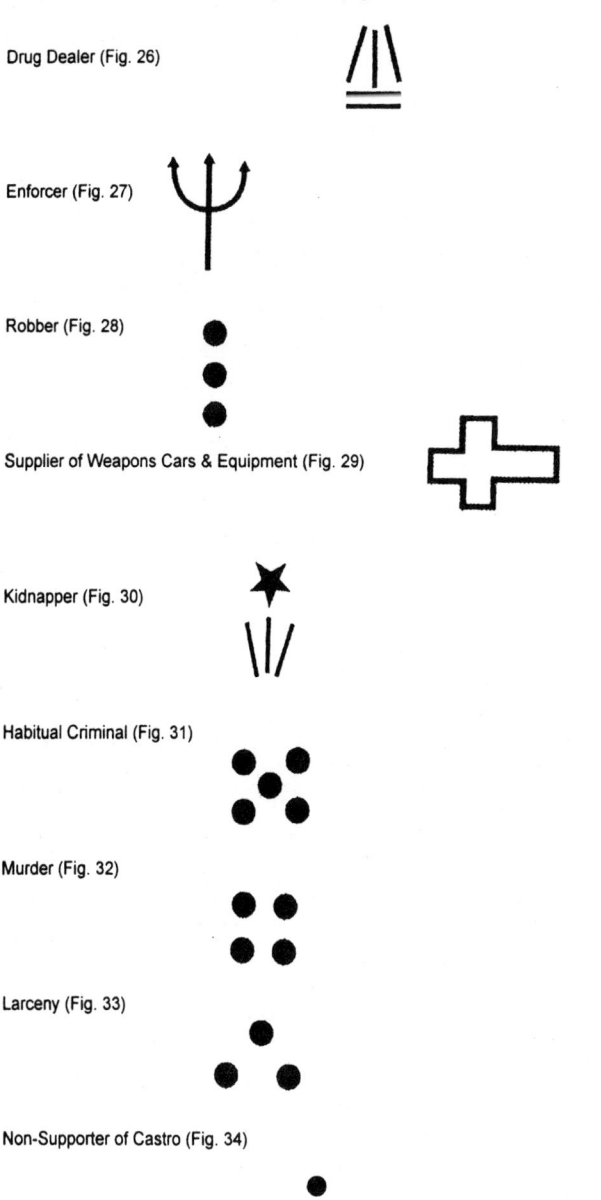

Drug Dealer (Fig. 26)

Enforcer (Fig. 27)

Robber (Fig. 28)

Supplier of Weapons Cars & Equipment (Fig. 29)

Kidnapper (Fig. 30)

Habitual Criminal (Fig. 31)

Murder (Fig. 32)

Larceny (Fig. 33)

Non-Supporter of Castro (Fig. 34)

Robbery (Fig. 35)

Latin Kings (Fig. 36)

The Latin Kings originated in Chicago and is the largest and oldest Hispanic *street* gang. Even though the name implies Latin membership, it is now recruiting whites. Latin Kings are associated with the Texas Syndicate and are involved in narcotic trafficking and robberies.

The Latin Kings use a five and a three pointed crown in their tattoos and graffiti. Most Mexican factions will use the five pointed crown while most Puerto Ricans will use the three pointed crown. (Note the upside down pitchforks, which is a sign of disrespect to the Folk Nation.

Mi Raza Unida (Fig 37)

Mi Raza Unida means My Race United. This prison gang originated in Nevada but has ties in other states. The prison gang also goes by the name of *"Aguila"* which means *"eagle"*. The word "Aguila" has several slang meanings when used such as for law enforcement officers. (IE: They have sharp eyes like an eagle and are watching.) Also to keep a sharp eye open for the law.

The tattoo is similar to the Mexican Mafia (EME) but are not known to affiliate with them.

Graphics and excerpts provided courtesy Mark S. Dunston from his book "Street Signs", which is available from The Constable Group, Inc.

Mara Salvatrucha (MS) *(Salvatrucha LIT: "Trout Saver")*

The Mara Salvatrucha (MS) has become the fastest growing, hardcore criminal street gangs and has spread to coast to coast *("Trucha" means trout in Spanish. In gang context "trouts" are very smart, wary and hard to catch.)* They are more mobile geographically than any other Hispanic group. They originated from a group of Salvadoran youth who had migrated to the U.S. to escape the civil war which ended in 1992. The gang has now spread into Canada as well. Many older members are "*veterano's*" and are trained in special weapons and military training and will act as the "enforcers". Due to their propensity for violence they pose an extreme threat to law enforcement. The "MS" identifies itself with the number "13" (trece) and the "MS" tattoos, along with the name or abbreviation of their specific clique IE: "La Eme Ese--Tre'Ce," MS 13", ("Sur 13" or "Sureno", indicate Southern California), "WS" (Westside Mara Salvatrucha from Los Angeles). It is common to see "MS" in large letters across the abdomen with "Sur 13". Gang members are now setting in small towns as well as large cities.

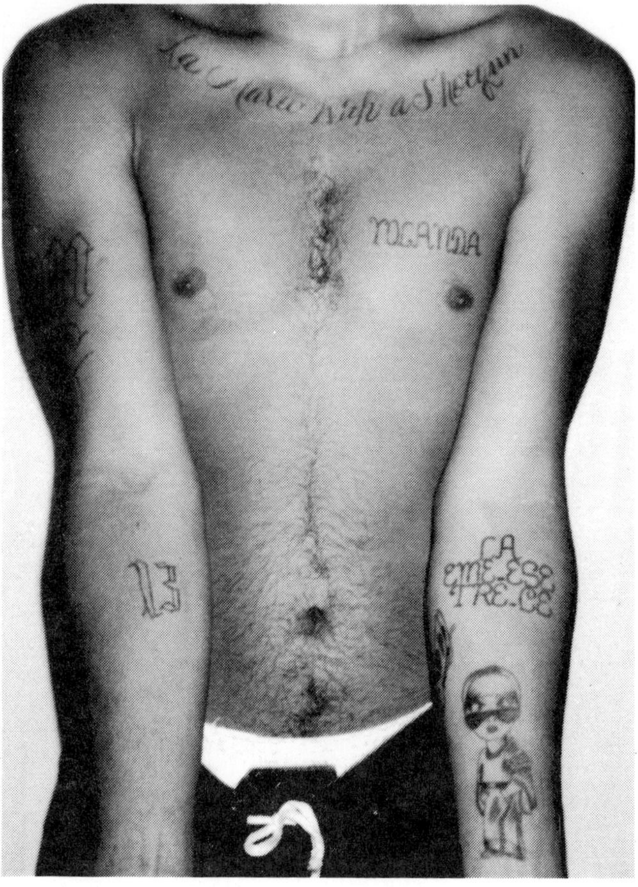

Some of the body tattoos of the "**Mara Salvatrucha**" (**MS**) (Fig. 38)
Photo courtesy Sgt. Bill Valentine, Nevada State Prison (Sgt. Valentine is the author of the Gang Intelligence Manual).

Author's note: If a tattoo with the letters "TJ", "Colonos 36", "Sur", the wearer is from a gang in Tijuana, Mexico. Colonos means 'Colonists' from the 36th Street South area. In Mexico "Colony" is the same as "The Barrio" or "the neighborhood".

106

It is common to see "MS" across the abdomen in large letters. *(Fig. 39)*

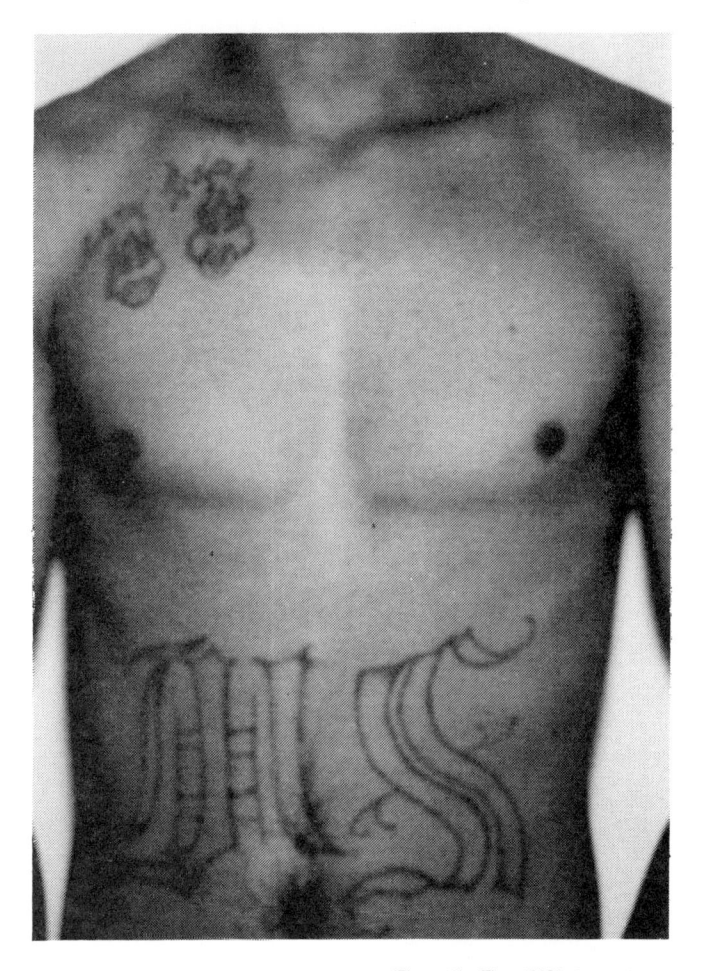

(Fig. 40) The "MS" have been associating themselves with one of the symbols of devil worship as dipicted in this actual wall graffiti. Pentagrams and other symbols of devil worship are also seen in their tattoos and "placas". Their hand sign is formed by the first three fingers pointed downward to form the letter "M" or turned up to represent the devil's pitchfork. It is not uncommon for groups to practice the dark side of Afro-Carribean religions in the furtherance of their criminal enterprises such as Voodoo, Santaria, Brujería and the very dark, Palo Mayombe from Africa. It is common to mix many of these religions together for use to cast spells on enemies, rival gangs or law enforcement officers.

(Fig. 41) **Mara Salvatrucha Street Gang graffiti.**
(Photo courtesy Detective Richard Duran, LAPD Gang Unit)

(Fig. 42) **Gang graffiti of the "Mara Salvatrucha (MS)** Note the 13 SUR
(Photo courtesy Sgt. Bill Valentine, Nevada State Prison)

ORGANIZATIONAL STRUCTURE

(Have subject print names at appropriate level)

PRINT NAMES OF PEOPLE IN ORGANIZATION.
Deletrea los nombres de los personas en la organización.
(Day-lay-TRAY-ah lohs NOHM-brays day lohs payr-SOH-nahs ehn lah ohr-gah-nee-zah-SYOHN)

LIST BY IMPORTANCE.
Registrelos por importancia.
(Ray-GEES-tray-lohs pohr eem-pohr-TAHN-see-ah)

WHAT IS HIS (YOUR) JOB?
¿Cual es su [su] trabajo?
(Kwahl ays soo [soo] trah-BAH-hoh)

PRINT YOUR NAME.
Deletrea su nombre.
(Day-lay-TRAY-ah soo NOHM-bray)

NAME YOUR BOSS.   BOSS- jefe (HAY-fay)
Nombre su jefe.
(NOHM-bray soo HAY-fay)

BOSS OF BOSSES Mero o mero (MEH-roh oh MEH-roh)

_____

_____ _____

_____ _____ _____

_____ _____ _____ _____

ITEMS OF INTEREST. TERMS FOR POLICE.

(INTERNATIONAL)	Polizonte	(Poh-lee-ZOHN-tay)
(MEX)	Policia	(poh-lee-SEE-ah)
(MEX)	Placa	(PLAH-kah)
(MEX) Federal Police	Federales	(Fay-day-RAHL-ays)
(Chile)	Carabinero	(kah-rah-BEE-nay-roh)
(Chile)	Paco	(PAH-koh)
(Argentina)	Gendarme	(shawn-DAHR-may)

SOCIAL SECURITY PREFIX NO'S / ASSIGNED STATES

PREFIX	STATE		PREFIX	STATE	
001-003	NH		486-500	MO	
004-007	ME		501-502	ND	
008-009	VT		503-504	SD	
010-034	MA		505-508	NE	
035-039	RI		509-515	KS	
040-049	CT		516-517	MT	
050-134	NY		518-519	ID	
135-158	NJ		520	WY	
159-211	PA		521-524	CO	
212-220	MD		525,585	NM	
221-222	DE		526-527-800-801	AZ	
223-231	VA		528-529	UT	
232-236	WV		530	NV	
232 *(30)	NC		531-539	WA	
237-246	232 NC		540-544	OR	
247-251	SC		545-573-602-626	CA	
252-260	GA		574	AK	
261-267 589-595	FL		575-576	HI	
268-302	OH		577-579	DC	
303-317	IN		580	VIRGIN ISLANDS	*(01-18)
318-361	IL		580		
362-386	MI		581-584	PUERTO RICO	*(-20-)
387-399	WI			PUERTO RICO	
400-407	KY		585		
408-415	TN		416-424	AL	*(01-18) GUAM
425-428 587-588	MS		586		
429-432	AR		*(20-28)	AM. SAMOA	
433-439	LA		586		
440-448	OK		*(60-78)	PHILIPPINES	
449-467	TX		587	MS	
468-477	MN		602-626	CA	
478-485	IA		700-729	RR. RET. BD.	

* INDICATES THE CENTER DIGITS OF SOCIAL SECURITY NUMBERS.

WHAT IS YOUR SOCIAL SECURITY NUMBER?
Cual es el número de su seguro social?
(Kwahl ays el NOO-may-roh day soo say-GOO-roh soh-see-AHL)

DELEGATIONS OF ASSIGNMENTS

CASE # _____ INCIDENT TYPE _____
CASE OFFICER _____ RADIO# _____ CELL PH# _____
LOCATION# 1 _____
LOCATION# 2 _____
SUSPECT #1 _____ DOB _____
SUSPECT #2 _____ DOB _____
SUPERVISOR _____ RADIO # _____ CELL PH# _____
COMMAND POST PH# _____ DISPATCH PH# _____
S.W.A.T. SUPERVISOR _____ RADIO # _____
BOMB TECH _____ RADIO # _____
AMBULANCE RADIO# _____ FIRE TRUCK RADIO # _____
AIRCRAFT RADIO # _____ HELICOPTER RADIO# _____
PRIORITY RADIO CHANNEL _____ MISC. RADIO #'s _____
SEARCH WARRANT READ BY _____ TIME _____ RECEIPT LEFT? Y__ N__
EVIDENCE OFFICER _____ PHOTO \ VIDEO OFFICER _____
DIAGRAM OFFICER _____ DOG HANDLER _____
ANIMAL CONTROL _____ RADIO TECH _____
TRANSPORT OFFICERS _____
PROSECUTOR _____ PH# _____
PRESS RELEASE OFFICER _____

EQUIPMENT / PERSONNEL

- ❏ A.P.C. & Radio # _____
- ❏ Air Life on Standby
- ❏ Aircraft / Helicopter
- ❏ Ammunition (Extra)
- ❏ Animal Control
- ❏ Barricades
- ❏ Bolt Cutters
- ❏ Bomb Tech
- ❏ Cameras / Film / Videos
- ❏ Cell Phones
- ❏ Children Present
- ❏ Door Key
- ❏ Evidence Kits
- ❏ F.I.R.Sheets/Citations/Booking Shts.
- ❏ Female officer for Female Search
- ❏ Field-test Kits
- ❏ First Aid Kits
- ❏ Food & Water
- ❏ Gas / Gas Masks
- ❏ Maps / Diagrams
- ❏ Marked Cars / U.C. Cars
- ❏ Protective Equip.
- ❏ Radio's
- ❏ Rifles / Shotguns
- ❏ Sign In Sheets
- ❏ Slimjims
- ❏ Spike Strips
- ❏ Tape Recorders / Tapes
- ❏ Translators
- ❏ Warrants / Arrest / Search

BRIEFING

- ❏ Basic Case Details
- ❏ Designation of Entry/Cover Teams
- ❏ Designation of Door Key Man
- ❏ Designation of interview teams
- ❏ Dogs Present (vicious Y/N)
- ❏ Latest Intel
- ❏ Entrances/Exit's (Diagrams)
- ❏ Hospital (location of)
- ❏ Fire and EMT's on Standby
- ❏ List of Officers/Agencies Involved
- ❏ Location & number of suspects
- ❏ Marked Car assignments
- ❏ Names and ID of suspects
- ❏ Photo's of informants
- ❏ Photo's of suspects
- ❏ Photo's of U.C. officers
- ❏ Probation Officers
- ❏ Radio Silence & Secure Freq.
- ❏ Sign in/out of personnel
- ❏ Special Operations (Briefing)
- ❏ Support Agencies (CSD)
- ❏ Suspect Vehicles
- ❏ Suspect's criminal record
- ❏ Suspect's armed
- ❏ Suspects present
- ❏ Suspect's wanted
- ❏ Suspects violent (Y/N)
- ❏ Staging Details
- ❏ Traffic Control (Assignments)
- ❏ Vehicles Present at Location

SLANG AND COLLOQUIALISMS

(Slang and colloquialisms will vary from area to area and from gang to gang).

Words used to warn an individual/accomplice of impending discovery, danger or something about to happen that will affect their freedom or safety. This is vernacular, often used by street people that will affect their freedom or safety. This is vernacular, often used by kind and should not used but listened for. (Note: Much of the slang is of a Mexican influence but several are used in many countries where Spanish is spoken).

WORDS THAT MEAN
Watch Out, Beware, Be Prepared, Lookout

¡Aguas! (AH-goo-ahs)
Lit:--waters

Al alba (al AL-bah)
Lit:--contrary/dawn of day

En guardia (en goo-AHR-dee-ah)
Lit:--on guard

Ensapea (TEX-MEX slang)
(ESS-nah-peh-ah)

Ponte abusado
(POHN-teh ah-boo-SAH-doh)
Lit:--get wise/get on the stick

Trucha (troo-CHAH)
Lit:--trout (Be wary like a fish.)

EX: **Ponte trucha guey, nos esta watchando la jura.**
Cool it / straighten up dummy / the cops are watching us.

Ensapea pendejo, esconde el polvo.
Wise up dummy, hide the coke.

¡Aguas! Hay va la pinche migra.
Lookout! There goes the damn cops.

ABUSE WORDS — to describe weak individuals held in low esteem.

Darío (Dah-REE-ree-oh)
Lit: a proper name

Fácil (FAH-seel) Lit: easy

Culero (KOO-lehr-oh)
Lit: asshole
Slang for: a jerk, or a person who commits anal sex.

Kool-Aid (TEX-MEX slang for a jerk)

Chapete (CHAH-peh-teh)

Safado (Sah-FAH-doh)

SLANG FOR "YES"

Simón (See-MOHN)
Sirol (see-ROHL)
Yesca (YES-kah)
Orale (OH-rah-leh)

SLANG FOR "NO"

Chale (CHAH-leh)
Nel (nehl)

Naranjas (oranges)
(nah-RAHN-hahs)

Nixon (NEEK-sohn)

MARIJUANA SLANG

Yierba (YEHR-bah) Lit: Weed
Yesca (YES-kah) (slang)
Toque (TOH-que) Lit: Shock
Verdura (vehr-DOOH-rah)
Lit: Vegetation
Mota (MOH-tah) Lit: small knot of cloth
Grifa (GREE-fah)
Lit: italics in printing

COCAINE SLANG

Los Goodies
Lit: the goodies

El Producto (proh-DOOK-toh, el)
Lit: the product

The touch to the eye with the index finger is an international symbol that the police are watching. It may also be used as a signal to "Watch the cop and get ready to attack". In other ethnic groups this can mean the person is crazy or stupid.

El Polvo (POHL-voh, el)
Lit: the powder

El Masca Dientes
(MAHS-kah DEE-EHN-tess)
Lit: The tooth chewer

La Gringa (GREEN-gah)
Slang for gibberish; or American female

El Saca Moco
(SAH-kah MOH-koh, el)
Lit: The booger remover

HEROIN SLANG

Chiva (CHEE-vah) Lit: Female goat

Tecate (the-KAH-teh) a brand of beer

El Shoot it

Veneno (veh-NEH-noh) Lit: poison

Tumba (TOOM-bah) Lit: tomb

Negra (NEG-rah)
Lit: negro female or black object

Mescla (Slang for Speedball)
(MEHS-clah) Lit: mixture

EX: ¡Me esta poniendo chichona!
I'm tired of this crap!

Estoy hasta el copete con tus chingaderas.
I'm up to here with your B.S.

PRE ATTACK VERBAL CUES

Madre, en la (MAH-dreh, en lah)
Lit: in the mother

Canosa, en la (KAH-noh-sah, en lah)
Lit: in the grey-haired female

Sumele (SOO-meh-leh)
Slang for: stick it in

Chinga, una (CHEEN-gah)
Slang for: a beating

Putazo (poo-TAH-soh)
Slang for: a strike, kick, punch, usually without a weapon

Curada, una (KOO-rah dah, ooh-nah)
Slang for: a beating

Suenale (SOO-EHN-ah-leh)
Slang for: making noise while striking another person, "smacking" someone

Vergazos (VEHR-gah-zohs)
Lit: animal penis

Descuentalo (dehs-KOO-EHN-tah-loh)
Lit: to discount

Guante (GOO-AHN-teh) Lit: glove

Dóblalo (DOH-blah-loh)
Lit: to fold/bend

Baba, tumba la
(BAH-bah, TOOM-bah lah)
Lit: knock the drool off

Rebote (reh-BOH-teh) Lit: rebound

EX: Let's beat him up. Go for it.
EX: ¿Lo descuentas tu o yo?
Are you going to take him out or am I?

EX: Dale en la madre con el cohuete.
Shoot him/her.

Examples of words used by cholos, old gangsters (pachucos), and some wanna-be type vatos (street guys).

Sofoque (soh-FOH-keh)
Slang for: dimwit, 2 bricks shy of a load, or not having both oars in the water. In Tex-Mex used for dummy / crazy person.

Huey (also written as guey or buey)
(way) Lit: ox
Connotes: Oxen pull plows, therefore dumb;, or oxen have big testicles, yet are often castrated.

SLANG USED BY DRUG USERS OR TRAFFICKERS

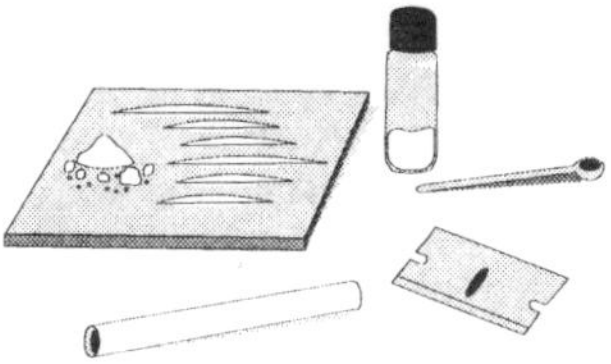

Destrampado (dehs-trahm-PAH-doh)
Meaning: messed up on drugs

Coco (koh-koh)
Meaning: wired up on cocaine

Estar Cocodrilo (ess-TAHR koh-koh-DREE-loh)
Lit: being a crocodile
Slang for: being on the nod, as crocodiles yawn as they bask in sun.

Estar eléctrico (ess-TAHR eh-LEHK-tree-koh)
Meaning: wired on cocaine

Grifo (GREE-foh) high on grass

¿Te persinaste? (teh pehr-see-NAHS-teh)
Lit: Did you cross yourself?
Meaning: Religious hand gesture, the last part being fingertips touched to lips as if smoking/toking.

Narizaso (nah-ree-SAH-soh)
Slang for: a snort, a "noseload."

Desluzado (DEHS-luh-sah-doh)
Slang for: blacking out

Darse las tres (DAHR-seh lahs tres)
Slang for: doing the sign of the cross/smoking grass

Lucas McKane: (high on grass)

Mandado a la verga (mahn-DAH-doh a lah VEHR-gah)
Lit: Sent to the animal penis
Slang for: being really messed up on alcohol/drugs or having life kick the crap out of you.

Pico caído (PEE-koh KAH-ee-doh)
Meaning: turned down bill, i.e. head down, in the pits from a bum trip, hangover or to be impotent.

Quijada (KEE-hah-dah) Lit: Jaw
Slang: numbing of the gums from coke.

Línea (LEE-nee-ah) a line of coke

De aguas (deh ah-KEH-yahs)
Meaning: feeling good with or w/o drugs.

Vato del planeta X (VAH-toh del plah-NEHT-as ex)
Slang for: the dude from planet X, or a spaced out dude.

Vasilar (vah-SEE-lahr)
Meaning: screw around

Tirar tripa (TEE-rahr TREE-pah)
Lit: throw tripe
Slang for: barfing, throwing up

Chompa (CHOM-pah)
Slang for: the mind

Jale de aguas
(HAH-leh deh ah-KEH-yahs)
Slang for: good drugs

WORDS USED TO EXPRESS FRUSTRATION WITH EXTENSIVE QUESTIONING

Chichona (chee-CHOH-nah)
Lit: large breasted female

Fastidiado (fahs-tee-DEE-ah-doh)
Lit: to feel disgust

Hozico, el (oh-SEE-koh, el)
Lit: the mouth of an animal

Copete, hasta el (KOH-peh-teh, as-tah el)
Lit: to the forelock of a horse.
Slang for: comb of a rooster, as with a hand/palm gesture over the top of his head

Estufas, ya (ess-TOO-fahs, yah)
Lit: stoves, enough
EX: "that's enough."

Pepe (PEH-peh)
Lit: diminutive for Jose

Pendejo (PEHN-deh-hoh)
Lit: hair above the pubis/groin. To call someone an "asshole."

EX: Oye culero, cortale con el pedo, dile la neta a la placa porque parece que ese cabron te trae de los huevos.
Hey dummy, cut the crap, tell the cop the truth because it looks like that bastard has you by the testicles.

114

GANG AND JAILBIRD TALK

No hay pedo (noh ay PEH-doh)
Lit: there is no fart
Slang for: it's alright, it doesn't matter

Puro pedo (POO-roh PEH-doh)
Lit: pure fart Slang for: B.S.

Sacale los pedos
(SAH-kah-leh lohs PEH-dohs)
Lit: take his farts out
Slang for: scare the crap out of him

Pélale el ojo (PEH-lah-leh el OH-ho)
Lit: peel his eye
Slang for: keep an eye on him

Sin Bolas/Huevos
(seen BOH-lahs/ WEH-vohs)
Lit: without balls/eggs
Slang for: no courage

Aguitate (ah-GWEE-tah-teh)
Slang for: chill out

Aguitado (ah-GWEE-tah-doh)
Slang: dismayed, depressed, give up

Suerealo (soo-REH-ah-loh)
Slang for: study it, check him out

Azules (ah-SOO-lehs)
Lit: the ones in blue
Slang: policemen

Jale (HAH-leh)
Slang for: the stuff/thing/contraband

Escupe (ess-KOO-peh) Lit: to spit
Slang for: rifle/shotgun

Cohuete (KOH-et-eh)
Lit: rocket/firecracker
Slang for: firearm

Fierro (fee-EHR-oh) Lit: iron
Slang for: handgun (older slang)

La de puneta (lah deh POON-nyet-ah)
Slang for: shotgun or to masturbate

Veduque (veh-DOO-keh)
Slang for: knife

La pica (lah PEE-kah) Slang for: knife

El filero (el FEE-lehr-oh)
Slang for: long knife

Manoplas (man-OH-plahs)
Lit: from manopla/gauntlet
Slang for: brass knuckles

La Jura (lah HOO-rah)
Slang for: the cops

La chota (lah CHOH-tah)
Slang for: the cops

Capiro (KAH-pee-roh)
Slang for: cop

Bronca (brohn-KAH)
Slang for: bad situation/problem

Tecos (TEH-kohs)
Lit: from the word tecolote/owl
Slang: Cops, like owls, are looking around with very big eyes

La perica (lah peh-REE-kah)
Lit: female parrot
Slang for: the rap, B.S., distracting talk

El rollo (el ROH-yoh) Lit: the role
Slang for: B.S., rap, distracting talk

Juegale la mente
(HOO-EGG-ah-leh lah MEHN-teh)
Lit: play with his mind
Slang for: mind games; or concocting a story for a scam or alibi

Pinto (TT's) (PEEN-toh)
Slang for: ex-convict

Pinta (PEEN-tah) Slang for: prison

Pintado
(PEEN-tah-doh)
Slang for: ex-convict
Also: something/someone painted or tattooed.

¿Traes cola?
(tries KOH-lah)
Lit: Do you have a tail?
Slang for: Are you on probation?

Rifa
(REE-fah)
Lit: raffle
Slang for: getting over, such as unexpected parole or early out due to prison overcrowding or I.N.S. deportation in lieu of time imprisoned/joint.

Bote
(BOH-teh)
Lit: can
Slang for: prison

Calentar cemento
(KAH-lehn-tahr seh-MEHN-toh)
Lit: to heat cement
Slang for: doing a long term in the joint

Cantar
(kahn-TAHR)
Lit: to sing
Slang for: spilling your guts, confessing;

NOTE: It is not uncommon for Hispanic prison inmates to slash the face of an informant with a razor blade, thus marking him as a "snitch."

¿Qué debes?
(keh DEH-bess) Lit: What do you owe?
Slang for:
What crimes have you committed that you haven't paid for / been caught for/or found guilty of.

Relaje
(reh-LAH-heh)
Slang for:
snitch, informant, uncool

¿Estabas en la carrucha?
(ess-TAH-bahs en lah kah-ROO-chah)
Slang for:
Were you a gang member in prison?

Maderista
(mah-dehr-EEST-ah)
Slang for: con man, from Maderista - A person who followed President Madero

Aquí cayeron tus huevos
(ah-KEE kah-YEH-rohn toos WEH-vohs)
Slang for: you're caught by the balls and you're not getting out of this

Juégatela fría
(HOO-egg-ah-tehl-ah FREE-ah)
Slang for: play it cool

Pintar huellas
(peen-TAHR WEH-yahs)
Lit: paint tracks
Slang for: making tracks / to escape

Slang

The slang is not meant to be all inclusive and may have different meanings in different geographical areas inside and outside of the U.S. Even though the majority of the slang are of Mexican influence, many are used in other countries.

A drunk	Vato mamado	(**VAH**-toh mah-**MAH**-doh)
Activity, damn activity	La Chinga	(**LAH CHEEN**-gah)
Aids	Sida	(**SEE**-dah)
AK-47 Assault Rifle	cuerno de chivo	(koo ehr no deh **CHEE**-voh)

(Means "Goat Horn" because the clip is curved like a goat horn).

Alcohol	Alcohol	(ahl-**KOHL**)
Alcohol (To drink)	Inflar	(een-**FLAR**) Lit: To inflate
Alert	Abusado	(ah-boo-**SAH**-doh)
All the way	Total	(toh-**TAHL**)
Always (forever)	Siempre	(see-**EHM**-pray)
American	Americano	(Ah-may-ree-**CAH**-noh)
Angel Dust	Angelito	(Ahn-hay-**LEE**-toh)
Arm tracks	Alacranes	(ah-lah-**KRAH**-nehs) Lit: Crab Tracks
Arrested I.E. busted	Torcido	(tohr-**SEE**-doh)
Ass	Culo	(**KOO**-loh)
Ass, kiss my	Lámeme el culo	(**LAH**-meh-meh ehl **KOO**-loh) Lit:: Lick my ass
Ass, pain in the	Desmadre	(dehs-**MAH**-dreh)
Ass fucker	Coño	(**KOH**-nyoh)

Used in the Caribbean, Cuba, PR, Dominican Republic, etc., not so much in Mexico

Ass, get off my	Ya estuvo	(yah ehs-**TOO**-voh)
Ass kisser	Mamón	(mah-**MOHN**)
Ass kisser	Lambíon	(Lahm-bee-**OHN**)
Ass kisser	Lambiache	(Lahm-bee-**AH**-cheh)

This is a deragatory term used toward a Hispanic police officer.

Assassin	Asesino	(ah-seh-**SEE**-noh)
Assassin (Child)	Sicario	(seh-**CAH**-reeoh) (Columbian Term)
Assassin (Hit man)	Gatillero	(gah-tee-**YAY**-roh) (Trigger Man)

Execution Patterns and Interpretations	
SHOT TO THE FOREHEAD	Indicates the mark of a good shooter and lets others know they can be hit at a distance.
SIDE OF THE BODY	A final insult to the recipient. The shooter wants the person to know who committed the act. It is often a contact wound.
NAPE OF THE NECK	Traditional execution in Mexico (No brain splatter).
CORNER OF EYE	A bad debt and almost always involved with drugs.
DIRT STUFFED IN THE MOUTH	Definitely a revenge killing. The killer is sending the message "You will eat dirt when you go to your grave."

Asshole	Sieso	(SYEH-soh)
Asshole	Culero	(koo-LEHR-oh)
Asshole	Pendejo	(PEHN-deh-hoh)
Backup or to help	Esquina	(ays-KEE-nah)
Backup or to help	Vaqueta	(vah-KEH-tah)
Bad Experience	Que gacho	(Kay GAH-choh)
Bad Situation	Caca (also bad drugs)	(KAH-cah) Lit: Shit
Badge	Placa	(PLAH-kah)
Bag, small	Borrego	(Boh-RAY-goh) Lit: Pig Skin
Bastard	Bastardo	(bahs-TAHR-doh)
Bastard	Pinche	(PEEN-chay)
Beat, to	Dar una chinga	(dahr OO-nah CHEEN-gah)
Big mouth individual	Ozicón	(oh-see-KOHN)
Bindle	Papiro	(pah-PEE-roh)
Bitch	Cabrona	(kah-BROH-nah)
Black	Negro	(NEH-groh)
*Derogatory Terms for blacks		
Black	Pina	(PEE-nah)
Black Person	Chanate	(Chah-NAH-tay)
Black Person	Mayate*	(Mah-YAH-tay)
Black Person	Mayuga*	(Mah-YUH-gah)
Black Person	Chuntaro*	(Chun-TAH-roh)
Black People	Terones	(Tay-ROHN-ees)
Black People	Tinto	(TEEN-toh)
Blow his head off	Vuélale los sesos	(VWAY-lah-leh lohs SEH-sohs)
Body	Cuerpo	(KWAYR-poh)
Bodyguard	guarda espaldas	(GWAHR-dah es-PAHL-dah)(shoulder pad)
Bomb	Bomba	(BOHM-bah)
Booze	Pisto	(PEES-toh)
Booze, to drink	Pistear	(Pees-tay-AHR)
Boss	Jefe	(HAY-fay)
Boss, big	Mero chingón	(MEH-roh cheen-GOHN) Lit: Top Fucker
Botanica (not slang)		(boh-TAH-nee-kah) (Retail shop specializing in Santeria paraphernalia and herbs.
Boy (or man or guy)	Vato	(VA-toh)
Boy friend	Ruco	(ROO-koh)
Brave, to be	Tener huevos	(teh-NEHR WAY-bohs) Lit: To have balls
Breasts	Tetas	(TEH-tahs) means nipples
Breasts	Las mamas	(Lahs MAH-mahs)
Bribe	Mordida	(mohr-DEE-dah) (Lit: bite)
Broke (no money)	Andar amolado	(ahn-DAHR ah-moh-LAH-doh)
Brother (in a gang)	Carnal	(Cahr-NAHL) Lit: Of the same flesh
Sister (in a gang)	Carnala	(Cahr-NAHLAH) Lit: Of the same flesh
Brotherhood, the	El barrio	(ehl BAH-rryoh)

English	Spanish	Pronunciation
Bullet	Bala	(BAH-lah)
Bullshit	Puro pedo	(POO-roh PEH-doh) Lit: Pure Fart
C/S	Consafos	(Kohn-SAHFOHS)
C/S (means "The same to you & anything you write goes back to you twice as bad")		
California	Califas	(Cah-LEE-fahs)
Calm Down, Asshole!	¡Cálmate Culero!	(CAHL-mah-tay coo-LEHR-oh)
Car (or Bomb)	Ranfla	(RAHN-flah)
Car	Carucha	(Cah-ROO-chah)
Car, a junker	Carcancha	(Cah-CAHN-chah)
Cause, the	!Viva La Causa!	(VEE-vah lah KAHS-sah)
Chance	Chansa	(CHAHN-sah)
Cheat, to	Chapusear	(chah-poo-seh-AHR)
Check him out!	¡Wáchalo!	(WAH-chah-loh)
Chicano Brotherhood	Chicanismo	(Chee-cahn-EES-moh)
Chicano's	Eses	(EES-EEHS) Brothers
Chicken shit	Pinche	(PEEN-cheh)
Cigarettes	Frajos	(FRAH-hohs)
Co-Father or Godfather	Compa	(COHM-pah) Not slang
Cocaine, rock	Piedra Blanca	(PYEH-drah BLAHN-kah)
Cocaine, powder	Talco	(TAHL-koh)
Cocaine, powder	Polvo	(POHL-voh) Lit: Powder
Cocaine, a line of	Línea de blanca	(LEE-neh-ah deh BLAHN-kah)
Cocaine	Blanca	(BLAHN-kah)
Cocaine	Coca	(COH-cah)
Code of silence	Código del mudo	(KOH-dee-goh dehl MOO-doh)
	Lit: Code of the Deaf Man	
Cold turkey	Enferma	(ehn-FEHR-mah)
Cold Blooded Dude	Gacho	(GAH-choh)
Colors	Colores	(koh-LOH-rehs)
Con man	Chafo	(CHAH-foh)
Con Job	Chafear	(chah-feh-AHR)
Contract killing	Contrato	(kohn-TRAH-toh)
Control, we	Controlamos	(kohn-troh-LAH-mohs)
Control	Controlar	(kohn-TROHL)
Convict	Pintado	(peen-TAH-doh)
Cool (to be)	La Onda	(lah OHN-dah) Lit:On the same wave length
Cool it	Ya estuvo	(yah ehs-TOO-voh)
Cop Out, (Don't)	No copeas	(No koh-PAY-ahs)
Correctional officer	Placa	(PLAH-kah)
County Jail	El bote del Condado	(Ehl BOH-tay dehl kohn-DAH-doh)
Cousin(& High Quality)	Primo	(PREE-moh)
Coward	Culero	(koo-LEH-roh)
Crazy	Loco	(LOH-koh)
Crazy man	Vato loco	(VAH-toh LOH-coh)
Criminal Activities	La Torcida	(lah tohr-SEE-dah)
Criminal	Criminal	(kree-mee-NAHL)
Cross out marks	Puta marks	(POO-tah mahrks)
Cross out marks	Desplacar	(dehs-plah-KAHR)
Dangerous/Reckless Person-	Lumbre	(LOOM-breh)
	Means mean, light, fire, flame etc.	
Death sentence	Sentencia de muerte	(sehn-TEHN-syah deh MWAYR-teh)
Death	La huesuda	(lah way-SOO-dah) Lit: Bones
Deep trouble	Atorado	(ah-toh-RAH-doh) Lit: Stick
Depressants, on	(De bajada	(deh bah-HAH dah) Lit: On the way down
Depressed	Deslusado	(dehs-loo-SAH-doh) Lit: Flame out
Devil	Pingo	(PEEN-goh)
Drink, a	Birria (booze)	(BEEHR-ee-ah)Spanish/English Beer
Drive by shooting	Tiroteo de pasada	(tee-roh-TEH-oh deh pah-SAH-dah)
Drug smuggler	Contrabandista	(kohn-trah-bahn-DEES-tah deh)
Drug Addiction	Drogadiccion	(droh-gah-deek-see-OHN)
Drug dealer	Tirador	(tee-rah-DOHR)
Drug dealer	Traficante	(Trah-fee-KAHN-tay)
Drug outfit (kit)	Equipo	(eh-KEE-poh)

Drug withdrawal	Enfermo	(ehn-FEHR-moh) Lit: Sick
Drug money	Lana sucia	(LAH-nah SOO-syah) Lit: Dirty Wool
Drugged or stoned	Estar cocodrilo	(ehs-TAHR koh-koh-DREE-loh)
Lit: Like a crocodile. Like a crocodile basking in the sun		
Drugged or stoned	Drogado	(droh-GAH-doh)
Drugs, free sample	Pilón	(pee-LOHN)
Drugs, bad i.e. bunk	Mierda	(MYEHR-dah) Lit: Shit
Drugs, bad	Caca	(KAH-cah) Lit: Shit
Drugs, get off of	Tirar la cruz	(tee-RAHR lah croos)
Lit: To throw off the cross (Christ carrying the cross)		
Drugs, cut or diluted	Cortar drogas	(kohr-TAHR DROH-gahs)
Drugs, high quality	Fina	(FEE-nah)
Drunk	Pedo	(PEH-doh)
Eat, to	Refinar	(Ray-fee-NAHR)
Enough!	¡Estufas!	(ehs-TOO-fahs)
Enough!	¡Ya basta!	(yah BAHS-tah)
Evil Person	Maleante	(mah-lay-AHN-tay)
Ex-convict	Pintado	(peen-TAH-doh)
F-XIII		
The tattoo worn by the Florencia Southern (Surenos) L.A. California Stree Gang and originated with Mexican Nationals. The tattoo will be worn on the forearm, chest, stomach or at times on the thigh and is common in Roman numerals F-XIII. They are allignded with the Mexican Mafia. Their rivals are the Florencia (Nortenos) F-XIV which originated with legal aliens.		
False! (i.e. bullshit)	¡Puro pedo!	(POO-roh PEH-doh) Lit: Pure Fart
Family,(criminal)	La familia	(lah fah-MEE-lyah)
Fart	Pedo	(PEH-doh)
Father	Jefito	(Hay-FEE-toh) Lit: Chief (Diminutive-Affectionate)
Federal cop	Federal	(feh-deh-RAHL)
Felony	Felonía	(feh-loh-NYAH)
Fight, a	Pleito	(PLAY-toh)
Fight	Pedo	(PEH-doh) Lit: Fart
Fight, to	Bailar	(Bah-EE-lahr) Lit: To Dance
Fight, to	Arranque	(ah-RAHN-kay) Lit: To start up
Final blow (to kill)	El Gran Chingaso	(El Grahn Cheen-GAH-soh)
Fighting blows	Chingasos	(cheen-GAH-sohs)
Finger, to	Dedo	(DEH-doh)
Firearm	Cohuete	(koo-EH-tay) (Used by "Crips" too.)
Firearm(Do you have a?)	¿Traes cohuete?	(TRAH-ays koh-EH-tay)
Firearm / Revolver	Fogón	(foh-GOHN)
Fix, a (a drug dose)	Curada	(koo-RAH-dah)
Food	Refin	(REH-feen)
Fraud	Fraude	(FROW-deh)
Friend, Associate	Camarada	(Cah-mah-RAH-dah)
Friend	Compa	(COHM-pah) Short for compadre
Friend / Brother	Carnal	(KAR-nahl)
Fuck you!	¡Pélamela!	(PEH-lah-meh-lah)
Fuck your mother!	¡Chinga tu madre!	(CHEEN-gah too MAH-dreh)
Fuck, a	Chingado	(cheen-GAH-doh) (Noun)
Fuck over, to	Chingar	(cheen-GAHR)
Fuck, him up	Chingaso	(cheen-GAH-soh)
Fuck it!	¡Carajo!	(kah-RAH-hoh)
Gang	Ganga	(GAHN-gah)
Gang Colors	Placa	(PLAH-kah)
Gang Signs/Graffiti	Señas	(SEHN-yahs)
Gang Fight	Rumbar	(ROOM-bar)
Gang Initiation	Cliquiar	(Klee-kay-ahr)
Gang Language	¿El lenguaje?	(ehl lehn-goo-AH-hay)
When asked as a question is slang for "Do you speak the gang language?" or meaning, "Are you a gang member?"		
Gang Talk (Mexican)	Calo	(CAH-loh)
Gang Life	Cargar la Cruz	Lit: To carry the cross

120

Meaning "You are going to have to bear the cross. You are going to pay the price".		
Gang Life (to give up)	Tirar la Cruz	Lit: To throw off the cross
Gang Member, fellow	Homeboy, Homie, Home	
Gang Neighborhood	Varrio	(BAHR-ree-oh)
Gang, Sub-group	Clique	(KLEE-keh)
Gang Pants	Los Tramados	(Lohs trah-MAH-dohs) Lit: The fixed up ones
Gang Dress	Los Trapos	(LOHS TRAH-pohs)
Gang Boy	Cholo	(CHOH-loh)
Gang Girl	Chola	(CHOH-lah)
Garrote	Garrote	(gah-RROH-teh)
Get rid of him	Descuentalo	(dehs-KWAYN-tah-loh)
Get lost	Vete a la verga	(VEH-teh ah lah VEHR-gah) Lit Go to the dick
Girl or Sissy	Chavala	(Chah-VAH-lah)
Girlfriend, main	Ruca	(ROO-kah)
Girlfriend	Jaina	(HAH-een-ah)
Go to hell	Vete a la chingada	(VEH-teh ah lah cheen-GAH-dah)
God damned	Chingado	(cheen-GAH-doh)
God	Dios	(dyohs)
Godfather	El Padrino	(ehl pah-DREE-noh) Can also be a Priest of Santeria, a Santero. One patron and intiator.
Graffiti	Placa	(PLAH-kah)
Gram (drug)	Gramo	(GRAH-moh)
Greeting (like Hey Bud!)	¡Oye compita!	(OH-yeh cohm-PEE-tah)
Hallucinating	Estar en las nubes	(ehs-TAHR ehn lahs NOO-behs)
Hand signing	Señando	(seh-NYAN-doh)
Hang him	Cuélgalo	(KWAYL-gah-loh)
Hashish	Hachís	(ah-CHEES) (Letter H in alphabet)
Hashish	Concentrada	(Kohn-sehn-TRAH-dah) Lit: concentrate
Hashish	Dura	(DOO-rah)
Hat or cap	Gora	(GOH-rah) (Knit watch cap)
Hell	Infierno	(een-FYEHR-noh)
Hepatitis B	Hepatitis B	(eh-pah-TEE-tees beh)
Herion	Carga	(KARH-gah)
Heroin (china white)	Chiva	(CHEE-vah)
Heroin (tar)	Negra	(NEH-grah)
Hey Dude! (or Man)	Ese Vato	(EH-say vah-toh)
Hiding place	Clavo	(KLAH-boh)
High Quality	De Categoria	(Day kah-teh-goh-REE-ah)
Homosexual	Joto	(HOH-toh)
Homosexual	Maricon	(Mahr-ee-KOHN)
House	Canton	(kahn-TOHN)
House	Chante	(CHAHN-teh)
Hustler	Talon	(TAH-lohn)
Hyper, (on uppers)	Estar eléctrico	(ehs-TAHR eh-LEHK-tree-koh)
"I AM"	Soy	(soy)
Idiot	Idiota	(ee-DYOH-tah)
Idiot	Menso	(MEHN-soh)
Idiot	Tonto	(TOHN-toh)
Illegal	Ilegal	(ee-leh-GAHL)
Illegal allien	Mojado	(moh-HAH-doh)
Illegal allien	Broncs (derogatory)	Also: No Way Ho-say
Immigration (INS)	La Migra	(Lah MEE-grah)
Immigration card	Mica	(MEE-kah)
Informer	Chota	(CHOH-tah) (Can also mean "Cop")
Inform, to	Pillar	(pee-YAHR) Lit: To snag
Inform, to	Rajar	(RAH-ahr) Lit: To split open
Informer	Soplón	(soh-PLOHN) Lit: Big Blower
Informer	Rata	(RAH-tah) Lit: Rat
Informer	Raton	(RAH-tohn) Lit: Big Rat
Informer (traitor)	Relaje	(Ray-LAH-hay) Lit: Relaxer, Joker
Informer (triator)	Snizzle	(SNEEZ-lay)
Informer (Chicano)	Vendido	(Vehn-DEE-doh)

NOTE: It is not uncommon for Hispanic prison gangs to attack informers with razor blades and slash their face to mark them as informers.

Inhalants (paints)	Meterse pinturas	(meh-TEHR-seh peen-TOO-rahs)
Inhale drugs (snort)	Meterse drogas	(meh-TEHR-seh DROH-gahs)
Injection	Inyeccion	(eehn-yeck-see-OHN) Not slang
Inject (to yourself)	Picarse	(pee-KAHR-say) (**stick yourself**)
Intoxicated	Andar perruskia	(ahn-DAHR peh-roos-KYAH)
Intoxicated	Cuete	(koo-et-tay)
Intoxicated	Pedo	(PEH-doh)
Intoxicated	Borracho	(Boh-RAH-choh)
Intoxicated by drugs	Anda Lucas	(Ahn-dah LOO-kahs)
It's against the law	Es contra la ley	(ehs KOHN-trah la lay)
It's over!	¡Ya stuvo!	(yah STOO-voh)
Jacket	Chamara	(Chah-MAH-rah)
Jail	Cárcel	(KAHR-sehl)
Jail	Bote	(BOH-teh)
Jail	Tanque	(TAHN-keh)
Jail, to be locked up	Torcida	(Tohr-SEE-dah)
Jailer	Carcelero	(kahr-seh-LEH-roh)
Job	Cameo	(kah-MEH-oh)
Job, the	Jale	(HAH-leh)
Joke, to	Bromear	(broh-meh-AHR)
Junkie (Lit: Owl)	Tecate (tay-KAH-tay) (Also for Cop, Beer, Big eyes)
Kidnapper	Secuestrador	(seh-kwehs-trah-DOHR)
Kilo (2.2 lbs)	Kilo	(sehn-TAH-voh)
Kilogram (drugs)	Un entero	(oon ehn-TEH-roh) Pure/Uncut
Kill	Matar	(mah-TAHR)
Kill (to)	Quebrar	(kay-BRAHR) (Lit: To break)
Killing, a (a hit)	Contrato	(kohn-TRAH-toh)
Kill him	Bájalo	(BAH-hah-loh)
Kill (to)	Bajar	(bah-HAHR) Lit: To lower
Kill him!	¡Chingatelo!	(CHEEN-gah-teh-loh)
Kill him!	¡Descuentalo!	(dehs-KWAYN-tah-loh) Lit: To Discount
Kill him	¡Pártele la madre!	(PAHR-teh-leh lah MAH-dreh) Lit: Split his mother open

Kiss Ass	Lambión	(lahm-bee-OHN)
Knife	Filero (Fila)	(FEE-lah)
Knife	Pica	(PEE-kah)
Knife	Pinaldo	(peh-NAHL-doh) The knife used for the sacrificing of animals used in Santeria.
Knife or stick as a weapon - arma blanca		(AHR-mah BLAHN-koh)
Laborer	Obrero	(oh-BREH-roh)
Later	al rato	(ahl RAH-toh)

Later Man	al rato, ese	(ahl **RAH**-toh, eh-say)
Lawyer	Abogado	(ah-boh-**GAH**-doh)
Lazy	Huevon	(**WEH**-vohn)

This is a Mexican slang only. In the rest of Latin American this is one of the most insulting names you could call some one. (Lit: Big balled, one so stupid that his balls get in the way. The purpose to list this slang is to alert and warn an officer he is being called this insulting word. As with all of the derogatory slang, it is not to be used by an officer as it will inflame or escalate tensions.

Lesbian	Marimacho	(mah-ree-**MAH**-choh)
Lesbian	Jota	(**HOH**-tah)
Letter, Card	Carta	(**KAHR**-tah)
Liar	Mentiroso	(mehn-tee-**ROH**-soh)
Long Live (or live)	Viva	(**VEE**-vah)
Long prison term	Sentencia chingona	(sehn-**THEN**-syah cheen-**GOH**-nah)
Look Here! (or at this)	Aqui	(ah-**KEE**) Look at this graffiti
Lookout a (the eye)	El Ojo	(el **OH**-hoh) Lit: The eye
Lookout, a	El gafas	(ehl **GAH**-fahs) (The spectacle)
Lookout!	¡Wacha!	(**WAH**-chah)
Low Riding	Means gangstering among gangsters	
LSD	Acido	(**AH**-see-doh)
M (letter)	Eme (Mex. Mafia)	(**AY**-may)
Machine gun	Metralla	(meh-**TRAH**-yah) Lit: Machine Gun Fire
Mad	Enojado	(Eh-noh-**HAH**-doh
Mad, to be	Andar león	(ahn-**DAHR** leh-**OHN**)
Mad or upset	Atetado	(Ah-teh-**TAH**-doh) Lit: Tits Up
Mafia	Mafia	(**MAH**-fyah)
Man, crazy	Vato loco	(**VAH**-toh **LOH**-koh)
Man (boy or guy)	Vato	(**VAH**-toh)
Marijuana butt	Chicharra	(Chee-**CHAHR**-rah) Lit: Buzzed
Marijuana	Yierba	(**YEHR**-bah)
Marijuana	Sacáte	(sah-**KAH**-tay
Marijuana	Zacate	(zah-**KAH**-tay)
Marijuana	Yesca	(**YEHS**-kah)
Marijuana	Grifa	(**GREE**-fah)Lit: A fire hydrant spouting
Marijuana (joint)	Gallo	(**GAH**-yoh) Lit: Rooster
Marijuana butt	Besicha	(beh-**SEE**-chah)
Married	Joined	(Joined A Gang)
Mask	Careta	(kah-**REH**-tah)
Medicine	Medicina	(meh-dee-**SEE**-nah)
Mercenary	Mercenario	(Mehr-seh-**NAH**-ryoh)
Methamphetamine	Cranke	(**KRAHN**-keh)
Mex. Nationals in US	Chuntaros	(Choon-**TAH**-rohs)
Mexico (Occupied)	Aztlan	(Ahtz-**LAHN**) and Mystical Atlantis
Misdemeanor	Infracción	(een-frahk-**SYOHN**)
MM	La Eme (Mex. Mafia)	(lah **AY**-may)
Moco rag	Trapo	(**TRAH**-poh)Moco means booger or snot.

The bandana is folded lengthwise, just over the forehead, and tied in the back. It will vary in color have commonly will have the member's gang name embroidered on the front. (Unless it is at a funeral it will be black). The bandana is also a display of pride of their heritage. The "stingy" brim or the baseball hat will be worn and frequently will have their nickname on the bill.

Money	Lana	(**LAH**-nah) Lit: Wool
Money (or change)	Feria	(fehr-ee-ah) Lit: Market day change
Money Order	Giro	(**HEE**-roh)
Mother	Jefita	(Hay-**fee**-tah) Lit: Little Chief
Mother fucker	Coño de tu madre	(**KOH**-nyoh deh too **MAH**-dreh)

Lit: Your mother's coño. This is Carribbean Spanish only. Not Mexican.

Movement, the	La Movida	(Lah Moh-**VEE**-dah)
Murderer	Asesino	(ah-seh-**SEE**-noh)
Mushrooms (drug)	Hongos	(**OHN**-gohs)
MVL(My Crazy Life)	Mi Vida Loca (...)	(mee **VEE**-dah **LOH**-kah)
N (The letter)	Ene (Norte) N. Cal.	(ay-nay)

Name	Placa	(PLAH-kah)
Narcotic cop	Narco	(NAHR-koh)
Narcotics or Guns	Herramientas	(eh-rrah-MYEHN-tahs) Lit: Tools
Narcotics	Narcoticos	(Nahr-KOH-tee-kohs) Not slang.
Narcotics	Lucas	(LOO-kahs)
Needle	Aguja	(ah-GOO-hah)
Needle	Clavo (nail)	(KLAH-voh)
Needle	Punta	(POON-tah)
Neighborhood (turf)	Barrio	(BAHR-ree oh) Lit: Neighborhood
Nervous	Andar culeco	(ahn-DAHR koo-LEH-koh)
NF Gang Member	Farmero	(Fahr-MEH-roh)
NF (The letters)	Ené Efe (Nuestra Fam.)	(AY-nay AY-fay) Prison Gang
Nganga (not slang)	A priest or object consecrated in the Kongo religious traditions of Cuba. (Can be a cauldron or kettle).	(GANG-gah)
Nickname	Apodo	(ah-POH-doh)
No	Nel	(nehl)
No	Nixon	(NEEK-sohn)
North	Norte	(NOR-teh)
Nothing	Nada	(NAH-dah)

Numbers

8 ocho	Herion (8th letter in the alphabet)	(OH-choh)
13 trece	South, "M" for Marijuana, Mex. Mafia (13 letter in alphabet	(TREH-seh)
14 catorce	North	(kah-TOHR-seh)
15 quince	"M" 15th letter in Spanish alphabet, Mex, Mafia', Mani.	(KEEN-seh)

Obey	Obedece	(oh-beh-DEH-seh)
Of	de	(deh)
OK or Alright!	¡Horale!	(OH-rah-lay)
One and Only	Nomas	(NOH-mahs)
Ounce (drugs)	Pedazo	(peh-DAH-soh) (Mex. Ounce)Lit: A 15th
Outfit	Riata	(REE-ah-tah) Lit: Reata
Outfit	Pistolo	(Pees-TOH-loh)
P/V (Forever)	Por Vida	(Por VEE-dah)
Package	Quete	(KEH-tay)Short for paquete(Package)
Paranoia	Paranoia	(Pah-rah-NOY-ah)
Party, to	Rumbear	(room-beh-AHR) Lit: To dance the rhumba
PCP	PCP	(pahs)
Peace	Paz	(peh seh peh)

"Pee Wees" or "Lil' Winos" - In street gangs young male gang members ranging in ages from 10-13. Age 14-22 are made up of the hardcores who are involved in gang related nature. Anyone who survives to 23 becomes a "Veterano". *NOTE:* If two members have the same nickname they will refer to each other such as "Cruz" which may refer to an older member while "Lil' Cruz" make reference to a younger member emulating the older member with the same nickname.

Penis	Hueso	(WEH-soh) Lit: Bone
Penis	Verga	(VEHR-gah) Lit: Root
Penis	Chile	(Chee-Lay)
Penis	Casco	(KAHS-koh) Lit: Hood
People smuggler	Pollero	(poh-YEH-roh) Lit: Chicken runner

"Pendleton Shirts" are normally buttoned at the collar and cuffs. Officers should be aware that the remaining front buttons are left open so concealed weapons can be easily removed. T-Shirt are worn in the summer and are several sizes to large which allows the tail to conceal weapons in the waistband.

Pill Head	Pildo	(PEHL-doh)
Pills	Pastillas	(Pahs-TEE-yas)
Pimp	Alcahuete	(ahl-kah-WAY-teh)
Pipe	Pipa	(PEE-pah)
Piss on him!	¡Que se joda!	(keh seh HOH-dah) Lit: Screw Him
Piss off!	¡Véte a la verga!	(VEH-teh ah lah VEHR-gah) Lit: Go back to the root (penis)
Plague	Placa	(PLAH-kah)
Poison	Veneno	(veh-NEH-noh)

Police	Placa	(**PLAH**-kah, lah) (Badge)
Police	Chota	(**CHOH**-tah)
Police	La jura	(lah **JOO**-rah) (To Swear)
Police	Marrano	(mah-**RRAH**-noh) (Pig)
Police Oath Taker	Jura	(**HOO**-rah)
Police	Perro	(**PEHR**-roh) (Dog)
Police	Tecolote (Owl)	(teh-koh-**LOH**-teh) Undercover cop
Police	La ley	(lah leh) Lit: The law
Police Station	Estación de policía	(Ehs-tah-**SYOHN** deh poh-lee-**SYAH**)
Police (derogatory)	Los pinchas placas	(Lohs **PEEN**-chays **PLAH**-kahs)
Poor, to be	Pobreza	(poh-**BRAY**-zah) (Poverty)
Powder, the	Polvo	(**POHL**-voh) Cocaine
Price	Precio	(**PRAY**-see-oh)
Prison	La Pinta	(lah **PEEN**-tah)
Prisoner	Pinto	(**PEEN**-toh)
Probation officer	El probe	(ehl **PROH**-beh) probe is also short for probation
Race, the United	La Raza Unida	(Lah **RAH**-zah oo-**NEE**-dah) (National Mexican American Political Party based in San Antonio, TX
Race, the	La Raza	(lah **RAH**-sah)
Really	De veras	(deh **BEH**-rahs)
Records	Rolas	(**ROH**-lahs)

Rest in Peace-Translated in Spanish "en pas descance" (ehn pahs dehs-**KAHN**-say). Will be worn by many Cuban Marielitos in the form of the intitials of "E.P.D." on a tattoo of a tombstone with the name of a love one or a "brother" who has died.

Revenge / Payback	Revancha	(Ray-**VAHN**-chah) Lit: The flip side
Right on	Bacán	(Bah-**KAHN**)
Room	Cuarto	(Koo-**AHR**-toh)
Roster		List of Gang Members/Nicknames
Rule, We control/rule	Rifamos	(Ree-**FAH**-mohs) Lit: We raffle
Rule, to control/rule	Rifa	(**REE**-fah) Lit: The raffle
Rule, They control	Rifan	(**REE**-fahn) Lit: They raffle
Rush from drugs	Triliado	(Tree-**LYAH**-doh)
S (The letter)	Ese	(**AY**-say)
Safe house	Gúarida	(Gwah-**REE**-dah)
Sale	Barata	(Bah-**RAH**-tah) Lit: Cheap
Sale	Ganga	(**GAHN**-gah)
Santeria	(SAHN-tah-ree-ah)	The Way of The Saints(Saint Worship)
Scam (What's the)?	¿Como esta el rollo?	(**KOH**-moh ess-**TAH** el **ROH**-yoh)
Scared	Escamado	(ehs-kah-**MAH**-doh)
Scar (to)	Escamar	(Ehs-**KAH**-mahr)
Screwed, you've been	Te chingaron	(tay cheen-**GAH**-rohn)
Secret gang language	El lenguaje	(ehl lehn-**GWAH**-heh)
Sets		Sub-division of a larger gang
Sexual Intercourse	Canquear	(Kahn-hay-**AHR**) Lit: To exchange
Shield	Placa	(**PLAH**-kah)
Shit	Pedo	(**PEH**-doh) Lit: Fart
Shit, I don't give a Shit	Me vale madre	(meh **BAH**-leh **MAH**-dreh)
	Mierda	(**MYEHR**-dah)
Shoes (Kicks)	Carcos	(**KAHR**-kohs)
Shoot	Tira	(**TEE**-rah)
Shooting, drive by	Tiroteo de pasada	(Tee-roh **TEH**-oh deh pah-**SAH**-dah)
Shut up!	¡Cállate el ozico!	(**KAH**-yah-teh ehl oh-**SEE**-koh)
Silent Treatment, the	Leva	(**LEH**-vah)
Sing, to (inform)	Cantar or rata	(kahn-**TAHR**) (**RAH**-tah)
Smart or cunning	Zorro	(**ZOHR**-roh) Lit: Like a fox
Smuggled goods	Contrabando	(kohn-trah-**BAHN**-doh)
Smuggler, alien	Coyote	(koh-**YOH**-teh)
Soldier	Mafioso	(mah-**FYOH**-soh)
Son of a bitch	Hijo de puta	(**EE**-hoh deh **POO**-tah)
South	Sura	(**SOO**-rah)

English	Spanish	Pronunciation
South	Sur	(soohr)
Also Southern California	Sura Califas	(SOO-rah Cah-LEE-fahs)
Spanglish	A person who mixes the Spanish with the English. One who does this is called a "Pocho" (POH-choh)	
Split his head open!	¡Pártele la cabeza!	(PAHR-teh-leh lah kah-BEH-sah)
Stab him!	¡Súmelei	(SOO-meh-leh)
Stash	Escondite	(ehs-kohn-DEE-teh)
Steal, to	Hambar	(ahm-BAHR)
Stimulants	Estimulantes	(ehs-too moo-LAHN-tehs)
Straight Person	Firme	(FEER-may)
Stupid	Pendejo	(Pehn-DAY-hoh)
Supplier	Conexión	(Koh-nex-see-OHN)
Suspect	Sospechoso	(sohs-peh-CHOH-soh)
Talk, to rap	Cabollar	(Kah-boh-YAHR)
Talk, distracting	La pantalla	(lah pahn-TAH-yah)
Tar Heroin	El Dragon Negro	(ehl drah-GOHN NEH-groh)

English	Spanish	Pronunciation
Tatto's	Tatuajes	(tah-TWAH-hehs)

Tattoos, are a "*Red Flag*" that the individual is a gang member or has done time in jail. They frequently can be used to identify the member's gang, clique and nickname. The tattoo(s) may appear on the neck, wrists, arms, hands, chest, legs, thighs or even the face. The tattoo's may be of insects, spiders, animals, snakes, serpents, and spiders. The wearer feels it depicts the trials and tribulations of life in the "*barrio*" or in prison. The tattoo's serves another purpose, to show the wearer's "machismo", maleness, or toughness and often is an intimidation to others.

English	Spanish	Pronunciation
Tear his eyes out!	¡Sácale los ojos!	(SAH-kah-leh lohs OH-hohs)
Testicles	Tanates	(tah-NAH-tehs)
Theft	Robo	(ROH-boh)
Thief	Ratero	(ah-TEH-roh)
Thirteen	Trece	(TREH-seh)
Three	Tres	(trehs)
Time, doing	Estar pintado	(ehs-TAHR peen-TAH-doh)
Tip	Gangs	
Texas Syndicate (TS)	Ese Te	(ay say tay) (Texas Prison Gang)
Toilet or Crap	La Crepa	(lah CREH-pah)
Trouble	Pedo	(PEH-doh) Lit: Fart
Trouble maker	Picabuche	(Pee-kah-BOO-chay) Lit: Throat Cutter
Trouble (to start)	Torear	(Toh-ray-AHR) Lit: To tempt the bull(bullfighting)
Truth (tell the)	¡A la neta!	(ah lah NEH-tah) (Right to the nitty gritty)
Uncle Tom (derogatory)	Tío taco	(TEE-oh TAH-coh)
Undercover cop	Narco	(NAHR-koh)
Up your ass!	¡Métetelo en el culo!	(MEH-teh-teh-loh ehn ehl KOO-loh)
Vagina	Panocha	(pah-NOH-chah)
Venereal disease	Purgación	(poor-gah-SYOHN)

English	Spanish	Pronunciation
Veteran gangster	Chuco (Pachuco)	(CHOO-koh) Short for the Pachuco of the 50's
Veteran gangster	Veterano	(veh-teh-RAH-noh)
Vice-President	Visa	(VEE-sah)
Warning (to give)	Alambrazo	(ah-lahm-BAHR-zoh) Lit: Phone Call
Waste him!	¡Descuéntalo!	(dehs-KWAYN-tah-loh) Discount Him
Watch out (get with it)	Trucha	(TROO-chah) Lit: Trout
Watch out(deep trouble)Aguas		(ah-GWAHS) Lit: Waters

Watch Out!	Aguila!	(ah-GEE-la) Lit: Eagle (Also slang for a cop as they have eyes like eagles. Also slang for the MRU Street Gang)
Watch him!	¡Wáchalo!	(WAH-chah-loh)
We are	Somos	(SOH-mohs)
Weakling i.e. wimp	Debilucho	(deh-bee-LOO-choh)
Weapons or Drugs	Herramientas	(eh-rrah-MYEHN-tahs)
Weapons	Armas	(AHR-mahs)
Weedhead	Un grifo	(oon GREE-foh) Lit. Fireplug/Hydrant
What are you going to do about it? ¿Y'Que?		¿eee kay? Lit: And so?
What's Happening	¿Que paso?	(Keh PAH-soh) Lit:What happened?
Where you from?	¿Dónde?	(DOHN-deh)
White Person	Bolillo	(Boh-LEE-yoh) Lit: White Bread
White Man	Gabacho	(gah-BAH-choh)
White Woman	Gabacha	(gah-BAH-choh)
Whites or Anglos	Sabanas	(SAH-ban-ahs) Lit: Sheets also KKK
Whites or Anglos	Gabachos	(Gah-BAH-chohs)
Whites or Anglos	Hueros	(Hoo-AIR-ohs)
Lit: Those of a light complexion, could be Latin also not necessarily American or white.		
Whore (male homosex).	Puto	(POO-toh)
Whore	Puta	(POO-tah)
Whorehouse	Congal	(kohn-GAHL)
Whorehouse	Casa de Putas	(CAH-sah day POO-tahs)
Wife's Boyfriend	Sancho	(SAHN-choh)
Wilding (to commit)	Paca	(PAH-kah) Lit: Hay bale
Worthless	Bale	(BAH-leh)
Wow	Híjole	(EE-hoh-leh)
Yes	Simón	(see-MOHN) Lit: A BIG YES
Yes	Chale	(CHAH-leh) Comes from échale (OK)

(SEE DRUG SECTION FOR MORE SLANG)

PAROLE AND PROBATION

ARE YOU ON PAROLE / PROBATION?
¿Está Ud. bajo probación?
(Ess-**TAH** oo-**STEHD** **BAH**-hoh pro-bah-see-**OHN**)

ARE YOU ON PROBATION? (SLANG)
¿Traes cola?   Lit: Are you dragging a tail?
(tries **KOH**-lah)

WHERE?   **WHAT FOR?**
¿Dónde?   ¿Para qué?
(**DOHN**-day)   (**PAH**-rah kay)

WHO IS YOUR PAROLE / PROBATION OFFICER?
¿Quien es su official de probación?
(kee-**EHN** ees soo oh-fee-see-**AHL** day proh-bah-see-**OHN**?

YOU ARE UNDER ARREST FOR....
Usted está arrestado por....
(Oo-**STEHD** ess-**TAH** ah-reh-**STAH**-doh pohr....)

ASSAULT
Asalto
(ah-**SAHL**-toh)

CARRYING A CONCEALED WEAPON
Llevar arma oculta   (escondida)
(yeh-**VAHR** **AHR**-mah oh-kool-**TAH** [ays-kohn-**DEE**-dah]

EX-CONVICT IN POSSESSION OF A FIREARM
Ex-reo en posesión de arma de fuego
(ex REH-oh ehn poh-sez-SYOHN day AHR-mah)

(OR)   **FOR HAVING A FIREARM**
Por tener arma de fuego
(Poor tay-NAIR AHR-mah de FOO-ay-goh)

DRIVING WITH A SUSPENDED DRIVER'S LICENSE
Manejar con licencia suspendida
(mah-neh-HAHR kohn lee-SEHN-see-ah soos-PEHN-dee-dah)

DRIVING WHILE UNDER THE INFLUENCE OF AN INTOXICANT.
manejar tomado
(mah-neh-HAHR toh-MAH-doh)

POSSESSION OF NARCOTICS
Posesión de narcóticos
(poh-sez-SYOHN day nahr-KOH-tee-kohs)

VIOLATING YOUR.....   **PROBATION / PAROLE**
Violar su.....   probación (same word for parole)
(vee-oh-LAHR soo.....)   (proh-bah-see-OHN)

RESTRAINING / STALKING ORDER
Orden de Restricción
(OHR-den day ray-strick-see-OHN)

THERE ARE DRUGS PRESENT IN YOUR BLOOD   /   URINE
Hay drogas presentes en su.............. sangre / orín
(ay DROH-gahs pray-SEHN-tays ehn soo..... (SAHN-gray) (oh-REEN)

THERE IS A WARRANT FOR YOUR ARREST.
Hay una orden de arresto para usted.
(Eye OO-nah OHR-dehn day ah-REHS-toh PAH-rah oo-STEHD)
(SEE "CRIMES AND DESCRIPTIONS" for other crimes).

DID YOU DO IT?   (ADVISE OF RIGHTS IF APPROPRIATE)
¿Lo hizo Ud?
(Loh EE-soh oo-STEHD)

A SAMPLE OF YOUR BLOOD / URINE IS REQUIRED
Se requiere una muestra de su sangre / orín
(say ray-KEE-ay-ray OO-nah moo-AYS-trah day SAHN-gray / OH-reen)

YOU WILL BE NOTIFIED OF THE RESULTS
Se le avisarán de los resultados
(say lay ah-vee-sahr-AN day lohs ray-sool-TAH-dohs)

128

IF YOU REFUSE YOUR PAROLE / PROBATION WILL BE REVOKED
(Use for Searches also)
En caso de que se rehuse su probación se revocará
(Ehn **CAHS**-oh day kay say ray-**OO**-say soo proh-bah-see-**OHN**
ray-voh-cahr-**AH**)

I AM NOT REQUIRED TO HAVE A WARRANT?
No requiero una orden de registro / cateo
(No ray-**KEY**-ahr-oh **OO**-nah **OHR**-dehn day reh-**HEE**-stroh / kah-**TAH**-oh)

I AM GOING TO SEARCH YOUR.......(See "Consent to Search for list)
Voy a registrar / catear su......
(Voy ah reh-**HEES**-trar / cah-**TAY**-ahr soo.....)

WE HAVE A SEARCH WARRANT.
Tenemos una orden de registro / cateo.
(Tehn-**EH**-mohs **OO**-nah **OHR**-dehn day reh-**HEE**-stroh / kah-**TAY**-oh)

YOUR PAROLE / PROBATION IS REVOKED
Su probación está revocada
(Soo proh-bah-see-**OHN** es-**TAH** ray-voh-**CAH**-dah)

YOUR PAROLE / PROBATON / DEPORTATION HEARING WILL BE ON THE
Su audiencia de probación / deportación será el:
(Soo ah-oo-dee-**EHN**-see-ah day proh-bah-see-**OHN** day-pohr-tah-see-**OHN**
say-**RAH** ehl:)

____ OF	_____	199__	AT	_____
____ de	_____	199__	a las	_____
____ day	_____	199__	ah lahs	_____

YOU MAY BE DEPORTED
Quizas Ud. será deportado (a)
(Kee-**SAHS** oo-**STEHD** seh-**RAH** day-pohr-**TAH**-doh (dah)

YOU WILL BE DEPORTED
Ud. será deportado (a)
(oo-**STEHD** seh-**RAH** day-pohr-**TAH**-doh (dah)

YOU CANNOT BAIL
No puede salir bajo fianza
(noh **PWAY**-deh sah-**LEER** **BAH**-oh **FYAHN**-sah)

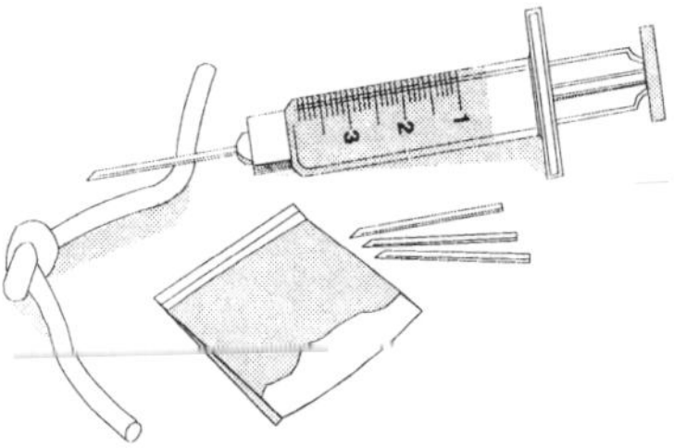

DRUG GLOSSARY AND CATEGORIES OF DRUGS

(Street slang and terms will vary from local to local)

ARE YOU ON MARIJUANA?	¿Estás grifo?	(es-STAHS gree-FOH) (fountain)
ARE YOU GOING TO A DOPE DEAL?	Jale (work); ¿Vas a hacer un trato?	(HAH-lay) (vahs ah ah-SAYR oon TRAH-toh)
ARE YOU HOLDING?	¿tienes jale?	(tee-EHN-ays HAH-lay) (P.V.C.)
ARE YOU TAKING COKE?	¿Estas eléctrico	(es-STAHS ee-LEHK-tree-koh)
ARE YOU ON THE NOD? (H)	¿Estas cocodrilo	(es-STAHS koh-koh-DREE-loh) (Are you like a sleepy crocodile basking in the sun?)
BUSINESS WITH NON-HISPANICS	hacer business	(ah-SAYR biz-nez)
CENT	centavo	(sehn-TAH-voh) (A KILO OF DOPE (2.2)
DO YOU HAVE DOPE ON YOU?	¿Traes jale?	(TRAH-ays HAH-lay)
FINGERNAIL OF SNORT	uñazo	(oon-YAH-soh)
FLUNKY (DRUG RUNNER)	menso	(MEHN-soh)
FRONTED DRUGS	por en frente	(pohr ehn FREHN-tay)
INJECT (TO)	picarse	(pee-KAHR-say) (stick yourself)
JUNKIE	tecate	(tay-KAH-tay)(beer or owl/big eyes)
LARGE DOPE DEAL	un jalón	(oon hah-LOHN)
LINE OF COKE	linea	(LEE-nee-ah)
NARCOTICS COP	narco	(NAHR-koh)
PREMIUM	de pilón	(pee-LOHN)=N/C Good Business
SOUTH TO NORTH MULING	ir para arriba	(eer PAH-rah ah-REE-bah)
SMALL DOPE DEAL	jalectio	(hah-lay-SEE-toh)
TO FIND DRUGS	hallar jale	(ah-YAHR HAH-lay)
TO GO FAR SOUTH TO GET	ir bien para abajo.	
TO GO NORTH TO GET	ir para arriba	(eer bee-YEHN PAH-rah ah-BAH-hoh)
TO GO SOUTH TO GET	ir para abajo	(eer PAH-rah ah-BAH-hoh)
WET FINGER DAB OF DRUGS	Dedal	(der-DAHL) (Thimble Full)
WHOLE (Uncut)	Entero	(ehn-TAY-roh)

(* Indicates Nystagmus present)

Depressants	(*Alcohol, Marijuana, *Barbiturates except Valium)
C.N.S. Stimulants	(Cocaine, Meth)
Hallucinogens	(LSD, Peyote, PCP)
*Phencyclidine	(PCP)
Narcotic Analgesics	(Heroin)
*Inhalants	(*Toluene; in glue and paints)
Cannabis	(No nystagmus present in Narcotics, Stimulants, Cannabis, or Hallucinogens)

Note: Pupil dilation references are approximations. Pupil size is dependent not only on the drug taken, but the number taken and quantity used. References are for standard pharmaceutical quality.

INDICATIONS OF DRUG USAGE

<u>ALCOHOL</u> alcohol (ahl-koh-OHL) (Booze, brew, juice, cool one, sauce, vino, barooski, and others) User may appear happy, excited, confused, passive, aggressive, uncoordinated, incoherent, drowsy, sluggish. May have drooping eyelids, slurred speech, and general state of intoxication. One of the most widely abused addictive drug. Frequently, ingested by individuals involved in motor vehicle accidents, assaults, robberies, rapes, and many other crimes. *Duration of dosage varies. Detectible in urine. (6.5 mm pupil dilation). Orally taken but can be injected.*

DRUNK	borracho	(boh-**RRAH**-choh)
INTOXICATED	intoxicado	(een-toh-xee-**KAH**-doh)
DRUGGED	endrogado	(ehn-droh-**GAH**-doh)

CANNABIS: Canabis (kah-**NAH**-bees)

MARIJUANA, HASHISH, AND HASH OIL. Rebound dilation, slurred speech, impaired attention process and divided attention tasks. Bloodshot eyes, odor of substance about person, stimulated appetite, at times disoriented, mild confusion, released inhibitions, reddening of the nasal and throat areas. *Duration varies with strength but averages 2-4 hours. Can be smoked, eaten, combined in food, or sometimes injected. Pupils may be slightly dilated. Detectible in urine.*

DEPRESSANTS Depresivos (day-prehs-**EE**-vohs)

ALCOHOL, BARBITURATES, NON-BARBITURATES, CANNABIS, AND OTHERS THAT INDUCE SLEEP. Thick slurred speech, drunken behavior without odor of alcohol inability to perform simple mental or physical tasks, uncoordinated, at times disoriented, drowsy, sluggish. (Ex: Quaalude, seconal, phenobarbital, Tuinal, Librium, Valium. *(Pupils 6.5 mm)*

HALLUCINOGENS Alucinates (ah-loo-see-**NAHN**-tays)

LSD, PEYOTE, PSILOCYBE MUSHROOMS, MESCALINE, PCP, ETC. Hallucinations, memory loss, mental misperceptions of surroundings and self identity, dazed, paranoia, body tremors, flashbacks, poor coordination, reddening of the face, sweating, tearing,disorientation, muscle twitching, speech difficulty, yawning, misconception of time, dizziness, blurred vision, headaches, nausea, impaired hearing, seizures, and general dazed appearance. *Duration varies. Pupils dilated 6.5 mm)*

INHALANTS Inhalantes (ehn-ah-**LAHN**-tays)

PAINTS, (GLUE-Cola (KOH-lah), WHITE OUT, BENZENE, FINGERNAIL POLISH, GOLD AND SILVER SPRAY PAINT, COOKWARE COATINGS, LEATHER COATINGS, HAIR SPRAYS, AND OTHERS. Produce variety of effects including blockage of oxygen to the brain. Most noticeable causes: Residue or odor of substance about person, drunken behavior, confusion, thick or slurred speech, poor attention span, nausea may be present. *Inhalants frequently sprayed into plastic bread wrappers and placed over nose and mouth to be inhaled. Duration may last from 5-8 hrs. Pupils normal.(refer to "SOLVENTS").*

NARCOTICS Narcóticos (nahr-**KOH**-tee-kohs)

NATURAL OR SYNTHETIC GROUPS. (OPIUM, MORPHINE, HEROIN, CODEINE, HYDROMORPHONE, METHADONE, MEPERIDINE, DEMEROL, ETC.). Sleepy, droopy eyelids, dry mouth, drowsiness, facial itching with scratching,
euphoria, poor coordination, needle marks on body, slurred or thick speech. *Pupils constricted (-2.9mm), can be snorted, smoked, injected, or orally. Duration 3- 6 hours but varies.*

STIMULANTS   Ectimulantes   (ây-stee-moo-LAHN-tays)

AMPHETAMINES, METHAMPHETAMINE, COCAINE, RITALIN, DEXEDRINE, PRELUDIN, ETC. Restlessness, increased alertness, talkative, anxious, excitation, rapid and rambling speech, euphoria, insomnia, loss of appetite, grinding of teeth, dry mouth, redness to nasal area if "snorting" & appear to have a runny nose, impaired decision making processes, over confident, paranoia. **PUPILS DILATED 6.5MM**

NAME, STREET NAME and DEFINITION

BARBITURATES (Barbs, blues, downers, reds-rojas (ROH-hahs), red devils-Coloradas (koh-loh-RAH-dahs), yellow jackets-Amarillas (ah-mah-REE-yahs), (Rainbows a combination of pills called reinbos (REH-EEN-bohs) in capsules and tablets. Refer "DEPRESSANTS" above for Symptoms of Abuse. *(Oral, injected, or taken rectally. Duration varies from 1-16 hrs. Detectible in urine.*

COCAINE Cocaina (Koh-kah-EE-nah) (100 Milligram is average street dose(Coke, flake, lines, blow, base, girl, toot, snow, dust, nose candy, white, perica, ghetto blaster, La Dama Blanca(Cocaine-Freebase type), greengold, **crack, coca.**) A white, crystalline alkaloid powder extracted from dried cocoa leaves of S. America. Used as a local anesthetic. Anesthetizes tissue and constricts blood vessels during surgery to cut blood loss. Excitable, talkative, euphoria, loss of appetite, and insomnia. Users appear to have a runny nose or a cold. Sold in the form of Cocaine hydrochloride. Conversion to base of Crack makes it volatile when heated and will vaporize for smoking. Risk of heart attack and liver damage. Smoked, sniffed, injected. Dosage varies 1½ to 2 hours. Present paste added to tobacco or marij. Popular in Latin America. (Cocaine normally can be detected in blood within 8 hours) *NOTE: Av. 175 kg of dried cocoa leaves will produce 1 kg of almost pure Cocaine.*

ADDITIONAL SLANGS AND TERMS

Bindle -	bolsita	(bohl-SEE-tah)
Newspaper bindle	papiro	(pa-PEE-roh)
Brick -	ladrillo	(lah-DREE-yoh)
Dime Bag -	una bolsa	(OO-nah BOHL-sah)
Gram -	Gramo	(GRAH-moh)
½ Gram -	Medio gramo	(MEH-dee-oh GRAH-moh)
Nickel Bag -	un cinco	(oon SEEN-koh)
Ounce -	onza	(OHN-sah)
1/2 Ounce -	media onza	(MEH-dee-ah OHN-sah)
1/4 Ounce -	Cuarto de onza	(KWAHR-toh deh OHN-sah)
Outfit -	equipo	(eh-KEE-poh)
Needle -	aguja	(ah-GOO-hah)
Spoon -	cuchara	(koo-CHAH-rah)
Pipe -	pipa	(PEE-pah)

COCAINE AMOUNTS
DURATION OF DOSE/30-40 MIN. EFFECTS FROM 1-2 HRS.

Girl	1/16 gram
Quarter	1/4 gram of powder
Five-0	$50 of Cocaine
Half	$50 = 1/2 gram of powder Cocaine
Fifty	$50 = 1/2 gram of rock Cocaine
G-rock	One gram of rock Cocaine
Double up	$40 of rock Cocaine for $20 (competition)
Bindle	Paper or foil folds (usually 1/8 oz)
Twenty	$20 of rock Cocaine
(Doub)	" " and (Two-O)
8 Ball	3.5 grams/ 1/8 oz. slang name: Able

CODEINE (School boy)

In capsule, tablet, and liquid form. Alkaloid found in opium. Most Codeine is produced from Morphine. Pain killer. *(Taken orally but can be injected. Duration 3-24 hours. Detectible in urine.*

DEMEROL   (Cubes)

Meperidine (Pethidine) used medically as an analgesic and sedative. *DURATION 4-8 HOURS (ORAL & INJECTION)*

DILAUDID (Dillies, Little D, Big D, Drug Store Heroin) -

Hydromorphone - used medically as an analgesic. Derivative of Opium. In tablet and liquid form. 2-8 times more potent than Morphine. *(ORAL & INJECTED) DURATION 3-24 HOURS DETECTIBLE IN URINE.*

ETORPHINE

Derivative of Opium. 1000 times more potent than Morphine. Used by veterinarians to immobilize large wild animals. Strictly regulated. Duration varies. Detectible in urine. *DURATION VARIES. DETECTIBLE IN URINE.*

FENTANYL (China White, Persian White)

Can be taken in capsule, powder, or tablet forms. Appears to similar outward symptoms like Heroin. Substance is addictive. *(ORAL AND INJECTION) DURATION VARIES SUBSTANTIALLY. DETECTIBLE IN URINE.*

HASHISH   haxis (ax-EES)

(Goma de Mota, Hash, Soles, kif, leb, shish, sole) Secretions of the cannabis plant, which are collected, dried, and then compressed into a variety of forms, such as balls, cakes, or cookie-like sheets. Has 3% THC content. **DURATION - 2-4 HOURS (SMOKED AND ORAL) (OTHER TYPES OF): (Black Russian, Blond Lebanese, Pakistani, Black Afghani, Moroccan, Kashmir)** Indicates both quality and area of production. **HASH OIL** Process of repeated extraction of plant materials to yield a dark liquid. Contains 20% THC content. 1-2 drops on a cigarette is equal to 1 joint. Symptoms of abuse same as Marijuana. *Smoked or ingested. Duration 2-4   hours. DETECTIBLE IN URINE.*

HEROIN   heroína (ay-roh-EEN-ah) (20-30 Milligrams daily for physical dependency)(Chiva, Horse, smack, H, stuff, boy, junk, thing, jive, polvo, Estuffa, Caballo, Hombre, Scag) Diacetylmorphine. Derived by modification of chemicals contained in Opium. Synthesized from Morphine. Pure Heroin is a white

powder with a bitter taste. Illegally it varies in color from white to dark brown from impurities or additives such as food coloring, cocoa, or brown sugar. A single dosage (bag) is about 100 mg. and is 5% pure. Cut is sugar, starch, powdered milk, and quinine. (Injected, sniffed, smoked) Duration 3-6 hrs. Detectible in urine. Derivatives include morphine, Codeine, Dilaudid, Methadone. (See Opium) (Concrete - Slang for White Heroin from Mexico) Brown Heroin also called Mexican Brown, Mexican Horse.

AMOUNTS

Booger 2/10 gram
Balloon Balún (bah-LOON) Grams in balloon for packaging or quick ingesting
Packet 13 balloons - packet
Bindle Foil folds (usually 1/8 oz)
Bag - Bolsa (BOHL-sah) Single dosage unit; weight 100 mg; 5% purity

HEROIN (TAR) Obscura, Negra, Tootsie roll, gum, chiva, goma, Mexican, Mud, boy, Mexican Gum, Gum) Note: Mexican slang for informer is Rat - rata

Pedazo (peh-DAH-soh) (piece)   1p = 25 (28 N/A) X 40 (Y) X 40 = 1 B/O)

A dark colored, narcotic, tar-like sticky substance; a crude form of heroin illicitly made in Mexico containing impurities such as hydrochloride, opium, alkaloids, acetylated opium, acetylated codeine and insoluble plant products of the opium poppy. It commonly smells of vinegar, may be sticky like roofing tar or hard like coal, and is dark brown to black. Purity is 40-80%. (Cut is burnt cornstarch) (INJECTED).

HEROIN (China White, SEA, SWA) White heroin is usually from SE Asia.

KETAMINE (ketaject, Ketalar) A legal prescription drug intended for use as an anesthetic. Close relative of PCP(similar effects). Duration can be for days.

LSD ácido (AH-see-doh) (Acid, blotter, windowpane, paper, pane, purple haze, stars, wedges, microdots, blue double dome, yellow sunshine, white mini-micro dots, micro-dots) Lysergic Acid Diethylamide (LSD-25) A hallucinogenic drug, semisynthetic, derived from lysergic acid, a chemical in ergot (the) fungus that attacks cereal grains. Causes hallucinations, illusions, poor perception of time and space, panic reactions, and psychosis. Flashbacks are common. Taken by capsule, tablets, powder, or liquid. Commonly found on sugar cubes and paper carriers. Taken by mouth normally and measured in micrograms. *Duration 8-12 HRS. (Oral) Not detectible in urine)(Pupil Dilation 6.5 mm) AMOUNTS 1 Hit (Dose varies)*

MARIJUANA Marijuana (mah-ree-hoo-AH-nah) (Smoke, grass, greenbacks, shake, (leftover scraps after a harvest), pot, sativa, Indica, mota, weed, Mexican weed, redheads, sinsemillia, ganja, whack, reefer, Thai stick, Acapulco Gold, punta, roja, negra) Originally used for rope, seed in feed mixtures, an oil in paint, 3 times more potent when smoked then taken orally. Produces feeling of relaxation, well being, hunger, changing emotions, sensory imagery, impaired memory, dulling of perception. Wild domestic plants contain .5% concentration of THC. Sinsemilla contains up to 20% THC content. SE Asian "Thai Sticks" consist of marijuana buds bound on short sections of bamboo. Smells of burned rope.
Duration 2-4 hrs. (Smoked & Oral) DETECTIBLE IN URINE
T.H.C. Tetrahydrocannabinol: one of the 61 cannabinoids contained in the resin synthesized by the marijuana plant.

AMOUNTS

Dime	$10 of marijuana	
Nickel	$ 5 " "	
1/2 O.Z.	1/2 ounce of Marijuana	
" O. Z."	1 ounce of Marijuana	
Kilo	2.2 pounds of Marijuana	

MARIJUANA TERMS DESCRIBING THE STRAIN & AREA OF PRODUCTION

(Columbian, Oaxacan, Thai, Panama Red, Mexican Red Hair, Kona Gold, Maui Wowi, Acapulco Gold)

<u>CLONING</u> Cutting from a superior quality plant (sinsemilla), rooting and placing it in rich soil. Genetically identical; will have same THC content; 4-5 harvests yearly.

<u>SINSE</u> Sinsemilla - derived from two Spanish words: "sin" meaning "without", "semilla" meaning "seed". Prepared from unpollinated female plant.

MDA, MDMA, DOM (Ecstasy, LOVE DRUG)
Methylenedioxymethamphetamine. An amphetamine variant which causes hallucinations and appears to have effects like amphetamines. **DURATION IS VARIABLE. DETECTIBLE IN URINE.**

MESCALINE - SEE PEYOTE (PUPILS DILATED APPROX., 6.5 mm)

METH (Crank, meth, crystal meth, crystal, crank, speed, go, fast, uppers, bennies, jelly beans, wake ups)
Methylamphetamine: An amine derivative of amphetamine that is used in the form of crystalline hydrochloride (stimulant). "Speed Freak" is a person who takes drug by injection. Originally used for narcolepsy and weight control. Restlessness, increased alertness, talkative, anxious, excitation, rapid and rambling speech, euphoria, insomnia, loss of appetite, grinding of teeth, dry mouth, appear to have cold with a runny nose, over confident, paranoia, insomnia. *Pupils dilated 6.5 mm. Duration varies from 2-12 hrs., depending on dosage. Present in urine. Methadrine metadrina (meh-tah-DREE-nah) Speed anfetamina (ahn-feh-tah-MEE-nah)(Meth can be detected in urine from 48-72 hours after taking)*

AMOUNTS
Dime bags -	Avg .1 gram; purity approx. 25-35% (varies in locale)
Bindle -	Paper folds usually containing 1/8 oz
Eightball -	1/8 oz

<u>ICE</u> **(Glass, Crystal)** A clear, crystal-shaped, solid form that looks like glass. May have yellow cast or look milky. *Ingested by smoking. Depending on quality, one dose varies in duration & may last anywhere from 2-24 hrs. Often sold in heat sealed cellophane packets.*

METHADONE (Dolophine, Dollies)
A synthetic drug in tablet and liquid form, similar to Morphine only in it's effect. Used in detoxification of Heroin addicts. *(Oral & Injected. Duration 12-25 hrs. Detectible in urine.*

METHAQUALONE (Mex Quas, Quaaludes, ludes, 747's, sopor)
Normally in tablets but found as white powder or capsule. Symptoms are same as barbiturates. *(ORAL OR INJECTED) DURATION 4-8 HRS. DETECTIBLE IN URINE.*

MISC (Speedball)
Heroin/coke or heroin/crank combination; no particular weight measurement. **(Travel Agent)** Dealer in Hallucinogens **(Turkey or Bunk)** An imitation drug sold as a real one. **(Tin)** A small amount of opiate.

MORPHINE morfina (mohr-FEE-nah) (M, Morf, Miss Emma) A principal derivative of Opium. Odorless, tastes bitter, and darkens with age. White crystals, tablet, and liquid forms. One part Morphine base makes one part Heroin. Codeine is a derivative. Duration 3-24 hrs. (Oral, smoked, injected) Detectible in urine.

OPIUM Dover's Powder. Used as a pain killer and antidiarrheal. Milky fluid that oozes out of incisions in unripe seedpod of the poppy. Dried to produce Opium gum. 25 alkaloids of which two are Morphine and Codeine. Dark brown in color. 10 parts Opium make one part Morphine base. One part Morphine Pod contains 80 mg of Opium. (8 mg Heroin) DURATION 3-6 HRS SINGLE DOSAGE (SMOKED & ORAL).

PERCODAN (Perks) An analgesic & anti-diarrheal.
Duration 1-4 hrs (Oral & Inject)

PEYOTE & MESCALINE (Mesc, buttons, cactus) Mescaline, derived from the peyote plant buttons, which produces hallucinations, psychedelic effects, and poor perception of time and distance. Can cause emotional instability, psychosis, and panic reactions. Obtained from fleshy parts or buttons of the plant. Ground to a powder and taken orally. Duration 8-12 Hrs. Psilocybin is variable. Orally in capsules, tablets or raw buttons from Peyote Cactus. *Not present in urine.*

PHENCYCLIDINE (PCP)
(Juice, dusters, Angel Dust, Super Grass, Killer Weed, Embalming Fluid, Rocket Fuel, loveboat, ozone, wet one, hog, pour, water, crystal, wac. A PCP cigarette dipped in PCP is called a Shem, kool, lovely, & stick) Used in veterinarian medicine as a powerful anesthetic. A white crystalline powder that causes bizarre and violent behavior (contaminants can cause it to be tan to brown with consistency ranging from a powder to a gummy mass). Sold in tablets/capsules/liquid/powder forms. Commonly put on leafy material for smoking or ingestion. Sweating, illusions, repetitive speech, hallucinations, confused, drowsiness, can be violent and combative, drowsiness, blank stare, non-communicative, incomplete verbal responses, misconception of time and space, muscle rigidity, unresponsive, can tolerate extreme pain with little acknowledgement, inability to perform simple mental tasks, aggressive personality. Can cause psychosis, psychotic behavior, psychological dependence. *Duration of dose can vary from hours to days. Pupils dilated. Can be snorted, injected, smoked, ingested. Detectible in urine.*

PSILOCYBIN / PSILCCCYN (Mexican Mushrooms, shrooms, mushrooms, Magic, Magic Mushrooms) Brown mushrooms that contain the natural hallucinogen psilocybin, chemically related to LSD. Sold frozen, fresh, cooked, or dried and taken orally. Can also be ingested in capsule and tablet form. DURATION 4-6 hrs but may vary.
(NORMALLY TAKEN ORALLY) CANNOT BE DETECTED IN URINE.

SOLVENTS Gasoline, model airplane glue, nail polish, lighter and cleaning fluids, and numerous types of adhesives. Inhalation causes drunken behavior with loss of appetite, nausea, sneezing, nose bleeding, bloodshot eyes, fatigue, extreme thirst, and with chronic use appears to impair and damage the brain. *Duration depends on product.*

TRANQUILIZERS (Big T's, T's, V's) Symptoms same as barbiturates. In tablet and liquid forms. *(Oral or injected) Duration 4-8 hours. Detectible in urine.*

VALIUM (Mother's helper) Anti anxiety, anti-convulsant, sedative hypnotic.
DURATION 4-8 HRS. (ORAL)

Note: Hispanic Street Gang Slang "vato loco" (VAH-toh LOH-koh) or crazy man. Usually a hard core with a record of violence. (Copo=Corporal in Carribean)

ARM TRACKS- alacránes (ah-lah-CRAH-nays) (TRAH-kehs)
BUTT OF A MARIJUANA CIGARETTE- pitillo (pee-TEE-yoh) (**butt**)
CON JOB- palitorque (pehl-ee-TOHR-kay) to be smooth or leverage to twist
GOOD STRONG MARIJUANA- "yerba buena" (YEHR-bah boo-ay-nah)
PEOPLE SMUGGLER - "pollero" (poh-YERH-oh)
    Lit: A Chicken farmer but means a coyote at the border)
RUSH FROM TAKING DRUGS - "quique" (**KEY**-kay)
SMUGGLED GOODS (cigrettes or stolen goods) "fayuca" (fah-YOU-kah)
TO BE OUT OF MONEY - "liso" (**LEE**-soh) (Lit: smooth)

"A good narc never shares guns, dogs, wives or informants."

PRICE LIST OF CONTROLLED SUBSTANCES

(Prices are that of Oregon and will vary due to purity rate and locale. Prices for individual locales may be inserted).

DRUG	TYPE	DESCRIPTION	QUANT	PRICE ($)
COCAINE	**CRACK**	Rock	.5g	45-60
			1.g	80-100
			1 OZ	750-1100
	POWDER		.25g	20-35
			.5g	40-60
			1.g	60-120
	8 Ball		3.5g	160-350
			1/16 Oz	100-150
			1 OZ	800-1500
			1 LB	16000-36000
			1 KILO	22000-40000

PACKAGING - *Vials, foil, heat sealed bags, zip lock bags, cellophane bags. Kilo's wrapped in plastic, fiberglass casting, duct and electrical tape, multi-colored paper or plastic wrap, cellophane etc.*

CODEINE			Tab	3-25
DEMEROL			Tab	5-6
DILAUDID			Tab	25-60
HASHISH			1 grm	10
			1 OZ	200
PACKAGING - Foil, vials, paper			1 **LB**	1920
HEROIN	**TAR**		.25 grm	50-100
			1 grm	100-240
		Balloon	1 grm	100-550
			1 OZ	2200-4000
			1 LB	40000-70000
		Mexican Brown	1 **KILO**	35,000-100,000

PACKAGING - Tinfoil, Cellophane, Balloons, wrapped in duct and electrical tape etc.

| **LSD** | Blotter | 1 hit | $1-5 |

(In Oregon 1 ounce cost $110 and can be converted to 80,000 hits)

PACKAGING - Usually on a carrier substance such as paper

MARIJUANA	Cigarette or joint	1	3-10
		1 g	10-15
SHAKE		.25 OZ	10-45
		.5 OZ	40-55
		1 OZ	125-400

Joint (Rooster) Gallo (**GAH**-yoh) or leño (**LEH**-nyoh)
Lid (Boot) Bote (**BOH**-teh)

BUD		1 grm	10-20
		1 OZ	200-300
		.25 LB	**$500-550**
		1 LB	1500-4000

PLANTS   1 Starter Plant 10-25 (Germinates 6-7 days)
100 Starter Plants 2000
1 Fully Matured Plant (high quality)   1000-2000

(Marijuana Plants -Planta de marijuana
(**PLAHN**-tah   deh mah-ree-**UAH**-nah)
(1 mature plant yields 3/4 to 1 Lb of dried material)

PACKAGING - Plastic baggies, paper, paper folds, plastic bags, paper packages, plastic and paper in assorted colors.

| **MDMA** | | .25g | $30 |

METH	**POWDER**	.25g	20-25
		.5g	40-60
		1g	60-100
	8 BALL	3.5 grm	150-300
		1 OZ	1000-1600
		1 LB.	10000-16000
		1 Kilo	25,000
ICE		1 g.	250-400
	8 Ball	3.5g	900-1200
		.25 OZ	1900-3000
		.5 OZ	4000-5000
		1 OZ.	5200-8000

PACKAGING Sealed Bags, Paper, Paper Folds, Plastic Bags in assorted colors

PRECURSOR Methlamine 1 GAL. $800

PSILOCYBIN MUSHROOMS 1g   15
                                                                   1 OZ   100-250
                                                                   1 LB   600-875

PACKAGING Plastic bags or baggies

VALIUM   1 Capsule $3
                                                  1 Pill $3

CHEMICALS ASSOCIATED WITH "METH LABS"

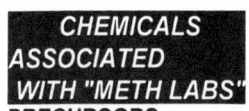

PRECURSORS (A raw material for a controlled substance that becomes part of the finished product. Precursors controlled by each state)

- 1-phenyl-2-bromopropane
- 2-phenyl-1-bromoethane
- Acetaldehyde
- Acetic Anhydride
- Acetic Acid
- Acetonitrile
- Acetylphenylacetonitrile
- Allybenzene
- Allyl Chloride
- Aluminum
- Aluminum Chloride
- Ammonia
- Ammonium Formate
- Ammonium Acetate
- Amphetamine
- Aniline
- Anthranilic Acid
- Benzaldehyde
- Benzene
- Benzyl Methyl Ketone
- Benzyl Chloride
- Benzylcyanide
- Bromobenzene
- Butylamine
- Chloroacetone
- Cyclohexanone
- Ephedrine
- Ethyl Acetate
- Formamide
- Formic Acid
- Freon (F-12)
- Hydrochloric Acid
- Hydroxylamine Hydrochloride
- Isatoic Anhydride
- Magnesium
- Magnesium Turnings
- Manganous Carbonate
- Manganous Chloride
- Methyl Acrylate
- Mercuric Chloride
- Methyl Acrylate
- Methyl Methacrylate
- Methyl Benzyl Ketone
- Methylamine
- Monobromobenzene
- N-(1-phenethyl)-piperidin-4-one
- N-(1-phenethyl-4-piperidinyl)aniline
- N-(1-phenethyl-4-piperidinyl)-4-fluoroaniline
- N-(4-piperidinyl)aniline
- N-1-(2-phenylisopropyl)-4-piperidiyl)aline
- N-1-(2-phenylisopropyl)-piperidin-4-one
- N-AcetylaNthranillic Acid
- N-methylformamide
- Nitric Acid
- Nitroethane
- Ortho-nitrotoluene
- Ortho-toluidine
- P-2-P(Phenyl-2-Propanone)
- P-Fluoroaniline
- Palladium Black
- Phenethylamine
- Phenylacetic Acid (Cat Urine Smell)
- Phenylmagnesium Bromide
- Phenylpropanolamine (HCl)
- Pheynlacetone
- Phosphoric Acid
- Piperdine
- Propionic Anhydride

REAGENTS (Reacts chemically with one or more precursors, but does not become part of the finished product).

- Acetic Acid
- Aluminum Chloride
- Aluminum
- Aluminum Grit/Foil
- Ammonium Chloride
- Ammonium Hydroxide
- Benzenesul
- Butylamine
- Calcium Hydroxide
- Carbon
- Copper Sulfate
- Ferric Chloride
- Formic Acid
- Hydriodic Acid
- Hydrobromic Acid
- Hydrochloric Acid (Anhyd.)
- Hydrochloric Acid

SOLVENTS (Does not react chemically with a precursor or reagent and does not become part of the finished product.)

2,2,4-Trimethylpentane
Acetic Acid
Acetone
Acetonitrile
Benzene
Chloroform
Diethyl Ether
Ethanol
Ethanol (ETOH)
Ether
Ethyl Ether

CHLOROFORM - Clear colorless very watery liquid; sweet, heavy medicinal odor; usually found in metal can or bottle. Contact may cause burns to skin & eyes. Fumes produce dizziness, weakness and anesthesia. Excessive inhalation produces liver damage & can be fatal. Speed in removing material from skin is off **extreme** importance. Flush eyes for 15 minutes.

ACETONE - A clear, colorless liquid; very watery with pungent sharp odor; usually found in metal can or bottle. Irritating to eyes and respiratory system. Causes headache, dizziness and unconsciousness. May be absorbed through the skin. **Flammable & combustible.**

Hexane
Freon (Tetra Hydrogenfluron)
Iso-Octane
Isopropyl Alcohol
Methanol (MEOH)
Pyridine
Sodium Hydroxide
Sodium Methoxide
Tetra Hydrogenfluron (Freon-12)
Toluene

OTHER CHEMICALS

Acetic Acid (Glacial)
Aluminum Foil
Biphenyl
Charcoal
Cyclohexylpiperidine
Diethyl Ether
Distilled Water
Dry Ether
Ethanol Alcohol
Ethanol
Hydriodic Acid
Hydrogen Gas
HYDROGEN SULFIDE (EGG SMELL) (Danger get out)
Iodine
Magnesium
Methamphetamine Hydrochloride
Methyl Alcohol
Methylamine
Petroleum Ether
Phenol
Phenylacetoacetonitrile
Phenylcyclohexanol
Phenylcyclohexene
Phenylethanol
Potassium Cyanide
Potassium
Salt
Sodium / Potassium Hydroxide
Thynal Chloride
White Phosphorous
Yellow Phosphorous
Sodium Sulfate
Sodium Cyanide
Sodium Bicarbonate
Sodium / Magnesium Sulfate
Sodium / Potassium Hydroxide
Sulfuric Acid
Thallium (III) Nitrate
Thonium Nitrate
Thionyl Chloride
X-Acetylphenylacetonitrile
X-methylstyrene
Sodium Sulfate
Sodium Acetate
Sodium Acetate (Catalyst)
Sodium Acetic (Anhyd)
Sodium Cyanohydroborate
Sodium Hydroxide (Flake Caustic Soda)
Sodium Acetate (Anhydrous)
Sodium Bisulfite
Sodium (Metal)
Sodium Chloride
Sodium Sulfate
Sodium Acetate
Sodium Hydroxide
Sodium Borohydride
Sodium Carbonate
Sodium Methoxide
Sodium
Sodium Amalgam
Red Phosphorus
Randy Nickel
Pumice
Phosphorus Oxychloride
Potassium Iodide
Potassium Cyanide
Potassium Carbonate
Platinum Oxide
Platinum Chloride
Phosphorus Pentoxide
Phosphorus Trichloride
Phosphoric Acid
Phosphorus Pentachloride
Perchloric Acid
Palladium on (Barium) Sulfate
Palladium Black
P-Toluene Sulfonic Acid
Nitric Acid
Molecular Sieve 3a
Mercury / Copper
Mercuric Chloride
Manganous Carbonate
Manganous Chloride
Magnesium Sulfate
Magnesium Turnings
Lithium Aluminum Hydride
Iodine
Iron Filings
Hydrogen Chloride Gas
Hydrogen Gas

ETHER- Clear watery liquid with pungent sweet odor; usually found in cans. If can appears rusty *DO NOT TOUCH*. Very flammable. Explosive if vapors confined. **Flame will follow vapors; sparks from light switches may ignite fumes.**

LEAD ACETATE- White, grayish or brownish color; commonly in powder form; odorless to slight vinegar smell;
usually obtained in 5 lb. quantity, usually in paper bag or box. Inhaling dust will cause dizziness or unconsciousness & is irritating to skin and eyes.

MERCURIC CHLORIDE- White opaque crystals or powder; usually comes in small jar or box. Used as a catalyst to start the chemical reaction. **Very poisonous if inhaled or injected; dust very irritating.**

METHYLAMINE- Clear liquid, ammonia or fishy smell; usually found in quart or gallon bottles. Irritant to eyes, respiratory system, & **burns skin**.

MURIATIC ACID- Clear liquid, if it is in it's original bottle it will have a blue cap on it; usually in pint to 5 Gal. size. Contact may cause burn to skin/eyes. Harmful if inhaled. **Fire may produce irritating or poisonous gas.**

PHENYL-2-PROPANONE (P2P)- Yellow, watery to oily liquid; slightly heavier than water and insoluble in water with a sweetish odor.

PHENYLACETIC ACID- Shiny white powder or crystals with cat urine smell. Usually found in cardboard containers (this chemical will test positive for Methamphetamine.) Inhalation of dust is poisonous. **Fire will produce toxic fumes.**

PHOSPHORUS- (Amorphous, Red)- Brownish red powder; usually found in cardboard containers in pint size. Flammable, combustible material. Can be ignited by heat, sparks or flame. Burns rapidly with flare burning effect.

Cap colors of Acids and Bases

Red - Nitric Acid	**Brown** - Acidic Acid	**Blue** - Hydrochloric Acid
Yellow - Sulfuric Acid	**Green** - Ammonia Hydroxide	

HELPFUL TERMS WHEN DEALING WITH DOGS

CAREFUL !
cuidado!
(kwee-**DAH**-doh)

AGGRESSIVE ?
Bravo ?
(**BRAH**-voh ?)

GRAB YOUR DOG !
agarra su perro!
(Ah-**GAHR**-ah   soo   **PAY**-roh)

DANGEROUS ?
peligroso?
(Pay-lee-**GROW**-so ?)

DOES YOUR DOG BITE ?
su perro muerde ?
(soo **PAY**-roh   **MWHERE**-day ?)

COLLAR
cadena
(ca-**DAY**-nah)

DO THEY BITE?
Muerdan?
(moo-**AYR**-dahn)

LEASH
lazo
(**LAH**-soh)

SPANISH ALPHABET

Alphabet consists of the same letters as the English alphabet AND these four additional characters: CH, LL, Ñ, and RR. [Asterisks (*) denote the letter name]

A	(ah)	*a. A in ah
B	(bay)	*be. B and V are pronounced the same (most of the time)
C	(say)	*ce. Ex: Civil. Hard like C in "country," all other times
CH	(ch)	*che. Like in "church".

(As of January 1996 the Spanish Royal Academy has eliminated "CH" as an actual letter of the Spanish alphabet, but it is still commonly used.)

D	(day)	*de. Da in dare; th in there
E	(ay)	*e. Has two sounds, E and A EX: Bet and Cafe
F	(ay-ray)	*efe. Similar to English
G	(hay)	*ge. Before vowels A, O, and U. Ex: gasolina (gasoline). Before E, I, and G is pronounced like H in House.
H	(ah-chay)	*hache. H is silent
I	(ee)	*i. Like the I in the English word machine
J	(hoh-tah)	*jota. (H sound) Like the letter H in house. Ex: Jose
K	(kah)	*ka. Letter found only in foreign words
L	(ehl-ay)	*ele. Similar as English
LL	(ehl-yay)	*elle. Considered a single symbol. On Mexican border, it is pronounced like the English letter Y
M	(ay-may)	*eme. As in English
N	(ay-nay)	*ene. As in English
Ñ	(ay-nyay)	*eñe. It sounds like the "NY" in "canyon"
O	(oh)	*o. Similar to English
P	(pay)	*pe. Similar to English
Q	(koo)	*qu(cu). Q is followed by U and is silent. The QU has same sound as K.
R	(ay-ray)	*ere. Similar to English. Beginning of word is slightly trilled. Would sound like this: rrest (rest).
RR	(ay-ray)	*erre. Strongly trilled
S	(ay-say)	*ese. **Similar to the S in sister**
T	(tay)	*te. As in English
U	(oo)	*u. As a vowel like the OO in Moon
V	(bay)	*ve. See the letter "B"
W	(doh blay oo)	*doble ve. Letter only appears in foreign words.
X	(ay kiss)	*equis. Ex: Exit. Sounds like English "S" before consonants. Some people pronounce the "X" before a consonant like the word "exit". Mex. sounds like the English "H".
Y	(ee-gree-ay-gah)	*i-griega. Alone it means "and" and sounds like the English long "E". Used as a consonant it is pronounced like the "Y" in "yes".
Z	(zeh-tah)	*zeta. Same as C before E or I.

TRIVIA - During the last century when U.S. Troops were in Mexico they frequently sang the popular son, "*Green Grow the Lilacs.*" The Mexicans overhearing the Americans sing tried to repeat some of the lyrics and "*Green Grow*" came out sounding like "*Gringo*." Hence the song was associated with the American "*Gringo*."

COMMON ERRORS MADE BY SPANISH SPEAKERS IN ENGLISH

1. The b and the v are confused as in base-vase
2. The v is pronounced as f as in have-haf; leaves-leeafes
3. The voiceless th sound is pronounced as s or t as mouth-mouse; think-sink; thank-tank
4. Pronounces the voiced th sound as d as these-dose; then-den
5. Pronounces ch sound as sh as catch-cash; chair-share; shoes-choose; wish-witch
6. Pronounces sh sound as ch as in fish-fich; ship-chip
7. Pronounces sh sound as ch as in measure-meacher; garage-garache
8. Pronounces z sound as s as in prize-price
9. Pronounces voiced s as in voiceless s as in rice-rise; his-hiss
10. The sp sound is said as esp as in spool-espool; special-especial
11. The final d sound is pronounced as t as in ride-write; bid-bit
12. The final t sound is pronounced as d as in classmate-classmade; sight-side
13. Pronounces the j sound as ch as in jar-char; joke-choke
14. Pronounces y sound as j as in yellow-jello; yet-jet
15. Pronounces g sound as ck as in bag-back; pig-pick
16. Pronounces the w sound as gw as in woman-gwman; wry-gray
17. Pronounces ng sound as nng as in bring-bringg; hang-hangg
18. Final ed is often omitted or mispronounced as in walked-walkked; curled-curlt

PROBLEM VOWEL SOUNDS:

1. Pronounces EE as I as in sheep-ship; feet-fit; neel-nild; cheek-chick
2. Pronounces I as EE as in did-deed; pill-peel; pick-peek
3. Pronounces OO sound as U (OO) as in pool-pull
4. Pronounces O as U as in bought-but; caught-cut
5. Pronounces A as O as in late-lot; gate-got
6. Pronounces A as in O as in hat-hot; map-mop
7. Pronounces E as A as in let-late; met-mate
8. Pronounces U as O as in done-dawn; cut-cot; duck-dog
9. Pronounces the U (OO) sound as OO as in pull-pool

"Girls tend to marry men like their fathers, that is why mothers cry at weddings."

SURVIVAL SPANISH ® COGNATES

Note: In reference to the following guide, almost all English words have the same meaning in Spanish. There are exceptions in the spelling in Spanish.

WORDS ENDING IN: "AL"
FATAL, HABITUAL, MUNICIPAL, SEXUAL, TERMINAL,
INDIVIDUAL, CENTRAL, LEGAL, SEVERAL, CRIMINAL,
PATERNAL, MATERNAL, EXTERNAL, MENTAL, VERBAL,
PATERNAL, MATERNAL, CONTROVERSIAL, PENAL, VITAL, RADICAL,
IDENTICAL, ANIMAL, CULTURAL, CRUCIAL, DENTAL

NOUNS ENDING IN: "OR"
MOTOR, COLOR, EXTERIOR, INTERIOR, SUPERIOR, PASTOR,
(if English word ends in TOR and preceded by a vowel change to DOR)
IE: RADIADOR, INDICADOR, ALTERNADOR, ASPIRADOR

NOUNS AND ADJECTIVES ENDING IN: "AR":
SIMILAR, RADAR, VERNACULAR, PARTICULAR

NOUNS AND ADJECTIVES ENDING IN "NT" ADD "E"
AGENTE, RESIDENTE, VIOLENTE, INCONSISTENTE,
NEGLIGENTE, PERTINENTE, EXIGENTE, INFORMANTE,
INCIDENTE, SIGNIFICANTE, COMPETENTE, ACCIDENTE

NOUNS ENDING IN "SION" (PRONOUNCED "see-OWN")
PERMISSION, VERSION, CONCLUSION, DECISION, DIVERSION

NOUNS ENDING IN "TION" CHANGE TO "CION" (see-OWN)
IE: DESTINATION TO "DESTINACION". Etc.
IDENTIFICATION, DIRECTION, PROTECTION, NOTIFICATION,
DETENTION, INFORMATION, CONTRADICTION, NATION

ADJECTIVES ENDING IN "BLE" PROCEEDED BY A VOWEL
(PRONOUNCED "BLAY") INOPERABLE, IMPROBABLE,
INDISPUTABLE, INELIGIBLE, VISIBLE, INTOLERABLE

NOUNS ENDING IN "MENT" ADD "O"
MOMENTO, DOCUMENTO, ARGUMENTO, DETRIMENTO

NOUNS AND ADJECTIVES ENDING IN "IC" ADD "O"
MEDICO, ANTISEPTICO, ALCOHOLICO, PUBLICO, FORENSICO,
EROTICO, PACIFICO, DIBETICO, DRASTICO, NEUROTICO,
DOMESTICO, CAUSTICO, LUNATICO, ERRATICO

NOUNS AND ADJECTIVES ENDING IN "CT" ADD "O"
IMPACTO, DIRECTO, PERFECTO, CONFLICTO, INCORRECTO,
CORRECTO, PRODUCTO, IMPERFECTO

NOUNS WHICH END IN "ITY" CHANGE TO "IDAD"
CAPACIDAD, OBSCENIDAD, COMPLICIDAD, BRUTALIDAD,
PROBABILIDAD, IDENTIDAD, ACTIVIDAD, MINORIDAD

NOUNS ENDING IN "CY" CHANGE THE "Y" TO "IA". (AFTER A
CONSONANT SUCH AS "LY" TO "LIA", "TY" TO "TIA" AND SO ON.
AGENCIA, URGENCIA, EMERGENCIA, RESIDENCIA, FAMILIA

An actual call to 911 in Bend, Oregon in 1995:
"Is it illegal to haul manure across state lines?"

WORDS THAT ARE SPELLED ALIKE OR ALMOST ALIKE IN SPANISH AND ENGLISH, YET MEAN THE SAME THING IN AT LEAST ONE DEFINITION (and some "Alcohol & Drug Cognates")

abdomen	inferior	**Alcohol / Drug Cognates**	fatal
abrasión	informal		fatiga
acidental	instructor		federal
actual	instrumental	(See if you can guess the word's meaning.)	felón
admirable	interior		fiasco
adorable	labor		gramo
alcohol	local		habitual
animal	mamá	abuso	hangar
antena	manual	adicción	hiperactividad
anual	maternal	agresividad	hipodérmica
apendicitis	melón	alcohol	horrible
aplicable	metal	alerta	horror
área	motor	brutal	hospital
artificial	múltiple	calibre	inspector
atlas	municipal	canon	infección
auto	negro	cápsula	intensiva
automóvil	no	cartel	intoxicación
balance	normal	causa	intoxicado
canal	numeral	cigarrillos	irritabilidad
capital	ocasión	colisión	judicial
casual	opinión	combinación	legal
central	oral	confesión	marca
cereal	original	concentración	material
chocolate	particular	conducta	memoria
circular	paternal	confusión	mental
civil	peculiar	contaminación	miserable
color	permanente	control	misión
coordinación	personal	criminal	náusea
comisión	plural	crisis	negociable
comparable	popular	cruel	oficial
conclusión	posible	culpable	omisión
considerable	postal	depresión	pánico
cónsul	prior	detectivo	paranoia
convoy	probable	dificultad	percepción
cuestión	profesional	diversión	plan
chasis	radio	**Drogas**	planta
decisión	región	Acido	pulso
detector	regular	Alucinates	pupila
diván	religión	Anfetamina	resultado
doctor	reversible	Canabis	revólver
error	revocable	Cocaína	rifle
evasión	rural	Codeína	rufián
expresión	sensible	Cranke	severa
extensión	sexual	Depresivos	tableta
factor	similar	Estimulantes	tensión
familiar	simple	Haxis	terrible
favor	sofá	Heroína	terror
favorable	superior	Inhalantes	vómito
final	suspensión	Marijuana	
flexible	total	Morfina	
fórmula	tractor	Narcóticos	
gas	trío	emocional	
general	triple	euforia	
gradual	trivial	exceso	
guardián	usual	explosión	
honor	verbal		
horizontal	versión		
hotel	visión		
imposible	visual		
impresión	vital		
individual	vocal		

"The reason we have such a high crime rate is that too many parents tie up their dogs and let their kids run loose."

INFINITIVE AND PRESENT TENSE VERBS ONLY

NOTE: **There are two verbs for "to be".** *Ser* describes a permanent condition. *Estar* describes location or a temporary condition. (Use *haber* only in compound sentences).

	ser (to be)	**estar** (to be)	**haber** (to have)
(yo) I	soy	estoy	he
You (fam.) (tú)	eres	estás	has
You(form.) usted	es	está	ha
He/She (él / ella)	es	está	ha
We (nosotros)	somos	estamos	hemos
You (pl.) ustedes	son	están	han
They (m) ellos	son	están	han

THREE CATEGORIES OF REGULAR VERBS

	ends in AR hablar (to speak)	**ends in ER** comprender (to comprehend)	**ends in IR** escribir (to write)
I (yo)	hablo	comprendo	escribo
You (fam.) (tú)	hablas	comprendes	escribes
You(form.) usted	habla	comprende	escribe
He/She (él / ella)	habla	comprende	escribe
We (nosotros)	hablamos	comprendemos	escribimos
You (pl.) ustedes	hablan	comprenden	escriben
They (m) ellos	hablan	comprenden	escriben

FOUR IRREGULAR VERBS TO LEARN

	poder (to be able)	**ir** (to go)	**ver** (to see)	**tener** (to have)
yo	puedo	voy	veo	tengo
tú	puedes	vas	ves	tienes
usted	puede	va	ve	tiene
él/ella	puede	va	ve	tiene
nosotros	podemos	vamos	vemos	tenemos
ustedes	pueden	van	ven	tienen
ellos	pueden	van	ven	tienen

ser (to be) (permanent)

I AM	NOSOTROS (We are)
SOY	**SOMOS**

HE IS (el)		
SHE IS (ella)		(ellos)
YOU ARE (Usted) (Formal)	**ES**	(ellas) **SON** (They are)
YOU ARE (Tu eres) (Familiar)		(Ustedes)

ESTAR (to be) (temporary)

I AM	NOSOTROS (We are)
ESTOY	**ESTAMOS**

HE IS (el)		
SHE IS (ella)		(ellos)
YOU ARE (Usted) (Formal)	**ESTÁ**	(ellas) **ESTÁN** (They are)
YOU ARE (Tu estás) (Familiar)		(Ustedes)

SIMPLE CONJUGATION OF "AR", "ER", and "IR" REGULAR VERBS IN THE PRESENT TENSE

Use the diagrams to conjugate regular verbs listed on the following pages. These diagrams will assist you in making a visual image that will make conjugation easier. *(Refer to the previous page of charts for samples of conjugations.)*

HABL**AR** (Singular-Present Tense)
(To Speak)

I (Yo)			NOSOTROS (We)
	O	**AMOS**	

HE IS (el)			(ellos)	
SHE IS (ella)	**A**	**AN**	(ellas)	**(They)**
YOU ARE (Usted) (Formal)			(Ustedes)	
YOU ARE (Tu hablas) (Fam.)				

COMPREND**ER** (Singular-Present Tense)
(To comprehend or to understand)

I (Yo)			NOSOTROS (We)
	O	**EMOS**	

HE IS (el)			(ellos)	
SHE IS (ella)	**E**	**EN**	(ellas)	**(They)**
YOU ARE (Usted) (Formal)			(Ustedes)	
YOU ARE (Tu comprendes) (Fam.)				

ESCRIB**IR** (Singular-Present Tense)
(To write)

I (Yo)			NOSOTROS (We)
	O	**IMOS**	

HE IS (el)			(ellos)	
SHE IS (ella)	**E**	**EN**	(ellas)	**(They)**
YOU ARE (Usted) (Formal)			(Ustedes)	
YOU ARE (Tu escribes) (Fam.)				

NOTE: These diagrams will not be of use when conjugating irregular verbs which are denoted with an asterisk (●) on the following pages of verbs.

LIST OF VERBS (Lista De Verbos)

SURVIVAL SPANISH® SHORTCUTS TO EXPAND YOUR VERB USAGE WITH OUT VERB CONJUGATION. Let me show you an easy way to learn "**Survival Spanish**" without the tedious method of verb conjugation. Let's say I am a police officer and I want to advise a suspect I want to search his car. (Prior to asking for consent). I would use the word for "**I Want**" which is "**Quiero**" (KEE-air-roh). Now I select the verb (from the list) to search, "**Registrar**" (ray-hee-STRAR) and add it. To that I add what I want to search. In this case it would be: "Your car," su carro (soo CAH-roh):

I WANT TO SEARCH YOUR CAR
Quiero registrar su carro
(KEE-air-roh ray-hee-STRAR soo CAH-roh)

Now let's say I have probable cause or exigent circumstances and do not need to ask for consent but want to tell the suspect "**I AM GOING TO SEARCH YOUR CAR.**" All I have to do is to preface the verb with "Voy a" which means "I AM GOING TO". IE:

I AM GOING TO SEARCH YOUR CAR
Voy a registrar su carro
(Voy ah ray-hee-STRAR soo CAH-roh)

Now let's say I want to tell a suspect that my partner wants to search his car. The word for He, She or it wants, is "**Quiere**" (KEE-air-ray). All I have to do is add the verb, "registrar", and add "su carro." IE:

HE (SHE OR IT) WANTS TO SEARCH YOUR CAR
Quiere registrar su carro
(KEE-air-ray ray-hee-STRAR soo CAH-roh)

ABANDON	(abandonar)	ANNOUNCE	(anunciar)
ABUSE	(abusar)	ANNOY	(disgustar)
ACCELERATE	(acelerar)	ANSWER	(contestar; responder)
ACCEPT	(aceptar)	APOLOGIZE	(excusarse;disculparse)
ACCOMPANY	(acompañar)	APPEAL	(apelar)
ACCUSE	(acusar,)	APPEAR	●(aparecer; presentarse)
●ACQUIT	(absolver)	APPEAR	(look like) (*parecer)
ADMIT	(admitir)	APPLY	(aplicar)
ADMIT (Medical)	(internar)	APPROACH	(acercar(se)
ADVISE	(aconsejar)	ARGUE	(discutir)
AGGRAVATE	(agravar)	ARISE	(surgir)
AGITATE	(agitar (se)	AROUSE	(excitar)
●AGO (time)	(hacer)	ARRANGE	(acomodar)
AGREE	(acordar)	ARREST	(arrestar)
AID	(ayudar)	ARRIVE	(llegar)
AIM	(apuntar)	●ASK FOR	(pedir)
●ALERT	(advertir)	ASK	(preguntar)
ALLOW (let)	●(consentir; permitir)	ASSIST	(asistir)
ALTER	(alterar)	ASSOCIATE	(asociar)
ALTERNATE	(alternar)	●ASSUME	(suponer)
ANGER	(enojar; indignar)	ASSURE	(asegurar)

148

ATTACK	(lograr)	COMMIT SUICIDE	(matarse)
ATTEMPT	(intentar)	COMMUNICATE	(comunicar)
ATTEND	(asistir; atender)	COMPARE	(comparar)
AVOID	(ceder, guardar(se)	COMPENSATE	(compensar)
BAN	(prohibir)	COMPLAIN	(lamentarse)
BATHE	(bañar)	COMPLETE	(cumplir; terminar)
●BE ABLE, CAN	(poder)	CONCEAL	(ocultar)
BE OVER	(acabar)	CONDEMN	(condenar)
●BE BORN	(nacer)	●CONFESS	(confesar)
BE MISSING, LACK	(faltar)	CONFIDE IN	(abrir a/con; fiar)
●BE	(Ser; Estar)	CONORM TO	(conformarse con)
●BEGIN	(comenzar)	CONFISCATE	(confiscar)
●BEGIN	(empezar)	CONFRONT	(enfrentarse)
BEHAVE	(comportar)	CONFUSE	(confundir)
●BELIEVE	(creer)	●CONSENT	(consentir)
BITE	(morder)	CONSULT	(consultar)
BLAME	(culpar)	CONTAMINATE	(infectar)
BLEED	(sangrar)	●CONTAIN	(incluir)
●BLESS	(bendecir)	CONTEND	(contender)
BLOCK	(impedir)	CONTINUE	(continuar)
BLOW	(soplar)	CONVICT	(condenar)
BOTHER	(molestar)	CONVINCE	(convencer
BREAK, TEAR	(romper)	COOK	(cocinar)
BREAK	(quebrar)	CO-OPERATE	(colaborar)
BREATH IN	(aspirar)	CORRECT	(corregir)
●BRING	(traer)	COST	(costar)
BUILD	(construir)	●COUNT OR TELL	(contar)
●BURN	(quemar)	COVER	(cubrir)
BURY	(sepultar)	CRASH	(chocar)
BUY	(comprar)	CRY	(llorar)
CALL, BE CALLED	(llamar)	CURE	(curar(se)
CAMP	(acampar)	●CURSE	(maldecir)
●CARRY	(traer)	CUT	(cortar)
CARRY, TAKE	(llevar)	DANCE	(bailar)
CATCH / PICKUP	(coger)	DECIDE	(decidir)
CATCH	(agarrar(se)	DECEITFUL	(engañar)
CEASE	(cesar)	DECIDE	(decidir(se)
CHANGE	(cambiar)	DEFEND(oneself)	(defender(se)
CHARGE	(cobrar)	DELIVER	(entregar)
CHEAT	(engañar)	DESCRIBE	(describir)
CLAIM	(reclamar)	DESIRE	(desear)
CLEAN	(limpiar)	●DESTROY	(destruir)
CLOSE	(cerrar)	●DETAIN	(detener)
COLLABORATE	(colaborar)	DETERMINE	(determinar)
COLLECT	(recollectar)	●DETEST OR HATE	(maldecir)
COLLIDE	(chocar)	DIE	(morir(se)
COMBINE	(combinar)	●DISAPPEAR	(desaparecer)
COME	(venir)	●DISCOVER	(descubrir)
COMMAND	(mandar)	DISCUSS	(discutir; consultar)
COMMENT	(comentar)	DISMANTLE	(desmantelar)
COMMIT	(cometer)	DISPLAY	(mostrar)

HESITATE	(vacilar)	PROTEST	(protestar)
HELP	(ayudar)	PROTECT(watch)	(guardar)
●HEAR	(oír)	PRONOUNCE	(pronunciar)
●HAVE	(tener)	PRODUCE	(producir)
HAVE BREAKFAST	(desayunar)	PRINT	(imprimir)
HAVE LUNCH	(almorzar)	PRICK, STING(to)	(picar)
GRAB	(agarrar)	PREVENT	(prevenir)
●GO	(ir)	●PRETEND	(fingir)
GO FOR A WALK	(pasear)	PLEASE	(gustar)
●GO TO BED	(acostar(se))	PHONE	(telefonear)
GO OR AMBLE	(andar)	PERSUADE	(persuadir)
GO DOWN	(bajar)	●PERMIT	(permitir; consentir)
●GIVE UP	(rendir)	PAY	(pagar)
●GIVE	(dar)	PASS	(pasar)
●GIVE BACK	(devolver)	PAIN	(doler)
GET UP	(llevantar)	OWE	(deber)
●GET	(traer)	ORDER	(mandar; ordenar)
GAMBLE(away)	(jugarse)	OPERATE	(manejar)
●FURNISH	(amueblar)	OPEN	(abrir)
FUNCTION	(funcionar)	OCCUPY	(ocupar)
FREE	(librar)	●OBEY	(obedecer)
FOUND	(fundar)	NEED	(necesitar)
FORGET	(olvidar)	NAME	(llamar)
FORCE	(obligar)	MOVE	(mover)
●FOLLOW	(seguir)	MANUFACTURE	(fabricar)
FLY	(volar)	LOWER	(bajar)
FIT	(caber)	LOOK AT	(mirar)
FIRE(set on)	(incendiar)	LOOK FOR	(buscar)
FINISH	(terminar)	LOCATE	(situar)
FIND GUILTY	(condenar)	LOAD	(cargar)
FIND	(encontrar)	LIVE	(vivir)
FIND OUT	(averiguar)	LISTEN	(escuchar)
FILL	(llenar)	LIE (tell a)	(mentir)
FIGHT	(pelear)	LEAVE	(salir)
●FALL	(caer)	LEAVE,LET,ALLOW	(dejar)
EXTINGUISH	(extinguir)	LEARN	(aprender)
EXPLAIN	(explicar)	●KNOW (something)	(saber)
EXCEED	(exceder)	●KNOW (someone)	(conocer)
ESCAPE	(escapar; salir)	KILL	(matar)
ENTER	(entrar)	JUMP	(saltar)
EARN	(ganar(se))	INVITE	(invitar)
EAT	(comer)	INVESTIGATE	(averiguar)
●DROP	(caer(se))	INTERVIEW	(entrevistar)
●DRIVE	(manejar, conducir)	INSPECT	(inspeccionar)
DRINK	(beber)	INJECT	(inyectar)
DRESS	(vestir)	INFORM	(informar)
DREAM	(soñar)	INDICATE	(indicar)
DOUBT	(dudar)	IMPLICATE	(comprometer)
●DO, MAKE	(hacer)	IGNITE	(encender)
DIVORCE	(divorciar)	HIT	(pegar)
DIVERT	(desviar)	HIDE	(ocultar(se))

150

PURCHASE	(comprar)
●PURSUE	(seguir)
PUSH	(empujar)
PUT AWAY, GUARD	(guardar)
●PUT	(poner)
QUESTION	(preguntar)
QUESTION (to doubt)	(dudar en)
RAPE	(violar)
●READ	(leer)
RECOGNIZE	(reconocer)
●REGRET, FEEL	(sentir)
REMEMBER	(recordar)
REMEMBER	(acordar(se)
REMOVE	(quitar)
REPEAT	(repetir)
REPORT	(informar)
●REQUEST	(pedir; solicitar)
REQUIRE	(obligar)
RESCUE	(librar)
RESIST	(resistir)
REST	(descansar)
RESTRICT	(limitar)
●RETURN	(vover; regresar)
REVEAL	(manifestar)
REVOLT	(rebelarse)
ROB	(robar)
RUN	(correr)
RUN AWAY	(escaparse)
●SAY, TELL	(decir)
●SEE	(ver)
SEEK PROTECTION	(ampararse)
●SEIZE, GRASP	(coger)
SELL	(vender)
SELL ON CREDIT	(fiar)
SELL ONESELF	(venderse)
SENTENCE	(condenar)
SEPARATE	(separar; apartar)
SHOOT	(tirar)
SHOOT OR FIRE	(disparar)
SHOW	(enseñar; mostrar)
●SHUT OR CLOSE	(cerrar)
SIGN	(firmar)
SILENT (to be)	(callarse)
SIT DOWN	(sentar)
●SLEEP	(dormir)
SMOKE (cigarettes)	(fumar)
SOUND, RING	(sonar)
SPEAK	(hablar)
SPEED UP	(acelerar)
SPEND	(gastar)
STAGGER	(tambalear(se))
STAND UP	(levantarse)
●START	(comenzar)
STAY OR REMAIN	(quedar)(se)
STEAL	(robar)
STOP	(parar)
●STRIKE	(dar de; pegar)
STUDY	(estudiar)
SUBDUE	(someter)
SUBMIT	(someter)
SUMMON	(convocar)
SUPPLY	(suplir)
SURRENDER	(rendirse; entregarse)
SUSPECT	(sospechar)
SUSPEND	(suspender)
SWEAR	(jurar)
SWEAR (curse)	(maldecir)
SWINDLE	(engañar)
TAKE, DRINK-	(tomar)
TAKE OUT	(sacar)
TALK	(hablar)
●TEACH, SHOW	(enseñar; instruir(se))
TELEPHONE	(telefonear)
●TELL	(decir, contar)
TESTIFY	(testificar)
THERE IS/ARE (helping verb)	(haber)
●THINK-	(pensar)
THREATEN	(amenazar)
TOSS/THROW	(echar)
TOUCH	(tocar)
●TRANSLATE	(traducir)
TRAVEL	(viajar)
TRUST	(confiar)
TRY	(tratar)
TURN OFF	(apagar)
TURN	(virar)
UNDERSTAND	(comprender)
●UNDERSTAND	(entender)
UNDRESS	(desvestirse)
USE	(usar)
VACILLATE	(vacilar)
VIOLATE	(violar)
VISIT	(visitar)
WAIT	(esperar)
WALK	(caminar; andar)
WANT	(●querer; desear)
WARN	(avisar)
WASH	(lavar)
WATCH	(mirar; ver)
WATCH OVER	(guardar)
WIN, GAIN, EARN,	(ganar)
WORK	(trabajar; funcionar)
WOUND	(herir)
WRITE	(escribir)

● Denotes irregular verbs

(se) when added to the end of a verb changes meaning to be reflexive IE:
To kill (Matar) To kill oneself (Matarse)

NATIONALITIES

American- Americano (ah-meh-ree-KAH-noh)
Word and abbr. for a person from the United States is called Estadoulidense (EE.UU.) (ays-tah-doh oo-nee DEN-say)

Argentinean-	argentino	(ahr-hehn-TEE-noh)
Bolivian-	boliviano	(boh-lee-bee-AH-noh)
Chilean-	chileno	(chee-LEH-noh)
Chinese-	chino	(CHEE-noh)
Colombian-	colombiano	(koh-lohm-bee-AH-noh)
Costa Rican-	costarricense	(kohs-tah-ree-SEHN-seh)
Cuban-	cubano	(koo-BAH-noh)
Dom. Republic-	dominicano	(doh-mee-nee-KAH-noh)
Ecuadorian-	ecuatoriano	(eh-kwah-toh-ree-AH-noh)
Guatemalan-	guatemalteco	(gwah-teh-mahl-TEH-koh)
Honduran-	hondureño	(ohn-doo-REH-nyoh)
Japanese-	japonés	(hah-poh-NEHS)
Mexican-	Mexicano	(meh-hee-KAH-noh)
Nicaraguan-	nicaragüense	(nee-kah-rah-GWEHN-seh)
Panamanian-	panameño	(pah-nah-MEH-nyoh)
Paraguayan-	paraguayo	(pah-rah-GWAH-yoh)
Peruvian-	peruano	(peh-RWAH-noh)
Puerto Rican-	puertorriqueño	(pwehr-toh-ree-KEH-nyoh)
Russian-	ruso	(RROO-soh)
Salvadoran-	salvadoreño	(sahl-bah-doh-REH-nyoh)
Spanish-	español	(ehs-pahn-YOHL)
Uruguayan-	uruguayo	(oo-roo-GWAH-yoh)
Venezuelan-	venezolano	(veh-neh-soh-LAH-noh)

TIME FOR A LITTLE HUMOR ABOUT TRANSLATIONS

Here is a look at how shrewd American business people translate their slogans into foreign languages: From "American Demographics" magazine:

When Braniff translated a slogan touting its upholstery, "Fly in Leather," it came out in Spanish as "Fly Naked."

Coors put its slogan, "Turn It Loose," into Spanish, where it was read as "Suffer From Diarrhea."

Chicken magnate Frank Perdue's line, "It takes a tough man to make a tender chicken," sounds much more interesting in Spanish: "It takes a sexually stimulated man to make a chicken affectionate."

When Vicks first introduce its cough drops on the German market, they were chagrined to learn that the German pronunciation of "v" is "f," which in German is the guttural equivalent of "sexual penetration."

Not to be outdone, Puffs tissues tried later to introduce its product, only to learn that "Puff" in German is a colloquial term for a whorehouse.

The Chevy Nova never sold well in Spanish speaking countries. "No Va" means "It Does Not Go" in Spanish.

When Pepsi started marketing its products in China a few years back, they translated their slogan, "Pepsi Brings You Back to Life" pretty literally. The slogan in Chinese really meant, "Pepsi Brings Your Ancestors Back from the Grave."

When Gerber first started selling baby food in Africa, they used the same packaging as here in the USA--with the cute baby on the label. Later they found out that in Africa companies routinely put pictures on the label of what is inside since most people can not read.

PATRON SAINTS

Name	Date	Name	Date
Apolinar	1-8	Cirilo	3-18
Apolonia	2-9	Ciro	1-31
Apolonio	4-10	Clara	8-12
Aquileo	5-12	Claudio	6-6
Aquilino	1-29	Clemente	11-23
Arcadio	1-12	Cleto	4-26
Aristeo	9-3	Clotilde	6-3
Armando	8-27	Coleta	3-6
Artemio	10-20	Columba	12-31
Arturo	12-15	Concepcion	12-8
Asteria	8-10	Conrado	11-26
Atalo	3-10	Consorcia	6-22
Atanasia	8-14	Constancio	3-11
Atanasio	5-2	Constantino	3-11
Atenedoro	10-18	Contanza	2-17
Augusto	10-7	Cornelio	9-16
Aurea	8-24	Cosme	9-27
Aurelia	9-25	Crescencia	6-15
Aurelio	11-12	Crescencio	4-19
Ausencio	12-18	Crisanto	10-25
Avertano	2-25	Crisoforo	4-20
Balbina	3-31	Crisogono	11-24
Aaron	7-1	Baltasar	6-20	Crispin	10-25
Abdias	11-19	Barbara	12-4	Crispina	12-5
Abdon	7-30	Barsilio	6-14	Cristina	7-24
Abraham	3-16	Bartolome	8-24	Cristobal	7-25
Abundio	7-11	Basilisa	4-15	Cruz	5-3
Acacio	5-8	Beatriz	4-15	Cutberto	3-20
Adalberto	4-23	Beda	5-27	Damaso	12-11
Adelaida	12-16	Benigno	2-13	Damian	4-12
Adolfo	9-27	Benito	3-21	Daniel	7-21
Adrian	3-5	Benjamin	3-31	Daria	10-25
Agapito	9-20	Bernabe	6-10	Dario	12-19
Agaton	12-7	Bernado	8-20	David	12-29
Agustin	8-28	Bernardino	5-20	Defina	12-24
Alberto	4-8	Bibiana	12-2	Delfino	12-24
Albino	3-1	Blas	2-3	Demetrio	12-22
Aldegunda	1-30	Bonifacio	5-14	Diego	11-13
Alejandro	4-24	Braulio	3-26	Dimas	3-26
Alejo	7-17	Brigida	10-8	Dionisia	12-6
Alfonso	10-30	Bruno	10-6	Dionisio	10-9
Alfredo	1-12	Bulmaro	7-20	Domingo	8-4
Alicia	6-23	Calixto	10-14	Domitila	5-12
Alvaro	2-19	Camerino	8-21	Donaciano	5-24
Amado	9-13	Camilo	7-18	Donato	8-7
Amador	4-30	Candido	2-2	Dorotea	3-28
Amalia	7-10	Canuto	1-9	Doroteo	6-5
Amancio	4-8	Carlos	11-4	Ediiberto	2-24
Amando	2-6	Carmen	7-16	Edmundo	11-16
Ambrosio	12-7	Casiano	8-2	Eduardo	10-13
Ana	7-26	Casilda	4-9	Efren	6-18
Anacleto	7-13	Casimiro	3-4	Eleazar	8-23
Anastasia	4-15	Castulo	3-26	Elena	8-18
Anastasio	1-22	Catalina	4-30	Eleucadio	2-14
Anatolio	7-3	Catarina	11-25	Eleuterio	2-20
Andres	2-4	Catedra	4-22	Eligio	12-1
Angel	10-1	Cayetano	8-7	Eliseo	6-14
Angela	5-31	Cayo	4-22	Elpidio	3-4
Aniceto	4-17	Cecilia	11-22	Elvira	1-25
Anselmo	4-21	Celestino	4-6	Emelia	5-30
Antelmo	6-26	Celia	10-21	Emeterio	3-3
Antero	1-3	Celso	4-6	Emigdio	8-5
Antioco	10-15	Cenobio	10-30	Emilia	4-5
Antolin	9-2	Cesareo	2-25	Emiliano	8-8
Antonino	5-10	Cipriano	9-26	Emilio	5-22
Antonio	1-17	Cira	8-13	Emperador	7-17
Antonio	6-13	Ciriaco	2-8	Enedina	5-14

Engracia	4-16	Gelasio	11-21	Juan Bautista	6-24
Enrique	7-15	Genaro	9-19	Juan de Dios	3-8
Epifanio	4-7	Genoveva	1-3	Juana	
Epitacio	5-23	Gerardo	10-3	Francisca	8-21
Erasmo	1-25	Germán	5-28	Opundo	11-14
Ernestina	11-11	Geroncio	5-9	Judas	10-28
Ernesto	11-7	Gertrudis	11-15	Julia	5-22
Espiridion	12-14	Gervasio	6-19	Julián	1-9
Estanislao	5-7	Gilberto	2-4	Juliana	6-19
Esteban	11-28	Giliberto	12-31	Julieta	7-30
Esther	1-1	Godeleva	7-6	Julio	12-20
Eufrasia	1-13	Gonzalo	10-10	Justa	7-19
Eulalia	2-12	Gordiano	11-15	Justa	9-26
Eulogio	3-11	Gorgonio	9-9	Justino	4-14
Eusebio	8-14	Graciano	12-18	Justo	7-14
Eusebio	8-6	Gregorio		Justo	
Eustaquio	5-3	Magno	3-12	Juvenal	5-3
Eustasio	3-29	Gregorio N.	5-9	Ladislao	6-27
Eustorgio	4-16	Guadalupe	12-12	Lamberto	9-17
Eutamia	3-20	Guadencia	2-12	Largo	8-8
Eutimio	12-24	Guillermo	6-25	Laura	10-19
Euduqio	3-14	Gumesindo	1-13	Laurencio	11-14
Eva	12-2	Heladio	2-18	Lázaro	12-17
Evaristo	10-26	Heliodoro	7-3	Leandro	2-27
Evodio	9-5	Heraclio	8-8	Leobardo	1-18
Ezequiel	4-10	Herculano	11-7	Leocadia	12-9
Fabian	1-20	Heriberto	3-16	Leodegario	10-2
Facundo	11-27	Hermes	8-28	León Magno	4-11
Fausta	9-20	Hermelinda	10-28	Leonardo	11-6
Faustino	2-15	Hermenegildo	4-13	Leoncio	8-1
Fausto	9-6	Herminio	4-25	Leonilla	1-17
Febronia	6-25	Heron	10-17	Leopoldo	11-15
Federico	3-2	Hesiquio	11-18	Leovigildo	8-20
Felicitas	3-6	Higinio	1-11	Liborio	7-23
Felipe de Jesús	2-5	Hilario	2-28	Librado	8-17
Felipe (NERI)	5-26	Hilarion	10-21	Lidia	8-3
Felix	11-20	Hipólito	8-13	Lino	9-23
Fermin	7-7	Hoglinio	1-11	Liova	9-28
Fernando	5-30	Honorio	12-30	Longinoe	3-15
Fidel	6-1	Hortensia	1-11	Lorenzo	8-10
Fidencio	11-16	Hugo	6-1	Loreto	12-10
Filemón	3-21	Humberto	3-25	Lourdes	2-11
Filiberto	8-22	Ignacio de Loyola	7-31	Lucas	10-18
Filogonio	12-20	Ignacio MR.	2-1	Lucía	12-13
Filomena	7-5	Ildefonso	1-23	Luciano	1-7
Flavia	10-5	Inés	1-21	Lucina	6-30
Flavio	5-7	Inocencio	6-22	Lucio	3-4
Flora	6-9	Inocente	12-28	Lugarda	6-16
Florencio	10-27	Irene	4-5	Luis Rey	8-25
Florentina	6-20	Irene	10-20	Lydia	8-3
Florentino	10-16	Irenelo	6-28	Macario	1-2
Florina	5-1	Isaac	6-3	Macedonio	3-10
Floro	10-26	Isabel	7-8	Macrina	1-14
Focas	3-5	Isaías	7-6	Magín	8-19
Foilan	10-5	Isidoro	4-4	Malaquías	11-3
Fortino	8-12	Isidro	5-15	Mameto	5-11
Fortunata	10-14	Jacinto	8-17	Manuel	6-17
Francisco de Asís	10-4	Jacinto	9-11	Marcelina	7-17
Narciso		Jerónimo	9-30	Marcelino	6-2
Javier	12-3	Jesús	12-25	Marcelo	1-16
Fulgencio	1-16	Joaquín	8-16	Marcial	7-3
Gabino	2-19	Joel	7-13	Marco	6-18
Gabino	10-25	Jonás	9-21	Marcos	4-25
Gabriel	3-24	Jorge	4-23	Mardonio	12-23
Galdino	4-18	José	3-19	Margarita	10-17
Galo	10-16	Jovita	2-15	María	9-12
Gaudencio	1-22	Juan AP.	12-27	Magdalena	7-22

Name	Date	Name	Date	Name	Date
Maria Magdalena de la Luz	5-29	Perdecto	4-18	Severiano	2-21
Mariana	4-17	Perfecto	4-18	Severo	2-1
Marina	7-18	Petronila	5-31	Sidonio	8-23
Marino	12-26	Pilar	10-12	Silvano	2-10
Mario	1-19	Pio	5-5	Silverio	6-20
Marta	2-23	Placida	10-11	Silvestre	12-31
Martin	11-11	Placido	10-5	Silviano	5-4
Martina	1-30	Platon	4-4	Simeon	2-18
Martiniano	7-2	Plutarco	6-28	Simon	10-28
Martiniano	1-2	Policarpo	1-26	Sinforiano	8-22
Mateo	9-21	Pomposa	9-19	Sofia	9-18
Matilde	3-14	Ponciano	11-19	Sofonias	12-3
Maura	11-30	Porfirio	9-15	Sostenes	11-28
Mauricio	9-22	Praxedes	7-21	Sotero	4-22
Maurilio	9-13	Primitivo	6-10	Susana	5-24
Mauro	1-15	Prisciliano	1-4	Susana	8-11
Maximiano	8-21	Procopio	7-8	Taide	10-19
Maximiliano	10-12	Procopo	4-9	Tecla	9-23
Maximino	6-8	Proculo	12-9	Tedoro	10-29
Maximo	5-11	Prospero	7-29	Tedoro	11-9
Melesio	2-12	Protasio	6-19	Telesforo	1-5
Melito	4-24	Proto	9-11	Teodora	4-1
Meliton	4-1	Prudenciana	5-19	Teodula	2-17
Melquiades	12-10	Prudencio	4-28	Teofanes	3-12
Menas	11-11	Quintin	10-31	Teofilo	2-16
Merced	9-24	Quirino	6-4	Teresa	10-15
Micheas	1-15	Rafael	10-24	Teresita	10-3
Miguel	9-29	Ramon	8-31	Tiburcio	8-11
Milburga	2-23	Ranulfo	5-27	Tiburcio	9-9
Modesto	6-15	Raymundo	3-15	Tigrio	1-12
Moises	9-4	Refugio	7-4	Timoteo	1-24
Monica	5-4	Regina	9-7	Tirso	1-28
Mucio	5-13	Regulo	3-30	Tito	2-6
Nabor	7-12	Remato	11-12	Tomas	12-21
Narciso	10-29	Remedios	9-1	Toribio	4-16
Natalia	7-27	Remigio	10-1	Tranquiliano	7-6
Nazario	6-12	Ricardo	4-3	Trinidad	6-9
Nemesio	10-31	Rita	5-22	Ubaldo	5-16
Nemorio	9-7	Roberto	6-7	Urbano	5-25
Nestor	2-26	Rodrigo	3-13	Ursula	10-21
Nicandro	6-7	Roman	8-9	Valente	5-21
Nicanor	1-10	Romualdo	2-7	Valentin	2-14
Nicasio	10-11	Roque	11-17	Valeriano	4-14
Niceforo	2-9	Rosa	8-30	Venancio	5-18
Nicolas de B.	12-6	Rosalia	9-4	Venustiano	12-30
Nicolas de Tolent.	9-10	Rosario	10-7	Verulo	2-21
		Rosendo	3-1	Vicente	7-19
Noe	11-10	Rufina	7-10	Victor	7-28
Norberto	6-6	Rufino	7-19	Victoria	12-23
Obdulia	9-5	Rufo	11-28	Victoriano	11-8
Obilon	4-29	Ruperto	3-27	Victorico	12-11
Octaviano	3-22	Rustico	10-9	Vidal	4-28
Odon	11-18	Rutilo	6-4	Virginia	1-31
Ofelia	4-2	Sabas	12-5	Vital	11-4
Onesimo	2-16	Sabina	8-29	Vito	6-15
Otilia	12-13	Sabino	12-30	Wenceslao	9-28
Pablo	6-29	Sador	2-20	Wilfrido	10-12
Paciano	3-9	Salome	10-22	Zacarias	11-5
Palemon	1-11	Salustia	9-14	Zeferino	8-26
Panfilo	6-1	Sanson	6-27	Zemalda	6-5
Pascasio	2-22	Santiago	7-25	Zenon	6-23
Pascual	5-17	Saturino	11-29	Zenon	7-9
Patricio	3-17	Saturnino	11-29	Zita	4-27
Paula	6-18	Seapion	11-14	Zozimo	12-26
Paulino	6-22	Segundo	6-1		
Paulino	10-10	Serapia	9-3		
Pedro	6-29	Serapion	11-14		
Pelagia	3-23	Sergio	10-7		
		Servando	10-23		

> "The cheapest way to have your family tree traced is to run for public office."

HINTS ON HISPANIC NAMES

Hispanic people use the surname of both parents. Neither is ever considered to be a middle name. In the case of an illegitimate child, usually the surname of the mother only is used. The surname of the father *precedes* that of the mother, and the two surnames should be connected by a hyphen.

Example: Jose CAMPOLI-Garcia. Jose is the given name; CAMPOLI, the surname of the father, and Garcia, the surname of the mother. In addition, variations exists as follow below:

Jose Garcia Campoli
Jose Campoli G.
Jose G. Campoli
Jose Campoli
Jose Garcia

Legally a Hispanic female retains her maiden name after marriage, but it is common practice to drop the surname of the mother and to add that of the husband joined by the preposition "de."

EX: María CAMPOLI-Garcia marries Carlos VILLA-Tovar and is known as María CAMPOLI de Villa.

Prior to her marriage she was known as: María CAMPOLI-Garcia
after being married as: María CAMPOLI de Villa
and if her husband dies, as: María CAMPOLI Vda. de Villa
(Vda., viuda - widow)

If the person gives only one surname, it will be necessary to obtain full and correct name. A Hispanic person who has resided in the U.S. may anglicize his or her name. Remember that a person's signature is not necessarily his full and correct name. This is particularly true of persons whose signatures are written with many flourishes. If in doubt, he or she should be asked to write it.

Due to similarity of the sounds of certain letters, differences in the spelling of proper names will be encountered.

Note: Official U.S. Government listing of last name of paternal parent is uppercase and underlined and maternal last name in lowercase, not underlined.

(Vincent Bugliosi (right) and Senior Trooper Bob Dent posed together to announce the release of their respective books.

Bugliosi is the author of "Helter Skelter" & "The Sea Will Tell." He is the former L. A. prosecutor who convicted Charles Manson and his infamous family.)

"Bob Dent has provided an excellent and much needed tool for today's public safety professional, and as such has performed a valuable public service. I highly recommend this manual, which will promote officer safety, improve community relations and provide an effective method of communicating with Spanish speaking peoples."

Vincent T. Bugliosi (Author)

"With more than 31 years of experience in simultaneous interpreting, translations and transcriptions in at least 8 languages for the United Nations, World Court, embassies, consulates and numerous multi-national companies in more than 9 countries, never have I found any comparable handbook for law enforcement personnel. This manual will fill a void for all agencies dealing with Hispanics, whether it be in East Los Angeles, CA, South Dade County, FL, the Yakima Valley of Washington State or the Rio Grande Valley of South Texas. I consider it a privilege and an honor to have been able to collaborate with Bob Dent on this needed endeavor."

Frank T. O'Hearn, Ph.D.
Former United Nations and Presidential Interpreter / Translator

"This publication is a good example of the author's loyalty and dedication in the police profession. His vision in producing this factual, innovative, and easily referenced Spanish translated field use book, is not only to make the job easier and safer for the police officer, but also for the Hispanic community to understand law enforcement officers.

The public expects today's law enforcement officer to be well trained and responsive to their needs. This book meets that expectation and will enhance the professional image and standards of law enforcement organizations."

Emil Brandaw - Superintendent
Oregon State Police (Retired)

"Bob Dent's book is the right book at the time. The increasing number of Spanish-speaking members of our community has made it inevitable that law enforcement officers and other public personnel who have little fluency in Spanish will come into contact with Spanish-speaking people on a more and more frequent basis. Bob's easy to carry quick reference book gives all of us an opportunity to communicate with Hispanic-speaking individuals in common and emergency situations. This quick reference book should be a must have 'for people in the business'."

Kenneth C. Bauman (Assistant U.S. Attorney, District of Oregon)

About the Author

Robert Dent is a retired Oregon State Police Senior Trooper from Bend, Oregon. The 29-year veteran served in the Criminal, Narcotic and Patrol Divisions. The Oregon Narcotics Enforcement Association previously chose him as the regional "*Officer of the Year*" for his achievements and dedication to the field of narcotic investigations.

He also authored the **Multi-Lingual Field Manual for Public Safety Professionals**, and recently co-authored **Silent Universal Signals for Public Safety and Educational Professionals**, with Commander Alan Morris (former Director of Training, US Navy SEAL Training Academy.) Dent also produced the training video "*Interactive Survival Spanish - High Risk Vehicle Stops*".

He has appeared on and provided training to the Law Enforcement Television Network, Fire & Emergency Television Network, Corrections USA Television Network and Professional Security Television Network. He is a member and former staff instructor for the American Society of Law Enforcement Training and was recently selected (from a field of 7000 trainers worldwide,) to receive the prestigious "**Ed Nowicki Lifetime Achievement Award.**" He is a member of the: International Narcotic Officers Association, International Association of Counter terrorism & Security Professionals, International Police Association, National Tactical Officer's Association, American Association of State Troopers, National Association of Independent Publishers and the Oregon State Police Officer's Association. He travels extensively, training members of city, county, state and federal public safety agencies on "**Survival Spanish®** and in addition, how to silently communicate using *Silent Universal Signals*®

He is founder and president of *The Constable Group, Inc.* and *Executive Director of The Constable Public Safety Memorial Foundation, Inc.*, the latter being a non-profit organization designed to assist the families and children of public safety officers killed in the line of duty. Dent is an Executive Board Member of the Kidnapped and Hostage Program, Inc. of Florida and an Ex-Officio Board Member of the Oregon Public Safety Memorial Fund. He has received commendations for successful philanthropic and legislative efforts from former President George Bush, Oregon Gov. John Kitzhaber, the American Association of State Troopers, Oregon Association of Chief's of Police, Oregon State Police and recently nominated by the National Board of Directors of the Concerns of Police Survivors for the National Distinguished Service Award.

"Our character is what we do when we think no one is looking."

Introduction and Acknowledgments

After reviewing this manual a few people have suggested that I shorten it by omitting some of the persons mentioned in the credits. I did not agree. I did not compile the credits to impress anyone, as the success of this publication will be determined by its contents. I want to give credit where it is justly deserved.

Sincere appreciation is extended to all the law enforcement officers and other criminal justice personnel whose requests for this manual have made it a worthwhile endeavor. The following credits represent only a scant reflection of the contributions made, for many people have given to this manual in terms of suggested content and organization. Others have contributed encouragement and support. I would like this manual to be viewed as a combined effort by interested people named and unnamed, who have strong convictions of professionalism and integrity. I owe them for their ideas and the motivation to put it in writing. Most importantly my wife Kathy; daughters Desiree' and Mandi; brothers Skip, Doug, Jack and Gary; and

A little Angel named "Jeannie" (In Memory)

Vincent T. Bugliosi, Author and Prosecutor of Charles Manson & Family
Francis (Bud) Mullen, Former Administrator, U.S. Drug Enforcement Agency
Joella West (Hollywood entertainment attorney)
John J. Bellizzi, Jr. Exec. Director, International Narcotic Enforcement Officers Assoc.
Lynn Lundquist, Oregon Speaker of the House of Representatives
Representative Ben Westlund, R-Bend, OR
Senator Neil Bryant - R-Bend, Oregon
Steve Newman, Exec. Director - Pacific Northwest International Trade Association
Dr. Frank O'Hearn, Former United Nations Interpreter/Translator - Madras, Or.
Brian Gerold, Public Safety Training Consultant
Ira Wilsker, Dir. Correctional Officer Training, Regional Police Academy, Lamar University, TX
Ken Bauman, U.S. Dept. of Justice, Assistant U.S. Attorney, District of Oregon

Mike DeChene, National Criminal Justice Reference Service, Wash. D.C.
Ed Nowicki, Past Exec. Dir. of The American Society of L.E. Trainers
Joseph J. Truncale, The American Society of Law Enforcement Trainers
Mayer Nudell, Exec. Dir., Int'l Association of Counterterrorism & Security Professionals
Kathryn E. Sulewski, Managing Editor, FBI Law Enforcement Bulletin
Andy Andrews, TV Talk Show Host of Fox TV's "A Matter of Fact."
Phil Donegan, Supervisory Senior Resident Agent, FBI, Eugene, OR
Ron Stuart, Special Agent, Federal Bureau of Investigation, Bend, OR
Emil "E.E." Brandaw, Superintendent, Oregon State Police, (Retired)
Superintendent Homer Kearns, Salem-Keizer School District, Salem, Or
Anne Crockatt (Mother of Rene Clodfelter)
Loyd and Lolita Clodfelter (Parents of Bret Clodfelter).
Jerry Mortimer and John Molnar, Hare Publications and Police Magazine
Bob Shotwell, The Oregonian Correspondent
Brandy Ruem and Janet Dayton of Police Magazine
Major Jim Willis, Dir. Ore. State Police, Intergovernmental Services Bureau
Ron Moore, Program Director, Fire and Emergency Television Network
Bruce Cameron, Editorial Director, Law and Order Magazine
Sgt. Sandy Slowik (Gang Intel.) Arizona DPS, Thomas Slowik (Training Coordinator Regional Counterdrug Training Academy, NAS Meridan, Mississippi
Ursula Miller, Special Serv.Div., Arizona DPS (Phraseology for Truck Inspection Section)
Sgt. Bill Vallentine, Nevada State Prison (Provided photo's of "Mara Salvatrucha" (MS)
Detective Richard Duran, LAPD Gang Unit (Provided photo's of 'Mara Salvatrucha" (MS)
Oregon State Fire Marshall Bob Garrison - Salem, OR
Assistant Chief Scott Majers - Redmond Fire Department
Henry LaSala, Supervisory Training Officer Specialist, USFS, Redmond, Ore.
Jeanne Canfield - State Chair for Mothers Against Drunk Driving - Sherwood, Ore.
Major Leroy Hyder, OSP, Director, Game Division, GHQ, Salem, OR (Ret.)
Senior Trooper Bill Lyons - Oregon State Police, Salem, Oregon
Chief Herbert Hawkins - Newberg, Oregon Police Department (In Memory)
Major Don Gallagher - Oregon State Police (In Memory)
Lt. Don Bussey, Oregon State Police (Retired)
Kaye Straube, Executive Secretary, OSP, Bend, OR   (Graphics Design for manual)
Chief James Soules, Prineville P.D., Prineville, OR
Chief Lane Roberts, Redmond, Oregon PD
Lt. Larry Kanski - Redmond Oregon PD
Rick Nissen, CPA - Redmond, Or
Richard and Margie Rollins - Redmond, Or
Sgt. Pat Gregg, Oregon State Police - Bend
Sgt. Ken Hauge, Oregon Army Nat. Guard / OSP Dist. V HQ, Bend, OR
Agent John Putnam - US Border Patrol
Lt. John Santana - Texas Department of Corrections
Dick Stein- Former President - NW Gang Investigators Assoc.
Don and Mary Jo Purkerson, Prineville, Oregon
Dave Jones Productions, Bend, Oregon
Norm and Donna Nielsen, Bend, Oregon and
Steve Albrecht, San Diego Police Officers Association
Suzanne Lawrence, National We Care Foundation - Dallas, Texas

Special appreciation to Carl Westcott, Glenn Dryfuss, Robert Smith, Dave Smith (aka J.D. "Buck" Savage), and Sharon Griffith of the Law Enforcement Television Network for their kind support and encouragement.

Purpose

My motivation in compiling this manual was sparked from the on-duty murders of fellow police officers. I saw a need for a basic, concise, easy to use tool that incorporated the most often used Spanish phrases under a wide variety of circumstances. . I focused my attention on a manual designed for use by the *"Troops"* in the field, while encompassing the majority of terms that would be useful in actual field situations by a multitude of public safety professionals. Being a former law enforcement officer myself, I desire to promote realistic, effective communication while enhancing the user's safety, whether it be providing assistance to the public or diffusing a life threatening or potentially dangerous situation. My goal is to enhance basic communication between public safety personnel and non-native speakers such as people in business, foreign visitors, immigrants with language difficulties, emergency service agencies and many others. This kind of service is becoming increasingly important with the growing numbers of international travelers, migration and the increase in international crime.

Most books written for the specific requirements of law enforcement and other public safety personnel are written by people who have little or no field experience. (I have consulted with many active undercover police officers and criminal informants regarding the slang contained in this manual. The slang accurately relates the verbiage used by the criminal element. Specific investigative techniques for law enforcement have been omitted for obvious reasons but I have concealed encrypted information the manual which I disclose during on site training that will provide techniques for its maximum usage).

It is not possible to adequately translate all the dialects, slang and colloquialisms that may be encountered in the field. The manual has been translated in the most common way used to facilitate communication with the largest number of people possible. It is not intended to replace the need for a fluent interpreter. However, it will be effective for persons who need to communicate at a very basic level. At times, the need to use this manual will be under life threatening circumstances where even a few minutes of waiting for an interpreter could cost a life.

The manual can be used by police officers, the military, firefighters, EMT's, educators, trainers, parole and probation officers, community relation services, wildlife resource officers, corrections personnel, courtroom personnel, children's services, Department of Motor Vehicle Investigators, truck inspectors, District Attorneys, security officers, and other public and private agencies where there is a need to effectively communicate with Spanish speaking people.

The phrases in the manual are first in English, then Spanish, followed by the phonetic pronunciation. The emphasized syllable is capitalized and in bold print. In the event the person being communicated to does not understand, he or she may read the written translation. The person may then respond orally or in writing for later translation. If the response is not understood, the person communicated to can be asked to select an answer from the appropriate section (many of the questions may be answered "yes," or "no.")

The manual should be indexed for quick reference with indexing tabs which may be attached to the individual language pages. For often used phrases the user may choose to highlight in red the priority phrases, yellow the cautionary ones and blue for phrases often used.

My challenge has been to give the reader useful techniques and tools to effectively attain desired goals with Spanish speaking persons. Audio cassette language tapes have been developed for and follow specific areas of the manual. It is very important that the user practice with the tapes to insure that the phrases are pronounced correctly. For administrators, this is a much more cost efficient method of teaching basic, useful phrases. It is also a most effective way of retaining the information, as the manual and tapes provide a ready reference.

I have made every effort to avoid the impression that any one ethnic group is more involved in crime than another. As with any race, the majority of the people are intelligent, honest, respectful, and hard working. We also know that there are those who have no respect for the law and comprise the criminal element. It is this criminal element that poses the greatest danger to public safety officers.

"When you invite trouble, it is usually quick to accept."

Cultural Awareness Is Really A Matter of Honor

I have observed all types of people and ethnic groups under the best and worst conditions. My conclusion is that no matter what race or profession involved, fatalities more often were caused by inappropriate remarks or insults. History has repeatedly shown us that if you take away a person's dignity, respect, or honor, he may take away your life.

Webster defines "Honor," as *"The willingness to regard or treat others with respect and dignity"*. Honor has several synonyms such as integrity, courtesy, dignity, honesty, virtue and principle. All of these elicit voluntary co-operation while dishonesty, discourtesy and dishonor breed contempt and escalation of tensions.

In this ever changing society of multi-ethnics, some things never change and we can learn from them. It is almost a universal trait that honor is a code of principally male dignity and esteem. A common courtesy extended to an individual by virtue of age or position often brings with it distinction and recognition which conveys respect and wisdom from the giver. The old adage *"talk is cheap"*, is very valuable in gaining co-operation in a potentially life threatening situation. Often a simple gesture of respect or concern gives the recipient a feeling of importance and honor.

Within this manual I have provided some cultural tips that can make the difference between a positive or negative outcome under a wide variety of situations. These *"Cultural Tips"* provide a simple tool in assisting the reader in achieving the desired goals. To have a basic understanding of the values of the Hispanic culture will give needed insight into the attitudes, perceptions and expected patterns of behavior. This will help not only in common interactive communication with the law abiding citizen, but as a tool that can be effectively used to defuse a potentially dangerous situation.

Are you aware of what your body is saying?

As important as language is in communication, perhaps even more important are all those ways in which we communicate inadvertently without speaking: our posture, our body and hand positioning; our gestures, our facial expressions, the look of the eyes, how we walk, our clothing or uniform mean many different things to different cultures. Even the surroundings where we talk have a communicative function. While words can be manipulated, gestures and body language are a lot harder to control. This nonverbal cue of communication is important because we commonly are unaware of its influence, perception, interpretation or impact. When there are unintentional nonverbal misunderstandings, we often don't have the luxury of additional time to identify or correct them. In certain professions this can have tragic and permanent consequences. Often the nonverbal body language cues not only support and confirm the intentions of our spoken words but amplify them. Body language can also contradict what we are trying to say with enough force that the listener fails to hear the real message. Simply put, **actions speak louder than words and often say all the wrong things.** All these nonverbal cues are related to feelings of being treated fairly and honorably. This equates to co-operation or resistance. Without this perception of being "honorably treated", voluntary co-operation will be elusive.

The U.S. population increased 1% last year. That's a 2.5 million increase (up to 261,653,497) with net migration from overseas accounting for one third of the increase. The nation is projected to grow by another 2.7 million during the coming year. With 2,972 different spoken languages in the world, the need for this manual in the public safety arena and other areas is self-evident.

Spanish Cultural Tips

The majority of the Hispanics are Roman Catholics. Many still rely on the parish priest to act as their representative, and look upon him as a potential, if not active, leader. Women and children continue to frequent Mass more often than men, at least on Sunday and Sacraments such as Baptism, Confirmation and the Holy Eucharist. Many are highly religious in the sense that they have a strong belief in God and Jesus Christ as Redeemer of mankind. Those in lower socio-economic levels tend to rely strongly on the belief that their plight may indeed be the will of God--"Es la voluntad de Dios." This point of view strongly influences their daily lives.

Family is likely to be the single most important social unit in life. It is usually at the core of thinking and behavior and is the center from which his or her view of the rest of the world extends. Even with respect to identification of one's self, self identity is likely to take second place after the family. For example, an individual is seen first as a member of the Hernandez or Mendoza family before he or she is seen as Juan or Jose, that is, before he or she obtains more personal acceptance. Thus to an extent the individual may view himself or herself much of the time as an agent or representative of the family. In many respects this means the person must behave correctly, as it is a direct reflection upon the family and if inappropriate could somehow reflect adversely bringing dishonor or disgrace.

The nuclear family, consists of husband, wife, children, and the extended family. Encompasses grandparents, uncles, aunts, and cousins. In addition to these members, the extended family concept also includes compadres who are the godparents of the children. For each child there may be a different set of compadres. The relationship between parents and compadres is very similar to that between the parents and other adult relatives where there is mutual respect and interchange of help and advice. Among extended family members there is often much communication, visiting, sharing, and closeness of relationship. Such family members are expected to call upon one another and help one another whenever the need arises.

Respect and obedience to elders and male dominance are common traits. The husband is the head of the household. He tends to be independent from the rest of the family. Few decisions can be made without his approval or knowledge. He is free to come and go as he pleases with little explanation to other family members. In essence the father represents authority within the family. All other family members are expected to be respectful of him and accede to his will or direction. An important part of his concept of machismo or maleness, is that of using his authority *within the family in a just and fair manner*. Should he misuse his authority, he will lose respect within the community.

In relating to his children the father frequently serves as the disciplinarian. He assumes responsibility for the behavior of the family members in or outside of the home. Misbehavior by another family member is a direct reflection on the father even though he might not have been present at the time of the misconduct.

Traditionally, the wife is supposed to be completely devoted to her husband and children. Her role is to serve the needs of her husband, support his actions and decisions, and take care of the home and children. In substance she represents the nurturing aspect of the family's life and it is usually highly respected and revered. The mother holds a very special place. She depends upon her sons to take care of her in her old age. It is part of the son's responsibility (machismo) to do so and to defend her honor at all times. Any implication of an insult to one's mother is a serious provocation. Even the Spanish word for "mother," *"madre,"* in certain contexts can be provocative. Care should be taken when using the word; the alternative "mamá" is often safer. Traditionally her life tends to revolve around her family and a few close friends.

There is usually a close continuing relationship between mother and children, which perpetuates throughout her life. In contrast to the father and his relationship to the children, the mother continues to be close and warm, serving and nurturing even when her children are grown, married, and have children of their own. Relationships between mothers and daughters and other female relatives are usually close. Hispanics have a tradition of honor and respect for the aged. While traditions are strong Hispanics are experiencing social changes in the way they view family relations and male and female traditional roles.

Children are not permitted to be disrespectful and are taught this at an early age. They are given responsibility and are often assigned tasks or responsibilities according to their age and ability, which they are expected to assume. Whatever the responsibilities assigned the children, they are real and usually necessary for the welfare of the family. Therefore a feeling of importance as a family member and inter-dependence are developed from an early age onward. Much of the individual's self-esteem is related to how he perceives and others perceive him carrying out his assigned family responsibilities. Boys are especially directed to look after and protect their sisters outside of the immediate home environment.

There is much more physical contact between members of the same sex in than is common in the U.S. Men greet each other with an *(abrazo)* embrace, women may kiss. Hugs, pats on backs, and other physical contact are an important part of communication. The handshake is the universal greeting in both Mexico, Spain and much of Latin America. The physical distance between people when engaged in conversation is also closer than in the U.S. More frequent physical contact and greater physical proximity sometimes make another ethnic withdraw, often without being aware of doing so. In his effort to keep to what he considers a comfortable conversational distance, he may also unintentionally communicate emotional or social distance. (Also, the hands are used in self expression more extensively than in the U.S.).

Culturally a Hispanic averts the eyes as a gesture of respect when contacted by authorities, and is not indicative of evasiveness. Although Hispanics pride themselves on the ability to argue persuasively. Talking your way out of something or to be "silver tongued" is an admirable trait.

The uniqueness of the individual is valued. As a quality which is assumed to reside within each person and which is not necessarily evident through actions or achievements. It is closer to the notion of "soul" than "character." That inner quality which represents the dignity of each person must be protected at all costs; any action or remark that may be interpreted as a slight to the person's dignity is to be regarded as a grave provocation. Moreover, since an individual will most often regard himself or herself first of all as a part of a family and only secondarily as a member of his or her profession, trade or organization, a slight to any other family member will be as provocative as a direct insult.

Keep in mind that many Hispanic men do not like being given orders or arrested by female officers in particular if it is in front of family or friends. Many Hispanics will tend to side with other Hispanics during confrontation or conflict. It is the honorable thing to do and is expected.

There are more than 300,000,000 people who speak Spanish and live in twenty countries. It is estimated that by the year 2000, Spanish will be the language of more than 500,000,000 people. (Approx., 30,000,000 Spanish speakers in the United States).

Spanish is written the same in Spain, Mexico and Latin America. There are differences in pronunciation of some words and in the use of idioms and of course slang. In Spain there are four official languages consisting of Castillian, Basque, Galican and Catalan, with Castillian being the most common. *(Note: In both Latin America and Europe it is common to list a date (IE: Date of Birth) with the day first, then the month and year. January 2, 1950, e.g. becomes 2-1-50).*

It is impossible within the confines of this manual to discuss all of the cultural differences of the many Spanish speaking countries in the world. Because of the number of Mexican citizens in the U.S. and Mexico's close proximity, the culture and its people warrant further discussion.

As expected, Spanish is the official language of Mexico. There are differences in the pronunciation of some words and in the use of idiomatic expressions of course. It is estimated to be as many as 100 Indian languages spoken there such as Nahuatl, Tzotzil, Otomi, Maya, Zapotec, Mextec, or Tzeltal. It is common for those who speak these languages to also speak Spanish. Mexicans are known for their proud Spanish and Indian heritage (It is estimated that 60 percent of the population of Mexico, are of mixed Spanish and Indian descent, 30 percent being predominantly Indian. (Excerpts from: Good Neighbors - Communicating with the Mexicans, by John C. Condon Intercultural Press Inc.)

Other interesting cultural differences and tips:

1. **_Time_** is at the service of people and not people controlled by time. The Hispanic is never late; when he arrives is the time he chooses to be appropriate. Hispanics do not worship the hands of the clock as Anglos do and feel life is made more complicated by impatience.

2. **_People_** are more important than projects or business. Therefore, the cultivation of relationships often take precedence over the production of works.

3. **_Belief in Religion_** or a superior being colors all decisions made which sometimes seems like a personal decision is not being made. It is not unusual in Hispanic homes to find a small altar in a closet or corner of a room with statues of saints and candles burning for various reasons. Some candles are lit for the saints and others for protective spirits.

(NOTE: The criminal element will often use these same type of altars for summoning protective spirits to protect their illegal activities from law enforcement. A large number of these criminals practice the dark side of such religions as Santeria, Brujeria and or Palo Mayombe in the furtherance of their criminal enterprises. Some of these extremists pose a dangerous threat to law enforcement authorities).

4. **_Extended Family_** is a network of support, influence and relationships who need to be considered when working with the Hispanic person.

5. **_Hispanics are a communitarian people;_** whatever they do is for the community instead of the individual. Once trust has been established, Hispanics will be more informal, characterized by warm, intense interactions.

6. **_Competition is a low priority_** but Hispanics work together so that the result is "ours" not "mine".

7. **_A sense of "verguenza" or saving face_** is often mistaken for shyness but pride and honor are high priorities.

8. **_Ability to celebrate life_** with song and dance amidst suffering, poverty and adversity has meant cultural survival. (A Hispanic may make an offer of food or drink during a home visit. To refuse this offer may signify rejection of the hospitality).

9. **_Children are considered a blessing_**, that is one of the reasons why family planned parenthood is not considered a value.

10. **_The Hispanic elderly are respected_** not only for their age, their experience but also because they are the culture's historians.

11. The *respect for nature* and the use of natural herbs and medicine are part of spiritual and physical healing.

12. *Expressions of feelings* are through song, poetry, art and dance. The inner privacy of the person is to be respected and not pried into.

13. *The male in the Hispanic family is the protector,* the disciplinarian, and the female is the teacher, the role model, the bearer of cultural and religious values.

(NOTE: Many Mexican-Americans are proud to be American and prefer to be called Mexican-American rather than Mexican).

In Mexico a handshake (normally a soft handshake) or a nod of the head is quite common (men should let a woman first offer a handshake) and may touch the forearm or elbow with the free hand. Among friends and family a full embrace is quite customary. Women often will greet each other with a kiss on the cheek.

Mexicans are more open and demonstrative than North Americans and body space is much closer than those of Westerners. Mexicans are known for their hospitable, friendly, and polite greetings and value sincerity and honor in relationships.

Tips on body language and gesturing:

- To indicate "No", shake the hand from side to side with the index finger extended with the palm facing outward.

- As in the U.S., "thumbs up" means "O.K."

- Never indicate the height of a person by extending the arm out with the palm down. This is used to designate the height of an animal. Instead use the handshake position to illustrate a person's height.

- To summon others extend the arm with the palm down and curl the fingers repeatedly inward.

- It is impolite to toss an object to another person, always pass it. To do so is considered impolite, offensive, and a lack of manners.

- For a man to stand with his hands on his hips gives the impression of a challenge or hostility and can escalate a situation.

- It is very rude and offensive to make a "V" with the index and middle finger with the palm toward the face with the "V" over the nose. The male person receiving this gestured message is called a "Cornudo". It signifies "your wife has been unfaithful".

- Placing the hand against the forehead in a horizontal position indicates the person is frustrated, fed up or is in over his head. *(The criminal element will use this as a signal to warn an accomplice of impending discovery when confronted by the police. It may also mean a signal to flee or attack the police officer.)*

- Another gesture law enforcement officers should be aware of is the touch to the corner of the eye with the index finger. This may be used as a signal to an accomplice that the police are watching or approaching. It may also be used as a signal from one suspect to another to watch the officer or prepare to attack. (Criminals will also use a shrill whistle to pass the alarm from one house to another that the police are nearby or approaching).

- Many North American gestures are understood by Mexicans so be careful with your gestures.

I have learned as a police officer that often during an initial contact with any individual, regardless of race, the way a person is greeted determines the tone of how that contact will progress. It is just as important to end the contact respectfully as a first impression is a lasting one. This last impression can set the the tone for the next officer who may come into contact with the individual at a later time. It almost goes without saying that there are times during high risk encounters that the officer needs to make that same first impression that he is in control by firm, professional commands. This command presence is its own form of communication and can prevent the encounter from escalating into an uncontrollable force. The confident, accurate use of command phrases can promote officer safety and avoid tragic misunderstandings.

I have been a police officer for 25 years and early in my career I was ambushed and seriously injured. I soon came to realize that experience was the greatest of all teachers, but the lessons are often sudden, harsh and sometimes fatal. Over the years I have seen too many police officers lose their lives needlessly from lack of or inadequate training. Some of them have been my friends. Those of us who have stared directly into the cold, dark, unforgiving eyes of realism are able to profit from even a fleeting glimpse. As a professional trainer, I feel it is a responsibility of all trainers, regardless of their profession, to share their experience with others. The inexperienced will learn quicker and avoid the tragic mistakes that realism and experience have so brightly exposed. An intelligent person learns from his or her mistakes but it is even a smarter person who learns from the mistakes of others.

Several years ago I decided to share my experiences and what I had learned from others. I know there was a widely recognized need to train public safety personnel to learn and speak short succinct survival phrases to promote officer safety and professionalism, while providing an effective tool to bridge the language barrier. I wanted the book and training to be realistic and designed to be easy to learn instead of the traditional, often tedious method of instruction of grammar, structure, and useless vocabulary that is soon forgotten under high stress.

There is a widely recognized need among all public safety officers for the ability to communicate with non-English speaking people under a variety of circumstances while promoting officer safety. Sometimes these circumstances are life threatening, not only to the officer, but to the suspect or even the law abiding citizen. Public Safety Officers may confront this need on a daily basis. They face the potential tragic risk for misunderstandings when dealing with non-English speaking people. Learning simple basic words can reduce those high risk situations. The language barrier has long separated public safety personnel from communicating with varied ethnic groups, a barrier that sometimes threatens or costs a life. All too often it will cost the life of an officer who has received no training in basic survival phrases. Survival phrases encompass a broad spectrum:

- The ability to commit to memory basic, succinct commands and phrases that can make the difference between a simple arrest and a deadly confrontation. This ability provides the officer with the tools to gain control of situations where he has never had control before. (A recent FBI study disclosed that 65% of officers killed were unable to properly control persons or situations).

- The ability to promote officer safety, improve community relations and provide an effective, simple method of communicating.

- The ability to ask an injured person to point to an injury, such as the neck. (This would indicate to the officer or paramedic should not move the person, thus avoiding additional injury).

- The ability to communicate to a frightened child at an accident scene that his mother or father will be o.k.

- The ability to communicate in a basic polite manner in order to elicit co-operation and respect while diffusing a potentially dangerous situation.

- The ability to make all involved persons aware, through actions and speech, that the officer is fair and impartial. It can be very frustrating for an officer to carry out a professional investigation if his communication or attitude is misinterpreted by the victim, witness or suspect.

Officers should be aware that the foreign born may have misconceptions about the police and judicial system. They may be completely ignorant of the American judicial system as well as their own. The presumption of innocence is not part of many other judicial systems. Some foreigners may be too timid to interact widely with persons outside their immediate community and linguistic group. They may fear the police. Police as professionals should earn and develop the confidence of the migrant or non-English speaking person. Regardless of perception of guilt, differing cultural values and national origin, officers should acknowledge the humanity of those they encounter. Ongoing training is crucial to learn about differing cultural perspectives. Understanding these perspectives can enhance the officer's personal safety during escalation of tensions. Communities of immigrants are highly cohesive and rumors of problems with any police officer are often perceived to affect the entire community. An investigation approached with professionalism will withstand the scrutiny of open court and enhance the reputation of the officer and his profession within the community. (Remember many Latin American countries do not have full freedom of the press and many Hispanics tend to pay more attention to information received by word of mouth than do Anglos).

Each day officers who are not properly trained lose court cases because they have failed to correctly advise a person of their rights or ask for consent to search as mandated by law or departmental policies. Officers, through no fault of their own, often cannot communicate with victims to obtain timely information, therefore criminal suspects frequently go free.

Because they cannot effectively communicate with non-English speakers, even at a basic level, emergency medical personnel cannot ask accident victims where they are injured, and sometimes law enforcement officers are injured or killed through not or misunderstanding.
There is a need to properly train police officers on the slang, profanities, gestures, and body language used by the criminal element. The use of profanity and recognizable body language *(silent and too often deadly communication)* are often an early warning indicator, or *"RED FLAG"*, that the encounter is progressing beyond the bounds of polite conversation. Officers must be able to recognize these *"Trip Wires"* of potential violence changing just like the language itself. The need to provide frequent updated training to stay abreast of the street vernacular and the *"Silent Language"* is of paramount importance to officer safety and survival. The *"Troops"* in the field must be educated and made aware of the words/phrases and coded gesturing used by a suspect to warn an accomplice of impending discovery, danger or action anticipated by the officer that will affect their freedom. The majority of slang contained in this manual is to be listened for, not to be used. (As mentioned earlier, the inappropriate use of the slang may escalate the encounter **with inappropriate and undesirable results**).

The conception that having a **qualified foreign language officer speaking officer** available for interpretation for a non-language speaking officer is not a viable solution to the problem. **Adequate training is**. Any officer working in a bilingual setting should be able to listen to and recognize slang and profane words and possess the ability to interpret basic cultural body language. Body language frequently amplifies a person's intentions. The officer's life may be at stake as well as his fellow officers' lives.

I am told by administrators that they have a foreign language speaking police officer available to translate for a non language speaking officer. If one is not available, one can be called to the scene or a telephone translation service can be used. I then point out to the administrator that **the officer in the field cannot wait** for the officer to arrive to command the suspect to: *"Drop the gun!"*, *"Put your hands up!"*, *"Don't move!"*, *"No talking!"*, etc. Nor can he wait to tell an accident victim not to move or to where he is injured". The increased interaction with many ethnics requires that officers are prepared to assess and respond quickly to a multitude of scenarios. Few agencies currently are providing the training to accomplish this complicated task.

I hope that I have not left the impression that people of any ethnic groups are more involved in crime than others, as this is not true. The vast majority of any ethnic group is very respectful, intelligent and hard working.

Professional trainers are given the responsibility to provide the highest quality of training possible. We must be willing to use and adapt unique, progressive ideas to achieve our goals in the ever changing challenges that lie before us. The public expects today's Public Safety Professionals to be well trained and responsive to its needs. Meeting that expectation shall enhance the professional image and improve the standards of law enforcement and other public safety agencies.

I sincerely believe if everybody would treat each other with respect, dignity and fairness, many of our problems in this world would cease to exist. If you follow these simple suggestions, what ever your profession, you will be doing your part to make this world a better place.

1. **Speak to people.** There is nothing as nice as a cheerful word of greeting. Foreigners are very appreciative when you attempt to communicate in their language even if you don't speak it fluently. Learn the basic greetings contained in this manual to convey respect. Believe me it will make your job easier.

2. **Smile at people.** This universal form of communication is understood by every culture known to mankind. It takes little effort, costs nothing and reaps big reward. It will help change the stereotype that law enforcement officers are insensitive, uncaring and cold.

3. **Call people by name.** The sweetest music to anyone's ear is the sound of their own name. Show respect by using the appropriate title the person deserves.

4. **Be respectful, friendly and helpful.** It will assist in gaining voluntary co-operation. The first impression is a lasting one and sets the stage for what follows.

5. **Relate to people and use empathy.** Speak and act as if everything you do were genuine pleasure. Be patient and place yourself in another person's shoes.

6. **Be genuinely and wholly interested in people.** Watch your body language. Actions speak much louder than words and often say all the wrong things.

7. Be generous with praise/cautious with criticism. Learn the cultural differences of each ethnic group. Always leave them an out for saving face even if you're right.

8. Be considerate with the feelings of others. It will be greatly appreciated and remembered. (We frequently come into contact with the same person again).

9. Be thoughtful of the opinions of others. There are 3 sides to a controversy, yours, the other fellow's and the right one. Be reasonable and don't stereotype any race.

10. Be alert to give service with honesty. Be known as a person of integrity, and keep your word.. What counts most in life is what we do for others without asking for anything in return. Remember, reward arrives when it is not summoned for.

After all .... its just a matter of honor.

"The great man shows his greatness by the way he treats the little man."

TYPES OF INTERPRETING AND TRANSLATING

SIMULTANEOUS: The type of interpreting a competent interpreter can furnish contemporaneously with the spoken English words to the non-English speaking participant. It implies a verbatim or word-for-word interpretation as near in time to the speaker's words as possible. Simultaneous translation is required where the testimony relates to facts or events of which the non-English speaking party has personal knowledge and where he can be of assistance to his own attorney.

CONSECUTIVE: A method wherein first a question is asked and translated and then the answer is given and translated. Interpretation usually follows the completion of a sentence or statement. This type is most frequently used when the non-English speaking person is on the witness stand. It would also be required where a witness testifies in English about facts within the personal knowledge of the non-English speaking party.

SUMMARY: A method of translation which summarizes the essence of testimony given either at frequent intervals or at the end of the proceedings. The Bilingual Court Proceeding Bill would not permit this type of translation in a criminal case. But in a civil case, depending on the nature of the factual issues, there may be certain preliminary testimony which need not be translated word for word. The laying of formal foundations for receipt in evidence of an official report or hospital record may be such a situation, if the party has no personal knowledge of the circumstances under which the report was made or the record kept. Similarly, a summarized translation may be sufficient if the testimony is technical or scientific in nature and the party is not himself a qualified technician or scientist in this particular specialty. (Court instructions may call for verbatim interpretation. A practical limitation is that relatively few interpreters are available who can provide verbatim United Nations-type translation).

INTERPRETED INTERVIEWS: Plan your general line questioning and ask follow-up questions as you would do with an English speaking interviewee. Placement of the tape recorder is crucial. Often investigators make the mistake of keeping the tape recorder too close to themselves. This results in over amplification of the investigator's voice. Often what is of most importance to the court is the exact communication of the person being interviewed not the interviewer. Another problem is background noise. Faint noises such as telephones, furnace noise and moving furniture may be enough to make the tape unintelligible. Interviews should be conducted under controlled circumstances.

It is important at the onset of the interview, to make all parties aware that the interpreter is fair and impartial. It can be extremely frustrating for an officer to carry out a professional investigation if his communication or attitude is misinterpreted by the victim, witness, or suspect. Victims or witnesses may hesitate to speak with police officers. Ongoing training is crucial to learn about differing cultural perspectives. Inadvertent misinterpretation of body language, attitude and escalation of tensions, can interfere with an investigation.

A given individual may or may not be aware that gestures he considers universal may in fact have quite different significance in our country. Officers should be aware of this when giving hand signals or interpreting or using gestures.

Officers may unwittingly elicit hostility or escalate tensions by being perceived to "challenge" men they are interviewing or their families. Examples of actions which may be perceived to represent insults or challenging behavior may include: touching or patting a Latino on the face, beckoning a person with the index finger instead of the whole hand, failing to give due respect to elders or ignoring them and dealing only with younger family members who speak English, acting brusque or hurried when no emergency exists, being perceived as rude, over-familiar or making ironic insinuations during interviews. These errors may extinguish any desire to co-operate. You may avoid escalation of tensions or violence in the cross cultural police encounter when interviewing by avoiding appearing rushed at all costs. Take time whenever possible for a few niceties such as complimenting the parents on their well behaved children or expressing admiration for some handiwork or centerpiece in the home, etc. *(NOTE: Touching little girls, even in a friendly way is taboo, and is simply not done by strangers).*

Take time to listen attentively to a convoluted roundabout explanation as answer to your question. If you do not believe the story, do not tell the person he is lying. Simply express sincere disappointment or fruit feelings that the person would make what appears to you to be a blatant attempt to deceive you. When arresting an individual, be very formal and correct, even in the face of abusive statements. (Courtesy; in part Diane Schneider of the U.S. Dept. of Justice, Community Relations Service, Seattle, WA.)

"Luck favors the backbone, not the wishbone."

Dynamic Memory Channeling® - Recall Under High Stress

There's a lot of talk in today's news about the so called "3 Strikes & Your Out" concept in the sentencing of felons. In law enforcement we don't have the "luxury" of 3 strikes. Often the police officer has only one strike available. Police officers who "strike out" strike out in one of three areas. They either:

- **Fail to Practice a Plan**
- **Fail to use Proper Tactics**
- **Failed to Anticipate Danger (ignoring 6th Sense Survival Instinct)**

Strike out with any one of the three, and you well could be out of the game. It's just not enough to use good tactics. You've got to be mentally prepared and know and practice your plan before you need it. It involves knowing and recalling succinct survival phrases under a multitude of conditions.

First you need to know about the dynamics of learning and the effects of high stress on quick recall. (These learning points are applicable to all public safety personnel not just law enforcement officers). Officers who have a strong sense of confidence in their ability to speak these phrases are better able to focus efforts on the demands of the situation than officers who don't.

Let's take a look at some recently released statistics from the FBI who interviewed 54 convicted law enforcement killers. This is what they had to say about the slain officers:

- **65 % of the slain officers failed to control persons or situations**
- **41 % of the slain officers made improper approaches**
- **66% of officers killed were alone.** (Many officers in this country patrol alone with no immediate backup available). One killer said he evaluated the officer's lack of command presence prior to the killing. He said, "The officer was not authoritarian and did not take and control of me. He was a willing participant in his own death."

Having the proper command presence both physically and verbally can make the difference between a suspect submitting peacefully or an escalation to a deadly confrontation. Let's speak for a moment about the most effective method of learning, retraining and recalling commands. I am going to show you how you mentally rehearse a scenario with detail. First jump inside the scenario and picture in your minds eye, you are the officer in the scenario. What commands are you going to give. Imagine what it will look, sound and feel like to respond and control the dangerous situation. Visualize yourself successfully responding to the situation (always with a positive / winning outcome). Build your self-confidence with flexibility and learn to be adaptable. Mentally rehearse many different scenarios. **Remember confidence in a skill is directly related to the number of times the skill has been performed in the past.** Remember that mental rehearsal does not take the place of physical practice. It is very important you visualize the situation you want to control and then see, hear and speak the command firmly, and with authority. Research has shown that with "Dynamic Memory Channeling©" and practice, the brain actually builds neural pathways to memory banks which facilitates faster recall. When the brain recognizes an event it triggers recall of training that has been practiced and experienced. Advantages

168

of mental rehearsal, is that it allows more practice and mistakes can be made without suffering the actual consequences.

Mental rehearsal and the use of visual *"mnemonics"* (associating the unfamiliar with the familiar) is an easy way of learning and retaining key phrases. All you have to do is use your imagination. Let me give you some examples.

Let's say you know very little Spanish and as a police officer in the course of your duties you will be asking for consent to search a car. This is the scenario: You are on patrol in your brand new Chevrolet Camaro patrol car. You see a vehicle weaving all over the road. You stop the vehicle and observe the operator is extremely intoxicated and smell a strong odor of marijuana coming from the vehicle (you have already introduced yourself, advised the individual of the purpose of the stop and have obtained his drivers license). You now would (or later in the contact) ask for consent to search. This is a way to use visual *"mnemonics"* to remember and recall the phrases:

MAY I SEARCH?
¿Puedo esculcar?
(**PWAY**-doh ehs-**KOOL**-cahr)?
(Is **COOL** car!)

All you have to do is to remember "puedo" means "May I" and "esculcar" means to search. Now think of your new Camaro and you know it "IS **COOL** CAR"

Here is another way to say:

MAY I SEARCH ?   (Ray he's a **STAR**!)
¿Puedo registrar?
(**PWAY**-doh ray-hees-**STRAR**)?

Remember that "puedo" means.......   "May I". Another way to say search is "registrar". Now picture in your mind that the person you have stopped is named "Ray". Ray has been drinking and he feels like he's a star. Now follow the phonetics to make the approximate pronunciation.

Here is a third way of saying:

MAY I SEARCH _____?   (Caught the **AIR**!)
¿Puedo catear _____?
(**PWAY**-doh kah-tay-**AHR**_)
(Remember when you smelled the odor of marijuana.
Your nose "caught the air")

Now depending on circumstances and what you asking consent to search for, you may select from the list below. Use your imagination and make up your own *"mnemonics"*. I will give a few hints below but only a few. You need to practice and visualize.

YOUR CAR	- su carro	(soo **KAH**-roh)
YOUR BUILDING	- su edificio	(soo ay-dee-**FEE**-see-oh)
YOUR HOUSE	- su casa	(soo **KAH**-sah)
YOUR PERSON	- su persona	(soo payr-**SOH**-nah)

THAT? - aquello (ah-**KAY**-yoh)   *(POINT TO ITEM)*

THIS? - esto   (**AY**-stoh)

UNDERSTAND?	**UNDERSTAND?**
¿Comprende?	¿Entiende?
(kohm-**PREHN**-day)	(Ehn-tee-**EHN**-day) (n t **N** day)

This is an easy one to remember:

ANSWER YES OR NO   Conteste sí o no (Kohn-**TEHS**-tay see oh noh)

169

Since you speak very little Spanish you want to limit the response to one you under stand, a simple "yes," (si) "or," "no" (o). So picture in your mind you are going to have a contest today with Ray to have him answer "yes." or "no."

Even though the sounds of the two languages are never exactly the same, with practice (and listening to the audio tapes) you'll have no problems in reading the phonetics in such a way to make yourself understood. The examples above are of course for law enforcement officers will feel like a hog on roller skates but with practice you will be associated and recalling phrases in no time at all).

Before I move on I want to provide you (if you are a law enforcement officer) with a couple more "mnemonics" that may save your life. I have provided these mnemonics in my training and have had officers call and tell me it alerted them they were going to be attacked. I feel it is worth sharing these **"RED FLAGS"**, or **"FATAL WORDS"** with you.

You may be in a situation that you may hear one of these words when dealing with the criminal element.

KILL HIM!
Matele
(MAH-tay-lay)

The killer of the bull is a "matador". (Slang in English for a State Trooper is "bull". So visualize the matador is going to kill and lay the bull down. Thus **"Matele"**. (Matelo for male and Matela for female. Matele can apply to either sex).

Now let's say the "Matador" is going to stab the bull with a sword or knife.

A knife is a **"Pica"** (PEE-kah).
The person who stabs the bull is called a "Picador".
Visualize the "Picador" is going to take a "pica" (reminds you of an ice pick) and he is going to lay you down thus:
¡Picale!

STAB HIM!
¡Picale!
(PEE-kah-lay)

(Picale applies to either sex)

STAB HIM
¡Picalo!
(PEE-kah-loh)

STAB HER
¡Picala!
(PEE-kah-lah)

EFFECTS OF STRESS ON MENTAL RECALL

Let's talk about the effects of stress on mental recall performance. Stress reduces your response capability with all too often fatal consequences. It is well documented that in sterile training sessions, reaction time is slowed when minimal stress is applied. That is why excellent recall in training environments cannot be compared to the realism of field applications. The student must receive immediate, positive feedback while under simulated field stress. This builds confidence and enhances mental and physical reaction time. It is a fact that stress has less effect on practiced skills that are mastered under conditions of perceived danger. Perceived danger or loss of control increases stress and causes physiological changes to prepare for the fight or flight mechanism with increased adrenal secretions. Automatic responses to danger are found more often in officers who use mental rehearsal techniques.

170

The goal of this training is to change inaction into reaction through automatic and reflexive responses that can save your life. At times the responses can be used proactively to prevent, control and de-escalate dangerous confrontation. Be prepared to take control and always, **expect the unexpected.**

We are now going to discuss the pre-attack verbal and non verbal cues that you may confront in the field. The ability to recognize theses red flags, the trip wires that indicate danger are of extreme importance. This ability is called **"Survival Awareness Communication"** and it is the art of hearing and seeing what is, and what is not being said. Remember that 35% of communication is by the spoken word and 65% is by body language.

Body language amplifies the suspect's intentions often through involuntary & unconscious movements, which if recognized, can be a warning to you. The ability to interpret and recognize body language is as important as learning basic survival phrases themselves.

It is important to note that you should not attempt to actually use the field manual during a high risk situation. Learn the phrases by reading the manual, and listening to the associated survival audio language tapes in your patrol car or at home. This is one of the most cost effective ways for agencies to train their personnel.

I wrote this manual to promote officer safety by reducing the time between what is perceived and reaction and response time. The information in this manual is realistic, job specific and logical to give you the ability to evaluate, assess and control life threatening encounters. This knowledge and skill, when learned, gives you the power to persuade, control, respond to and prevent a deadly confrontation. Verbal command presence is its own form of communication.

Many agencies send their officers to college to learn languages that are not specific to our profession. The problem is that many institutions don't teach law enforcement terminology or methods to promote officer safety.

There is an overwhelming need to provide training in a verbal force continuum with an effective supplement or alternative to physical confrontation. Periodic training and testing in these areas as well as regimented, standardized, basic survival phrase courses are needed.

Keep up your skills and learn the phrases you will use the most often. Observe native speakers and do not hesitate to use them as your mentors. Remember to enunciate distinctly, accurately, and succinctly.

I sincerely care about your safety and I hope I have given you the tool to perform your job more safely.

Remember....

Luck prefers a prepared mind and the biggest threat to you,

.....is you.

Practice, practice, and more practice.

You have nothing to lose

.... but your life.

Remembering / One mans dedication to fallen officers' survivors

By DOUG BATES

(USA BEND, OR) When a police officer anywhere is killed in the line of duty, Bob Dent mourns along with his fellow officers then does something about it.

A tragedy several years ago -- the fatal shooting of Dent's friend and colleague, a young Oregon State Police trooper named Bret Clodfelter - set in motion a chain of events that stunned Pacific Northwest law enforcement and changed Dent's life. He still has trouble talking about the 1992 shooting at Klamath Falls, Oregon, but what really haunts him is the death of Clodfelter's wife, Rene', who took her own life one year after her husband died, as law enforcement, corrections, security, school resource officers, parole and probation etc.

They had been married just 33 days when Bret Clodfelter (33 years old) was killed, Dent recalls, his voice trailing off. Dent, a retired Oregon State Police Senior Trooper living in Bend, has seen his share of friends fall to the bullets and knives of criminals and has long been involved in providing emotional support to the families of officers killed while serving in harm's way. It was the Clodfelter case, however, that galvanized his commitment and compelled him to dedicating his private life to this cause by setting up a non-profit foundation that raises money to help people such as Rene' Clodfelter deal with the grieving process.

His philanthropic efforts have brought international awards, television and radio appearances, articles written by national and international magazines with commendations from former President George Bush and Oregon Governor John Kitzhaber to name a few. However, Dent is quick to give the credit to individuals who support him, as he requires any donation given be accompanied by the donor's name and address. He handles all correspondence himself, keeping administrative costs near zero, and personally forwards the contributions and names of the contributors to the grieving family. "I want the families to know who each individual is," Dent says. "Too often, those responsible for goodwill and charity seldom get the credit they deserve. Letting these families know the many people who share in their grief offers the family support and comfort."

Dent recalls that Clodfelter died in his patrol car after being shot four times in the back of the head by one of three men riding in the back seat. The young trooper was giving the men a ride after arresting one of them for driving while under the influence of an intoxicant.

A fallen officer's survivors are part of the police family, he says, but after the funeral, after the honor guards, after the outpouring of support, there's often a sudden break in contact with the department. Yet, the loss goes on for years -- for a lifetime. "For those families left behind", Dents says, "there are no tolling bells, no names on a silent sacred wall, no solemn ceremonies with bagpipers and their Amazing Grace," but they too have made a terrible sacrifice. It is important these families receive help in bringing closure to a tragic time in their lives. Society owes this debt to them."

To help out, Dent has established the Bend-based **Constable Public Safety Memorial Foundation, Inc.** Since 1995, with a board of directors headed by Rene' Clodfelter's mother, Dent has been raising funds to assist such families. Contributions mainly help pay for survivors' travel expenses to the National Law Enforcement Officer's Memorial Services and the Concerns of Police Survivors Grieving Seminars in Washington, D.C.

Dent also donates part of the proceeds of sales of two foreign language manuals, a hand signaling manual, training videos and a buckle he has produced, to the foundation he created.

Clodfelter's death, says Dent, illustrates the need for officer training in foreign languages and other forms of essential communications. In the moments before the shooting, the three men in the rear of the patrol car were conversing in Spanish, and the young trooper might have realized the danger he was in, had he understood some of what was being said. "Experience is the greatest of all teachers, but its lessons are often sudden, harsh and all too often fatal," Dent says. "Law Enforcement is a profession that gives you the test first, then the lesson."

Dent receives no salary from the foundation he founded and has so far been paying postage, telephone and travel costs out of his own pocket.

Recently, Dent arranged an Oregon appearance by Vincent Bugliosi, the famed author and former Los Angeles prosecutor. Bugliosi wrote the best-selling book "Helter Skelter," recounting his successful prosecution of the Charles Manson case, and several other true-crime books including a recent best-seller, "Outrage," regarded by critics as the best book published on the O.J. Simpson murder case.

Bugliosi, moved by Dent's work, agreed to waive his speaking fee with all the proceeds going to the foundation. Dent arranged for Bugliosi's airfare to Bend to be paid by criminals convicted of assaulting police officers, resisting arrest or eluding officers, through an arrangement with Dennis Maloney, director of the Deschutes County Community Justice Department. Bugliosi has since been appointed as an honorary board member of the foundation.

Dent met Bugliosi at a conference several years ago. The prosecutor subsequently endorsed Dent's books and training tapes. The two became friends but it was the cause that brought Bugliosi to Bend, Dent says.

"For some reason many people mistakenly believe that the spouses, children, parents and co-workers who survive the law enforcement deaths are somehow more prepared for their losses than are other people. Nothing could be further from the truth." Dent said.

Since the foundation was created in 1995, it has provided assistance to surviving families in Washington, Idaho, Oregon and as far away as Florida. Ironically, within 45 days of the Bugliosi fundraiser, three of Dent's friends and fellow Oregon State Police officers were killed in the line of duty. Dent says the $16,000 raised from the Bugliosi fundraiser is being used to help the three families as well as other recent surviving families in Oregon, Washington and Idaho.

Dent tells of heartwarming stories about the generosity of others such as a Bend woman who heard about the foundation and the Bugliosi fundraiser. There's the story of the elderly widowed woman who sends the foundation $100 every month from her Social Security check. "She told me her husband and brother had passed on," Dent says, "and her contributions make her feel worthwhile, to be able to help these families."

Dent has not stopped with just police families to help; with support from Oregon State Representative Ben Westlund, **"The Fallen Officer's Bill"** was recently signed into law by Governor John Kitzhaber after winning unanimous approval from the House and Senate. The law, written by Dent and Westlund, gives help to families of other public safety professionals like firefighters, correctional and juvenile officers; and parole and probation personnel. The law makes convicted criminals and those that put officers at risk, pay to help the families of slain or incapacitated public safety officers. The newly passed law requires those convicted of felonies, misdemeanors, infractions and violations to pay a $1.00 assessment. The law established the **"Public Safety Memorial Fund Board,"** and is administered by members of the Oregon Department of Public Safety Standards and Training Executive Board. The board was appointed by Oregon's Governor. Dent was appointed as an "Ex-Officio" board member and volunteers his time and assistance to help administer the new law.

Dent said, " We are making criminals and those who violate the law more responsible for their illegal acts. They should bear the cost of this bill, not the law abiding taxpayer." The genesis of the fund is not just living expense money. It's four-year college scholarships for the spouse and children. It's for funeral expenses, it's therapy and meetings with other survivors." Also included in the law is: a $25,000 cash benefit to be paid within 14 days of the officer's death; fully paid health and dental benefits; 12 house mortgage payments; and catastrophic injury benefits.

Dent says he intends to get legislation passed nationally and internationally. He has been invited to appear on a number of national and international television networks to gamer support. More than 10 other states and a number of foreign countries have contacted Dent about the law.

The intense 50 year old, clearly enjoys the lectem -- an aptitude that shows up in training videos he has produced -- and you get the feeling that in another life he might have made an excellent classroom teacher. Inevitably, in today's cynical world, the time-consuming behind-the-scenes efforts of someone like Dent cause eyebrows to raise. What's the motivation here? It's clearly a simple one, found in the man's own terse explanation: "I cannot forget the looks, the tears on the faces of all the innocent young women with children, grieving a lost husband and father suddenly taken, older couples who have unfortunately outlived their son or daughter, brothers, sisters. And it saddens me greatly. I've just been to too many funerals. I hope that my small foundation can ease the pain and suffering just a little. Nothing equals the smiles and hugs from the family and fellow officers you help. No honor or award can replace the twinkle in the eye or the smile on the face when you know you've touched someone's heart... it is the right thing to do." Dent said.

In memory of Bret and Rene' Clodfelter... You and others like you will not be forgotten.

**Robert Dent
Exec. Director**

Bates is the Editorial Director for the Oregonian newspaper in Portland, Oregon.
(Article reprint permitted with appropriate author credit.)

Contributions to Dent's foundation may be mailed to:

Constable Public Safety Memorial Foundation, Inc.

P.O. Box 6415, Bend, OR 97708 (Visit him website for more information at:

http://www.survival-spanish.com

174

Victim Assistance Phone Numbers

Adam Walsh Child Resource Center	714-898-4802
Alcohol - Drug Help Line	800-621-1646
Alcohol / Drug Help Line	800-621-1646
Center for Crime Victims / Survivors	813-535-1114
Child Find of America	914-255-1848
Children of Alcoholics	415-431-1366
Cocaine Abuse Hotline	800-Cocaine
Concern for Dying	212-246-6962
Concerns of Police Survivors	301-599-0445
Constable Public Safety Memorial Foundation, Incorporated	Attn: Robert Dent, Exec. Dir. PO. Box 6415, Bend, Or 97708
Crime Victims Research Ctr.	803-792-2945
Crime Stoppers International	505-294-2300
Justice for Murder Victims	415-905-6419
Make A Wish Foundation	800-772-9474
Mothers Against Drunk Driving	800-438-6233
Nat. Poison Control Center	800-962-1253
Nat. S.I.D.S. Center	312-663-0650
Nat. Center for Missing Youth	800-782-SEEK
Nat. Victims Center	703-276-2880
Nat. Organaniz. for Victims Asst.	703-276-2889
Nat. Child Safety Council	517-764-6070
Nat. Hospice	703-243-5900
Nat. Center for Missing/Exploited Children	800-843-5678
Nat. Police Memorial	703-827-0518
Nat. Center for Missing Youth	206-771-7335
Parents of Murdered Children	800-962-1253
The White House	202-456-1414
US Supreme Court	202-479-3000
Vanished Children's Alliance	408-971-4822

Also Available from the Constable Group, Inc.

The Multi-Lingual Field Manual for Public Safety Professionals.

This compact expandable manual contains 30 of the most useful pages from the Complete *Spanish Field Reference Manual for Public Safety Professionals*. Translated into 11 languages by the World Trade Center School of Languages, Portland, Oregon. This manual contains Spanish, Russian, Vietnamese, Korean, Chinese and Cambodian with the following language inserts: Japanese, Hungarian, Italian, German and French
(ISBN #1-883339-01-4)
(For more information go to: www.Survival-Spanish.com)

Rights of Foreign Nationals

Article 36 of the Vienna Convention on Consular Relations (VCCR) confers specific rights on all foreign detainees and prisoners as follows:

- Must immediately inform detainee of right to seek consular assistance.
- Must also notify the consulate if the detained foreign national so requests (Notification is not mandatory unless requested)
- Exception: Consulate must be notified if any unaccompanied juvenile is arrested or detained.
- Consular officers have the right to visit detainee and to arrange for his or her legal representation. *Don't forget this international treaty pertains to you if you are in a foreign country.*

176

"SURVIVAL SPANISH"® HIGH RISK VEHICLE STOPS©

In this interactive training video you will be taken on a realistic journey into the realm of a dangerous high risk vehicle stop where you become part of the video and are forced to take control to survive.

The **"Red Flags and Trip Wire"** words of danger are explored that are often used by the Hispanic criminal element. The words and phrases learned can save your life and adaptable for use in many fields of the public safety arena such as police, corrections, parole and probation etc.

A SYNOPSIS OF THE FILM This video was viewed by the U.S. Department of Justice National Criminal Justice Reference Service. It is an objective review of the film and is not an official endorsement by that agency. The review is as follows: This video instructs law enforcement officers in the use of Spanish phrases and words appropriate for a high risk vehicle stop. "The video provides interactive instruction as users are given learning tasks in the course of the video presentation. The video opens with a simulated vehicle stop in which two Latino males suspected of having stolen the car are stopped. The officer fails to control the situation with Spanish commands and is subsequently killed by one of the suspects. The instructor notes the importance of gaining command of a situation through commanding and clear communication. Given the growing number of Hispanics in the population who cannot understand English, the instructor advises that officer safety requires learning critical command phrases and words in Spanish. The instructor first outlines the learning technique that is best for learning speech and behavior under high stress. It involves mental rehearsal, visualization, and the repetition of the behaviors appropriate for high-risk situations. The core of the instruction is a replaying of the simulated vehicle stop with the proper use of Spanish-language commands appropriate for having the suspects exit the vehicle and lie prostate on the ground away from their vehicle and a safe distance from the officer. The instruction also shows the English subtitle of each command followed by 3 second during users are to speak the Spanish translation. The Spanish word is then shown as both written and pronounced phonetically. The next segment of the tape provides instruction on the non-verbal body language that provides cues that a suspect is posing a danger, as well as verbal cues in Spanish that indicate a Spanish-speaking suspect is about to use a knife or gun." (Color VHS - 50 minutes with pre and post test for classroom or home study.)

"After initial instruction, you're stress tested by having to respond on your own to what you see under constant time pressure. *A ground breaking method...*

the Cadillac of all Spanish learning videos."

Dave Smith - Calibre Press

National Street Survival Seminars

New Release

Survival Spanish®
for
Public Safety Trainers®
(375 Slide PowerPoint Training CD)

This newly released, *Survival Spanish*® PowerPoint presentation is packed with invaluable information, insight and "no nonsense" techniques that are critical in learning and teaching Survival Spanish®. Written and produced by award winning author and trainer, Robert Dent, author of the "**Complete Spanish Field Reference Manual for Public Safety Professionals** (6th Ed.) This innovative and realistic training program provides a simple communications capability to bridge the language and cultural barrier, which enhances public service to the Hispanic community while saving lives.

Dent, a retired Oregon State Police Senior Trooper, designed the course for instructors to teach basic, entry level **Survival Spanish®** to a wide variety of public safety professionals. It encompasses the numerous situations, both common and life threatening, that public safety professionals encounter with Spanish speaking persons. This training helps avoid tragic misunderstandings, elicits voluntary cooperation and enhances the image of the public safety professionals. Using *learning cognates*, *mnemonics* and *"Dynamic Memory Linking®"* this "easy to teach" patented method is a practical way for learning, retaining and recalling commonly used Spanish words and phrases. The Survival Spanish® training method, addresses the relationship between sensory perception, the brain, "memory keys," and the rate of practice. Once learned, the **"Key"** for memory recall, evokes an appropriate learned response. Conceptual protocols for learning, remembering, and recalling practical and abstract concepts by means of cognitive association are retained by realistic practice and reinforced by immediate positive feedback, which this interactive training program provides.

Our materials circumvent the unnecessary and confusing grammar instruction found in most college courses. It is easy, efficient and cost effective. There are others who mimic the *"Survival Spanish®"* technique, but we are the leaders in the industry. (Typically, this course can be used as a 2-3 day stand-alone training program or can be used in conjunction with more in depth language courses.) *NOTE: The CD includes hundreds of pictures, illustrations, charts, speaker notes and pre and post tests. It is designed to be used in conjunction with the* **Complete Spanish Field Reference Manual for Public Safety Professionals (6th Ed.) and the "Interactive Survival Spanish - High Risk Vehicle Stops" video training tape.** (This CD and other training materials are useful for law enforcement, corrections, security, EMT's, parole / probation, firefighters, educators, military, juvenile and youth authorities and other public safety professionals.) For more information on topics go to: **www.Survival-Spanish.com**

New Releases

Silent Universal Signals for Public Safety and Education Professionals©
(Save Lives With Hand, Visual and Coded Communications)

by **Senior Trooper Robert Dent**
Oregon State Police (Ret.)

with

Commander Alan Morris, USN. (Ret.)
Former Director of SEAL Training
Naval Special Warfare Center

This unique 200 page 4" by 9" field manual contains revolutionary, easy to remember visual, auditory and coded signaling techniques for communicating between public safety and education professionals such as:

Law Enforcement; School Resource Officers; Teachers; Firefighters; EMS; Corrections and Youth Authority; Parole and Probation; Court Security; Emergency Response Teams; Search and Dive Rescue Personnel; Security, Personal Protection and Military Professionals; and many others. *(Contains hundreds of photographs, charts and illustrations.)* With

Free
20 Mile Signal Mirror

Turn page to learn more...

See how Commander Al Morris, Former Director of Training, U.S. Navy SEALs, (Ret.) uses a simple way of signaling for help over long distances. Learn this little known method of accurate "Targeting and signaling" that has been proven highly successful by the elite U.S. Navy SEAL Teams around the world. This mirror's brilliant, reflective, corrosive resistant surface is of the highest grade available, produced through a special patented process. This credit card size, polished stainless steel, signaling mirror will reflect light for 20 miles and can be carried in a wallet, purse, back or fanny pack.

The applicability of this mirror and signaling technique encompasses a broad spectrum of uses by professionals and non-professionals alike i.e. firefighters; EMS personnel; search and rescue; fish and wildlife resource officers; law enforcement; boaters; recreationalists; outdoorsmen and women; joggers; hikers; hunters; snowmobile enthusiasts; Boy / Girl Scouts and other youth groups; families; the hearing / speech impaired and many others. **A few examples of how useful this mirror and signaling techniques are:**

- **Families and Youth Groups:** Fewer children would be lost if they carried and used this mirror to aid in their recovery i.e. Can be used to signal their location if injured, to their family, passing vehicles or persons, aircraft, rescuers etc.

- **Educators:** When involved in school emergencies, staff can silently signal from inside a classroom (using overhead lighting) to responding emergency personnel, the location of the disturbance i.e. school shooting, hostage taking or other emergency.

- **Law Enforcement** - Law enforcement may use method to silently signal other public safety personnel; they may use it as an inspection mirror for hard to reach areas; a mirror for looking around a corner to see if the area is clear of a suspect or danger.

- This uniquely designed mirror comes with a color photograph, simple step-by-step instructions and an illustration that is adhered right on the back for easy reference. What better gift could you give to someone you care about?

"In the "Teams" we use what works, and we get to come home. I recommend that you use this handy credit card size signal mirror and simple aiming procedure.
Practice... and maybe you and yours can come home too!"

Al Morris
Commander, USN (Ret.)
Former Director of Training US Navy SEAL's

Another New Release

18 Silent Universal Signals

For

School Safety ©

The following standardized signals when posted and practiced, enhances teacher / staff / student or student leader communication under many types of situations such as, group activities, assemblies, field trips, or to safely and quickly direct students during fire drills, natural disasters or other emergencies. A full color, 11"x17" **educational bulletin board poster** with these signals and instructional guide can be ordered on the Internet at: **SilentSignals.com** *(Available in Spanish.)*

Attention and Quiet!
Silent!
Stand Up!
Move Over There!
Get Down!
Meet Here or There!
Leave or Evacuate!
Go!
Hurry!
Stop!
Come Here!
Me or I

I want
You
Nurse or Doctor
Teacher
Help Me!
I am being held!

(Turn page for more info)

"18 Silent Signals for School Safety," must be an essential ingredient of the safety and security plan for every school in America. This poster should be in every classroom in the country."

Homer H. Kearns, Ph. D.
Supt. of Schools, Salem, Oregon (Ret.)
Past President of the American Association of School Administrators

"Innovative, Comprehensive and Long Overdue... Silent Signals is a must for professional educators and all types of public safety personnel."

Vincent Bugliosi
(Author of Helter Skelter
and prosecutor of Charles Manson Family)

"No man has done more to ensure effective communication for public safety that Bob Dent. I am confident this **"Silent Signals"** and its associated training will save lives."

Dave Smith
Director of Education
Law Enforcement Television Network and
General Manager of Calibre Press

"As the world moves into the 21st Century, the need for accurate and efficient communication between public safety professionals constitutes one of the most crucial challenges of the new millennium. To meet that challenge, Robert Dent and Alan Morris have produced a reliable, simple and easy to learn method of silently communicating under all types of situations. This book, poster and associated training will revolutionize the way those in public safety communicate. Simply put, *"Silent Universal Signals"* will save lives and should be in the hands of everyone in America dedicated to safety."

Rep. Ben Westlund (R)
Chairman, Ways and Means
Public Safety Committee
Salem, Oregon

To order call 800-776-1950 or order on the Web at:
SilentSignals.com
Or e-mail us at: orders@SilentSignals.com

P784

(Reprinted from *"The Law Enforcement Trainer"*)

Pilot Program in Schools Uses Signals for Safety

Requests for training have been received from organizations around the world

by Gwen McEntire

Amid the chaos that surrounds a crisis, the most effective communication can often take place without one word being spoken. Robert Dent, recently retired Senior Trooper from the Oregon State Police (where he served more than 25 years), and Alan Morris, former Director of Training for the U.S. Navy SEALS, have developed cognitive signals for students and a wide array of public safety personnel. The purpose, simply put, is to save lives.

"We in public safety are given the test first and then the lesson," states Mr. Dent, who was seriously injured early in his career. He"d like to reverse that chronology for others in the public safety sector, and give students and educational staff an alternative way to communicate with emergency personnel. The idea of universal signals for safety was conceived by him about four years ago, and is comprised of uniquely cognitive gestures developed by Mr. Dent and Mr. Morris and include key American Sign Language signals. "This evolved from things I saw happening," says Mr. Dent. "I could see there was a need for improved communication between agencies responding to an emergency. I have seen too many people lose their lives needlessly from lack of, or inadequate, on scene communications capability." Additional considerations are that responding agencies are frequently on different radio frequencies, only one person can talk on the radio at a time, and using the radio can give away your location and compromise your safety.

He"d had success using signals in several incidents he"d encountered, including one when he signaled his rookie partner to "check for warrants" on a detained suspect. His partner after checking, signaled the "suspect was wanted." Dent then signaled to his partner to "take the advantage position," thereby maintaining control and increasing officer safety during the arrest. When his gestures worked, he thought of all the possibilities.

Columbine High School is one example where the efforts of emergency personnel were hindered by the inability to communicate with those inside. Response time was slowed significantly from the time police arrived at the school until a SWAT team was able to enter the building. Nobody knew where the gunmen were or how heavily they were armed. No one knew how many people had been shot. Police could see individuals in windows, but were unable to obtain critical information.

The "Silent Universal Signal" system provides a non-verbal form of communication that can be used in almost any situation. Gestures that signify that a child is being held against his or her will, or being threatened, could attract the attention of security officers or others who could intervene or provide assistance.

Signals are "common sense and easily learned," says Mr. Dent. A poster with 18 basic commands, from "silent" to "help me" and "come here" is hung in classrooms of participating schools as an immediate reference for students and teachers. In addition, specialized and other appropriate signals are taught to the teachers exclusively.

The program was launched May 25 at Elk Meadow Elementary School in Bend, Oregon, after Assistant Principal Bruce Reynolds saw a presentation at a Safe Schools Alliance meeting. He proposed implementing the program and received enthusiastic support from the principal and other staff at his school.

"We had our emergency procedures in place——our cell phones and special policies, but felt this fit the bill as one more way to keep our kids safe," says Mr. Reynolds. "We had our entire staff, teachers and support personnel, here for training."

It was outstanding. Bob and Alan did an incredible job." Everyone was amazed, he comments, at how much they learned in just two hours.

"You remember so much, but it"s all very logical. That"s what really helps," he states. Participants practice the signals and, in one demonstration, the trainer stands outside a window and gestures to communicate a message.

Posters are hung in Elk Meadow classrooms, and teachers are training students. A fire drill that was already planned was modified to be conducted in silence……"our goal is to move the kids outside absolutely silently," says Mr. Reynolds. Once students exhibit proficiency, a few additional signals will be taught.

Results from the training were immediate. One day after the program began, Mr. Reynolds saw a bus driver signal to another to ask if he had checked student IDs. The simple signal eliminated the need to shout or walk across the parking lot. Three other schools in Oregon are presently implementing the program.

Mr. Dent alludes to the silent signals used successfully by Native Americans for hunting and gaining tactical advantage over the enemy during battle. Street gangs and prison gangs, he notes, use their own form of sign language to counter the ability of law enforcement officials to anticipate their intentions. "Like the Native Americans, the 'tribes,' of public safety and education will benefit from a standardized silent communications protocol," Dent said.

The program is attracting interest from organizations throughout the country and abroad. United Nations peacekeeping forces have called for more information. Mr. Dent and Mr. Morris have trained an impressive array of public safety professionals, including a number of active or retired FBI agents, military intelligence officers, counter-terrorism officials, search and rescue, fire service professionals and are scheduled to train a cadre of personnel in Washington, D.C. this summer.

"This is not just for schools," notes Mr. Dent. "The potential magnitude is amazing." Recently the aviation industry has expressed an interest in the program's potential for handling incidents of air rage.

Mr. Dent's goal is to have the training become the silent communications standard common to ALL national and international public safety officials. This would include law enforcement officers, firefighters, corrections, parole / probation, educators, security and military professionals.

He has parlayed his expertise into other areas of communication as well, and wrote two multi-lingual field manuals to help public safety professionals converse in 11 different languages. "The Complete Spanish Field Reference Manual for Public Safety Professionals" won an award for "Best Book of the Year for Content" by the National Association of Independent Publishers. He has written articles that were published internationally about the importance of officer safety, and the need for improved language and non-verbal communications. The beauty of signals is their universality, he states.

"We can standardize and teach this intuitive system to people who speak any language such as multi-national peace keeping forces. The signals are cognitive and, once you see them, you'll remember them." He describes the method of training as "dynamic memory channeling," i.e. each signal easily links to others.

With the increase in crisis situations, crime and unpredictable violence, he sees non-verbal communication as becoming increasingly important.

"The ability to add this dimension to our communication repertoire can make the difference between a simple encounter and a deadly confrontation," he says. "The signals aren't meant to replace traditional means of communication, but to supplement them in situations where safety and security are an issue."

At the Web site, www.silentsignals.com, people can learn about the program, order an instructional guide, or a wall chart that depicts the basic signals. The 160-page book comes with a universal signaling mirror that can be seen up to 20 miles away.

Part of the proceeds from training materials and manuals is allocated by Mr. Dent to the Constable Public Safety Memorial Foundation, Inc. He founded the fund to assist the families of law enforcement officers who are killed in the line of duty.

(Reprint from "The Law Enforcement Trainer" the Official Journal of the American Society of Law Enforcement Trainers.) For reprint permission, e-mail Gwen McIntyre at: gmcentire@erols.com

Bob Dent to Receive Lifetime Achievement Award

After more than 25 years with the Oregon State Police, and being exposed to the best and absolute worst in people, Senior Trooper Bob Dent remains steadfast in his belief that most are kind, and that anything is possible. Others say he makes things happen, and that his belief serves as the catalyst for what he has accomplished during life.

Dent was nominated by American Society of Law Enforcement Training Board member Dave Smith who, years ago, recruited him as a member of the organization. According to Smith's nomination, Dent "took the pain of a personal loss and converted it to positive energy to create life-saving law enforcement training."

Smith first met Dent when he worked with him helping to produce a training video on Survival Spanish in the early 90s for the Law Enforcement Television Network. A close friend of Dent's had been murdered on a stop because he could not understand the suspects plotting. Bob believed that if officers knew key words they could possibly survive similar situations, and also could provide better service to the Spanish-speaking community.

The programs were well received..."before long the anecdotes were rolling in of law enforcement and corrections officers who had avoided serious injury or death by understanding key words," writes Smith. Dent continued to develop materials, and now has field manuals published in 11 foreign languages. One was awarded "Best Book of the Year for Content" by the National Association of Independent Publishers. He is considering writing a manual in Arabic, which would include a section about cultural diversity.

He expanded his work in communication and collaborated with Alan Morris, former Director of Training for the U.S. Navy SEALS, to develop the "Silent Universal Signals" system. This non-verbal communication can be used in almost any situation. Dent and Morris have been contacted by schools, pilots, and many public safety professionals around the globe.

Dent has been driven to continue his work with one purpose in mind...to help save the lives of innocent people. He says he's been to too many funerals. (Dent has donated approximately $40,000 in books and training videos to law enforcement agencies across the country that are limited by small training budgets.)

For those who have died in the line of duty, he found a way to reach out to their survivors and introduced the Fallen Officer's Bill. According to its provision, payment is assessed from convicted criminals and that money is directed to the families of slain or incapacitated public safety officers. The Bill has been signed into law in Oregon, and Dent has been contacted by troopers from approximately 20 other states who are either interested or already pursuing legislation through elected representatives.

His Constable Public Safety Memorial Foundation, Inc., was founded in 1995 without much fanfare and, according to Smith, with the humility he has shown throughout their friendship. Family members of slain officers from across the country have been helped with funds from the non-profit organization.

"He has shown the deepest humanity for those he knows only as the loved ones of fallen officers and reached out to help without regard to personal gain or recognition," writes Smith.

Good deeds have a way of resonating beyond the individual, and Dent has been recognized by numerous notable individuals, including former President George Bush and Oregon Governor John Kitzhaber. He received commendations from former FBI Director William Sessions, the American Association of State Troopers, and the Oregon Association of Chiefs of Police, along with many other awards throughout his long and distinguished career. (Reprinted from the Sept./October issue of *"The Law Enforcement Trainer"* magazine of the A.S.L.E.T.) For reprint permission e-mail the author Gwen McIntyre at: gmcentire@erols.com)

VOCABULARY

●* denotes verb form (to do)

A

a lot of-	mucho	(MOO-choh)
abduct-	raptar	(rahp-TAHR)
about-	acerca de	(ah-SEHR-kah day), tocante (toh-KAHN-tay)
abuse-	abuso	(ah-BOO-soh)
accessory cómplice	(KOHM-plee-say)
accident-	accidente	(ahk-see-DEHN-tay)
accomplice- cómplice	(KOHM-plee-say)
accusation- acusación	(a-ku-sa-SYOHN)
acknowledge- reconocer	(reh-koh-noh-SAYR)
addict-	adicto	(ah-DEEK-toh)
address-	dirección	(dee-rehk-SYOHN); domicilio (doh-mee-SEE-lyoh)
admit-	admitir	(ahd-mee-TEER)
admission-	admisión	(ahd-mee-SYOHN)
advice-	aviso	(ah-BEE-soh)
●advise-	avisar	(ah-bee-SAHR)
a few-	unos pocos	(OO-nohs POH-kohs)
affidavit- declaración	(deh-klah-rah-SYOHN)
after-	después de	(dehs-PWEHS day)
afternoon- la tarde	(TAHR-day)
in the afternoon- por la tarde (pohr lah TAHR-day)
this afternoon- esta tarde (EHS-tah TAHR-day)
tomorrow afternoon- mañana por la tarde (mah-NYAH-nah pohr lah TAHR-day)
afterwards- después, luego (dehs-PWEHS LWAY-goh)
again-	otra vez	(OH-trah vehs)
against-	contra	(KOHN-trah)
age-	edad	(ee-DAHD)
ago-	hace	(AH-say)
●agree to-	acordar	(ah-kohr-DAHR)
agreement- acuerdo	(ah-KWEHR-doh)
airplane-	avión	(ah-BYOHN)
airport-	aeropuerto; or
	- puerto aereo (S. Amer.) (ah-air-poo-ehr-toh) / (PWEHR-toh ah-AYR-ee-oh)
alcohol - alcohol	(ahl-koh-OHL)
alias-	sobrenombre (SOH-bray-NOHM-bray);
	- alias	(AY-lee-ahs)
- apodo	(ah-POH-doh)
alien- extranjero	(ehs-trahn-HAY-roh)
all-	todo	(HOT-doh)
allow me- permítame	(pehr-ME-tay-may)
all right-	bueno	(BWAY-noh)
alone-	solo	(SOH-loh)
already-	ya	(yah)
always-	siempre	(see-EHM-pray)
America- America	(Ah-MEH-ree-kah)
American- Americano	(ah-meh-ree-KAH-noh)

B

baby-	bebé	(beh-BAY)
back seat- asiento trasero	(ah-SEE-ehn-toh trah-SEHR-oh)
bad-	malo	(MAH-loh)
very bad- muy malo	(mooy MAHL-loh)
badly-	mal	(mahl)
bag-	bolsa	(BOHL-sa)
baggage- el equipaje	(eh-kee-PAH-hay)
baggage check- contraseña	(kohn-trah-SAY-nyah)

179

---

ammunition- munición	(moo-nee-SYOHN)
and-	y	(ee)
ANGER-	enojo	(eh-NON-zhoh)
animal-	animal	(ah-nee-mahl)
another	otro	(OH-troh)
answer (n) respuesta	(rehs-PWEHS-tah)
Answer!-	¡Responda Ud.! (rehs-POHN-day oo-STEHD)
apartment- apartamento (ah-pahr-tah-MEHN-toh)
appeal-	apelación(ah-peh-lah-SYOHN)
●appear-	aparecer	(ah-pah-reh-SEHR)
apple-	manzana	(mahn-SAH-nah)
application- aplicación	(ah-plee-kah-SYOHN)
- solicitud (soh-lee-see-TOOD)
apprehend- arrestar	(ah-rehs-TAHR)
ARE THERE? ¿hay?	(AH-ee) or (I)
AREA-	área	(AH-reh-ah)
ARREST-	arresto	(ah-REHS-toh)
YOU ARE UNDER ARREST ¡Usted está arrestado! (oo-STEHD ehs-TAH ah-rehs-TAH-doh)
AS SOON AS POSSIBLE- Tan pronto que sea posible
as-	como	(KOH-moh)
●ask-	preguntar	(preh-goon-TAHR)
assault-	asalto	(ah-SAHL-toh)
assist me- ayúdame	(ah-YOO-dah-may)
assistance- asistencia	(ah-sees-TEHN-syah)
assistant- ayudante	(ah-yoo-DAHN-tay)
at-	en	(ehn)
at the same time- al mismo tiempo (ah-MEES-moh TYEMM-poh)
AT WHAT TIME?- ¿A qué hora? (ah kay OH-rah)
●attack(v) atacar
attempt (to)- tratar de (trah-TAHR day)
- haga empeño (AH-gah em-pay-nyoh)
attorney- licenciado (lee-sehn-SYAH-doh)
automobile- automóvil (ah-oo-to-MOH-veel);
carro	(KAHR-roh);
-coche	(koh-chay)

bail-	fianza	(FYAHN-sah)
bald-	calvo	(KAHL-boh)
bandage-	venda	(BEHN-dah)
bandit-	bandido	(bahn-DEE-doh)
bank-	banco	(BAHN-koh)
bar-	cantina	(kahn-TEE-nah);
	barra	(BAH-rah)
bathroom-	cuarto de bano	
	(KWAHR-toh day BAHN-yoh)	
battery-	batería	(bah-tay-REE-ah)
Be on time!-	llegues a tiempo	
	(YEH-gays ah TYEHM-poh)	
on time-	a tiempo (ah TYEHM-poh)	
bedroom-	alcóba	(ahl-KOH-bah)
beer-	cerveza	(sehr-BEH-sah)
before-	antes de	(AHN-tays day)
●begin-	comenzar	(koh-mehn-SAHR)
beginning-	principio	(preen-SEE-pee-oh)
behind-	detrás de	(day-TRAHS day)
●believe-	creer	(kreh-EHR)
believe it!-	creélo	(KREH-loh)
belly-	panza	(PAHN-sah)
belt-	cinto	(SEEN-toh)
beneath-	debajo de	(day-BAH-hoh day)
between-	entre	(EHN-tray)
big-	grande	(GRAHN-day)
billfold-	cartera	(kahr-TEHR-ah)
bird-	pájaro	(PAH-hah-roh)
birth certificate		
acta de nacimiento		
(AHK-tah day nah-see-mee-EHN-toh)		
blame (n)-	culpa	(KOOL-pah)
bleeding-	sangrando	(sahn-GRAHN-doh)
blind-	ciego	(see-EH-goh)
blonde-	rubio	(ROO-bee-oh)
blood-	sangre	(SAHN-gray)
body-	cuerpo	(KWEHR-poh)
bomb-	bomba	(BOHM-bah)
bond-	fianza	(FYAN-sah)
bondsman-	fiador	(fyah-DOHR)
border-	frontera	(frohn-TEH-rah)

Border Patrol- Patrulla de la Frontera
(pah-TROO-yah day lah frohn-TEH-rah)
slang- La Migra (lah MEE-grah)

boss-	patrón	(pah-TROHN)
bottle-	la botella	(lah boh-TAY-yah)
BOUGHS	-ramas	(RAH-mahs)
bottom-	fondo	(FOHN-doh)
box-	caja	(KAH-hah)
boy-	muchacho	(moo-CHAH-choh)
breathe!-	¡respire!	(rehs-PEE-ray)
brief-	breve	(BRAY-vay)
briefly-	brevemente	
	(bray-vay-MEHN-tay)	
briefcase-	cartera grande;	
	(kahr-TEHR-ah GRAHN-day)	
	maletín	(mah-leh-TEEN)
Bring!-	¡Traiga!	(trah-EE-gah)
bring it-	traigalo(a)	(trah-EE-gah-loh[lah])
broken-	quebrado	(kay-BRAH-doh);
	- roto (S. Amer.)	(ROH-toh)
brother-	hermano	(ehr-MAH-noh)
brother-in-law-	cuñado	(koo-NYAH-doh)

bruise-	contusión	(kohn-too-SYOHN)
brunette-	moreno	(moh-RAY-noh)
BRUSH	arbustos	(ahr-BOS-tohn)
BULL-	toro	(TOH-roh)
bullet-	bala	(BAH-lah)
bundle-	bulto	(BOOL-toh)
burglary-	robo	(ROH-boh)
burn (n)-	quemadura	
	(kay-mah-DOO-rah)	
●burn (v)-	quemar	(kee-MAHR)
bury it!-	entierralo	(ehn-TEE-ay-rah-loh)
bundle it-	envuelvelo	
	(ehn-voo-ehl-vay-loh)	
bus-	bús	(BOOS);
	camión	(kah-mee-OHN)
●buy-	comprar	(kohm-PRAHR)
by now-	ya	(yah)

C

cafe-	café	(keh-FAY)
●call (v)-	llamar	(yah-MAHR)
call (n)-	llamada	(yah-MAH-dah)
camp-	campamento	
	(kahm-pah-MEHN-toh)	
car-	carro	(KAHR-roh)
carry it-	llevelo(a)	(yeh-vay-loh[lah]);
	cargalo(a)	(kahr-gah-loh[lah])
cash-	dinero	(dee-NAY-roh)
CATCH-	alcance	(ahl-KAHN-say);
catch (to)-	alcanzar	(ahl-KAHN-sahr)
certificate-	certificado	
	(sehr-tee-fee-KAH-doh)	
chainsaw -serrucho mecánico		
(say-RRO-choh meh-KAH-nee-koh)		
change it-	cambialo	(KAHM-bee-ah-loh)
CHASE (n)-	caza	(KAH-sah)
chase it-	perseguelo	(pehr-SEE-gay-loh)
check (n)-	cheque	(CHEH-kay)
check it-	reviselo	(reh-VEE-say-loh)
CHIEF-	jefe	(HEH-fay)
cigarette-	cigarrillos	
	(see-gah-REEL-yohs)	
cigarette paper- papel de cigarrillos		
(pah-PEHL day see-gah-REEL-yohs)		
citation-	tiquete	(tee-KAY-tay)
city-	ciudad	(syoo-DAHD)
civil-	civil	(see-BEEL)
close it-	cierrelo	(see-ay-ray-loh)
CLOSE!	¡cerrado!	(seh-RAH-doh)
clothes-	ropa	(ROH-pah)
coat-	saco	(SAH-koh)
color-	color	(coh-LOHR)
Come!-	¡Venga!	(VEHN-gah)
COME HERE-		Venga aquí.
	(VEHN-gah ah-KEE)	
Come in-	Pase usted.	
	(PAH-say oo-STEHD)	
companion- compañero		
	(kom-pahn-YAY-roh)	
compartment- compartimiento		
	(kohm-pahr-tee-mee-EHN-toh)	
complaint-	queja	(KAY-hah)

●complete- completar (kom-pleh-TAHR)
comply- cumplir con
       (koom-PLEER kohn)
COMPREHEND? ¿Comprende?
       (kohm-PREHN-deh);
       - ¿Entiende?
       (ehn-tee-YEHN-deh)
conceal it- esconderlo (ehs-kohn-day-loh)

CONCEALMENT / HIDDEN AREAS
[See Drug Section]

concerning- tocante a
       (toh-KAHN-tay ah)
●confess- confesar (kohn-feh-SAHR)
conscience- conciencia
       (kohn-see-EHN-see-ah)
●consent (to)- consentir
       (kohn-sehn-TEER)
constable- policía (poh-lee-SEE-ah)
contact- contacto (kohn-TAHK-toh)
contents- contenido(kohn-tay-NEE-doh)
continually- continuamente
       (kohn-tee-nwah-MEHN-tay)
CONTRABAND- contrabando
       (kohn-trah-BAHN-doh)
contract laborer- bracero (brah-SEH-roh)
convict (n) - preso (PRAY-soh);
       presidiario (preh-see-DYAH-ryoh);
convicted- convicto (kohn-BEEK-toh)
       (keek-syohn-NAH-roh)
cook it- cocinelo(a) (koh-SEE-nay-loh)
cook (n)- cocinero (koh-see-NAY-roh)
cop- chota (CHOH-tah)
correct- correcto (kohr-REHK-toh)
-county- condado (kohn-DAH-doh)
court- tribunal (tree-boo-NAHL);
       corte (KOHR-tay)
courthouse- corte
       (KOHR-tay)
cousin- primo (PREE-moh)
cover it- cubrelo(a) (KOO-bray-loh[lah])
cowboy- vaquero (bah-KAY-roh)
-coyote- coyote (koh-YOH-tay)
COW- vaca (BAH-kah)
crazy- loco (LOH-koh)
credit card- tarjeta de crédito
       (tahr-HAY-tah day KRAY-dee-toh)
CRIME- crimen (KREE-mehn)
criminal- criminal (kree-mee-NAHL)
CRY- lloro (YOH-ray)
CRYING- llanto (YAHN-toh)
cut it- córtelo (KOHR-tay-loh)
cut (n)- cortada (kohr-TAH-dah)

D

dad- papá (pah-PAH)
DANGER- peligro (Peh-LEE-groh)
dark- oscuro (ohs-KOO-roh)
date (the)- la fecha (FEH-chah)
daughter- hija (EE-hah)
daughter-in-law - nuera(NWEH-rah)
dawn- amanecer (ah-mah-neh-SEHR)

day- día (DEE-ah)
-all day- todo el día
       (TOH-doh el DEE-ah)
-daily- diario (dee-AH-ree-oh)
-a few days- unos días
       (OON-ohs DEE-ahs)
deaf (to pretend to be)- hacerse el sordo
       (ah-SEHR-say el SOHR-doh)
deaf (person)- sordo (SOHR-doh)
-deaf mute- sordomudo
       (SOHR-doh-MOO-doh)
-deafness- sordera (sohr-DEH-rah)
decade- década (DAY-kah-dah)
●deceive (to)- engañar (ehn-gah-NYAHR)
-deer- venado (beh-NAH-doh)
defendant- acusado (ah-koo-SAH-doh)
demonstrate- demuestralo(la)
       (day-moo-EHS-trah-loh[lah])
departure- salida (sah-LEE-dah)
deposit it- depositalo(la)
       (day-poh-SEE-tay-loh[lah])
DEPRESSED- deprimido
       (deh-pree-MEE-doh)
description- descripción
       (dehs-kreep-SYOHN)
DESPERATE- desesperado
       (deh-sehs-pay-RAH-doh)
destination- destinación; or
       (dehs-tee-nah-SYOHN)
destino(S. Amer.) (dehs-TEE-noh)
detain him- detengalo (day-tehn-gah-lo)
detective- detective (day-tehk-TEE-veh)
DID YOU KNOW? ¿Supo? (SOO-poh)
DID YOU KNOW IT WAS THERE?
       ¿Supo que estaba allí?
       (SOO-poh kay ay-STAH-bah ah-YEE)
DID YOU PAY FOR IT? ¿Lo pagó?
       (Loh pah-GOH)
DID YOU STEAL THE _____?
       ¿Robó el _____?
       (roh-BOH el _____?)
DIFFERENT- diferente
       (dee-feh-REHN-tay)
DIFFICULTY- dificultad
       (dee-fee-kool-TAHD)
-dirty- sucio (SOO-see-oh)
DISAGREE- desacuerdo
       (days-ah-KWAYR-doh)
DISAPPOINTED- decepcionado
       (day-sehp-see-oh-NAH-doh)
-dispatcher - telefonista
       (day-leh-foh-NEES-tah)
DISSATISFIED- descontento
       (dehs-kohn-TEHN-toh)
DO IT AGAIN- hagalo(a) de nuevo
       (AH-gah-loh[ah] day noo-AY-voh)
DO LIKE THIS- de este modo
       (day AY-stay MOH-doh)
DO NOT BE AFRAID- No tenga miedo
       (Noh TEHN-gah mee-AY-doh)

181

DOCTOR- doctor (dohk-**TOHR**)
DOCUMENT- documento
(doh-koo-**MEHN**-tohs)
DOG- perro (**PEHR**-rch)
dollar- dólar (**DOH**-lahr)
DOMICILE- domicilio (doh-mee-**SEE**-lyoh)
DOOR, OPEN IT- Abre la puerta
(**AH**-bray lah **PWEHR**-tah)
-**DON'T OPEN IT!** No abras la puerta
(noh **AH**-brahs lah **PWEHR**-tah)
DOWN! ¡Abajo! (ah-**BAH**-hoh)

DRAW me a diagram where it is.
Dibújeme dónde está.
(dee-**BOO**-hah-may **DOHN**-day
ays-**TAH**)

Dress yourself! -¡vístese! (**VEE**-stay-say)
dress (n)- vestido (behs-**TEE**-doh)
●drive (to)- manejar (mah-neh-**HAHR**)
DRIVER- chófer (**CHOH**-fehr)
●**DROP (to)-** dejar caer
(deh-**HAHR** kah-**EHR**)
drop (of)- gota (**GOH**-tah)
DRUG DOG- perro de droga
(**PEHR**-roh day **DROH**-gah)
DRUGGED endrogado
(ehn-droh-**GAH**-doh)
DRUGS drogas (**DROH**-gahs)
TAKE DRUGS- tomar drogas
(toh-**MAHR DROH**-gahs)
DRUG ADDICT- drogadicto(a)
(droh-gah-**DEEK**-toh (-tah))
DRUG PUSHER- vendedor
(behn-deh-**DOHR**)
DRUG PUSHER- traficante de drogas
(trah-fee-**KAHN**-tay day **DROH**-gahs)
drunk- borracho (bohr-**RAH**-choh)
drunkard- borrachón (bohr-rah-**CHOHN**)
during- durante (doo-**RAHN**-tay)

E

earlier- más temprano
(mahs tehm-**PRAH**-noh)
early- temprano (tehm-**PRAH**-noh)
to be early- llegar temprano
(yeh-**GAHR** tehm-**PRAH**-noh)
east- este (**EHS**-tay)
eat!- ¡come! (**KOH**-may)
education- enseñanza
(ehn-seh-**NYAHN**-sah); (or)
educación (ay-doo-kah-**SYOHN**)
either- o (oh)
ELK- alce (**AHL**-say); ante (**AHN**-tay)
empty- vacío (bah-**SEE**-oh)
EMPTY OR PUT THINGS ON TABLE.
Ponga sus cosas en la mesa.
(**POHN**-gah soos **KOH**-sahs ehn lah
MAY-sah)
employee- empleado (ehm-pleh-**AH**-doh)
engine- motor (moh-**TOHR**)
ENGLISH- inglés (een-**GLAYS**)
ENOUGH- bastante (bahs-**TAHN**-tay)

error- error (eh-**ROHR**)
escape (n)- fuga (**FOO**-gah);
evening- tarde (**TAHR**-day)
in the evening- por la tarde
(**POHR** lah **TAHR**-day)
this evening- esta tarde
(**EHS**-tah **TAHR**-day)
tomorrow evening- mañana por la tarde
(mah-**NYAH**-nah pohr lah **TAHR**-day)
EVIDENCE- evidencia
(eh-bee-**DEHN**-syah)
examine- examine (ex-sah-**MEE**-neh)
excuse (n)- excusa (ex-**KOO**-sah)
EXCEEDING THE LIMIT-
exceda el limite
(ex-**SAY**-dah el **LEE**-mee-tay)
EXCUSE ME- Perdón (pehr-**DOHN**)
EXPLAIN- explíquelo (ex-plee-kay-loh)
expensive- costoso (koh-**STOH**-soh)

F

FAITH- (f) fé (fay)
FALSE- falso (**FAHL**-soh)
family- familia (fah-**MEE**-lyah)
farm- rancho (**RAHN**-choh)
farmer- ranchero (rahn-**CHAY**-roh)
FARM LABORER- labrador
(lah-brah-**DOHR**)
- trabajador agrícola
(trah-**BAH**-hah-door ah-**GREE**-koh-lah)
father- padre (**PAH**-dray)
father-in-law - suegro (**SWAY**-groh)
fault- culpa (**KOOL**-pah)
fast- rápido (**RAH**-pee-doh)
federal- federal (feh-deh-**RAHL**)
FEDERAL BUREAU /INVESTIGATION.
Oficina Federal de Investigaciónes.
(oh-fee-**SEE**-nah fay-day-**RAHL** day
een-vehs-tee-**GAH**-syohn-ays)
FELONY- felonía (feh-**LOHN**-ee-ah)
few- unos pocos (**OO**-nohs **POH**-kohs)
field- campo (**KAHM**-poh);
- fil (feel)
●fight pelear / luchar
●find out- descubrir (dehs-koo-**BREER**)
- saber (sah-**BEHR**)
find- hállalo(a) (**AY**-yah-loh [lah])
fine (n)- multa (**MOOL**-tah)
FINGERPRINTS- huellas digitales
(**WEH**-yahs dee-hee-**TAH**-lays)
finish!- ¡termina! (tehr-**MEE**-nah)
to finish- acabar (ah-kah-**BAHR**)
FIRE! ¡Fuego! (**FWAY**-goh)
firearm- arma (**AHR**-mah)
first- primero (pree-**MAY**-roh)
FIRST NAME nombre de pila
(**NOHM**-bray day **PEE**-lah)
FIRST TIME? ¿Primera vez?
(pree-**MAY**-rah vehs)
FISH (to)- pescar (pehs-**KAHR**)
(n)- pez (pehs)
FISHING POLE- palo de pesca
(**PAH**-loh day **PEHZ**-kah)

flight (escape) - fuga (FOO-gah)
flight (plane) - vuelo (BWEH-loh)
●fly (to) - volar (boh-LAHR)
floor- suelo (SWEH-loh)
food- comida (koh-MEE-dah)
FOLLOW ME- Sígame (SEE-gah-may)
fool- tonto (TOHN-toh)
foreigner- extranjero
  (ehs-trahn-HAY-roh)
forgery- falso (FAHL-soh)
forget it- olvídelo(a) (ohl-BEE-day-loh [lah])
form- forma (FOHR-mah)
forward- adelante (ah-day-LAHN-tay)
FRAUD- fraude (FRAH-oo-day)
free (adj)- libre (LEE-bray)
frequent (adj)- frecuente
  (freh-KWEHN-tay)
●frequent (v)- frecuentar
  (freh-kwehn-TAHR)
frequently- frecuentemente
  (freh-KWEHN-tay-MEHN-tay)
Friday- viernes (bee-EHR-nays)
FRIEND- amigo (ah-MEE-goh)
FROM- en (ehn)
Front Seat- asiento delantero
  (ah-SEE-ehn-toh deh-lahn-TAYR-oh)

G

GAME (animal)- caza (KAH-sah)
GAME (played)- juego (hoo-AY-goh)
GAME WARDEN- Guardian Forestal
  (gwahr-dee-AHN foh-rehs-TAHL)
gang- pandilla (pahn-DEE-yah)
gas station- gasolinera
  (gah-soh-lee-NEH-rah)
gather- júntense (HOON-tay-loh [lah])
Get dressed- vestirse (vehs-TEER-say)
GET IN- métese (MEH-teh-say)
get it- recógelo(a) (reh-koh-hay-loh [lah])
GET OFF- bájese (BAH-hay-say)
GET OUT (vehicle)- salir (sah-LEER);
  - apearse (ah-pay-AHR-say)
GET OUT!- ¡Fuera! (FWEH-rah)
Get out of the way- Quítarse (v)
  (kee-TAHR-say)
Get up!- ¡Levántese! (leh-VAHN-tay-seh)
girl- chica (CHEE-kah)
GIVE UP! ¡Ríndase! (REEN-dah-say)
GIVE UP? ¿Se rinda? (say REEN-dah)
give to me- dámelo(a) (DAH-may-loh)
muchacha (moo-CHAH-chah)
go - vete (VEH-teh)
GO AWAY- Váyase. (BAH-yah-say)
GO, LET'S- Vámonos. (VAH-mow-nohs);
GO OVER THERE- Vaya allá.
  (VAH-yah ah-YAH)
gold- oro (OH-roh)
gold ring- anillo de oro
  (ah-NEE-yoh day OH-roh)
GOOD- bueno (BWAY-noh)
GOODBYE- adiós (ah-dee-OHS)
- hasta la vista (AHS-tah la BEES-tah)
HOW- como (KOH-moh)
house trailer- casa de remolque
  (KAH-say day reh-MOHL-kay)
to the house- a la casa
  (ah lah KAH-sah)
to home- a casa (ah KAH-sah)
  (day lah KAH-sah)
from the house- de la casa (day lah KAH-sah)
from home- de casa (day KAH-sah)
at the house- en la casa
  (ehn lah KAH-sah)
at home- en casa (ehn KAH-sah)
house- casa (KAH-sah)
HOSPITAL- hospital (ohs-pee-TAHL)
hotel- hotel (oh-TEHL)
hour- hora (OH-rah)
in an hour's time- dentro de una hora
  (DEHN-troh day OO-nah OH-rah)
per hour- por hora (pohr OH-rah)
homicide- homicidio (oh-mee-SEE-dee-oh)
honest- honesto (oh-NEHS-toh)
holster- pistolera (pees-toh-LAYR-ah)
highway- carretera (kahr-reh-TAY-rah)
highest- sumo (SOO-moh)
HIDDEN- escondido (es-kohn-DEE-doh)
hide- esconderse (es-kohn-DEHR-say)
here- aquí (ah-KEE)
HELP!- ¡Socorro! (soh-KOH-roh)
HELP ME- ayúdame (ah-YOO-dah-may)
(on phone)- Diga (DEE-gah)
HELLO- Hola (OH-lah)
HEART- Corazón (Koh-rah-ZOHN)
hear me! - ¡óigame! (OH-ee-gah-may)
head- cabeza (kah-BAY-sah)

HAVE YOU EVER ____ BEFORE?
¿Alguna vez has ____ antes?
  (Ahl-GOO-nah vehz ahs ____ AHN-tays)

haul- transportar (trans-pohr-TAHR)
harvest- pizca (PEEZ-kah);
handcuffs- esposas (ehs-POH-sahs)

RELAX YOUR HAND!
¡Suelta la mano!
  (Soo-EHL-tah lah MAH-noh)

HAND- mano (MAH-noh)
HAND OVER- entréguelo(a) (ehn-TREH-gay-loh [lah])
hand grenade- granada de mano
hair- pelo (PEH-loh)

H

- disparo (dees-PAH-roh)
GUNSHOT- tiro (TEE-roh); (or)
GUN- fusil (foo-SEEL)
GUILTY- culpable (KOOL-pah)
guilt- culpa (ehn-SEHN-yah-may soo MEE-kah).
Enséñeme su mica.
Green card, show me your-

English	Spanish	Pronunciation
HUNT-	caza	(**KAH**-sah)
HURRY-	dé prisa	(day **PREE**-sah)
HURTING-	doliendo	(doh-lee-**EHN**-doh)
husband-	marido	(mah-**REE**-doh)
	esposo	(ehs-**POH**-soh)

I

I AM NOT ALLOWED TO _____.
No se me permite _____.
(Noh say **MAY** payr-**MEE**-tay _____.)

I AM GOING TO SEIZE THE _____.
Voy a confiscar el/la _____.
(Voy ah kohn-**FEES**-kahr el/lah _____.)

I CANNOT. No puedo.
(Noh **PWAY**-doh)

I WILL NOT HURT YOU.
No le haré daño.
(Noh lay ah-**RAY DAHN**-yoh)

I'M LOOKING FOR ___. Busco a___.
(**BOOS**-koh ah_____)

identification- identificación
(ee-dehn-tee-fee-kah-**SYOHN**)
identify it- identifiquelo(a)
(ee-dehn-tee-**FEE**-kay-loh[lah])

THIS IDENTIFIES IT AS BELONGING TO:
Esto lo identifica como que es de:
(**AY**-stoh loh ee-dehn-tee-**FEE**-kah **KOH**-moh kay ays day....)

ILL-	enfermo	(ehn-**FEHR**-moh)
illegal-	ilegal	(ee-lay-**GAHL**)

IMMIGRATION & NATURALIZATION (FEDERAL)
-La Migra (Lah **MEE**-grah); (or)
-Immigración y Naturalización (federal)
(Ee-mee-grah-**SYOHN** ee nah-too-rah-lee-zah-**SYOHN** [fay-day-**RAHL**])

immigration card-	mica	(**MEE**-kah)
immunity-	inmunidad	(een-moo-nee-**DAHD**)
important-	importa	(eem-**POHR**-tah)
NOT IMPORTANT-	No importa	(Noh eem-**POHR**-tah)
IN-	en	(ehn)
income-	ingresos	(een-**GREH**-sohs)
indict-	enjuiciar	(ehn-**HWEE**-syahr)
INDIFFERENT-	indiferente	(een-dee-feh-**REHN**-tay)
ineligible-	no elegible	(noh ehl-ay-**HEE**-blay)
Infection-	infección	(een-fehk-**SYOHN**)
inform-	informelo(a)	(een-**FOHR**-may-loh)
	aviselo(a)	(ah-**VEE**-say-loh)
informant-	informante	(een-fohr-**MAHN**-tay)
Information-	informes	(een-**FOHR**-mays);
-información		(een-fohr-mah-**SYOHN**)
informer-	informante	(een-fohr-**MAHN**-tay)
injunction-	mandato	(mahn-**DAH**-toh)
INJURED-	herido	(eh-**REE**-doh)
injury-	herida	(eh-**REE**-dah)
innocent-	inocente	(ee-noh-**SEHN**-tay)
inquire-	averigualo(a)	(ah-vehr-**EE**-gwah-loh[lah])
inside-	dentro de	(**DEHN**-troh day)
inspector-	inspector	(eens-pehk-**TOHR**)
instant-	instante	(eens-**TAHN**-tay)
insurance-	seguranza	(seh-goo-**RAHN**-zah)

INSURANCE CARD- Tarjeta de seguro
(tahr-**HAY** tah day seh-**GOO**-roh)
intentional- intencional
(een-tehn-syoh-**NAHL**)

Intercourse, sexual-
Relaciones íntimas, sexuales
(Ray-lah-see-**OH**-nays **EEN**-tee-mahs, sayex-oo-**AHL**-ays)

interior-	interior	(een-teh-**RYOHR**)
intersection-	cruce	(**KROO**-say)
intoxicated	intoxicado	(een-toh-xee-**KAH**-doh)
INVALID-	inválido	(een-**BAH**-lee-doh)
INVESTIGATE (to)-	investigar	(eem-behs-tee-**GAHR**)
investigation-	investigación	(eem-behs-tee-gah-**SYOHN**)
investigator-	investigador	(eem-behs-tee-gah-**DOHR**)
IS-	Es (ays);	Esta (ay-**STAH**)
Is there?-	¿hay?	(ay)
IS THIS YOURS?-	¿Es suyo?	(ess **SOO**-yoh)

IT'S AGAINST THE LAW.
Es en contra de la ley.
(Ays ehn **KOHN**-trah day lah lay)
ITEM- artículo (ahr-**TEE**-koo-loh)

J

jacket-	chaqueta	(chah-**KAY**-tah);
- chamarra		(chah-**MAHR**-ah)
JAIL (n)-	cárcel	(**KAHR**-sehl)
jewel-	joya	(**HOH**-yah)
jewelry-	alhajas	(ahl-**AH**-hahs)
	joyas	(**HOH**-yahs)
JOB-	trabajo	(trah-**BAH**-hoh)
join! -	¡únese!	(**OO**-nay-say)
judge-	juez	(hoo-**AYS**)
jury-	jurado	(hoo-**RAH**-doh)
just (adj)-	justo	(**HOOS**-toh)
JUST RIGHT-	exacto; correcto	(ex-**AHK**-toh; koh-**REHK**-toh)
- de punto		(day **POON**-toh)
JUVENILE-	juvenil	(hoo-beh-**NEEL**)

K

kidnap- raptelo(a) (rahp-tay-loh])
kill!- ¡mátelo(a)! (MAH-tay-loh[lah])
killer- asesino (ah-seh-SEE-noh)
Kilogram- kilogramo (kee-LOH-grah-moh)
kilometer- kilómetro (kee-LOH-meh-troh)
KNIFE, jack- navaja (nah BAY-hah)
KNIFE- cuchillo (koo-CHEE-yoh);
●know (to)- saber (sah-BEHR)
know it- sabelo(a) (SAH-bay-loh[lah])

L

LABORER- bracero (brah-SEH-roh);
-trabajador (trah-bah-hah-DOHR)
lady- señora (sehn-YOH-rah) (Mrs.)
señorita (seh-nyoh-REE-tah) (Miss)
lane- carril (kah-REEL)
last (final)- pasado (pah-SAH-doh)
last month- el mes pasado
(ehl MEHS pah-SAH-doh)
last night- anoche (ah-NOH-chay)
last time- última vez (OOL-tee-mah vayz)
last week- semana pasada
(seh-MAH-nah pah-SAH-dah)
last year- el año pasado
(ehl AH-nyoh pah-SAH-doh)
last name- apellido (ah-peh-YEE-doh)
late- tarde (TAHR-day)
lately- recién (reh-SYEHN)
later- más tarde (mahs TAHR-day)
to be late- llegue tarde
law- ley (LAY-ee)
law-gay (YAY-day)
law, civil- derecho civil
(deh-REH-choh see-BEEL)
law, criminal- derecho penal
(deh-REH-choh peh-NAHL)
LAWYER- abogado (ah-boh-GAH-doh)
LAWYER- licenciado
(lee-sehn-see-AH-doh)
-leader- líder (LEE-dehr)
-leave! ¡Salga Ud.!
(SAHL-goo-STEHD)
left- izquierdo (ees-KYEHR-doh)
leg- pierna (PYEHR-nah)
legal- legal (leh-GAHL)
legally- legalmente (lee-gahl-MEHN-tay)
lend- ¡prestal (prehs-tah)
less- menos (MEH-nohs)
LET'S SEE!- ¡Vamos a ver!
(VAH-mohs ah vehr)
- deje ver (DAY-hay vehr)
LET'S GO!- ¡Vamos! (BAH-mohs)
let- deja (DAY-hah)
LICENSE- Licencia
(lee-SEHN-see-ah)
LICENSE PLATE- placa (PLAH-kah)
●LIE (v)- miente (mee-EHN-tay)

M

Machine Gun- ametralleta
(ah-may-trah-yah-YAY-tah);
-ametralladora
(ah-may-trah-yah-DOH-rah)
MAFIA, AMERICAN- Mafia Americana
(mah-FEE-ah ah-mayr-ree-KAH-nah)
MAFIA, MEXICAN- Mafia Mexicana
(mah-FEE-ah meh-hee-KAH-nah)
Mad (angry)/- enojado
(ay-(hoh-HAH-doh)
mad (crazy)- loco (LOH-koh)
maiden name - apellido
●mail (to)- enviar (ehn-BYAHR)
MAIN BOSS- mero gallo
(MAY-roh GAH-yoh)
-mero-mero
(MAY-roh MAY-roh)
- jefe principal
(HAY-fay preen-see-PAHL)
mama- mamá (mah-MAH)
man- hombre (OHM-bray)
sir- señor (seh-NYOHR)
large man- hombrón (ohm-BROHN)
manager- director (dee-rehk-TOHR)
MANY- muchos (MOO-chohs)
map- mapa (MAH-pah)
MARIJUANA- Marijuana
(meh-reh-HWAH-nah)
MAYBE- quizás (kee-SAHS)
meal- comida (koh-MEE-dah)

---

light- luz (loos)
like (as)- como (KOH-moh)
LIKE THIS- así (ah-SEE)
like that- así (ah-SEE)
LIST- lista (LEES-tah)
LISTEN!- ¡Escuche! (ehs-KOO-chay)
little (adj)- pequeño (peh-KAY-nyoh)
a- little- un poco (oon POH-koh)
- live viva (vee-vah)
living room- sala (SAH-lah)
load (n)- carga (KAHR-gah)
load it-cargalo(a) (KAHR-gah-loh[lah])
locate (to)- localizar (loh-kah-lee-ZAHR)
LOCATION- localización
(loh-kah-lee-sah-SYOHN)
long term- a largo plazo
(ah LAHR-goh PLAH-zoh)
LOOK!- ¡Mire! (MEE-ray)
I'M LOOKING FOR ___. Busco a ___
(BOOS-koh ah--)
● look for- buscar (boos-KAHR)
look for it- Búsquelo (BOOZ-kay-loh)
● look forward to - anticipar
(ahn-tee-see-PAHR)
Look out! ¡Cuidado! (koo-ee-DAH-doh)
lookout (n) atalaya (ah-tah-LAH-yah)

meantime (in the)-	mientras tanto (mee-EHN-trahs TAHN-toh)		**MRS.**-	Señora (sehn-YOH-rah)

meantime (in the)- mientras tanto
(mee-EHN-trahs TAHN-toh)
mechanic- mecánico (meh-KAH-nee-koh)
MEDICINE- medicina (meh-dee-SEE-nah)
meet - encuentralo
(ehn-koo-EHN-trah-loh)
MEXICAN- Mexicano (masc.)
(meh-hee-KAH-noh)
Mexican Dollar- peso (PAY-soh)
midnight- medianoche
(meh-dyah-NOH-chay)
at midnight- a la medianoche
(ah lah meh-dyah-NOH-chay)
mile- milla (MEE-yah)
minor- menor (meh-NOHR)
minute- minuto (mee-NOO-toh)
mirror- espejo (ehs-PEH-hoh)
misdemeanor- crímen menor
(KREE-mehn meh-NOHR)
Miss- Senorita (sehn-yoh-REE-tah)
miss (to)- errar (eh-RAHR)
MISTAKE- error (ehr-ROHR)

You are mistaken- Ud. se equivoca
(oo-STEHD say eh-KEE-voh-kah)

Mister- Señor (sehn-YOHR)
molest (annoy)- moléstelo/la
(moh-LEHS-tay-loh/lah)
MOMENT- momento (moh-MEHN-toh)
JUST A SECOND- un momento
(oon moh-MEHN-toh)
Monday- lunes (LOO-nehs)
MONEY- dinero (dee-NAY-roh)
money (to spend)- gastar (gahs-TAHR)
money (to save)- ahorrar (ah-oh-RAHR)
money order- giro (HEE-roh)
MONTH- mes (mehs)
LAST MONTH- El mes pasado
(ehl mehs pah-SAH-doh)
monthly- mensual (mehn-SWAHL)
MORE- más (mahs)
morning- mañana (mahn-YAH-nah)
in the morning- por la mañana
(pohr lah mahn-YAH-nah)
this morning- esta mañana
(EHS-tah mahn-YAH-nah)

tomorrow morning-
mañana por la mañana
(mahn-YAH-nah por la mahn-YAH-nah)

yesterday morning- ayer por la mañana
(ah-YEHR pohr lah mahn-YAH-nah)

mother- madre (MAH-dray)
motor- motor (moh-TOHR)
motorcycle- motocicleta
(moh-toh-see-KLEH-tah)
motorhome- casa rodante
(KAH-sah roh-DAHN-tay)
mouth- boca (BOH-kah)
MOVE IT!- ¡Muévate! (moo-AY-vah-tay)
MR.- Señor (sehn-YOHR)

MRS.- Señora (sehn-YOH-rah)
MUCH- mucho (MOO-choh)
MUCH MONEY- mucho dinero
(MOO-choh dee-NAY-roh)
murder- homicidio (oh-mee-SEE-dee-oh)
MUTE PERSON- mudo (MOO-doh)
Deaf Mute- Sordomudo
(sohr-doh-MOO-doh)

N

●**NAME** (to)- nombrar (nohm-BRAHR)
name- nombre (**NOHM**-bray)
NARCOTIC- Narcótico
(nahr-KOH-tee-koh)
necessary- necesario(neh-seh-SAHR-yoh)
neck- cuello (KWEHL-yoh);
- pesquezo (pehs-koo-AY-zoh);
- cogote (koh-GOH-tay)
need- necesidad (neh-seh-see-DAHD)
needle- aguja (ah-GOO-hah)
neighbor- vecino (beh-SEE-noh)
NERVOUS- nervioso (nehr-bee-OH-soh)
NEVER- nunca (NOON-kah)
almost never- casi nunca
(KAH-see NOON-kah)
next próximo (PROHK-see-moh)
night- noche (NOH-chay)
at night- de noche (day NOH-chay)
last night- anoche (ah-NOH-chay)
night before last- anteanoche
(AHN-tay-ah-NOH-chay)
tomorrow night- mañana por la noche
(mah-NYAH-nah pohr lah NOH-chay)
tonight- esta noche(EHS-tah NOH-chay)
NO- NO (noh)
NO ONE- nadie (NAH-dyeh)
NO MORE- ya no (yah noh);
no más (noh mahs)
none- ninguno (neen-GOO-noh)
noon- mediodía (meh-dyoh-DEE-ah)
at noon- al mediodia
(ahl meh-dyoh-DEE-ah)
north- norte (NOHR-tay)
nose- nariz (nah-REES)
●notify - avisar (ah-vee-sahr)
nothing- nada (NAH-dah)
November- noviembre
(noh-VYEHM-breh)
now- ahora (ah-OHR-ah)
for now- por ahora (pohr ah-OHR-ah)
from now on- de ahora en adelante
(day ah-OHR-ah en ah-day-LAHN-tay)
number- número (NOO-may-roh)

O

OBEY!- ¡Obedézca! (oh-bay-DEZ-kah)
obtain- obtenga (ohb-TEHN-gah)
occasionally- de vez en cuando
(day vehs ehn KWAHN-doh)
OCCUPATION- ocupación
(oh-koo-pah-SYOHN)

occur-	ocurre	(oh-KOO-ray)
Of-	de	(day)
of course-	claro	(KLAH-roh);
- naturalmente		(nah-too-rahl-MEHN-tay)
- por supuesto		(pohr soo-PWEHS-toh)
off duty-	a franco	(ah FRAHN-koh)
OFFENSE-	ofensa	(oh-FEHN-sah)
OFFER (to)-	ofrecer	(oh-fray-SAYR)
officer-	oficial	(oh-fee-SYAHL)
often-	con frecuencia	
	(kohn fray-KWEHN-see-ah);
- a menudo	(ah meh-NOO-doh)
OK-	bueno	(BWAY-noh)
ON-	en (ehn); sobre	(SOH-bray)
once-	una vez	(OO-nah vehs)
AT ONCE!	¡En seguida!	
	(ehn seh-GHEE-dah)
once in a while- de vez en cuando	
	(day vehs ehn KWAHN-doh)
only-	sólo	(SOH-loh)
twice- dos veces (dohs VAY-says)
OPEN (to)- abrir (v)	(ah-BREER)
OPENI-	¡Abre!	(AH-bray)
CLOSE!	¡Cierre!	(SEE-ay-ray)
OPEN THE DOOR! ¡Abre la puerta!
	(AH-bray lah PWEHR-tah)
Opium-	opio	(OH-pyoh)
-or-	o (oh); u	(oo)
order-	orden	(OHR-dehn)
organization- organización	
	(ohr-gah-nee-sah-SYOHN)
other-	otro	(OH-troh)
OUT!	¡Afuera!	(ah-FWEH-rah)
outside-	fuera	(FWEH-rah)
OVER THERE! ¡Allá!	(AH-lah)
overdue-	sobrevencido	
	(SOH-bray-vehn-SEE-doh)
owe -	debe	(deh-BAY)
owner-	dueño	(dway-NYOH)

P

package-	el bulto	(BOOL-toh);
- paquete	(pah-KAY-tay)
PAIN-	dolor	(Doh-LOHR)
PANTS-	pantalones	
	(pahn-tah-LOH-nays)
papa-	papá	(pah-PAH)
PAPER-	papel	(pah-PEHL)
PARDON ME- Perdón	(pehr-DOHN)
parents-	padres	(PAH-drays)
PARKI ¡Estacione!	(ehs-tah-SYOH-nay)
PARK (to)- estacionar	
	(ehs-tah-syoh-NAHR)
partner-	socio	(SOH-syoh)
PASS-	pasar	(pah-SAHR)
PASSENGR-	pasajero	
	(pah-sah-HAY-roh)
PASSPORT, SHOW ME YOUR
Enséñeme su pasaporte.
(Ehn-SEHN-yah-may soo pah-sah-POHR-tay)
past-	pasado	(pah-SAH-doh)
PATRON SAINT- santo	(SAHN-toh)
Pay●	pagar	(pah-GAHR)
PAY ATTENTION- hacer caso
	(ah-SAYR KAH-soh);
- poner atención	
	(poh-NAIR ah-tehn-SYOHN)
Pay! -	¡Paque!	(PAH-gay)
pay day-	día de pago	(DEE-ah day PAH-goh)
payment-	pago	(PAH-goh)
pen-	lapicero	(lah-pee-SEHR-oh)
penalty-	pena	(PAY-nah)
pencil-	lápiz	(LAH-pees)
penetrate- penetrate	(pay-nay-TRAH-tay)
penetration- penetración	
	(pay-nay-trah-SYOHN)
penis-	pene	(PAY-nay)
penitentiary- penitentiaria	
	(peh-nee-ten-syah-REE-ah)
penny-	centavo	(sehn-TAH-voh)
- pinta	(PEEN-tah)
PERHAPS- quizá	(kee-SAH)
PERJURY- perjuno	(pehr-JOO-ryoh)
permit-	permiso	(pehr-MEE-soh)
permissions- permiso	(pehr-MEE-soh)
" with your- con permiso
	(kohn pehr-MEE-soh)
person-	persona	(pehr-SOH-nah)
petition-	petición	(peh-tee-SYOHN)
PHOTO-	foto	(FOH-toh);
- retrato	(ray-TRAH-toh)
PICK UP THE ....! ¡Levante .....!
	(lay-NHAHN-tay .....);
¡Recoge ....!	(ray-KOH-hay ......)
PICKER- pizcador (peez-kah-DOHR)
PICKING SEASON- pizca (PEEZ-kah)
picture-	foto	(FOH-toh)
PIECE-	pedazo	(peh-DAH-soh)
pimp- alcahuete	(ahl-kah-HOO-ay-tay)
PISTOL-	pistola	(pees-TOH-lah)
- sitio	(SEE-tyoh)
- lugar	(loo-GAHR);
plea (n)-	alegato	(ah-leh-GAH-toh)
plead- declaracion(day-klah-rah-SYOHN)
plead guilty- declararse culpable
	(day-klah-RAHR-say koo-PAH-bleh)
plead not guilty- declararse inocente
	(day-klah-RAHR-say ee-noh-SEHN-tay)
PLEASE-	por favor	(pohr fah-VOHR)
POCKET-	bolsillo	(bohl-SEE-yoh)
POINT!	¡Apunte!	(ah-POON-tay)
point out- señala/a	(sehn-yah-loh/lah)
police-	policía	(poh-lee-SEE-ah)
police station		
- estación de policía	
	(ehs-tah-SYOHN day poh-lee-SEE-ah)
- comisaría de policía	
	(koh-mee-sah-REE-ah day
	poh-lee-SEE-ah)
possess- tengalo	(tehn-gah-loh)

187

POST BOND/BAIL- poner fianza
     (poh-NEHR fee-AHN-sah)
pregnant - embarazada
prepare- prepárelo
    (pray-PAH-ray-loh/lah)
present- actual (ahk-TWAHL)
presently- actualmente
    (ahk-twahl-MEHN-tay)
Pretend- ¡Finge! (FEEN-hay)
prevent- prevenga (pray-VEHN-gah)
previous- previo (PRAY-vee-oh)
 - anterior (ahn-teh-ree-OHR)
previously- anteriormente
   (ahn-teh-ree-ohr-MEHN-tay)
price- precio (PRAY-see-oh)
prison- cárcel (KAHR-sehl);
 -prisión (pree-SYOHN);
(slang) - pinta (PEEN-tah)
prisoner- preso (PREH-soh);
 - prisionero
   (pree-syoh-NAY-roh)
●prohibit- prohibir (proh-ee-BEER)
 it is prohibited- es prohibido
    (es proh-ee-BEE-doh)
proof- prueba (PRWAY-bah)
●prosecute- procesar (proh-seh-SAHR)
●prove- probar (proh-BAHR)
●provide- proveer (proh-veh-EHR)
pure- puro (POO-roh)
purse- bolsa (BOHL-sah)
●PUT IN- meter en (meh-TEHR ehn)
●put- poner (poh-NEHR)

PUT YOUR THINGS ON THE TABLE.
Ponga sus cosas en la mesa.
(POHN-gah soos KOH-sahs en
     lah MAY-sah)

Q

QUESTION- pregunta (preh-GOON-tah)
 ASK A QUESTION.
 Hacer una pregunta.
 (AH-sehr OO-nah preh-GOON-tah)
QUICKLY- pronto (PROHN-toh)
QUIET DOWN. Callarse (KAH-yahr say)
quit- deje (deh-HAH)

R

ranch- rancho (RAHN-choh)
rancher- ranchero (rahn-CHAY-roh)
ranch foreman- mayordomo
    (mah-yohr-DOH-moh);
 - caporal (kah-poh-RAHL)
rapid- rápido (RAH-pee-doh)
rare- raro (RAH-roh)
rarely- raramente (rah-rah-MEHN-tay)
razor -navaja (nah-VAH-hah)
razor blade- hojita de afeitar
 (oh-HEE-tah day ah-fey-TAHR)
●READ (to)- leer (leh-EHR)
ready- listo (LEES-toh)

rear- trasero (trah-SEH-roh)
RECEIPT- recibo (reh-SEE-boh)
recent- reciente (reh-see-EHN-tay)
recently- recientemente
   (reh-see-ehn-tay-MEHN-tay)
recognize- reconozca
    (ray-koh-NOZ-kah)
record (n)- registro (ray-HEES-troh)
red-haired- pelirrojo (peh-lee-ROH-hoh)
refuse- nieguelo/la (nee-ay-gay-loh/lah)
registration - registro (reh-HEES-troh)
●**regular-** regular (reh-goo-LAHR)
regularly- regularmente
   (reh-goo-lahr-MEHN-tay)
relatives- parientes (pah-ree-EHN-tays)
●release- librar (lee-BRAHR)
REMAIN!- ¡quédese! (KAY-day-say)
remember- recorda (reh-KOHR-dah)
remember! - ¡acuérdese!
   (ah-koo-AIR-day-say)
REMOVE - quitese (KEE-tay-say)
rendezvous- cita (SEE-tah)
rent - alquile (ahl-KEEL-ay)
rent (noun)- renta (REHN-tah)
rental- renta (REHN-tah)
REPEAT- repita (ray-PEE-tah)
report- reporte (reh-POHR-tay)
request- petición (peh-tee-SYOHN)
requirement- requisito (reh-kee-SEE-toh)
residence-residencia(reh-see-DEHN-syah)
respond!- ¡responde! (rays-POHN-day)
rest room- lavabo (lah-BAH-boh)
restaurant-restaurante
   (rehs-toh-RAHN-tay)
RESTRAINING ORDER.
 Orden de Retención.
 (OHR-dehn day ray-tehn-SYOHN)
retain (it)- tengalo/la (tehn-gah-loh/lah)
return!- ¡vuelve! (voo-EHL-vay)
 I WILL RETURN-Ya vuelvo
    (yah BWAYL-boh)
●RETURN ITEMS (to)- devolver
    (deh-bohl-BEHR)
review- repaso (reh-PAH-soh);
REVOLVER- fusil (foo-SEEL)
 - revólver (reh-VOHL-behr)
RIFLE- rifle (REE-fleh)
right- correcto (koh-REHK-toh)
RIGHT? (truth)- ¿Verdad? (vehr-DAHD)
right (direction)- derecha(deh-REH-chah)
RIGHT AWAY- pronto (PROHN-toh)
river- rio (REE-oh)
road- camino (kah-MEE-noh)
rob- robe (ROH-bay)
robber- ladrón (lah-DROHN)
robbery- robo (ROH-boh)
round trip- viaje de ida y vuelto
(BYAH-hay day EE-dah ee BWEHL-tah)
ROUTE- rumbo (ROOM-boh)

S

sack- costal (kohs-TAHL);
 - saco (SAH-koh)

SALARY- salario (sah-LAH-ryo)
SALE- venta (VEHN-tah)
saloon- cantina (kahn-TEE-nah)
Saturday- sábado (SAH-bah-doh)
save him/her- sálvelo/la (SAHL-vay-loh/lah)
SAY AGAIN- repita (ray-PEE-tah)
scale- balanza (bah-LHAN-sah)
scar- cicatriz (see-kah-TREES)
SEARCH- esculque (ehs-KOOL-keh);
- registre (ray-HEES-tray)
SEARCH WARRANT Orden de Registro
(OHR-dehn day rah-HEES-troh)
Orden de Cateo
(OHR-dehn day kah-TAY-oh)
seat- asiento (ah-SYEHN-toh)
second- segundo (say-GOON-doh)
secure consigue (kohn-SEE-gay)
see (let's see it) - a verlo (ah VEHR-loh)
seed- semilla (seh-MEE-yah)
seek it- búsquelo (BOOS-kay-loh/lah)
SEIZE (it)- agárrelo/la (ah-GAR-ray-loh/lah)
sell it- véndelo/la (VEHN-day-loh/lah)
send it- mándelo/la (MAHN-day-loh/lah)
send it- envíelo/la (ehn-VEE-ay-loh/lah)
separate (adj.) separado
separate/- separarse (say-pahr-ehn-say)
sergeant- sargento (sahr-pah-RAH-doh)
SERIAL NUMBER- número de serie
(NOO-may-roh ehn SAY-ryeh)
seven- siete (SEE-eh-tay)
seventeen- diecisiete (dee-eh-see-SEE-eh-tay)
seventh- séptimo (SEP-tee-moh)
several- varios (BAH-ree-ohs)
sex- sexo (SEK-sos)
sexual contact- contacto sexual
(kohn-TAK-toh sek-SWAHL)
sexual penetration- penetración sexual
(peh-neh-trah-SYOHN sek-SWAHL)
●shave rasurarse (rah-soo-RAHR-say);
-afeitarse (S.Am.) (ah-fay-ee-TAHR-say)
sheriff- sheray (shay-REE-fay)
shirt- camisa (kah-MEE-sah)
shoe- zapato (sah-PAH-toh)
●shoot- disparar (dees-pah-RAHR)
shooting- tiroteo (tee-roh-TAY-oh)
shoplifting- ratería de tiendas
(rah-tay-REE-ah day tee-EHN-dahs)
short term- a corto plazo
(ah KOHR-toh PLAH-zoh)
short time- rato (RAH-toh)
shot- tiro (TEE-roh)
SHOTGUN- escopeta (ess-koh-PAY-tah)
shoulder- hombro (OHM-broh)
SHOW CAUSE- Demostrar causa.
(day-mohs-TRAHR kah-OO-sah)
SHOW ME!- ¡Demuéstrame!
(day-moo-EHS-trah-may)
●show (to) - mostrar (mohs-TRAHR)
- enseñar (ehn-sehn-YAHR)
SHUT UP!- ¡Cállase! (KAH-yah-say)

Spell!- ¡Deletrea! (day-leh-TRAY-ay)
SPEED- velocidad (veh-loh-see-DAHD)
SPEED LIMIT- velocidad máxima
(veh-loh-see-DAHD MAHK-see-mah)
- mahs days-SEE-toh
- más despacio.
SPEAK SLOWER- Hable más despacio.
(AH-blay MAHS days-PAH-see-oh);
Hable en voz más alta
(AH-blay ehn vohz MAHS AHL-tah)
SPEAK LOUDER-
SPEAK- hablar (ah-BLAHR);
SPANISH- Español (ehs-pahn-YOHL)
south- sur (soor) pus (poos)
●**I'M SORRY** Lo siento (loh SYEHN-toh)
●sorry- sentir (sehn-TEER)
sooner or later- tarde o temprano
(TAHR-day oh tehm-PRAH-noh)
as soon as- tan pronto que
(tahn PROHN-toh kay)
soon- pronto (PROHN-toh)
son-in-law - yerno (YEHR-noh)
son- hijo (EE-hoh)
- algunos (ahl-GOON-nohs)
algún (ahl-GOON)
●solicit- solicitar (soh-lee-see-TAHR)
sobriety test -prueba del alcohol
(kohn-trah-bahn-DEES-tah)
SMUGGLER- contrabandista
(kohn-trah-BAHN-doh)
SMUGGLED GOODS- contrabando
(pah-SAHR day kohn-trah-BAHN-doh)
SMUGGLE (to)- pasar de contrabando
(proh-ee-BEE-doh foo-MAHR)
NO SMOKING- Prohibido Fumar
●smoke (to) - fumar (foo-MAHR)
smoke (n) humo (OO-moh)
small - pequeño (peh-KAY-nyoh)
(eer mahs dehs-PAH-see-oh)
SLOW DOWN - ir más despacio
chico (CHEE-koh);
despacio (dehs-PAH-see-oh)
slowly- lentamente (lehn-tah-MEHN-tay);
slow- lento (LEHN-toh)
site- sitio (SEE-tyoh)
sit- (see-EHN-tay-say ah-KEE)
SIT HERE- siéntese aquí (see-EHN-tay-say)
SIT DOWN- siéntese (see-EHN-tay-say)
sister-in-law - cuñada (koo-NYAH-dah)
sister- hermana (ehr-MAHN-nah)
sir- Señor (seh-NYOHR)
since yesterday- desde ayer
(DEHS-day ah-YEHR)
since- desde (DEHS-day)
(see-mool-TAH-neh-ah-MEHN-tay)
simultaneously- simultáneamente
simultaneous- simultáneo (see-mool-TAH-nay-oh)
silver- plata (PLAH-tah)
SILENCE! ¡Silencio! (see-LEHN-see-oh)
SIGNAL- señal (seh-NYAHL)
SIGNATURE- firma (FEER-mah)
SIGN! - ¡Firme! (FEER-may)
sick- enfermo (ehn-FEHR-moh)

189

Spend! -	¡Gáste!	(GAHS-tay)
sperm-	esperma	(ess-**PAYR**-mah)
●SPIT-	escupir	(ehs-koo-**PEER**)
spoon-	cuchara	(koo-**CHAH**-rah)
sporadic-	esporádico	
	(ehs-poh-**RAH**-dee-koh)	

sporadically- esporádicamente
   (ehs-poh-**RAH**-dee-kah-**MEHN**-tay)
SPRAIN- torcedura(tohr-see-**DOO**-rah)
stab him/her- apuñale/la
   (ah-**POON**-yah-lay/lah)
●STAND (to)- estar de pie
   (ehs-**TAHR** day pee-ay)
STAND HERE. Párese aqui.
   (**PAH**-ray-say ah-**KEE**)
STAND UP! ¡Párese! (**PAH**-ray-say)
●start- empezar (ehm-peh-**SAHR**)
state- estado (ehs-**TAH**-doh)
STATEMENT- declaración
   (day-klah-rah-**SYOHN**);
   -dictado (deek-**TAH**-doh)
●STAY- quedarse (kay-**DAHR**-say)
●steal- robar (roh-**BAHR**)
still- aún (ah-**OON**)
stolen- robado (roh-**BAH**-doh)
STOP- alto (**AHL**-toh)
STORY- cuento (**KWEHN**-toh);
   - historia (ees-**TOH**-ree-ah)
stranger- extraño (ex-**TRAH**-nyoh);
   - extranjero (ex-trahn-**HAY**-roh)
street- calle (**KAH**-yay)
student- estudiante
   (ehs-too-dee-**AHN**-tay)
study- estudio (ehs-**TOO**-dyoh)
subject- sujeto (soo-**HAY**-toh)
subpoena- orden judicial
   OHR-dehn hoo-**DEE**-see-ahl)
subway- metro (**MAY**-troh)
SUITCASE- maleta (mah-**LAY**-tah)
SUM- suma (**SOO**-mah)
SUMMONS- citación judicial
(see-tah-**SYOHN** hoo-dee-see-**AHL**)
Sunday- domingo (doh-**MEEN**-goh)
sunrise- salida del sol
   (sah-**LEE**-dah dayl sohl)
sunset- puesta del sol
   (**PWEHS**-tah dayl sohl)
supper- cena (**SEH**-nah)
●supply- proveer (proh-veh-**AYR**)
SURNAME- apellido (ah-peh-**YEE**-doh)
●SURRENDER-rendirse(rehn-**DEER**-say)
surrounded -rodeado
Suspect- sospechoso
   (sohs-peh-**CHOH**-soh)
suspend him/her- suspendelo/la
   (soos-**PEHN**-day-loh/lah)
suspension- suspensión
   (soos-pehn-**SYOHN**)
SUSPICIOUS- sospechoso
   (sohs-peh-**CHOH**-soh)
sweater- suéter (**SWEH**-tehr)
SWITCH- cambiarse (kahm-**BYAHR**-say)
syringe- jeringa (hay-**REEN**-gah)

T

TABLE-	mesa	(**MAY**-sah)
Take!-	¡Tome!	(**TOH**-may)
TAKE NOTICE- fijese		(**FEE**-hay-say)
TAKE OFF (clothes)- quitese		
		(kee-tay-say)
TAKE OUT- sáquese la/el		
		(**SAH**-kay-say lah/ell)
take place- tener lugar		
		(teh-**NEHR** loo-**GAHR**)
TALK!-	¡Hable!	(**AH**-blay)
tattoo-	tatuaje	(tah-**TWAH**-hays)
taxi-	taxi	(**TAHK**-see)
telephone-	teléfono	(tay-**LAY**-foh-noh)
●TELL-	decir	(day-**SEER**)

TELL ME THE TRUTH.
 Digame la verdad.
(**DEE**-gah-may lah vehr-**DAHD**)

temporarily- temporáneamente
   (tehm-poh-**RAH**-nay-ah-mehn-tay);
  temporalmente(tehm-poh-rahl-**MEHN**-tay)
temporary- temporáneo
   (tehm-poh-**RAH**-nay-oh)
terminate!- ¡termine! (tehr-**MEE**-nay)
testify! - ¡ateste! (ah-**TEHS**-tay)
   - ¡atestigue! (ah-tehs-**TEE**-gah-way)
than- que (kay)
THANKS- gracias (**GRAH**-syahs)
that- ese (**EH**-say); que (kay)
THE- el, la, los, las
   (ehl, lah, lohs, lahs)
theft- robo (**ROH**-boh)
then- entonces (ehn-**TOHN**-says)
thief- ladron (lah-**DROHN**)
thing- cosa (**KOH**-sah)
Think!- ¡Piense! (pee-**EHN**-say)
this- este (**EHS**-tay); esta (**EHS**-tah)
THIS WAY- por aqui (pohr ah-**KEE**)
thousand- mil (meel)
Thursday- jueves (**HWEH**-vehs)
TICKET- boleto (boh-**LAY**-toh);
   - tiquete (**TEE**-kay-tay)
time- tiempo (**TYEHM**-poh)
  at the same time- al mismo tiempo
         (ahl **MEES**-moh **TYEHM**-poh)
● be on time- llegar a tiempo
         (yay-**GAHR** ah **TYEHM**-poh)
   - ser puntual (Sehr poon-**TWAHL**)
   first time- primera vez
         (pree-**MAY**-rah vehs)
   in an hour's time- dentro de una hora
         (**DEHN**-troh day **OO**-nah **OH**-rah)
   in the meantime- mientras tanto
         (mee-**EHN**-trahs **TAHN**-toh)
   in time- a tiempo (ah **TYEHM**-poh)
   last time- vez pasada
         (vehs pah-**SAH**-dah)
   on time- a tiempo (ah **TYEHM**-poh)
●spend time- pasar (pah-**SAHR**)
   time is up- es la hora
         (ess lah **OO**-rah)

timetable- horario (oh-RAH-ree-oh)
tire- llanta (YAHN-tah)
Title of ownership- título (TEE-too-loh)
TO - a (ah);
 para (PAH-rah)
● to spend money- gastar (gahs-TAHR)
today- hoy (oy)
toe- dedo del pie (DAY-doh dayl pee-ay)
together- juntos (HOON-tohs)
toilet- retrete (reh-TRAY-tay)
tomorrow- mañana (mah-NYAH-nah)
day after tomorrow- pasado mañana (pah-SAH-doh mah-NYAH-nah)
tomorrow morning- mañana (mah-NYAH-nah)
tools- herramientas (can mean guns) (eh-rah-mee-EHN-tahs)
(SLANG FOR DRUGS OR WEAPONS)
tonight- esta noche (EHS-tah NOH-chay)
TOO BIG- demasiado grande (day-mah-SYAH-doh GRAHN-day)
TOO EARLY- demasiado temprano (day-mah-SYAH-doh tehm-PRAH-noh)
TOO LATE- demasiado tarde (day-mah-SYAH-doh TAHR-day)
TOO LONG- demasiado largo (day-mah-SYAH-doh LAHR-goh)
TOO MANY- demasiado (day-mah-SYAH-dohs)
TOO SHORT- demasiado corto (day-mah-SYAH-doh KOHR-toh)
TOO SMALL- demasiado pequeño (day-mah-SYAH-doh peh-KAY-nyoh)
TOUCH! - ¡Toque! (TOH-kay)
DON'T TOUCH! ¡No toque! (noh TOH-kay)
TOW TRUCK- camión de remolque (kah-mee-OHN day reh-MOHL-kay)
TOWN- pueblo (PWEH-bloh)
traffic- tránsito
transport- transporte (trahns-POHR-tay)
travelling- viaje (BYAH-hay)
● translate -traducir
TREE árbo (AHR-bohl)
trespass- traspaso (trahs-PAH-soh)
trial- proceso (proh-SEH-soh)
trip- viaje (BYAH-hay)
trousers- pantalones (pahn-tah-LOH-nays)
truck- camión (kah-MYOHN)
troca (TROH-kah)
Trust me- tenga confianza en mi (TEN-gah kohn-fee-AHN-zah ehn mee)
TRUTH- verdad (vehr-DAHD)
Try! - ¡Trate! (TRAH-tay)
Tuesday- martes (MAHR-tehs)
turn around!-¡voltéese!(vohl-TAY-ay-say)
TURN LOOSE! - ¡Suélte! (soo-EHL-tay)
TURN OFF- apáguelo(ah-PAH-gay-loh)
twice- dos veces (dohs BEH-sehs)

Ū

uncle- tío (TEE-oh)

U

under- debajo de (day-BAH-hoh day);
 bajo (BAH-hoh)
UNDERSTAND? ¿Comprende? (kohm-PREHN-day)
UNITED STATES OF AMERICA
Estados Unidos de América (ehs-TAH-dohs oo-NEE-dohs day ah-MAY-ree-kah)
UNITED STATES OF BRAZIL
Estados Unidos de Brasil (ehs-TAH-dohs oo-NEE-dohs day brah-SEEL)
UNITED STATES OF MEXICO
Estados Unidos Mexicanos (ehs-TAH-dohs oo-NEE-dohs meh-hee-KAH-nohs)
until- hasta (AHS-tah)
UP- arriba (ahr-REE-bah)
urine- orina (f) (OO-soh)
use (purpose)- uso (OO-soh)
use it- úselo/la (OO-say-loh/lah)
usually- normalmente (nohr-mahl-MEHN-tay)

V

vagina- vagina (vah-HEE-nah)
VALID- válido (VAH-lee-doh)
valise- la maleta (mah-LAY-tah)
vehicle- vehículo (beh-EE-koo-loh)
verification- verificación (beh-ree-fee-kah-SYOHN)
VERIFY IT- verifíquelo/la (veh-ree-FEE-kay-loh/lah)
victim- víctima (VEEK-tee-mah)
view- vista (VEES-tah)
● violate (to)- violar (vee-oh-LAHR)
violation- violación (vee-oh-lah-SYOHN)
visa- visa (BEE-sah)
visit- visítelo/la (vee-SEE-tay-loh/lah)
VOID- nulo (NOO-loh)
VOLUNTARILY- voluntariamente (voh-loon-tah-ree-ah-MEHN-tay)
voluntary- voluntario (boh-loon-TAY-ryoh)
Vomit! - ¡Vomite! (von-MEE-tay)

W

WAGES- sueldo (SWAYL-doh)
waist- cintura (seen-TOO-rah)
Wait!- ¡Espere! (ehs-PEHR-ay)
waiter- mesero (meh-SAY-roh)
waiver- renuncia (reh-NOON-syah)
Wake up! - ¡Despiertá! (days-pee-AIR-tah)
WALK! ¡Ándale! (AHN-dah-lay)
WALLET- cartera (kahr-TAY-rah)
Warm him/her- avíselela (ah-VEE-say-lay/lah)
WARNING- aviso (ah-VEE-son)
WARRANT Orden (OHR-dehn)

WARRANT OF ARREST-
 Orden de arresto
 (OHR-dehn day ah-REHS-toh)

WARRANT OF DEPORTATION-
 Orden de deportación
 (OHR-dehn day day-pohr-tah-SYOHN)

●**WASH** (to) lavarse (lah-BAHR-say)
WASTE- gaste (GAHS-tay)
watch (n)- reloj (reh-LOH)
Watch out! ¡Cuidado! (kwee-DAH-doh)
water- agua (AH-gwah)
WEAPON- arma (AHR-mah)
Wednesday- miércoles
 (MYEHR-koh-lehs)
WEEK- semana (seh-MAH-nah)
 a few weeks- unas semanas
 (OON-ahs seh-MAH-nahs)
 next week- semana próxima
 (seh-MAH-nah PROHK-see-mah)
 - la semana que entra
 (lah seh-MAH-nah kay EHN-trah)
 weekly- semanal (seh-mah-NAHL)
WELCOME (You're) De nada
 (day NAH-dah)
WELL(water) pozo ((POH-zoh)
WELCOME! ¡Bienvenido!
 (bee-ehn-vehn-EE-doh)
west- oeste (oh-EHS-tay)
WHAT? ¿Cómo? (KOH-moh)
WHEN? ¿Cuándo? (KWAHN-doh)
WHERE? ¿Dónde? (DOHN-day)

WHERE IS THE _____?
 ¿Dónde está el _____?
 (DOHN-day ay-STAH ehl _____)

widow- viuda (bee-OO-dah)
widower- viudo (bee-OO-doh)
wife esposa (ehs-POH-sah)
while- mientras (mee-EHN-trahs)
white- blanco (BLAHN-koh)
WHO? ¿Quién? (kee-EHN)

wholesale- venta al por mayor
 (VEHN-tah ahl pohr mah-YOHR)

wholesale work- al por mayor trabajo
 (ahl pohr mah-YOHR trah-BAH-hoh)

WHY? ¿Por qué? (pohr KAY)
wife- esposa (ehs-POH-sah)
 - señora (sehn-YOH-rah)
window- ventana (vehn-TAH-nah)
wine- vino (VEE-noh)
with- con (kohn)

withholding, Are you?
¿Está Ud. reteniendo?
(Ay-STAH oo-STEHD
ray-tehn-ee-ehn-DOH)

within- dentro de (DEHN-troh day)

witness- testigo (tehs-TEE-goh)
woman- mujer (moo-HEHR)
 - señora (sehn-YOH-rah)

WOOD. madera (mah-DAIR-oh)
woods- bosque (BOHS-kay)
word- palabra (pah-LAH-brah)
●**work** trabajar (trah-bah-JAHR)
work labor (lah-BOHR);
 - trabajo (trah-BAH-hoh)
worker- obrero (oh-BRAY-roh)
workday-
 día de trabajo
 (DEE-ah day trah-BAH-hoh)

wound (n)- herida (heh-REE-dah)
●wound (v)-herir (heh-REER)
wrap it- envuelvelo/la
 (ehn-voo-EHL-vay-loh/lah)

wrist- muñeca (moo-NYAY-kah)
wristwatch- reloj de pulsera
 (reh-LOH day pool-SAY-rah)

WRITE!- ¡Escribe! (ays-KREE-bay)

WRITTEN NOTICE- aviso escrito
 (ah-VEE-soh ehs-KREE-toh)

Wrong- incorrecto(een-koh-REHK-toh)

Y

Year- año (AH-nyoh)
yearly- anual (ah-NWAHL)
yellow- amarillo (ah-mah-REE-yoh)
YES- sí (see)

yesterday- ayer (ah-YEHR)

 day before yesterday- anteayer
 (ahn-tay-ah-YEHR)

 since yesterday- desde ayer
 (DEHS-day ah-YEHR)

 yesterday morning- ayer por la mañana
 (ah-YEHR pohr lah mah-NYAN-nah)

yet- todavía (toh-dah-VEE-ah)

YOU DID IT! ¡Lo Hizo! (loh HEE-zoh)

YOU PASSED THE TEST.
Usted pasó la prueba.
(oo-STEHD pah-SOH lah pro-EH-bah)

young- joven (HOH-behn)

Z

ZONE- zona (SOH-nah)

(1) Please concentrate and stare at the 4 vertical dots in the center of the diagram for a full 30 seconds without blinking your eyes. (2) Then close your eyes and tilt your head back. (3) Keep them closed... you will see a circle of light appear, continue looking at the circle. E-mail the author with what you saw at:

Dent@SilentSignals.com

No part of this manual may be reproduced or transmitted in any form or by any means, electronic or mechanical, including photocopying, recording, or by any information storage and retrieval system, without the prior written permission by the author. To discourage copyright infringement, state of the art encrypted and coding have been incorporated into the text. Violators will be prosecuted to the fullest extent of the law. (Code #2-164BG-Block-470.)

Although this manual and associated audio learning tapes have been carefully and thoughtfully published, they cannot guarantee success. The manual and audio/video tapes are designed to assist public safety professionals and others to maintain and improve their professional competence. Consequently, the user agrees to indemnify and hold the Constable Group, Inc., harmless from any loss or claim resulting from the use or misuse of the manual or audio/video learning tapes. Every effort has been made to make this manual accurate as possible. However, there may be some typographical errors. Therefore, this text should be used only as a general guide and not as the ultimate source of information.

Payment: Purchase orders must be accompanied by a cheque or purchase order number. Payment in U.S. Funds only, may be made with cheque or money order. No C.O.D.s. Invoice Terms: Net 30 days. A late charge of 1.5 % per month will be charged on all accounts past 30 days. (Most orders shipped within 24 hours). Purchase Orders, Personal Checks, and Visa/MC Credit cards accepted.

Manual and audio / video tapes are published, produced and marketed by:
The Constable Group, Inc., PO Box 6415, Bend, Oregon 97708-6415;
Specializing in Officer Safety Training, Loss Prevention and Multi-Cultural Interaction.
(Federal Tax Identification Number: 93-1069387)

"Survival Spanish"® is a registered trademark of the Constable Group, Inc. It is a violation of federal U.S. Patent and and Trademark law to use the trademark without authorization.

ADVICE OF RIGHTS

YOU HAVE THE RIGHT TO REMAIN SILENT
Usted tiene el derecho de mantener silencio.
(Oo-**STEHD** tee-**EHN**-ay el deh-**REH**-choh day mahn-tay-**NAHR** see-**LEHN**-see-oh)

IF YOU GIVE UP THE RIGHT TO REMAIN SILENT, ANYTHING YOU SAY CAN AND WILL BE USED AGAINST YOU IN A COURT OF LAW
Si usted renuncia el derecho de mantener silencio, cualquier cosa que usted diga, se puede usar en contra de usted en una corte de ley.
(See oo-**STEHD** reh-**NOON**-see-ah el deh-**REH**-choh day mahn-tay-**NAHR** see-**LEHN**-see-oh, kwahl-kee-**AYR** **KOH**-sah kay oo-**STEHD** **DEE**-gah, say **PWAY**-day oo-**SAHR** ehn **KOHN**-trah day oo-**STEHD** ehn **OO**-nah **KOHR**-tay day lay.)

YOU HAVE THE RIGHT TO TALK TO A LAWYER BEFORE WE TALK TO YOU AND TO HAVE HIM PRESENT WHILE WE TALK TO YOU.
Usted tiene el derecho de consultar con un abogado y tenerlo presente durante la interogación.
(Oo-**STEHD** tee-**EHN**-ay el deh-**REH**-choh day kohn-**SOOL**-tahr kohn oon ah-boh-**GAH**-doh ee tehn-**EHR**-loh preh-**SEHN**-tay doo-**RAHN**-tay lah een-tay-roh-gah-**SYOHN**)

IF YOU CANNOT AFFORD TO HIRE AN ATTORNEY, ONE WILL BE APPOINTED TO REPRESENT YOU PRIOR TO QUESTIONING.
En caso de que Ud. no tuviera suficientes fondos para ocupar su propio abogado, la corte nombrará uno para usted sin costo alguno. Tambien usted tiene el derecho de tenerlo presente, si desea.
(Ehn **KAH**-soh day kay oo-**STEHD** noh too-vee-**AYR**-ah soo-fee-see-**EHN**-tays **FOHN**-dohs **PAH**-rah oh-koo-**PAHR** soo proh-**PEE**-oh ah-boh-**GAH**-doh, lah **KOHR**-tay nohm-brahr-**RAH** **OO**-noh **PAH**-rah oo-**STEHD** seen **KOH**-stoh ahl-**GOO**-noh. Tahm-bee-yehn oo-**STEHD** tee-**EHN**-ay ehl day-**REH**-choh day tayn-**AYR**-loh pray-**SEHN**-tay, see day-**SAY**-ah.)

DO YOU UNDERSTAND EACH OF THE RIGHTS EXPLAINED TO YOU?
¿Entiende usted cada uno de estos derechos que le acabo de explicar?
(Ehn-tee-**EHN**-day oo-**STEHD** **KAH**-dah **OO**-noh day **ESS**-tohs deh-**REH**-chohs kay lay ah-**KAH**-boh day ex-plee-**KAHR**)

HAVING THOSE RIGHTS IN MIND, WILL YOU TALK TO ME?
¿Con esos derechos en mente, hablará usted conmigo?
(Kohn **AY**-sohs day-**RAY**-chohs ehn **MEHN**-tay, ah-blah-**RAH** oo-**STEHD** kohn-mee-**GOH**)

I UNDERSTAND MY RIGHTS AND KNOW WHAT I AM DOING.
Entiendo cuales son mis derechos, y se lo que hago.
(Ayn-tee-**EHN**-doh koo-**AHL**-ays sohn mees day-**RAY**-chohs, ee say loh kay **AH**-goh)

I DO NOT WANT A LAWYER AND I AM READY TO GIVE A STATEMENT.
No quiero un abogado y estoy listo para dar una declaración.
(Noh kee-**AY**-roh oon ah-boh-**GAH**-doh, ee **AYS**-toy **LEES**-toh **PAH**-rah dahr **OO**-nah day-klah-rah-**SYOHN**)

NO PROMISES OR THREATS HAVE BEEN MADE.
No me han hecho promesas ni amenazas.
(Noh may ahn fohr-**MAY**-sahs nee ah-**MAY**-nah-zahs)

NO FORCED COOPERATION OR COERCION HAS BEEN USED AGAINST ME.
No me han forzado cooperar en este caso.
(Noh may ahn fohr-**ZAH**-doh koh-oh-pay-**RAHR** en AY-stay **KAH**-soh)

WHEN YOU SIGN THIS, YOU ARE NOT ADMITTING GUILT.
Cuando usted firma aqui, no admite culpabilidad.
(KWAHN-doh oo-**STEHD FEER**-mah ah-**KEE**, noh ahd-**MEE**-tay kool-pah-**BEEL**-ee-dahd)

BY SIGNING, IT MEANS YOU UNDERSTAND YOUR RIGHTS
Cuando ud. firma aqui, quiere decir que si entiende sus derechos.
(KWAHN-doh oo-**STEHD FEER**-mah ah-**KEE**, kee-**AIR**-ay day-**SEER** kay SEE en-tee-**EHN**-day soos day-**RAY**-chohs)

REQUEST FOR CONSENT TO SEARCH

MAY I SEARCH?
¿Puedo esculcar?
(**PWAY**-doh ehs-**KOOL**-cahr?)
(is COOL car!)

MAY I SEARCH ?
¿Puedo registrar?
(**PWAY**-doh ray-hees-**STRAR**?)
(Ray he's a STAR!)

MAY I SEARCH _____?
¿Puedo catear _____?
(**PWAY**-doh kah-tay-**AHR**__)
(Caught the air)

YOUR CAR	su carro	(soo **KAH**-roh)
YOUR BUILDING	su edificio	(soo ay-dee-**FEE**-see-oh)
YOUR HOUSE	su casa	(soo **KAH**-sah)
YOUR PERSON	su persona	(soo payr-**SOH**-nah)
THAT?	aquello	(ah-**KAY**-yoh)
THIS?	esto	(**AY**-stoh) (POINT TO ITEM)

IF PROBABLE CAUSE OR EXIGENT CIRCUMSTANCES EXIST:

I AM GOING TO SEARCH YOUR...
Voy a esculcar su................
(Voy ah ehs-**KOOL**-cahr soo......)

I AM GOING TO SEARCH YOUR
Voy a registar su..................
(Voy ah ray-hees-**STRAR** soo......)

(OR) I AM GOING TO SEARCH YOUR............
Voy a catear su ....
(Voy ah cah-**TAY**-ahr soo ....)

UNDERSTAND?	¿Comprende?	(kohm-**PREHN**-day)
UNDERSTAND?	¿Entiende?	(Ehn-tee-**EHN**-day)
ANSWER YES OR NO.	Conteste si o no.	(Kohn-**TEHS**-tay see oh noh)
IS THIS YOURS?	¿Es suyo?	(ess SOO-yoh)
DID YOU KNOW?	¿Supo?	(SOO-poh)
SIGN HERE	Firme aqui.	(**FEER**-may ah-**KEE**)

195

EMERGENCY PHONE AND DISPATCH PHRASES

DO YOU HAVE AN EMERGENCY?
Tiene emergencia?
(Tee-**EHN**-ay eh-mehr-**HEHN**-see-ah)

ANSWER YES OR NO
Conteste si o no
(Kohn-**TEHS**-tay see oh noh)

UNDERSTAND?
Comprende?
(kom-**PREN**-day)

DON'T HANG UP!
No cuelgues!
(Noh koo-**EHL**-gays)

WAIT!
Espere!
(ehs-**PEHR**-ay)

A SPANISH SPEAKER WILL TALK TO YOU
Una persona que habla Espanol hablara con Usted.
(**OO**-nah pair-**SOH**-nah kay **AH**-blah ehs-pah-**NYOHL**
ah-blah-**RAH** kohn **OO**-stehd)

(NOTE: If a Spanish speaker is not available, use below phrases)

I SPEAK A LITTLE SPANISH
Hablo poco español.
(**AH**-bloh **POH**-koh ehs-pah-**NYOHL**)

LISTEN!
Escuche!
(Ehs-**KOO**-chay)

SPEAK SLOWER
Hable más despacio.
(**AH**-blay mahs days-**PAH**-see-oh)

REPEAT!
Repita!
(Reh-**PEE**-tah)

ARE YOU IN DANGER?
Está usted en peligro?
(Ehs-**TAH** oo-**STEHD** en peh-**LEH**-groh)

IS THERE or ARE THERE INJURIES?
Hay heridos?
(**EYE** ehr-**EE**-dohs)

HOW MANY ARE INJURED?
Cuántos heridos hay?
(**KWAH**-tohs ehr-**EE**-dohs **EYE**)

DO YOU NEED A ....?
Nescecita......................?
(Nehs-seh-**SEE**-tah.......?)

WAIT!
Espere!
(Ehs-**PEHR**-ay)

AMBULANCE?	Ambulancia?	(Ahm-boo-**LAHN**-see-ah)
POLICE?	Policia?	(Poh-lee-**SEE**-ah)
FIREFIGHTER?	Bombero?	(Bohm-**BEHR**-roh)

WHERE DO YOU NEED THE.......? (Refer above)
Dónde necesita...........................?
(**DOHN**-day nehs-seh-**SEE**-tah....?)

COMPLETE ADDRESS
Dirección completa?
(dee-rehk-SEE-own kohm-PLEH-tah)

ONE NUMBER AT A TIME
Un número a la vez
(oon NOO-may-roh ah lah vehs)

0 cero (SEH-roh)
1 uno (OO-noh)
2 dos (dohs)
3 tres (trehs)
4 cuatro (KWAH-troh)
5 cinco (SEEN-koh)
6 seis (sayhs)
7 siete (see-EH-teh)
8 ocho (OH-choh)
9 nueve (noo-EH-veh)

HOUSE NO? número de casa? (NOO-may-roh day KAH-sah)
APARTMENT # número de apartamento (NOO-may-roh day ah-pahr-tah-MEHN-toh)
STREET? calle? (KAH-yay)
AVENUE? avenida? (ah-beh-NEE-dah)
ROUTE #? número de ruta? (NOO-may-roh day ROO-tah)
BOX #? número de caja? (NOO-may-roh day KAH-hah)
ROAD? camino? (kah-MEE-noh)
CITY? ciudad? (see-oo-DAHD)
or TOWN? pueblo? (PWEH-bloh)
STATE? estado? (ehs-TAH-doh) **or**
LOCATION? lugar? (loo-GAHR?)
MILES millas? (MEE-yahs)
BLOCKS manzanas (mahn-ZAH-nahs)
(or) CUADRAS – BLOCKS (KOO-ah-drahs)

IS IT? ¿Es? (EHS)

NORTH? norte? (NOHR-tay)
SOUTH? sud? (Sood)
  sur? (soor)
EAST? este? (ESS-tay)
WEST? oeste? (Oo-WEHS-tay)

OF de (deh)

CLOSE TO cerca de (SEHR-kah deh)
HIGHWAY carretera (kah-ray-TAY-rah)

YOUR PHONE NUMBER?
Su número de teléfono?
(Soo NOO-may-roh day tay-LAY-foh-noh)

197

WHAT IS YOUR ADDRESS? (Refer above)
Cuál es su domicilio?
(Kwahl es soo doh-mee-**SEE**-lyoh)

ARE YOU THERE?
Está usted ahí?
(Ehs-**TAH** oo-**STEHD** ah-**EE**)

THE AMBULANCE IS COMING!
La ambulancia viene!
(lah ahm-boo-**LAHN**-see-ah vee-**EHN**-nay)

POLICE ARE COMING!
La policia viene!
(Lah poh-lee-**SEE**-ah vee-**EHN**-nay)

FIRE FIGHTERS ARE COMING!
Los bomberos viene!
(Lohs bom-**BAY**-rohs vee-**EHN**-nehn)

STAY THERE!   ¡Qúedese allá!   (**KAY**-day-say ah-**YAH**)

DETERMINING DANGER OR EXIGENT CIRCUMSTANCES

ARE THERE WEAPONS?
Hay armas?
(Eye **AHR**-mas)

PISTOL	pistola	(pees-**TOH**-lah)
RIFLE	rifle	(**REE**-fleh)
SHOTGUN	escopeta	(ess-koh-**PAY**-tah)
KNIFE	cuchillo	(koo-**CHEE**-yoh)

IS THE SUSPECT PRESENT?
Está presente el sospechoso?
(Es-**TAH** preh-**SEHN**-tay Soh-peh-**CHOH**-soh)

IS HE OR SHE ARMED?
Tiene armas?
(Tee-**EHN**-ay **AHR**-mas?)

IS THE SUSPECT INSIDE?   (OUTSIDE?)
Es el sospechoso dentro?   (afuera?)
(Ess ehl sohs-peh-**CHOH**-soh **DEN**-troh)   (ah-**FOO**-air-ah)

DO YOU KNOW HIS / HER NAME?   **TELL ME**
Sabe el nombre?   Dígame
(**SAH**-beh ehl **NOHM**-bray)   (**DEE**-gah-may)

HOW MANY ARE THERE?
Cuántos hay?
(**KWAHN**-tohs **EYE**)

DID HE LEAVE ON FOOT?	**WHAT DIRECTION?**
Salió a pie?	Qué rumbo?
(Sah-lee-OH ah PEE-ay)	(Kay ROOM-boh)

DID HE LEAVE IN A CAR?	**WHAT COLOR?**
Salió en carro?	De qué color?
(Sah-lee-OH ehn KAHR-roh)	(Day kay koh-LOHR)

black	negro	(NEH-groh)	
blue	azul	(ah-SOOL)	
brown	café	(kah-FAY)	
dark	oscuro	(ohs-KOO-roh)	
gold	dorado	(doh-RAH-doh)	
gray	gris	(grees)	
green	verde	(BEHR-day)	
orange	anaranjado	(ah-nah-rahn-HAH-doh)	
pink	rosado	(roh-SAH-doh)	
purple	púrpuro	(POOR-poo-roh)	(or)
	morado	(moh-RAH-doh)	
red	colorado	(koh-loh-RAH-doh)	(or)
	rojo	(ROH-hoh)	
silver	plateado	(plah-teh-AH-doh)	
white	blanco	(BLAHN-koh)	
yellow	amarillo	(ah-mah-REE-yoh)	

VEHICLE PLATE #	**STATE?**
número de placa?	Estado?
(NOO-may-roh day PLAH-kah)	(Ehs-TAH-doh)

COLOR OF THE CLOTHES?
Color de ropa?
(koh-LOHR day ROH-pah)

SHIRT	camisa	(kah-MEE-sah)
JACKET	chaqueta	(chah-KAY-tah)
HAT	sombrero	(sohm-BREH-roh)
BLOUSE	blusa	(BLOO-sah)
SKIRT	falda	(FAHL-dah)
DRESS	vestido	(behs-TEE-doh)

IS HE INTOXICATED	**DRUGGED?**
Está intoxicado?	Drogado
(Ay-STAH een-toh-xee-KAH-doh)	(droh-GAH-doh)

IS HE VIOLENT? DID HE / SHE HIT YOU?
Es violento? El / ella le pegó?
(Ays vee-oh-LEHN-toh) (ehl / EH-yah leh peh-GOH?)

IS HE (OR SHE) SUICIDAL?
Tiene tendencia hacia el suicidio?
(Tee-EHN-ay ten-DEHN-see-ah AH-see-ah ehl soo-ee-SEE-dee-oh)

IS THE SUSPECT............?
¿Es el sospechoso ....?
(Ess ehl sohs-peh-**CHOH**-soh)

YOUR HUSBAND? Su esposo? (Soo ess-**POH**-soh)
YOUR BOYFRIEND? Su novio? (**NOH**-bee-oh)

IS THE SUSPECT..............?
Es el sospechoso ....?
(Ess ehl sohs-peh-**CHOH**-soh)

ANGLO	Anglo	(**AHN**-gloh)
ARABIC	Arabe	(**AH**-rah-bay)
HISPANIC	Hispano	(ees-**PAH**-noh)
INDIAN	Indio	(**EEN**-dee-oh)
NEGRO	Negro	(**NEH**-groh)
ORIENTAL	Oriental	(oh-ree-ehn-**TAHL**)

MALE (or) **FEMALE**
macho hembra
(**MAH**-choh) (**HEHM**-brah)

SHORT **TALL** **FAT** **THIN**
bajo alto gordo flaco
(**BAH**-hoh) (**AHL**-toh) (**GOHR**-doh) (**FLAH**-koh) (or)

AVERAGE término medio (**TEER**-mee-noh may-**DEE**-oh)

AGE **ONE NUMBER AT A TIME**
edad Un número a la vez
(eh-**DAHD**?) (oon **NOO**-may-roh ah lah vehs)

STAY THERE !
Qúedese allá!
(**KAY**-day-say ah-**YAH**)

THE POLICE ARE COMING
La policia viene.
(Lah poh-lee-**SEE**-ah vee-**EHN**-nay)

THE POLICE HAVE ARRIVED
La policia ya llegó
(Lah poh-lee-**SEE**-ah yah yeh-**GOH**)

OPEN THE DOOR!
Abra la puerta!
(**AH**-brah lah **PWHERE**-tah)

GO OUTSIDE
Salga afeura
(**SALH**-gah ah-**FOO**-air-ah)

RIGHT NOW!
Ahorita!
(Ah-oh-**REE**-tah!)

911 INQUIRIES ON HANGUPS AND CALL BACKS

DID ANYBODY THERE CALL 911?
Alguien llamo a 911?
(**AHL**-gui-en yah-**MOH** ah noo-**EH**-veh **OO**-noh **OO**-noh)

WAS IT A MISTAKE?
Fue un error?
(Foo-**AY** oon air-**ROAR**)

THE POLICE ARE COMING
La policia viene.
(Lah poh-lee-**SEE**-ah vee-**EHN**-nay)

MISCELLANEOUS PHRASES:

YOUR NAME?   **CALM DOWN!**
Su Nombre?   Cálmese!
(Soo **NOHM**-bray)   (**KAHL**-meh-seh)

UNDERSTAND?   **I DON'T UNDERSTAND**
Comprende?   No comprendo
(kom-**PREN**-day)   (noh kohm-**PREHN**-doh)

I DON'T KNOW   ¡No sé   (noh **SEH**)

ACCIDENT?   accidente?   (ahk-see-**DEHN**-tay)

TRAFFIC ACCIDENT?
Accidente de tránsito?
(ahk-see-**DEN**-tay day **TRAHN**-see-toh)

FIRE?   incendio?   (een-**SEHN**-dee-oh)

IS EVERYBODY OUT OF THE HOUSE?
Salieron todos de la casa?
(Sah-lee-**EH**-rohn **TOH**-dohs day lah **KAH**-sah)

LEAVE!   **RIGHT NOW!**
Salga!   Ahoritai!
(**SAHL**-gah)   (Ah-oh-**REE**-tah!)

HEART   corazón   (kohr-ah-**ZOHN**)

DO YOU HAVE HEART PROBLEMS?
Tiene problemas del corazón?
(Tee-**EHN**-ay proh-**BLEH**-mahs dehl kohr-ah-**ZOHN**)

HEART ATTACK?
Ataque al corazón?
(Ah-**TAH**-keh ehl kohr-ah-**ZOHN**)

(Refer to page 29 for additional phrases)